☐ WORKING POOR

WORKING POOR
Farmworkers in the United States

DAVID GRIFFITH and ED KISSAM

with Jeronimo Camposeco, Anna García,
Max Pfeffer, David Runsten,
and Manuel Valdés Pizzini

TEMPLE UNIVERSITY PRESS
Philadelphia

Temple University Press, Philadelphia 19122
Copyright © 1995 by Temple University. All rights reserved
Published 1995
Printed in the United States of America

⊗ The paper used in this book meets the requirements of the American National Standard
for Information Sciences—Permanence of Paper for Printed Library Materials. ANSI
Z39.48-1984

Library of Congress Cataloging-in-Publication Data
Griffith, David Craig, 1951–
    Working poor : farmworkers in the United States / David Griffith
    and Ed Kissam with Jeronimo Camposeco . . . [et al.].
      p. cm.
    Includes bibliographical references and index.
    ISBN 1-56639-238-1 (cl).—ISBN 1-56639-239-X (pb)
    1. Agricultural laborers—United States. 2. Migrant agricultural
    laborers—United States. I. Kissam, Edward, 1943– . II. Title.
    HD1525.G75   1995
    331.7'63'0973—dc20   94-9120

All photographs dated between 1937 and 1940 are from the U S Farm Security
Administration Collection, Prints and Photographs Division, Library of Congress.

FOR ROB WILLIAMS

in admiration of his dedication to improving the lives
of farmworkers by providing a forum
for their empowerment

Contents

Tables

Preface

Every year, during the hottest part of the summer, you can be sure that some conscientious newspaper reporter or broadcast journalist in a state like North Carolina, Ohio, Virginia, Pennsylvania, Iowa, or Missouri will put together a story, usually for the Sunday supplements, on the horrible living conditions of migrant farmworkers. We've all seen the photographs: dirty-faced adolescents pouring buckets full of tomatoes or potatoes into trucks; vermin-infested frame houses with no screens on the windows and no proper doors, or trailers whose curling, rusty edges threaten small children; an Indian-looking woman leaning against a doorjamb, an infant on her hip and another small child hiding behind her skirt. We've read about the low pay, long hours, debt schemes, abusive crew leaders, and apologetic farmers. We've learned how pesticides damage eyes and skin, how rain creates the despair of idleness, how tuberculosis and AIDS spread among migrant populations at rates alarmingly higher than among the general population. Of course we're touched and horrified by these scenes, these revelations. We empathize with these poor, diseased people over our Wallace Stevens Sunday morning ''complacencies of the peignoir, and late / coffee and oranges in a sunny chair.'' Maybe we draw some comfort from the inevitable qualification that no matter how bad conditions are on the farms of America they are far worse in Mexico, that here at least local clergy and volunteer health officials and teachers get out into the fields to dispense clothing, food, medicine, religion, and education.

These news reports may generate a flourish of child-labor law enforcement or housing inspections. They have led to special presidential and gubernatorial commissions on migrant workers. They may even cause a handful of agencies, temporarily or permanently, to make a sincere effort to upgrade living and working conditions for migrants. They have, certainly, resulted in continued public funding of programs directed toward migrants and in private initiatives to improve the welfare of the farmworking population in general. Yet the fact remains that these stories continue to be run, summer after summer, year after year, throughout the United States. Migrant farmworkers continue to be "good copy," precisely because they are the working poor, among the most abused and impoverished of workers that live among us—usually isolated and out of sight—for a short time each year.

We cannot claim that this book of case studies about farm labor communities and regions will initiate vast improvements in the lifestyles and work settings of farmworkers. We cannot claim that it is much more than a somewhat larger version of the Sunday supplement on migrants or the working poor, although we can recommend it on the grounds that, compared with journalism, it is somewhat more comprehensive and based on more rigorous methods of sampling, data collection, and analysis. More important, the research on which our analyses are based, beginning in 1988 and continuing into 1991, took place over a much longer period than most newspaper accounts and even many of the supposedly more "rigorous" analyses. We certainly hope that the time we have spent yields more in the way of improved living and working conditions in U.S. agriculture than a Sunday supplement. If not, we will be letting down those who invited us into "their" usually temporary living quarters—the nearly one thousand farmworkers and their neighbors we interviewed for this study. To these individuals we owe our greatest debt of gratitude. We hope we have represented your feelings, aspirations, and attitudes accurately. We write this for you.

The people we should name for providing help with this research are so numerous that we are sure to leave out a few. We apologize. Those whom it is impossible for us to forget, deserving our special thanks, are those many individuals, spread across many decent organizations and agencies, who dedicate their lives to improving the lot of farmworkers and the working poor. If we were forced to select one such individual for sincerity and objectivity, the person who would readily come to mind is Rick Mines. Rick supported this research through his active interest in our findings as well as in his official capacity as project monitor for the Office of the Secretary of Policy, U.S. Department of Labor, which provided funding for this research. His *National Agricultural Worker Survey* has provided valuable national data on the changing face of farm labor. Luckily, Rick is not alone in his dedication to producing sound, objective work on farm labor. Among the more effective in this regard are those who tirelessly collect depositions, testimonies, pay records, and other bits and pieces of information that help the working poor in their legal cases. These are the lawyers and outreach workers of the Rural Legal Services offices across the United States. In Florida, Rob Williams and Greg Schell have been and continue to be particularly supportive of this work. Their work has led to important victories for farm labor and improvements in working conditions and record keeping, much to the chagrin of some of the most abusive farm labor contractors and growers. In North Carolina, Mary Lee Hall provided background material that fleshed out processes we were observing and describing up and down the eastern seaboard.

The employment services and other county offices in each of the labor supply and demand regions contained many people who spent much time talking with us and providing the reports, numbers, and data sources at their disposal. Again, we must apologize for leaving out some of these individuals. In Florida, among those we remember to thank are Tim Navarez, Michael Wong, and Joe Huntsucker of the Florida Department of Labor and Employment Security; Louis Pelle of the Florida Department of Health and Rehabilitative Services; and Michelle Edwards of the Collier County Planning Department. Ms. Edwards was particularly helpful in providing maps, reports, and other materials that were essential for sampling in Immokalee. For their aid with the Parlier study, we express gratitude to Arcadio Viveros, mayor of Parlier; and to Larry Trujillo, author of a monograph on Parlier. At the Virginia Employment Service, we thank Bob Warren and Richard Crossen; at the Delaware Employment Service, Al Glover; and at the Maryland Employment Service, Bernard Ward.

Many people affiliated with the national system of Association of Farmworker Opportunity Programs and other agencies responsible for administering the Job Training Partnership Program provided leads on data sources and other forms of assistance. Carlos Saavedra, of the Migrant Education Program in Florida, provided excellent feedback on early reports.

During the preparation of this book, a number of individuals working for the Commission on Agricultural Workers gave us the opportunity and means to meet and discuss important issues facing farmworkers. For this we thank Luis Torres, Monica Heppel, and Shannon Hamm. Sandra Amendola was also helpful in this regard. Monica and Luis deserve special recognition for their tireless work of bringing together research of the commission and for continuing their efforts as founders of the Inter-American Institute for Migration and Labor in Washington, D.C.

Many people at East Carolina University's Institute for Coastal and Marine Resources and Department of Anthropology contributed to this work as well. First and foremost, Bill Queen, director of the institute, supported this research effort in innumerable ways, having the wisdom to recognize that the development of theory and method dealing with farm labor can draw on and contribute to the development of theory and labor related to the social and cultural issues facing coastal populations. Linda Wolfe, chair of the anthropology department, aided this project by allowing David Griffith to reschedule his teaching and advising responsibilities for the preparation of the original manuscript. For this, also, thanks go to his colleagues in the department, who not only supported scheduling changes but have contributed to his intellectual development in many overt and subtle ways: Lorraine Aragon, John Bort, Robert Bunger, John Byrd, Dale Hutchinson, Holly Mathews, and David Phelps.

We deeply appreciate Cindy Harper's smooth method of resolving many of the paperwork problems that inevitably arise in a grant such as ours. Kay Evans deserves equal thanks for similar reasons, as well as for her role in the data processing and statistical analysis, expertly entering the mountains of survey data into a complicated computer format for processing and analysis. Also, support for a variety of research, layout, data-processing, and other tasks came from John Brown, Vernon Kelley, Carol Ann Smith, and Amy Whitcher. Ann Smith brought to the manuscript her expert skills as a proofreader, derived from years of educational experience.

At Temple University Press, Doris Braendel offered excellent suggestions during the inevitably long and problematic time between her first receiving the manuscript and publication.

A project of this size can only amass a large debt of gratitude for a diverse and multitalented staff. We thank Dennis Porter at Micro-Methods, who administered the Department of Labor's grant. Joanne Intilli provided excellent professional research assistance in the form of statistical analysis and data management. Fieldworkers who deserve special mention include Erasmo Teran and Felix Peña in Texas; Macrina Cartenas, Rafael Alarcón, and Naomi Guerrero in California; Deborah Landau in New Jersey, Maryland, and Delaware; Guy Honore in Florida; and Trina Ramos Foster in Michigan.

David Griffith
Greenville, North Carolina

Ed Kissam
Sebastopol, California

PART I

Introduction

Chapter 1

The Formation
of Agricultural Labor
in the United States

Carol Gelderman's (1981) biography of Henry Ford opens with the observation that he was born into a rural society and died in an urban one. This transformation, in which Ford himself played a substantial part, frames the evolving role of new immigrants, refugees, and minorities in the U.S. farm labor force. This transformation was not restricted to the United States or even North America; depending on the historical period, the transition from a rural to an urban society initiated or contributed to demographic processes in Mexico, the Caribbean, Central America, and even some of the labor-exporting countries of the Pacific Rim. The resulting social and cultural changes have shaken many of the fundamental principles of rural life. Some of these changes have been liberating, such as those that have drawn women out of male systems of authority and domination, peasants throughout Latin America and the Caribbean out of abject poverty and serfdom, and African Americans and new immigrant Europeans out of debt peonage in the South (Daniel 1972; Adams 1979). Yet other changes have given less cause for celebration. Many of the population movements typically viewed as spontaneous responses to economic disparity have actually been stimulated by labor brokers, personnel departments, and others to staff high-turnover, hazardous, low-paying positions.

The rural-to-urban transition underlies much conventional thinking about farmwork and farmworkers. Historically, U.S. farm labor has been undercounted, misrepresented, largely hidden from public scrutiny, and poorly understood. With such notable exceptions as John Steinbeck's *Grapes of Wrath* and Edward R. Murrow's *Harvest of Shame,* the conditions and existence of U.S. farmworkers have been buried under complex ideologies that regard farming as a reified lifestyle at whose heart and hearth lies the American family, usually of German or Scandinavian heritage. Richard Rhodes's (1989) popular book *Farm,* which chronicles "a year in the life of an American farmer," is a case in point, portraying a struggling, inventive, entrepreneurial Kansas farm family that balances its heavy-equipment debt against Russian grain deals and storage problems. The featured farmer's neighbors are being forced into webs of debt, subsidy programs, preferential-marketing agreements, corporate capital, foreclosures, and auctions until, eventually, they are displaced from the land. These unfortunate neighbors contribute to the structural change in U.S. agriculture that has, since the 1930s, marked the passage of decades by fewer farms with larger acreages (Brooks, Kalbacher, and Reimund 1990). Foreclosures deepen the stoicism and significance of those farmers who remain, including Rhodes's farmers. Rhodes's depictions include new immigrants, yet in a way that reinforces the imagery of family and farming rather than calls attention to the abysmal living and working conditions of today's immigrant farmworkers.

> Tom Bauer's forebears came from central Germany, from a thousand-year-old German Catholic farming village in Hesse where half the town answered to some variation on the Bauer name. Franz Bauer, Tom's great-grandfather, arrived in the United States in 1855, when he was thirty years old, and made his way to St. Louis. He was one of some two and a half million Germans who emigrated to the United States in the first six decades of the nineteenth century, an emigration that swelled between 1848 and 1860 to a flood. The farmers among the immigrants brought with them German habits of husbandry that invested the rural American landscape with its most characteristic features, the single-family farmstead and the multipurpose barn. (Rhodes 1989:36)

Farm crises of the 1920s, 1950s, and 1980s have focused and refocused public attention on the plight of the U.S. farm family and farmer—often in opposition to corporate farming—without significantly raising the public's consciousness about either the characteristics or conditions of U.S. farmworkers. Yet the general public is not alone in its lack of accurate information about U.S. farmworkers. Some government reports of the last few years describe farmworkers as though they were the farmhands in *The Wizard of Oz:* white, happy, so attached to the farm family that they figured prominently in

Dorothy's dreams. These reports have been used by growers and growers' associations to support their claims that their workers are treated well, as in an excerpt from an agricultural-cooperative representative's letter written in response to a report on the conditions of Florida farmworkers. "As documented in an article entitled 'Unscrambling the Hired Farmworkers Stereotype,' [the U.S. Department of Agriculture] reported in 1979 that the typical U.S. farmworker is more likely to be white, a nonmigrant, and part of a family with annual income of $10,000 or more" (Barry 1990: app. F).

Social scientists, journalists, and others also have great difficulty accurately representing U.S. farm labor. Two principal reasons for this difficulty are the high proportions of illegal and new-immigrant workers in the farm labor force and the mobility and invisibility of migrant and seasonal farmworkers. The most reliable accounts of conditions of farmwork are provided by anthropologists and journalists who have actually lived with farmworkers (e.g., Friedland and Nelkin 1971; Heppel 1983; Heppel and Amendola 1992), yet even these become quickly dated as demographic, political, social, and cultural changes interact to alter the face of the U.S. farm labor force. Often, by the time powerful portraits of farmworker housing and crew dynamics and other features of farmworkers' lives become incorporated into academic, policy, and popular discourse—when they become "conventional wisdom"—they no longer apply.

A case in point is the notion of the three streams, which asserts that there are three basic farm labor migrations within the United States: an East Coast stream made up primarily of African American workers, from Florida through Georgia, the Carolinas, and on into the Northeast; a midwestern stream consisting of Chicanos or Mexicans, from Texas into the breadbasket states of Michigan, Wisconsin, Illinois, Iowa, and so on; and a western stream consisting primarily of Mexicans, from Mexico and the Southwest up through California's central valleys and on into Oregon and Washington. While some farm labor migrations still follow one of these three streams, a number of developments over the past thirty years have chipped away at how much the three-streams model represents reality. These include sociopolitical and technological developments both national and international in scope. For example, the end of the Bracero Program and other immigration policy changes of the mid-1960s influenced the face of the nation's low-wage labor and marked the beginning of significant new waves of immigrants. With changes in immigration policies in 1965, the United States and Canada became major destinations for Caribbean immigrants, displacing the importance of England, the Netherlands, and France as immigrant destinations (Richardson 1983). Overseas, during the 1950s and 1960s, the formation of new Caribbean states through independence movements also reoriented emigration pathways from colonial mother countries to North America. In some Mexican states, Green Revolution rural-development programs expanded grain production and displaced peasants from the land, forcing them into U.S. and Mexican labor markets (Hewitt de Alcantara 1976). These developments helped construct a labor force that today makes up the bulk of agricultural labor in both the United States and Mexico. The most recent national survey estimates that, in 1990, Mexicans constituted 92 percent of the foreign-born U.S. farm labor force and 57 percent of the total farm labor force (Mines, Gabbard, and Samardick 1991:16; see also Heppel and Amendola 1992; Commission on Agricultural Workers 1993a, 1993b, 1993c).

Political and economic developments and difficulties within the United States also altered the flow of farm labor migrants and the ethnic composition of work groups. The civil-rights movement of the 1960s, combined with the Vietnam War, rising inflation, and the growth of the service sector, led to increased nonagricultural hiring of African Americans, women, and others who had long supplied labor to seasonal agricultural operations. Mechanization, in part a response to spot labor shortages and growing fears of labor shortages, altered the character of labor demand for a number of crops and regions. Changes in cropping and land-use strategies, encouraged by commodity programs and the agricultural-research agendas of land grant colleges, affected farm labor migrants' seasonal destinations and schedules, cycles of employment and unemployment, and annual incomes. The development of irrigation techniques ushered in ecological changes that made possible large-scale fruit and vegetable farming in Florida, Texas, and the Southwest. Key pieces of legislation and court rulings aimed specifically at abuses of farm labor (e.g., U.S. Congress 1963, 1965, 1978) suggested that the federal government was taking a closer look at farm wages and working conditions. New and old political crises in Mexico, the Caribbean, and Central America stimulated labor migrations and refugee flows from those areas to the United States at the same time demographic and labor market changes were occurring within U.S. borders. These changes have combined to alter, fundamentally, the farm labor force and the place of agriculture in the United States, despite the fact that residual demographic and sociological features of agriculture and farm labor remain from earlier periods.

In the following sections we discuss three eras in U.S. agriculture. These eras are somewhat arbitrary in their boundaries yet are marked by important events that signaled emergent labor processes in perishable-crop agriculture, especially in farmworker communities of California, Florida, Texas, and Puerto Rico. We pay more attention to the earlier periods than to the years from 1964 to the present, since the latter is discussed in detail in the community studies of Part II. How the broad, sweeping processes outlined here interact with the local histories of labor supply and labor demand regions lies at the heart of the case studies we present.

Early Years: 1865 to 1940

Before World War II, farm labor throughout much of the United States consisted primarily of unpaid family and local workers, sharecroppers, and tenant farmers. African Americans in the South, Japanese and Chinese workers in the West, and migrant workers displaced by various economic or ecological disasters such as the dust bowl of the 1930s supplemented a predominantly "hired-hand," resident labor force ("Wartime Changes" 1945). In the northern harvests, seasonal labor demand during the summer months could be met with local high school students, since few alternative job opportunities existed. While Mexican workers were present in southern California and the Southwest, many Mexican and Mexican American families were forcibly repatriated during the Great Depression or swindled out of their landholdings early in the twentieth century (Massey et al. 1987; Jiobu 1988). During the latter part of the nineteenth century, many growers in the Southwest, particularly California, relied on Chinese and Japanese immigrants for farm labor as well (Runsten and LeVeen 1981; Thomas 1985). Around the turn of the century, U.S. expansion into Puerto Rico, Hawaii, the Philippines, and other parts of the Pacific and Caribbean also established these regions as potential sources for agricultural and other low-wage workers; today, most immigrant nurses come from the Philippines, and nearly the same number of Puerto Ricans live in Chicago and New York as live in Puerto Rico. The expansionist phase of U.S. history that brought Puerto Ricans and Filipinos into the U.S. labor force was accompanied by an increasing scrutiny of and preoccupation with rural life inside the continental United States. The administration of Theodore Roosevelt played an important role in the expansion of U.S. government influence abroad and into the nation's "country life." In 1908, Roosevelt commissioned the now famous *Country Life Report,* published a year later. The commission and its report reflected the growing self-awareness of the United States as an emerging world power. With many of the nation's resources in its rural areas, the U.S. government, increasingly dominated by urban and industrial interests

since the end of the Civil War, could not afford to allow these rural areas to
stagnate under the husbandry of Jeffersonian yeoman farmers with little interest in large-scale commercial production.

The Country Life Commission was designed, "not to help the farmer raise
better crops, but to call his attention to the opportunities for better business
and better living on the farm" (Country Life Commission 1909:2). Increasing
commercial activity ("business opportunity") meant expanding acreages,
adopting more-efficient methods of production, and either hiring more labor
or binding more labor to the land through share and service tenure arrangements. In most works on agriculture published during this period, tenant farming was associated with the construction of a stable agricultural labor force
and portrayed as a path of upward mobility.

> So long as the United States continues to be a true democracy it will have a
> serious labor problem. As a democracy, we honor labor, and the higher the
> efficiency of the labor the greater the honor. The laborer, if he has the ambition
> to be an efficient agent in the development of the country, will be anxious to
> advance from the lower to the higher forms of effort, and from being a laborer
> himself he becomes a director of labor. If he has nothing but his hands and
> brains, he aims to accumulate sufficient capital to become a tenant, and eventu-
> ally to become the owner, of a farm house. A large number of our immigrants
> share with the native-born citizen this laudable ambition. Therefore there is a
> constant decrease of efficient farm labor by these upward movements. (41–42)

Labor supply problems were already being solved with immigration, which
the *Country Life Report* characterized as "a growing tendency to rely on for-
eigners for farm labor supply" (Country Life Commission 1909:43). The
commissioners found this tendency disconcerting. They expressed a desire for
the United States to develop an efficient, permanent, and native agricultural
labor force and suggested that established landowners adopt methods of insuring a resident, as opposed to migrant, labor force. Foremost among their concerns was the perception that farmworkers, ostensibly because of their living
conditions, had a propensity for drunkenness.

> There is widespread conviction that the farmer must give greater attention to
> providing good quarters to laborers and to protect them from discouragement
> and from the saloon. The shortage of labor seems to be the least marked where
> the laborers is best cared for. The best labor, other things being equal, is resident
> labor. Such reorganization of agriculture must take place as will tend more and
> more to employ the man year round and to tie him to the land. The employer
> bears a distinct responsibility to the laborer, and also to society, to house him
> well and to help him to contribute his part to the community welfare. (44–45)

Few farmers followed the commission's recommendations, in part because of the commission's urban origins and the consequent mistrust its findings generated among farm folk. Also, farmers could not stop the continuing flow of rural-to-urban migrants, having little or nothing to compete with the higher wages, more stable employment, and more modern lifestyles of the cities (DuBois 1898; Lively and Taeuber 1939). Seasonal migrant labor assumed more and more of the harvest tasks and other important labor requirements between the time of the Commission's report and the 1920s. In many parts of the country, sharecropping, cash renting, and other forms of tenancy either declined or did not lend themselves to creating the stability that the Country Life Commission encouraged. Fite (1984) reports, for example, that "sharecroppers and tenants were continually looking for a better situation" (46). Other causes of the instability of tenancy were continuing emigration of tenants and sporadic ecological crises such as the boll weevil infestation through the Cotton Belt (Wynne 1943). During the time the commission observed rural life, moreover, most farmers were concerned that merchants and bankers had gained too much control over the distribution and marketing of food products. This was a time of feeble and frustrated attempts by farmers to become politically active and more tightly and effectively organized. The Grange, the Alliance, and the Farmer's Union represented three such attempts (Danbom 1979; Fite 1984).

Tenancy as a potential steppingstone to farm ownership slipped farther out of reach during this period, as the supply of new land for farming dwindled. Before 1910, much of the growth of farm output and farm productivity derived from bringing new land into production. As this practice slowed, domestic food supplies had to be supplemented with imports, and urban dwellers grew alarmed over rising food prices. Low-cost food had been and continues to be an important mechanism of social peace in the face of declining or stagnant wages for industrial workers. Low-cost food is also necessary if an industrial labor force is to remain healthy enough to reproduce itself. As the nation's industrial base expanded, it created a pressing need for low-cost food; producing food cheaply, in turn, depended on increasing productivity per acre and increasing food supplies to cities. This need laid the foundation for widespread political and economic support for commercial agriculture that would not only improve food supplies but also consume the products of industry: fertilizers, hybrid seed, farm machinery, financial services, and so on. As the United States prepared to enter the First World War, the need for increasing farm production and farm productivity became acute.

Each of these developments paved the way for a greater reliance on seasonal migrant farmworkers, especially workers with reduced consumption needs, willing to work for wages that fell from 70 percent of industrial workers' wages to 23 percent between 1910 and 1934 (Schwartz 1945:14). Sponsored by the War Department, Puerto Ricans became citizens in 1917, in time to be used in the First World War as well as to move freely between mainland agriculture, largely a spring and summer activity, and the sugar fields of Puerto Rico, which needed labor primarily during the late fall and winter months. In 1917 and 1918, to facilitate the flow of Mexican workers into agriculture, the U.S. government removed the head tax and other barriers to immigration (Schwartz 1945:25).

In addition to lending legitimacy to increased state intervention in labor market policy, the First World War played an important role in establishing a "modern" outlook within agricultural communities. This opened up agriculture even further to corporate farming, secured the place of land grant colleges in agricultural research, and justified the technological modernization of agricultural practices (Danbom 1979). A variety of rural and urban groups expressed their patriotism by attempting to mobilize for field work students, retired workers, women, and others who had never engaged in farm labor. Methods such as these could be relied on only with the impetus of war, however, which stimulated increased commercial production among farmers as much as it stimulated farmwork among citizens. With few exceptions, a great deal of farm production before the First World War was oriented less toward commerce than toward family sustenance, especially in isolated areas far from urban centers. And many areas were isolated, serviced by dirt roads or paths and fourth-class postal services. At the turn of the century in the South, for example, "one could travel for hundreds of miles throughout much of the region and never encounter a place of 8,000 or more population" (Fite 1984:31). Over the next few decades, largely because of a growing urban America's concern over the backwardness of a rural America that would not or could not provide cheap food to urban populations, concern spurred by war, agriculture was to engage in what Danbom (1979) terms a "resisted revolution" of technological change and modernization.

As early as the 1920s and 1930s, rural demographic and agricultural practices were changing in ways that pointed toward the increased use of hired farm labor in perishable-crop agriculture. In the South, the decline in sharecropping and tenant farming was accompanied by increased levels of African American and white emigration. The decrease in share tenancy reduced the local, resident labor supply that could be tapped during periods of peak labor demand on neighboring farms. According to Schwartz (1945):

The role of the tenure system in the determination of farmers' needs for hired seasonal workers arises chiefly from the connection between different forms of land tenure and the size of the resident labor supply. An agricultural community consisting of a large number of small family farms is likely to have more resident labor available for peak periods of crop work than is an agricultural community of equal areas consisting of large manager-operated enterprises. [T]enancy in cotton production assures plantation owners of a great pool of resident labor—consisting mainly of tenants' and sharecroppers' wives and children—who though idle most of the crop year are available at key periods of cotton chopping and cotton picking. On large corporation-owned fruit or vegetable farms, on the other hand, there is no idle labor available to reduce the need for seasonal employees. (18–19)

Technological developments also altered the character of agriculture, contributing to more sophisticated mechanization and changing cropping strategies, cultural practices, and the overall image of agriculture as a grain- or soybean-producing enterprise. Not the least important of innovations were complex financial instruments and arrangements developed to underwrite the expansion of commercial agriculture. Farmers used credit to purchase land, machinery, and inputs and to cover operating expenses, expanding yet another avenue for urban-industrial control over the development of agriculture as a commercial enterprise. In perishable fruits, nuts, vegetables, and other crops, hired and contracted farmworkers began to assume an ever-greater proportion of the workforce. Florida, Texas, and California required the largest farmworking populations, but migrants from these regions and Puerto Rico began supplying harvests throughout the northern United States in large numbers during the 1930s and 1940s. In the case studies in this volume—for example, in Berrien County, Michigan—farmers have relied on African Americans from the South; whites from Arkansas and Appalachia; Filipinos; and finally, after World War II, Mexicans, on whom they continue to rely today.

John Steinbeck left us an enduring portrait of agriculture during the 1930s in *The Grapes of Wrath,* and most of us know this decade for the widespread displacement of farmers from their land throughout the Midwest because of foreclosures and drought. These were the so-called dust bowl refugees, pouring from Oklahoma, Arkansas, and other midwestern regions into California and Texas. This was also a decade of developing and continuing industrial-labor unrest in the United States, the Caribbean, and Latin America. Organizational gains by labor caused industrialists to recruit African Americans, illegal aliens, and other minorities that had long been a mainstay of agricultural labor forces. The rural-to-urban movements of the 1930s built upon those of the two previous decades, with some notable differences. Stimulated by the First World War, between 1920 and 1930 the Mid-Atlantic lost 7.9 percent of its rural population through migration, and the East South Central region—including much of the Deep South—lost twice that much (15.8 percent) (Lively and Taeuber 1939). Although the Pacific states experienced net increases in their rural populations through migration, only 17 percent of counties nationwide shared this experience.

During the first part of the 1930s, rural emigration seemed to be slowing, from 600,000 a year during the 1920s to 120,000 a year in the period 1930–34. Again, rates and results of migration were unevenly distributed. Secondary migration (another move to a new location) seemed to be more common than return migration (going back to a place of origin), so that those who returned to the countryside were returning to farms near urban areas instead of to the farms and regions that had lost population a decade earlier. Hence, Lively and Taeuber (1939) note that:

> widespread variations in migration to and from farms occurred among the various geographic divisions of the country. The areas reporting net migration from farms during the 5-year period 1930–34 were, broadly speaking, the major agricultural regions—the areas producing cotton and wheat together with a section of the Corn Belt. Areas receiving a relatively large net migration to farms included the northeastern portion of the United States, the Appalachian Mountains, the Lake States Cut-Over Region, and the farm Northwest as well as scattered smaller areas. Although the total net movement from farms to villages, towns, and cities from 1930 to 1934 was only 600,000 persons, approximately 8 times as many persons actually moved to achieve this result, reflecting the constant interchange of farm and nonfarm population. (xvi)

Toward the end of the decade, public concern about the impoverished conditions facing California farmworkers grew to the point that a special commission, known as the La Follette Commission, was established to examine such farmworker issues as low wages, hazardous working conditions, and the problems of labor organizing (La Follette, Thomas, and Walsh 1941). Investigations were undertaken in other regions as well (e.g., Webb and Brown 1938; Holley, Winston, and Woofter 1940; Schwartz 1945). During this time, attention to farmworker problems emerged in particular as a result of the horrors that accompanied labor organizing during the 1930s and earlier. Strikes and other farmworker organizing activities, gathering legitimacy during depression years, stimulated reactions among growers that led to bloody confrontations throughout the United States between farmworkers and vigilante groups representing growers. In the South, the Southern Tenant Farmers Union emerged to organize tenants who, along with their family members, supplied much of the labor to cotton and other harvesting operations. In California, a number of union drives began to gain acceptance among farmworkers and related industries such as packing houses and canneries (Meister and Loftis 1977; Ruiz 1987). These gains proved short-lived. Wartime labor relations, seated in patriotic calls to arms and politically inspired economic expansion, allowed little room for grievance or complaint.

The War Years: 1940 to 1964

> We depend on misfortune to build up our force of migratory workers and when the supply is low because there is not enough misfortune at home, we rely on misfortune abroad to replenish the supply.
> —Commission on Migratory Labor 1951

If the depression years forced agricultural producers to reconsider using domestic workers, improving wages and working conditions, and recognizing the rights of workers to organize, U.S. involvement in World War II turned the clock back. Again, growers focused their recruiting efforts outside the United States, in particular, on Mexico. This was especially true in California and Texas, where domestic farmworkers leaving agriculture for the war effort were quickly replaced by Mexicans.

In a study of seasonal farm labor in the fruit and vegetable and sugar beet industries, Schwartz (1945) distinguished between "hired hands" and seasonal agricultural workers, a distinction that still describes many farm labor forces today. Before and during World War II, however, hired hands were those workers who considered themselves more like apprentices than mere wageworkers, gaining skills and experience in hopes of one day becoming independent farmers themselves. Often they were employed year-round and performed a variety of skilled farm tasks. Socially and culturally, hired hands were likely to resemble the farmers they worked for more than the disadvantaged workers we associate with farmwork today. It is likely, too, that they participated in celebrations and ritual observances along with their employers; sometimes they were the sons of neighboring farmers, working as hired hands until their fathers reached retirement age. Thomas (1985) also notes that the farm labor market was divided into those struggling to strike out on their own and those who, because of a variety of disadvantages, could never dream of tilling their own soil. Similar characterizations of farm labor have been made by other observers for this and other periods (e.g., Commission on Migratory Labor 1951; Mines 1974).

Today's equivalent of Schwartz's hired hands tend to be permanent employees or longtime returning migrant families with no more hope of farming their own land than the Chinese in California had during the 1870s. This distinction, however, is but one of many that describes divisions within the farm labor force and implies the existence of internal labor markets. Simply, the farm labor market has always been heterogeneous. Internal differentiation has rested, at various times, on ethnic background, residence (migrant vs. local), gender, attachment to farm labor, or legal status. Because of the active role of the U.S. government in the recruitment of foreign workers, during the early years of war, especially, legal status became the most important factor in establishing internal labor markets.

Growers throughout the United States worried that the war effort's demand for workers would lead to a severe reduction in the labor surpluses they had grown accustomed to during the depression (Rasmussen 1951). Thus, in 1941, the U.S. government allowed growers to import Mexican workers legally, beginning what later became known as the Bracero Program (Galarza 1977; U.S. Congress 1978). A similar but much smaller program, the British West Indies (BWI) Temporary Alien Labor Program, began a year later in the eastern United States, importing workers first from the Bahamas and later from Jamaica, Barbados, Dominica, St. Vincent, and St. Lucia (Griffith 1983). British West Indians worked in several crops east of the Mississippi River, while the Mexican "Braceros" worked throughout the western United States in cotton and fruits and vegetables.

Both of these programs allowed growers to import foreign nationals legally, work them as long as they needed them, and then send them back to their home countries during the off-season. Most workers were certified to work for a single grower or firm, which gave the programs the flavor of indentured servitude. During its peak, the Bracero Program admitted over four hundred thousand workers in a single year, while the BWI program, which still exists, never admitted more than twenty thousand workers in a given year. These government-sponsored programs supplemented continued flows of Latin American and Caribbean workers into U.S. agriculture.

Even during the war, state assistance in supplying foreign workers to agriculture was never a politically neutral issue. Again, Rasmussen (1951:43) points out that, with the war, growers feared less an absolute shortage of labor than a shortage relative to the surplus conditions that allowed them to keep wages low and working conditions poor. There were, however, sporadic labor shortages, and farm wages did grow during the war years, from 25 percent to 44 percent of industrial wages between 1940 and 1945, even though foreign nationals continued to be allowed into the country legally. Following the war, however, agricultural wages began to fall; by 1950, they were only 37 percent of industrial wages. Annual earnings were even worse, since mechanization of important crops such as sugar beets interrupted migrant itineraries and negatively affected the amount of work farmworkers could perform during the year (Commission on Migratory Labor 1951:17). If patriotism and rising production costs could justify the continuation of foreign-worker programs during World War II, the same justifications carried less political clout after 1945.

By the early 1950s, conditions in the fields warranted yet another executive examination of farm labor issues, particularly the plight of migrant farmworkers. The president's Commission on Migratory Labor (1951) emerged out of increasing concerns that foreign nationals in U.S. agricutlure, whether legal or illegal, constituted the principal cause of low wages for domestic farmworkers, their lack of employment security and social benefits such as unemployment insurance, their inefficient use in the fields, and their overall powerlessness. Despite these concerns, the Korean crisis again raised the prospect of possible food shortages from inadequate labor supplies (Commission on Migratory Labor 1951:25–27). The question facing the commission was whether the Korean crisis overseas was matched by a farm labor crisis at home. In short, should the government continue assisting growers by importing foreign farmworkers? The commission recommended that domestic workers could, and should, be utilized more efficiently, and it encouraged containing alien-labor programs at their 1950 levels. Like many commissions, the 1951 commission's recommendations were largely ignored. By the mid-1950s, the Bracero Program had risen to record levels of nearly half a million workers (Galarza 1964).

Several characteristics of the alien-labor programs begun during World War II were important in laying the groundwork for the state's role in supplying labor to perishable-crop agriculture. First, contract alien labor never provided more than 3 percent of the hired farmworkers in any year during the 1940s, yet Mexicans were utilized in twenty-four states and British West Indians in twenty-one states. Most of the Mexicans were concentrated in California, Washington, Idaho, and Oregon, most of the British West Indians in New York, California, and Florida. This pattern of broad geographical representation coupled with high concentrations of foreign workers meant that, in most regions, foreign contract workers constituted a supplemental rather than primary workforce. Despite this, contract workers received a disproportionate amount of attention from legislators and bureaucrats, primarily because the program involved turning the government into a labor contractor. Those writing for government audiences during this time were clearly uncomfortable with this role and encouraged more passive government involvement in supplying labor to growers (Commission on Migratory Labor 1951:iii). This came in the form of legalization.

> When the contracting of wetbacks was proposed by Mexico, the Immigration and Naturalization Service saw it as a threat to enforcement of the immigration law and opposed it. . . . A technique more insidious than ingenious was devised and put in effect by the agencies of the United States Government having responsibility for law enforcement and procurement of labor. In this improvisation, the Immigration and Naturalization Service would be allowed to ''deport'' the wetback by having him brought to the border, at which point the wetback would be given an identification slip. Momentarily, he would step across the boundary line. Having thus been subjected to the magic of token deportation, the illegal alien was now merely alien and was eligible to step back across the boundary to be legally contracted. (Commission on Migratory Labor 1951:52–53)

Such activities by government agencies illustrate the instrumental role of the state in supplying agriculture with labor. Despite a variety of special commissions and investigations, ultimately the state facilitated growers' access to cheap and docile labor from abroad. The legalization programs of the early 1950s simply lent legitimacy to the prevailing status quo of using foreign workers, primarily Mexicans, in agriculture.

Thus, the years 1940 to 1964 constitute a key ''formative'' period for U.S. agriculture's labor supply. Links with Mexican, Puerto Rican, and other overseas labor forces, although established earlier, were expanded during this period. Anglo workers declined in importance. African Americans maintained a continued presence in the South, East, and Northeast. It was during this period, too, that Texas, California, and Florida solidified their importance as labor supply states, and as what we have labeled ''nodes'' in international migration networks. Furthermore, with the increase in the importance of hired farm labor proportionate to family workers in areas of labor-intensive agriculture, we see a corresponding increase in labor intermediaries, including farm labor contractors and specialized associations and agencies. The year 1946, for example, marked the founding of the Glassboro Services Association, an agency that still imports Puerto Rican farmworkers into New Jersey and neighboring states. In Florida, the Florida Fruit and Vegetable Association helped with farm labor placement, particularly in the BWI program. Producers in California, Arizona, Texas, and other major agricultural states banded together to stem the growth of farm labor unions, to reduce their dependence on the processing sector, and to market farm produce more effectively. These developments created more effective grower organizations capable of influencing government policies regarding labor, immigration, and trade in agricultural production. At the same time, farm labor leaders and others sympathetic to farm labor issues realized that the Bracero Program and continued illegal immigration of Mexican nationals would continue to impede similar levels of organizational complexity and effectiveness among farmworkers.

Civil Rights and Foreign Workers: 1965 to 1992

The demand for new-immigrant, foreign, and largely illegal labor for agricultural services has, since the mid-1960s, become institutionalized in perishable-crop agriculture throughout most of the United States. Spearheading the illegal immigrant influx were Mexican nationals. Concentrated geographically and confined to specific groups of crops between 1940 and 1964, Mexican workers began migrating east and north across the continental United States during the mechanization of cotton harvesting through the 1950s and after receiving green cards in 1965. Until the late 1950s, the primary Latin presence in the East and Midwest was Puerto Rican. Beginning in the 1950s, however, Mexican workers began slowly working their way into agricultural services in almost every area where large numbers of seasonal workers were needed. Yet our community studies show that the process of ethnic succession in the nation's diverse agricultural labor markets is complex. In some crops and regions, to be sure, foreign Latino workers have displaced Chicanos, African Americans, Puerto Ricans, and others. In other regions, new immigrants and foreign workers have replaced domestic workers who have left the labor market; in still others, they play a complementary role.

Nevertheless, between 1965 and 1992, Mexican workers succeeded in establishing footholds in virtually every important perishable-crop production region in the country. In the chapters that follow we focus primarily on this period; here we merely point out some of the broad trends that have led to the current social and cultural complexion of the agricultural labor force.

Thomas (1985) argues that by the end of the Bracero Program, in 1964, the use of undocumented workers had already become so widespread in south-

western agriculture that most growers preferred "wetbacks" to the more captive but more highly regulated Braceros. As far back as 1950, observers noted
huge increases in the size of border cities, indicating the growth of border
crossings and deportations. Such increases ranged from 78 percent in Nogales
to 259 percent in Tijuana (Commission on Migratory Labor 1951:72). Mexican nationals supplemented Bracero crews primarily in California, the Northwest, Arizona, New Mexico, and Texas. After 1965, however, the termination
of the Bracero Program and the liberal granting of green cards to Bracero
workers fostered "pioneering" migrations into agricultural pockets throughout the United States. This marked the beginning of the large-scale geographic
dispersion of Mexican and other Latin workers. Tomato and muskmelon producers along the Mississippi Valley had begun shifting from local workers to
Mexican migrants around this time. Witnessing the loss of African American
workers to a developing tourist industry that culminated in the construction of
Disney World, vegetable growers in southern Florida and citrus growers in
central Florida also began turning to Chicano and Mexican workers from
Texas (Hudson 1979; Barry 1990). As African American and Spanish-speaking crew leaders took crews into spring and summer harvests up the eastern
seaboard, Latin workers began appearing in Georgia, the Carolinas, and Virginia's Eastern Shore (Heppel 1983). Factors both inside and outside of agriculture forced more and more growers to turn from their traditional labor
supplies to Mexican and, later, Central American and non-U.S. Caribbean
workers. A U.S. Department of Agriculture report published in 1967 cites
four factors affecting California's farm labor supplies in the immediate post-
Bracero era.

> (1) Termination of the importation of bracero (Mexican national) labor.
> (2) Rapid expansion of employment in industrial, commercial, service, defense
> activities, and movement of workers out of the farm labor force to those activi-
> ties, to the Armed Forces, and to manpower training courses.
> (3) Mechanization of the cotton harvest and resulting dislocations in the labor
> force. The displaced workers have generally avoided work in crops formerly
> done by foreign labor.
> (4) Development of machinery to harvest the cannery tomato crop. This will
> reduce the need for handpicked but will increase the demand for sorters on the
> harvesting machines. (Metzler, Loomis, and LeRay 1967:1)

Other factors contributing to demographic changes in the agricultural labor
force were the civil-rights movement and the continuing alliance between the
Democratic party and organized labor. The latter relationship, in particular,

resulted in sporadic successes for organized labor in farming (Mines 1974). While these developments began drying up or altering the character of traditional labor supplies (those involving members of minority groups and unpaid family workers) and labor relations in agriculture, factors in the sending countries—Mexico in particular—contributed to the construction of a foreign labor force. Continued poverty and unemployment in Mexico and other sending countries, exacerbated by so-called rural modernization programs, increased rates of peasant landlessness and promoted rural-to-urban and Mexico-to-U.S. migrations, particularly in the decades of the 1950s and 1960s (Hewitt de Alcantara 1976; Massey et al. 1987).

Because of the proliferation of illegal and legal foreign-born labor, government attempts to replace Bracero workers with domestic workers received a great deal of attention beginning in 1965. Converting from Bracero to domestic labor, however, involved significant infrastructural and social changes. Bracero workers had been an entirely male labor force and lived in dormitory-style housing. To attract domestic workers, growers would have to modify or replace existing structures to accommodate family workers. Further changes had to take place in supervision. Being foreign, "captive" workers, Braceros could be and were treated with authoritarian methods of labor control. Periodically, throughout the Bracero period, the Mexican government protested the treatment of Bracero workers in U.S. agriculture (Rasmussen 1951). During the supposed "transition" to domestic labor, various branches of the U.S. government attempted to institute training and "enhanced recruitment" programs. There were public programs designed to upgrade supervision and the quality of farm jobs, but they met with little success. Growers and farm contractors continued to recruit immigrant, minority, and disadvantaged labor, regardless of citizenship. Always they preferred those most vulnerable and least likely to leave the farm labor market.

Yet programs to upgrade farm jobs were not a waste. They succeeded in keeping attention focused on the abysmal living and working conditions facing farmworkers and generated sincere, if spotty, attempts by growers to improve labor relations. They also contributed to the growing sympathy for farmworker organizing that followed the rise of the United Farm Workers (UFW) and the temporary successes of farmworker boycotting activities. Union contracts were signed in many California locations and with Minute Maid (Coca-Cola) in Florida.

Throughout this period as well, the American consumer's dietary wants continued to change, with people favoring fresh over processed vegetables, paying increasing attention to consistency of product quality, and becoming mindful of preservatives and chemicals used for enhancing flavor, texture, or appearance. From 1970 to 1990, fresh-fruit consumption rose from 79.4 to 92.6 pounds per person, fresh-vegetable consumption from 177.0 to 190.8 pounds (USDA 1991). Responding to this increased demand, land grant colleges continued providing research to grow produce of high and consistent quality. Yet the relationships between labor demand in perishable-crop agriculture and technological developments is not a simple case of labor demand falling as technology improves. Many of the technological inputs created greater demand for hand labor by improving yields or creating new production tasks (Commission on Agricultural Workers 1993a:44). New inputs included drip irrigation; deleafing of grapevines; new seed varieties; deadlier pesticides; plastic mulches; and improved harvesting, handling, and packing equipment. Environmental regulations, tightening controls over some chemical inputs, altered the amount of labor needed in some harvests as well (Pfeffer 1992; Griffith and Camposeco 1993). Some fresh fruit and vegetable companies experimented with marketing products under brand names, although few succeeded in becoming well known among end consumers. Branding, of course, can backfire if there is no corresponding attention to quality, and attempts to maintain consistently high product quality in the fresh-fruit and vegetable markets frustrated mechanization of many harvests (Hamm et al. 1993).

Mechanizing harvests in highly perishable fruits, vegetables, and horticultural products has never been a simple or straightforward issue. Historically, the mechanization of crops such as sugar beets, tart cherries, and cotton has reduced seasonal labor demand, altered migrant itineraries, and forced some farmworkers out of the farm labor market altogether. In other cases where mechanization has been possible, because of the continued availability of cheap and docile labor, machines have not displaced hand labor. Despite this, historically, mechanization of harvests and other farming operations has been instrumental in changing the regional and seasonal character of labor demand across the country, but always technological innovations have been weighed against marketing and labor cost considerations. Overall, increasing consumer demand for fresh fruits, vegetables, and horticultural products has continued to translate into increased demand for hand labor.

Turning to new methods of labor recruitment and work organization as well as new labor supplies was not the only grower response to these crises. Many altered production strategies to reduce their farms' labor needs, changing patterns of land use. Others turned to sharecropping or new subcontractual arrangements among corporate farms, smaller family farms, and professional crews of workers (Wells 1987, 1990). Still others pioneered new marketing strategies that depended on entrepreneurial farmworkers, such as the professional watermelon or ''pinhooking'' crews, who buy the crop from the farmer, harvest it with their own crews, and sell it themselves, usually in farmers' market settings. ''U-pick'' operations became yet another alternative (Hansen, Griffith, and Butler 1981; Griffith 1988).

As we demonstrate in the chapters that follow, changes such as these alter the life chances for migrant workers, both creating new and dissolving previous job packages. These changes, in turn, initiate shifts in migrant schedules and itineraries. The current farm labor force enjoys a few entrepreneurial opportunities for small-scale harvesting and marketing of farm produce, sharecropping, and labor contracting that farmworkers of past periods could never hope to achieve. Yet most of the farmworkers of today suffer the same inhumane conditions and indignities of the past. Worker turnover and exit rates remain high. Incomes and working conditions are, by all accounts, abysmal. Farmworker housing continues to deteriorate. Paths of empowerment have been spotty, short-lived, and largely ineffective. Many early union gains were undermined by so-called sweetheart contracts with California growers, where union leaders negotiate contracts that increase membership without improving wages and working conditions (Martin 1989). By the late 1980s, the U.S. government, as part of the reform of immigration laws, established the Commission on Agricultural Workers to address questions such as farmworker empowerment, the employment and unemployment of foreign and domestic farmworkers, and the impact of the legalization programs of the 1980s on wages and working conditions in agriculture (U.S. Congress 1986; Commission on Agricultural Workers 1993a, 1993b, 1993c). Most of the commission's findings concur with those we present in the following chapters. Commission researchers, looking at important crops and regions across the country, encountered labor surpluses, stagnant or slowly increasing wages, continued reliance on foreign workers, and poor living and working conditions among farmworkers. This, for the most part, is the setting we encounter, describe, and explain in this book.

Research Settings and Methodological Issues

From the beginning, this examination parted with conventional methods of representing farmworkers and the farm labor market. Most previous studies of farmworkers lack the detail necessary to capture the variety of ways growers and farmworkers come together to prepare the ground and harvest, pack, and otherwise produce the nation's food. Studies that do give detailed descriptions of the social, cultural, and technical dimension of labor-intensive agriculture (e.g., Fischer 1953; Friedland and Nelkin 1971; Heppel 1983; Thomas 1985; Goldring 1990) often lack a national or even regional scope, confining their discussions to migrant crews, crops, states, or communities. We sought, principally by means of the research settings we selected, to balance the detail of local studies with the representativeness of national studies. This is similar to the approach used by the Commission on Agricultural Workers (1993a, 1993b, 1993c), with one critical exception. Whereas the commission studies were nationwide in scope, their survey techniques were less rigorous and comprehensive than ours. By contrast, the commission was able to study more crops and regions than we were, and there has been some overlap between our studies and that of the commission in terms of research sites. Thus, the work of the commission and our work complement one another.

For this work, we selected research settings in four areas with winter and spring growing seasons and three areas with summer growing seasons. The winter–spring growing areas are located in the major farm labor supply states of California, Texas, and Florida, and the Commonwealth of Puerto Rico. The summer growing areas were chosen by means of interviews, which uncovered historically important migrant destinations of farmworkers from the communities farther south. By observing employers and workers performing agricultural tasks at different points during the annual cycle of migration, rest, and work, we hoped to capture the broad range of work settings and social conditions facing the nation's farmworkers. At the same time, we wanted our findings to represent the larger populations of low-wage workers and growers in the communities studied. This demanded an "ethnosurvey" approach, as recommended by Massey et al. (1987), or a combination of ethnographic work, participant observation, rigorous sampling, and survey research (see Appendix).

Immokalee, Florida; Weslaco, Texas; and Mayagüez, Puerto Rico, were well known to us as communities that annually supply workers to growing regions of, respectively, the Delmarva Peninsula, southwestern Michigan, and New Jersey (see map). Because we considered Parlier, California, a major supply and demand farmworker community, we did not pair it with another community for this work. Each of these labor supply communities and labor demand regions is distinct from the others, yet the comparisons that emerge from the chapters that follow show a number of similarities. Immokalee and Parlier, for example, are commercial collection and shipping points for ag-

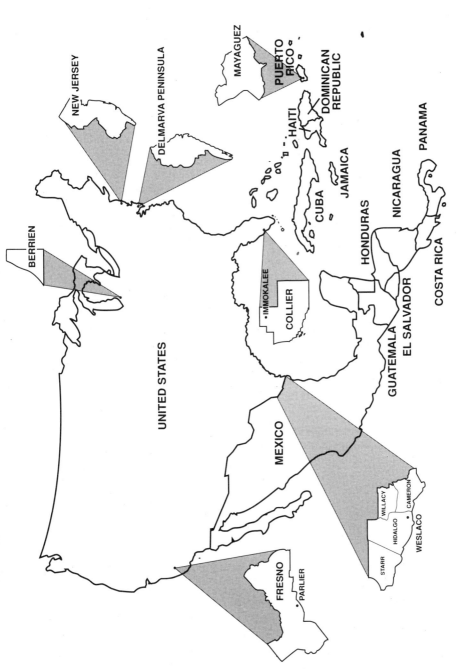

Map 1   Regions Selected for Study

ricultural produce as well as seasonal centers for large numbers of agricultural
workers. They are typical of towns situated in the heart of labor-intensive
agricultural growing regions, with packing sheds and produce storage facilities, many large neighborhoods of substandard housing, and predesignated
areas where farmworkers gather, early mornings, to board buses bound for
work in the fields. Both communities have been chronicled in other works,
including Edward R. Murrow's *Harvest of Shame* and doctoral dissertations
by Heppel (1983) and Bernstein (1986), and in more-recent publications
(Commission on Agricultural Workers 1993a, 1993b, 1993c; Heppel and
Amendola 1992).

Weslaco and Mayagüez are similar to one another for three reasons. First,
both communities have long histories of supplying workers to nearby and
distant harvests, yet recently they have seen their status as farm labor communities undermined by communities such as Immokalee and Parlier or, more
likely, by communities throughout Mexico and Central America, along with
Haiti and other parts of the Caribbean. Second, both communities have experienced low-cost housing initiatives that have allowed formerly migrant farmworking families to withdraw from migrant streams or from the farm labor
force altogether. A third similarity, directly related to the other two features
of these communities, is that they both include large numbers of bonafide
''domestic'' farmworkers, many of whom speak Spanish and are culturally
adept at getting along in the farm labor market and yet who, as noted, have
been displaced and replaced by foreign workers.

The labor demand regions we selected for study have been important northern migrant labor demand areas for decades. New Jersey's farms have imported Puerto Rican labor since before World War II yet have begun relying
more and more on Mexican, Central American, and Asian workers. The Delmarva Peninsula shows the remnants of an African American farm labor force
that has been slowly supplemented and displaced by Haitian and Mexican
workers. Michigan family fruit and vegetable farms have also relied on migrant labor for decades, experiencing the ethnic succession that has accompanied the decline of Texas agriculture from a Mexican American to an increasingly Mexican national workforce. Situated along the routes of complexes of
migrant streams and other destinations, these labor demand areas thus reflect
broader processes taking place among migrant farm labor forces throughout
the United States.

The mainland U.S. communities that we discuss are all partially linked by
migrant networks and provide good insight into the means by which common
dynamics operating under distinct local conditions can give rise to a variety

of labor market behaviors. As became clear in the course of our ethnographic work, events in one part of the country (e.g., the 1990 southern Texas freeze) may have effects that ripple through a number of other "linked" regions (e.g., Florida, Michigan, California, and Washington). The labor supply "home-base" areas studied (southern Florida, Puerto Rico, the lower Rio Grande Valley, and central California) probably are home to over half of the farm-workers residing year-round in the United States.

Organization of the Work

Chapters 2–8 are studies of the farm labor supply communities and the de-mand crop regions of the North. We have paired the studies so that each farm labor supply community study is followed by the study of the crop region it supplies with farm labor. The Parlier case study deviates from this pattern because the Central Valleys region of California, the largest perishable-crop-growing region in the country, constitutes both a supply community and a labor demand crop-region.

Chapter 9 includes descriptions of the farm labor force, the factors affect-ing continued labor supply, and the ways in which farmworker housing is linked to labor market dynamics. In the conclusion, Chapter 10, we present theories of low-income labor processes, immigration, resource use, and the implications of the growing use of subcontracting for power, resistance, and poverty in U.S. agricultural workplaces. This discussion examines, closely, farmworkers' networks, recruitment, farmworker decision-making, occupa-tional mobility, and farm labor contracting.

We do not claim to have captured fully all of the crucial features or factors underlying the changing dynamics of farm labor in the United States. Throughout this volume, we try to represent the complexity of what has be-come a predominantly transnational labor force, a population living and work-ing in two or more cultures, a people united not by language or history but by poverty and hardship, by injury, difficulty, and abuse. Yet the working poor we encountered and spoke with during this study never asked to be pitied or pampered. They waited hours and days to work hard and worked hard. They accepted low wages, rough working conditions, and crowded housing with a dignity that was nothing if not honorable. They deserve the respect of anyone who has ever relished the sweet fruits, tasted the crisp vegetables, or sipped the nectar or fermented beverages of rural America's orchards, vineyards, groves, and fields. If America's plain is, as the song says, fruited, it has become so less with a divine crown of brotherhood than a thorny crown of poverty and division.

Picking tomatoes in southern Maryland, 1938

Onion picker, Rio Grande Valley, Texas. © *1979 Ken Light*

Tomato pickers, Oceanside, California. © *1983 Ken Light*

Young onion picker, Rio Grande Valley, Texas. © *1979 Ken Light*

36 cents for 12 bunches. Green onion field, Salt River Valley, Arizona. © *1979 Ken Light*

African American workers in Homestead, Florida, 1938

Labor camp in southern Florida, 1938

Waiting to be paid. Tomato harvest, Homestead, Florida.
© *1983 Ken Light*

Migrant camp sign, Immokalee, Florida.
© *1982 Ken Light*

Cotton workers returning to southern Texas, 1939

Picking cucumbers, northwestern Ohio. © *1980 Ken Light*

PART II

The Community Studies

Chapter 2

Waves of Ethnicity
Immokalee, Florida

The formation, history, and current social, economic, and cultural complexion of Immokalee, Florida, have been intimately tied to eastern and midwestern agricultural-labor migrations, to political and economic developments in Latin America and the Caribbean, and to southern Florida agriculture. In many ways, this southwestern Florida community is a microcosm of the way agricultural labor is mobilized, organized, and set to tasks in labor-intensive agricultural operations throughout the United States. Like other farmworker communities, Immokalee imports labor from Texas, the Caribbean, Mexico, and Central America; but it also exports labor to agricultural harvests throughout the eastern and midwestern United States. The famous documentary *Harvest of Shame* features scenes from Immokalee in its portrayal of the low quality of life of the U.S. farmworker in the 1960s. Today, the media continue to portray Immokalee as a frontier city, usually contrasting its poverty with the affluence of Collier County's seat, Naples, or the tourist haven Marco Island. In the social and cultural context of Immokalee, many farmworkers learn what wages, working conditions, housing, transportation, and labor relations to expect in agricultural jobs in the United States, while growers and farm labor contractors learn about the work habits and attitudes of different groups of workers, comparing new and old immigrants, refugees, and minority and other workers with one another.

The population of Immokalee fluctuates like that of college or tourist towns. During the summer months, with few agricultural tasks to be done, the resident population reaches a low of eight thousand. It swells to between twenty-five thousand and thirty thousand during the winter citrus, flower, and vegetable harvests. These figures include farmworkers' dependents, others who accompany them and occupy positions of support in their households, and those who drift in and out of the farm labor force.[1] These numbers will rise through the 1990s as agricultural acreage expands throughout southwestern Florida.

Underlying Immokalee's poverty is its economic dependence on agiculture, which has increased in the past twenty years and continues to draw more and more workers into the area. More vegetable and citrus acreage has been put into production. New workers, with a variety of legal statuses, have come from the Caribbean, Mexico, and Central America. New technologies, cropping cycles, and enterprise mixes now tie workers to the region for longer periods. Over the past decade, Immokalee has become a major staging area for international labor migrants, who are drawn into the region by network ties and labor market information and who, at the season's end, are either deported or move into other parts of the United States. In this sense, the process of network formation, or "network-building," that occurs in Immokalee influences other migrant behaviors, such as synthesizing and judging labor market information; establishing relations with farm labor contractors, growers, or other migrants; or taking advantage of farmworker programs. Since the mid-1980s, understanding progressive network building in its social and cultural contexts has been considered fundamental in international migration studies (Portes and Bach 1985; Massey et al. 1987; Papademetriou et al. 1989; Portes and Böröcz 1989).

In addition to providing workers for agricultural tasks in Collier County, Immokalee residents and migrants commute to harvests in nearby Hendry and Lee counties, as well as to cities on Florida's rapidly developing west coast. Vans from hotels, restaurants, and construction companies in Fort Myers, Naples, and Marco Island come to Immokalee to recruit workers, who wait at specified places where farm labor contractors routinely pick up and assemble crews in the early morning.

Among the more important developments in the region's agriculture has been the movement of citrus groves farther south in the state, especially since the freezes of the early 1980s. During the 1980s, citrus acreage nearly doubled in Collier County, from 5,321 to 9,101 acres. When new trees fully mature in the 1990s, this increase will create a demand for an additional two thousand to three thousand workers. Between 1984 and 1990, growers in Collier, Hendry, and Lee counties expanded their acreages of tomatoes from 11,200 to 17,650 acres (a 57.6 percent increase) and peppers from 5,600 to 9,300 acres (a 66 percent increase). From this increased production, county planners foresee the need for an additional thirteen thousand to fourteen thousand workers; this growth will continue at least until the total agricultural-worker population living in and around Immokalee exceeds thirty thousand.[2]

Growth of this magnitude is certain to tax Immokalee's already inadequate housing stock and draw further political attention to and popular support for improving farmworker living conditions. At the center of public concern for farmworkers are the issues of health (Bernstein 1986), education (Florida Institute of Government 1988), and—most important, as increasing national attention is given to homelessness—housing (Florida. Collier County 1988). Less attention has been devoted to other, equally problematic features of farmworker living conditions. These include transportation problems, insurance, the anxieties of separation from families, the overlap between farmworking and underclass populations, and the labor market effects of farmworkers' creating new households in the United States while maintaining material and emotional connections with households in one or more distant locations. The survey, secondary-source data collection, and ethnographic work conducted in Immokalee was designed to address these aspects of farmworker living conditions within the more general context of Immokalee's low-wage labor force. Most of the quantitative data derive from 196 structured interviews distributed over several nationalities and even more ethnic groups. More than one-third (35.2 percent) of our sample were born in the United States, and almost the same proportion came from Mexico (32.1 percent). Another 15.3 percent were Guatemalan-born; 14.8 percent, Haitian-born; and the remainder, born in several countries of Central America and the Caribbean. Over half (53 percent) of the migrants in the sample are currently farmworkers; under 15 percent have never done farmwork. Their incomes and educational levels are relatively low, much of the work they perform is seasonal (one month of unemployment a year is relatively common), and 68 percent speak Spanish as their first language.[3] These are the characteristics of a population at the lower levels of the economy and society by nearly any standard. They are, in short, the working poor.

Housing and Households in Immokalee

One of the foremost problems facing the working poor, and especially farmworkers, is securing adequate housing. Solving this problem involves such related concerns as household size, composition, and other living arrange-

ments. Thus, we focus much of our discussion on the variations among different groups of workers in terms of families and households, and how those
variations have influenced and have been influenced by the farm labor market
in general. While much farmworker housing in the northern growing regions
is free, only a few workers in Immokalee (3 percent) receive free housing as
part of their terms of employment. Housing tends to be in high demand during
the winter tomato and citrus harvests, and competition for existing units is,
correspondingly, high. As such, housing becomes an important instrument of
labor control: providing access to housing is one means farm labor contractors
use to increase the reliability of workers in their crews.

From accounts throughout the United States, we know that farmworker
housing is substandard, unsafe, decrepit, and overcrowded. In Immokalee,
public condemnation of farmworker housing has already led to subsidized
housing developments (e.g., Farmworker Village), the building or renovating
of homes by private, nonprofit, self-help organizations (e.g., Habitat for Humanity), the provision of private low-cost housing (usually in the form of
trailer parks), and a proliferation of housing studies, land-use plans, and continued media attention that highlights Immokalee's slums. In May 1989, for
example, the *Naples Daily News* ran a five-part series on Immokalee's poor,
with the first part focusing on Immokalee's housing and social ills (May 21:
front page). In addition, the Pocket of Poverty Program, initiated by the state
legislature (House Bill 1454), has produced reports on the Florida farmworking population. One of these concluded that

> the best estimate of the number of housing units [in Immokalee] is 8,300 to
> 9,300; of these, 3,000 to 4,000 [around 40 percent] are unauthorized. . . . The
> 1980 U.S. Census reported a total of 2,181 substandard housing units due to
> overcrowding, lack of complete kitchen and lack of complete bathroom. . . .
> Housing professionals [now] estimate the need for 4,000 new housing units to
> correct current deficiencies. (Florida. Collier County 1988)

Our emphasis on farmworker housing derives from the overall importance
of housing in the lives and economic decisions of migrant farmworkers. Most
studies of the investment and consumption behaviors of international labor
migrants have found that building a house is the primary investment among
returning migrants (Portes and Bach 1985; Griffith 1986b; Massey et al.
1987). Once the house has been built and furnished, migrants have less incentive to migrate. Quality of housing constitutes a principal factor in the economic decisions of farm labor migrants within the United States as well. In
Immokalee, farmworkers who live in the subsidized and highly desirable

Farmworker Village are less likely than other farmworkers to enter the migrant stream. On the other hand, low-quality housing is easy to leave behind in search of better living conditions in northern, summer harvest regions, and it is clear that housing in the northern harvests is a key factor attracting or repelling farm labor. Information about housing in the labor demand regions of the North spreads rapidly through migrant networks. This phenomenon is not confined to southern Florida. In Jamaica, for example, peasants who wished to work in the British West Indies Temporary Alien Labor Program, who had never seen the labor camps of the southern Florida sugar plantations, accurately described company housing (Griffith 1983). In Virginia, we found that farmworkers tended to differentiate between growers on the basis of housing (Griffith 1988; see also Heppel 1983). And housing plays a significant role in relations between farmworkers and farm labor contractors, who provide labor camps to those working in their crews.

Underlying the styles, conditions, and terms of occupancy of Immokalee's housing are the seasonality, poverty, and powerlessness of much of its population. While the 1980 census reported 43.9 percent of the population living below poverty level (Florida. Collier County 1988), the 1980s and 1990s have seen influxes of Haitian and Guatemalan refugees, increased acreages of crops attracting migrants from Mexico and Caribbean, and other population trends that suggest increasing levels of unemployment, underemployment, and poverty. During the first half of the decade, average weekly incomes, instead of improving, dropped from $104 in 1980 to $70 in 1982, rising only to $102 by 1986. Our survey revealed that average weekly incomes during the harvest season were around $218, with slightly over one-third of the households earning $150 a week or less.

Immokalee resembles a densely populated inner-city ghetto far more than a small rural town. At the heart of one of the town's poorest areas is the principal supermarket parking lot, where farm labor contractors meet their crews in the early morning. Known to the U.S. Census Bureau as South Immokalee (Geo Cell 112502) and to the locals as "El Centro," this area that is the gathering place for farmwork is also known locally for its taverns and flophouses, for its drugs and prostitution, for its check-cashing services and drive-through liquor tunnels, and for its muggings, bail bondsmen, and the restless idleness of the chronic unemployed. South Immokalee encompasses around fifty blocks of dwellings, three blocks of agencies and businesses, and a few weedy vacant lots where muggers lurk, the homeless sleep, and drug addicts shoot or smoke dope. The poverty of South Immokalee spills across Main Street into the neighborhoods near the center, where the growers' association issues its *tarjeta blancas* (white identification cards certifying that the farm-worker has complied with I-9 immigration regulations that are necessary to work in the fields) and onto the block of the Redlands Christian Migrant Association. The most densely populated of South Immokalee's blocks has twenty-six mobile homes and two multifamily dwellings in an area that, in the middle-class neighborhoods of Immokalee, would contain between five and ten single-family units. Furthermore, the way this area and areas like it have been portrayed, statistically, by the U.S. Census Bureau demonstrates how little we can rely on census data for sampling and other purposes. Despite the short-comings of the census data, the Collier County Planning Commission relies on this data annually to estimate the size and character of its population. In February 1989, a private consulting firm conducted a field count and found Collier County's population estimates to be inaccurate in terms of both the number of dwellings in Immokalee and the number of individuals per dwelling. Regarding dwellings, the firm reports:

> The total count difference between the field survey taken in February, and the April 1, 1988 population estimate made by the County Planning staff is 1073 [with the latter overestimating the number]. . . . Much of the difference lies in Geo Cell 112502, the South Immokalee area. . . . Somehow the Census data indicated that there were over 1,200 units of multi-family housing in South Immokalee. Based on the consultant field work, the area only contains 402 units. (Immokalee Population Analysis 1989:3–4)

While overestimating the number of dwellings in South Immokalee, the Planning Commission and the Census Bureau underestimated the number of persons per household, estimating an average of 2.656 persons per household for South Immokalee. This was just under half of the estimate of the 5.97 persons per household derived from a survey of Immokalee's hourly and sala-ried employees in South Immokalee and substantially less than the estimate of 3.6 persons per household from a survey of 358 households throughout Immokalee.

Even the most recent and field-checked population estimates, however, can easily become obsolete in a matter of weeks in a town like Immokalee that is so dependent on labor-intensive agriculture. Changing weather conditions can affect population levels in a matter of days. The freeze of December 1989, for example, destroyed most of the tomatoes and other vegetable crops in the area, severely reducing labor demand for the harvests and leading to unem-ployment and emigration out of farmwork. Additional sources of instability and change in housing arrangements come from the formal and informal politics and economics that accompany labor recruitment, crew assembly, field supervision, and methods of payment in farmwork; these often underlie the terms of occupancy of a dwelling, influencing household composition. Despite the difficulty we encounter in coming up with accurate counts of housing units and people in Immokalee, we can describe some of the general parameters of Immokalee's housing.

First, 43.1 percent of all housing units in Immokalee are mobile homes, compared with 37.3 percent single-family dwellings, 15.4 percent multifamily dwellings, and 4.9 percent duplexes (Florida. Collier County 1988). The high percentage of mobile homes—a housing type common among farmworkers and low-wage workers generally—is clearly related to the farmworking basis of the economy. Combined with multifamily units, which are characteristic of tenement and public housing, nearly 60 percent of Immokalee's housing consists of types typical of impoverished populations. While the overall complexion of Immokalee's housing reflects general population trends, the distribution and relative proportions of housing types in Immokalee's various neighborhoods shows the community's internal differentiation.

South Immokalee, around El Centro, has much higher proportions of multifamily dwellings and mobile homes than the more affluent neighborhoods, testifying to the transience and poverty of residents in this heart of the farmworking population. Other neighborhoods, such as "La Rata" (the rat), are composed almost entirely of mobile homes and small houses built through years of acquisition of construction materials, as is typical of homes throughout the Caribbean, Mexico, and Central America. Most of Collier County's fifty-eight licensed labor camps are located in Immokalee; many are owned by farm labor contractors or members of contractors' families and are occupied by workers in their crews. This practice leads to highly complex households while further intertwining work and housing in the farm labor market. In one case, a small nuclear family—a man, woman, and their adopted infant daughter—lived with seven single Guatemalan men; all the men worked in the gladiola harvests under the supervision of the same crew leader. In this case, as well, all household members came from the same Guatemalan village and stayed together in Immokalee both on and off the job. Yet another Guatemalan farmworker described his housing as follows:

> I live here in a trailer camp behind the thrift store on the main street, not too far from Ninth Street [South Immokalee]. I live with four couples, five with me and my wife. They are from San Juan Ixcoy, Guatemala. There is a newborn there (born here in Naples). We pay for the motor home a hundred seventy-five dollars

a week. A teenager lives with us, and each person pays thirteen dollars and fifty cents for the rent. The motor home has three rooms, but we are in need: we divided each room in two spaces separated by a blanket.

Such descriptions of housing are common in the literature on farm labor and on new-immigrant and refugee populations generally (e.g., Friedland and Nelkin 1971). Housing may be the principal area in which new-immigrant populations contribute to the erosion of standards of living of native minority and poor populations. The so-called colonization that others describe in the context of the labor market (Martin 1989) may also be occurring in the housing market, as new immigrants exert upward pressure on rents while altering local cultural, linguistic, and social landscapes. Insofar as this change in the housing market has taken place in Immokalee, it has helped to create a variety of housing alternatives, including subsidized housing, for citizens and legal immigrants. Yet fewer than 7 percent of the families we visited lived in subsidized housing of any kind, evidence that low-income and new-immigrant populations lack knowledge about and access to the housing subsidies that are available. Low-income workers typically respond to housing costs by entering into creative living arrangements that include subletting rooms and dividing rooms up with blankets (Table 2.1). Young males and females, better able than families to tolerate crowded conditions, spend the least proportion of their income on housing.

Subsidies further complicate the terms of occupancy found in Immokalee. Because housing is so fundamental a part of farm labor markets, the various

TABLE 2.1 Cost of Housing by Farmworker Family Type (N = 196)

Family Type	Percent of Monthly Earnings Spent on Housing	Total Monthly Rent or Payments	Percent in Subsidized Housing
Lone male/female (N = 87)	20.40 (11.15)	132.62 (68.90)	6.3
Extended family (N = 46)	25.21 (16.88)	158.27 (101.40)	0
Nuclear family—working children (N = 31)	29.12 (22.8)	217.65 (101.26)	8.9
Working couple—no children or children only under 13 (N = 19)	21.93 (4.8)	173.75 (108.19)	0

Source: Immokalee survey data, 1989–90 (see Appendix).

Note: Figures in parentheses are standard deviations; thirteen cases were deleted because of missing data.

housing subsidies and programs in Immokalee have further differentiated and stratified the farm labor market, intensifying the divisions that are already there, based on legal status, ethnicity, and experience in the farm labor market. The various housing arrangements in Immokalee include labor camps, privately arranged housing, public housing, and self-help housing.

Labor camps are dwellings specifically for farmworkers, often occupied seasonally, and usually owned and operated by either growers or farm labor contractors. Because, as already noted, some labor camps are occupied on the condition that the tenant work for the owner of the labor camp, in this case, quite explicitly, one's housing dictates one's work. Most labor camps are oriented toward single males, though a small percentage of the units might be family housing. Many labor camps are houses that have been converted into dormitories.

Privately arranged housing is not necessarily owned or operated by a crew leader or tied to a specific occupation, and occupancy may not necessarily be contingent upon working in the farm labor market, let alone a specific crop. It is, as its name implies, simply housing arranged with private landlords, occupied because of a relationship with the current owner or tenant. This kind of housing, common in Immokalee, varies widely in quality, from hovels to fairly nice mobile homes. Rents in Immokalee tend to be steep, especially when figured as percentage of earnings. As illustrated in the description above, a three-room mobile home can rent for up to $175 a week—to people who may be making as little as $20 a day, sporadically.

Public housing consists of subsidized dwellings that are either free or inexpensive to rent, and that tend to be occupied on a number of conditions tied directly to one's earning power or behavior in the labor market. In Immokalee, Farmworker Village is the most famous public-housing project for farmworkers. It is occupied on the condition that a certain portion of the occupant's income come from farmwork. It seems to have been colonized by Latinos, reflecting the growing Latino presence in the eastern agricultural labor markets, though new units are being built specifically for African Americans.[4]

Self-help housing is provided with help from Habitat for Humanity, a nationwide organization that builds houses for families who normally would not qualify for loans from conventional sources, paying for their construction through volunteer and recipient labor (''sweat equity'') as well as private donations and low-interest financing.

Immokalee's households reflect the fact that its farmworking population is skewed heavily toward single males. Nevertheless, the idea that all the single males living in Immokalee are unattached or actually ''single'' is somewhat

misleading. "Single" males are often parts of crews who stay together
through the year and, because of such practices as cooperative cooking or
pooling of income for food and transportation costs, resemble a household.
They also may be parts of viable households that do not correspond to actual
dwellings or bounded units but are "transnational." In these contexts, individual household members interact and influence one another's lives through remittances, phone calls, and other material and emotional communications.
Household structures in Immokalee reflect the ways in which immigrant populations penetrate the U.S. labor market, especially those groups of immigrants
who, first, are highly geographically mobile and, second, consider their residence in the United States to be temporary (even when temporary means
twenty years). The growing proportion of young single males in the labor
force has, in the past ten years, been partially driven by developments on
the demand side of the farm labor market. Many growers have been actively
recruiting young Mexican workers into the harvests, preferring them to West
Indians, African Americans, and most other Latinos. Compared with these
other groups, Mexicans nationals—many of whom were legalized under recent immigration laws[5]—are less likely to travel with families. Puerto Ricans,
who are an almost completely adult-male work force, have also, historically,
been less likely to travel with families. Currently in the East, especially in the
summer harvests, both housing and network relationships select for single
males or, at the very least, adults without children. Households in Immokalee
reflect this preference, yet tend to be more complex because of Florida agriculture's continued reliance on family farmworkers. That is, while growers in
general have been relying more and more on Mexican nationals and young
single males, Florida agriculture, like Texas agriculture and parts of California
agriculture, continues to maintain housing and other infrastructural needs of
farmworking families. As a result, Immokalee farmworker households have
assumed transitional forms, with one of the more common arrangements consisting of a "core" family, who may be the principal occupant of a dwelling,
and a number of related or unrelated adult males. Families in Immokalee may,
in such a case, act as anchors for entire diffuse networks, the members of
which come and go depending on the availability of work.

   Virtually all studies of labor markets known for high concentrations of
new immigrants acknowledge the importance of households and networks in
migrants' job searches and other behaviors in the receiving economy and society. Because immigration is itself a transitional state, new immigrants are
particularly well suited to adapting their social-organizational forms to short-
term fluctuations in the housing and labor markets and long-term develop-

ments in the receiving economy. New immigrants to the farm labor force are faced with prearranged housing styles, rental conditions, and arrangements with farm labor contractors and growers that select for some family styles over others.

We argue that the two household types best adapted to the farm labor market—or, more strongly stated, most frequently selected by the farm labor market—are single-person (lone-male/lone-female) households and "anchor" households consisting of nuclear families and singles attached to the unit by virtue of kinship and friendship ties. Results of our research in Immokalee lend support to this thesis. Survey results revealed that, for the entire sample population, lone-male/lone-female (single) households were the most common (44.4 percent), followed by nuclear families (25.1 percent), and extended families. Among those who identified themselves as single, however, 76.5 percent are in the farm labor force and nearly half are migrant farmworkers, while 55 percent of those identified as living in extended (anchor) households are in the farm labor force and 45 percent are migrant farmworkers. This compares with 52.1 percent of nuclear families in the farm labor force (23.9 percent migrants), 36.4 percent of single mothers (18.2 percent migrants), and 31.6 percent of working couples (10.5 percent migrants). These figures support our proposition that single workers, primarily single males, and extended (anchor) households are the two social-structural forms most common in today's farm labor force.

Further support comes from the differences among the groups in their attitudes toward continuing in the farm labor market, which reflect their abilities to tolerate farmwork. Single workers, nuclear families with working-age children, and extended families showed more willingness to remain in farmwork than those from other family types. Specifically, 57.5 percent of lone workers, 22.3 percent of workers in nuclear families with working-age children, and 12.8 percent of workers living in extended families said they will continue performing farmwork. By contrast, only 5.3 percent of workers in families with small children and 2.1 percent of single mothers planned to stay in farmwork. Clearly, outside of anchor households, where elderly relatives are available to care for children, children are a burden to the farmworking lifestyle.

Ethnicity, Household Formation, and the Farm Labor Market

Ethnicity affects farmworker households as profoundly as the availability of housing, network ties, and relations with farm labor contractors. Many features of household formation and maintenance are explicitly cultural, such as ideas about postmarital residence, courtship and marriage, gender relations, and relations between generations. As such, we can expect to find differences among farmworker households based on ethnicity as well as expect that these differences will influence labor market behavior.

From the data on Immokalee's school system and school-aged population, we can estimate, roughly, the ethnic complexion of Immokalee, at least among that portion of the population (between 40 and 50 percent) that has school-aged children. Based on our own observations, however, the high proportions of single or lone Guatemalan and Mexican males would increase the proportions of Latinos in Immokalee relative to whites and African Americans. Nevertheless, the following figures reflect the ethnic breakdown of Immokalee's families: out of 4,089 students in Immokalee in 1989, 61.9 percent were Hispanic, 21.0 percent were white or native American, and 16.9 percent were African American. These students were distributed over three elementary schools, in which nearly 60 percent of the students were enrolled, one middle school, with 22.6 percent of the students, and one high school, with the remaining 17.8 percent of the students (Florida Institute of Government 1988). That the overwhelming majority of students attend elementary school (and are likely to be under eleven years old) suggests that many families in Immokalee are composed of young adults with young children.

The principal ethnic groups in Immokalee are Mexicans, Mexican Americans (Chicanos), African Americans, Guatemalans, and Haitians.[6] Each of these groups has had distinctly different experiences with their incorporation into U.S. society and the labor market, as they combine past kinship and family relations with the realities of a new or significantly altered setting. For African Americans, longtime natives to the area, changes in Immokalee and the farm labor market changes have created new social contexts and under mined their once-dominant position in the East Coast farm labor market. In contrast, Haitians are recent immigrants, most arriving within the past twelve to fourteen years, and Guatemalans are even more recent, with substantial increases only since the mid-1980s. Mexicans and Mexican Americans, however, have been in the farm labor force in Florida for at least the past twenty-five to thirty years, with significant numbers entering the citrus harvests in the early to mid-1970s and others coming to Immokalee as far back as the late 1950s (Hudson 1979).

Celebrations of Ethnic Identity and Interethnic Relations

Immigrant and refugee flows place heavy demands on ethnic and national identities of both host and immigrant groups. In a community as fluid as Immokalee, and in an employment setting as unpredictable as the farm labor market, commonplace activities often assume uncommon cultural dimensions and ethnic repercussions. Local dance halls in Immokalee sponsor well-known Mexican bands. New churches reproduce Haitian forms of Catholic worship. Young Guatemalan men practice native courtship and gift-giving rituals with local prostitutes. During our observations, we encountered a case of an automobile sale being used by Mexicans and Mexican Americans to reaffirm their collective presence in southern Florida. The dealership sponsoring the sale used the ethnicity angle in advertising, broadcasting ads on the major Spanish-language radio station and holding a raffle for a used car before the event and broadcasting over loudspeakers during the sale. The sale itself then attracted mostly Mexicans and Mexican Americans, along with a few Anglos; conspicuously absent were African Americans, Haitians, and Guatemalans.

A somewhat different form of the reinforcement of ethnic identity occurs among the Guatemalans, who sponsor festivals similar to those associated with village festivals in Guatemala. These tend to attract members of the same Guatemalan ethnic groups, such as Kanjobal speakers, from small pockets of Guatemalans all over Florida (Burns 1988). In recent years, however, such festivals have expanded to include a variety of other ethnic groups, suggesting that refugees will suppress some of their differences under shared circumstances of exile (Griffith 1993b; Burns 1993).

Such events enhance the power of Immokalee to attract workers from these various cultural backgrounds, further differentiating the labor force, complicating housing and neighborhood complexions, and leading to the growth of churches, restaurants, and other small enterprises oriented toward different ethnic groups. The receiving community's response to this is either to leave Immokalee (''white flight'') or to reaffirm its own identity through such activities as the annual African American festival in Belle Glade or the swamp cabbage festival in La Belle. Struggles over community identity can lead to strained relations between host and immigrant ethnic groups, especially when, as in Immokalee, immigrant groups are perceived to contribute to crime, alcoholism, prostitution, drug abuse, and related concerns about the health and welfare of the resident population.

Comparing farmworkers from different migrant and network backgrounds offers some insight into the selective pressures at work in the farm labor market. The international migrants in our survey (about one-third from traditional sending areas such as Mexico and about one-third from new sending regions such as Haiti and Central America) contributed more members to the farm labor force and to migrant streams within the country than did those born in the United States. At the same time, those international migrants who had been in the country longer (e.g., since before 1975) contributed fewer workers to the farm labor force and to migrant streams than the newer immigrants did. Specifically, 87 percent of the new immigrants from traditional sending areas (e.g., Michoacán, Mexico) worked in farmwork, compared with 75 percent of pre-1975 immigrants; 71.4 percent of immigrants from new sending regions (e.g., Haiti, Guatemala); 40 percent of migrants from Texas; and only 30.2 percent of local, U.S.-born residents of Immokalee, most of whom are African Americans. These groups were similarly ranked in terms of supplying workers to the harvest of the north: 69.9 percent of new immigrants from traditional sending areas, 41.7 percent of pre-1975 immigrants, and 42.9 percent of immigrants from new sending regions migrated north. Only 20 percent of the migrants from Texas and 9.3 percent of the locally born U.S. citizens migrated into the northern harvests. According to existing information about differences between new and old immigrants and native and immigrant workers, the results of other comparisons could easily have been predicted—for example, that new immigrants earn less than old immigrants and that native workers earn more than immigrants.[7]

Reflecting these labor market behaviors and cultural backgrounds, African Americans and Mexican Americans tend to have the most complex and extended families, though these are distinct from one another in gender relations, internal dynamics, and composition; Guatemalans and new-immigrant Mexican nationals have the least complex families, with many households composed primarily of single males. These newer immigrant groups often assemble into what we call "artificial networks," or networks that function in ways similar to networks based on village residence or kinship but that are extremely responsive to labor market developments and hence extremely fragile.

When Friedland and Nelkin conducted their research in the late 1960s, most of Florida's farmworkers and most farmworkers along the East Coast were African Americans.

It is difficult to establish how many migrant workers there are in the United States: census enumerations provide estimates varying from 400,000 to 2,000,000. The discrepancies arise largely from technical difficulties in the enumeration of a mobile people. The eastern stream is estimated at about 50,000 people. With the decline of the plantation economy, Negroes from agricultural communities in the south moved to a variety of areas, including the rich agricultural lands of Florida. There they now work in citrus or vegetables throughout the winter. During the summer, the available agricultural work is limited. Because few can subsist for four to five months on the meager income earned during the winter growing season, this group is the main source of the labor that moves north to harvest the crops in the northeastern United States.'' (Friedland and Nelkin 1971:3)

In a related essay, Nelkin (1970) acknowledges the extreme variation between crews in family and household size and structure, contrasting two crews that reflect the internal composition of the African American farmworker population. The first crew, of one hundred workers, included 93 percent singles (workers with no attachments to other workers in camp), while the second crew, of sixty-one workers, had only 32.8 percent singles. Other notable differences between the two crews were that in the first crew, mostly of singles, 50 percent were under twenty-five years old and nearly half (47 percent) were in the migrant stream for the first time; in the other crew, 29.5 percent were under twenty-five and only 4.9 percent had been in the migrant stream for the first time.

These two "types" of crews—the one consisting primarily of single individuals and the other of families or individuals with ties to others in their crews—are associated with the African American experience and African American family life in the South. A brief consideration of how these crew types and African American household and family structures are linked is important, because the predominance of African Americans in the East Coast harvests laid the groundwork for the subsequent use of other ethnic groups. In other words, many of the working and living conditions that prevail in today's harvests developed during the time when African Americans provided the principal labor source.

Anthropologists have long portrayed African American family life as "matrifocal" or female-centered, in that consanguineal ties—those established between siblings and others related through women—tend to be stronger than affinal ties, those established through reproductive or sexual relations (Stack 1971). The matrifocality of African American households, however, does not mean an absence of African American males in domestic units, no matter how much this image has become the stereotype in journalism and to some extent in social service offices throughout the country. Males are present in African American households, though their attachments are also either consanguineal (as brothers, sons, uncles, nephews, and cousins, if not as husbands) or less visible to social workers and social scientists than are the women and children for whom so many welfare programs have been designed (Leibow 1967; Gonzalez 1971). Sexual partners sometimes live apart or live together irregularly, leaving the impression of the absence of males. Within this domestic arena, relations *within* households are thus based primarily on consanguineal ties, while relations *between* households may be based on either affinal or consanguineal ties.

This apparent fluidity of household relations, with men able to attach themselves to and detach themselves from households with relative ease, has been noted throughout the Caribbean and interpreted as "weak" social structure. While such practices may indicate weak household structures, they are functional in labor markets that are unpredictable and require periodic geographical mobility. Research on relations between economic development and family life have shown repeatedly that household and even community structures come to reflect labor market demands in industries where workers are nonunionized, relatively disorganized, and powerless against capital (Wallerstein 1974; Portes and Walton 1981; Gordon, Edwards, and Reich 1982; Lamphere 1987). A dynamic exists between the labor market and family life; in time, each accommodates the other. Depending on the political and economic environment, however, either families must conform more to labor market demands or those who organize the labor market (in this case, growers) must recognize the needs of families and the structure of households and communities and attempt to adapt recruitment, housing, work schedules, and so on to these needs and structures. During periods of economic growth, with the creation of alternative job opportunities for farmworkers, growers become compelled either to access new labor supplies or to adapt their needs to prevailing household and family structures (Griffith 1983). During periods of high unemployment or labor surpluses, on the other hand, workers need to adapt their family lives to the demands of the labor market.

Farmworker households, as well as the success or failure of one or another ethnic group in the farm labor market, reflect these processes of revision and accommodation. Historically in the South and East, African American households have operated at a distinct disadvantage when negotiating for job offers in the farm labor market. Some observers have traced African American family life to the labor needs of slave plantations (Gonzalez 1971; Mintz 1971; Stack 1979). Faced with unpredictable labor markets requiring periodic migration for varying lengths of time, both in the South and in the Caribbean, it is likely that African American households maintained the internal flexibility and emphasis on uterine ties that characterized their households under slavery, yet adapted these practices so that men could move in and out of migrant streams with an ease and freedom unavailable to them under slavery. Here, however, we are less concerned with the historical precedents or functional components of African American household structure than with its probable effects on the organization of the farm labor market. In short, the farm labor market has selected for extremely fluid households where singles, either male or female, are able to attach and detach themselves to existing, stable (anchored) households in sending communities like Immokalee or in one of several other domestic and international locations. The presence of Puerto Ricans in U.S. farm labor markets has further contributed to summer-harvest labor markets being organized by and for single, unattached migrants with viable family lives in Puerto Rico—workers whom we refer to as "anchored singles."

In the light of this discussion, we should not be surprised to learn that contemporary research on Mexican households has emphasized their transnational nature and the continued relations between sending and receiving areas (Portes and Bach 1985; Massey et al. 1987; Chavez 1988; Portes and Böröcz 1989). In the context of the present study, moreover, we have been observing three phenomena that seem functionally related to these selective pressures: the continuing and developing grower preference for young Mexican nationals and Guatemalans in the farm labor market, the difficulties surrounding the use of Haitians in the farm labor market, and the increasing grower interest in, and expansion of, legal-alien labor programs (Barry 1990).[8]

Each of these developments, in a general way, can be related to the characteristic household structures and patterns of family life among Mexican nationals, Guatemalans, Haitians, and legal-alien workers. Briefly, with the exception of Haitians, each of these groups has penetrated U.S. society and its economy with extremely fluid patterns of family life in which singles—males primarily, but also females—are able to attach and detach themselves to more stable households in the United States or abroad with the ease that seems to have characterized African American and Caribbean households. This is most extreme with Jamaican H-2A workers who harvest sugarcane in counties near Collier, since they migrate only as singles, but high proportions of single males are also present in populations of Mexican nationals and Guatemalan refugees. These population characteristics are preadapted to the housing and labor market characteristics that emerged during the time growers relied primarily on U.S. African American households for their labor.

In contrast to these groups, many Haitian households have had difficulty in establishing a viable foothold in the harvests. This derives in part from the nature of Haitian assimilation in southern Florida. Many growers we interviewed view Haitians as particularly close-knit or "cliquish," as well as more litigious and more likely to collectively complain about working conditions (see also Griffith and Camposeco 1993; Richman 1992). Stepick and Portes (1986) found that Haitians who came to Florida during the late 1970s and early 1980s were severely discriminated against and forced to rely on their own community for housing, cultural orientation, and economic assistance during their first years in the country (see also Stepick and Stepick 1990). Furthermore, the more recent Haitian arrivals were often discriminated against by earlier immigrants from Haiti, much in the way the *Marielitos* (Cubans who arrived during the boatlift from Mariel, Cuba, in 1980) were not welcomed by the Cubans who had fled Castro's regime in the early 1960s (Glick-Schiller and Fouron 1990; Grenier 1990). This discrimination has created even more close-knit communities of Haitian farmworkers, in conformity with the ethnic-group adaptation model, which posits that ethnic boundaries become established and strengthened because of discrimination from the dominant group or groups (Jiobu 1988:2). The close-knit character of their community would clearly discourage the fluidity exhibited by Mexicans, Guatemalans, and African Americans.

We emphasize, however, that household structure alone cannot account for the presence and viability of specific ethnic groups in the farm labor market. If it could, growers would have had no reason ever to shift from using African Americans and Puerto Ricans to using Mexican nationals or Guatemalans. Instead, we argue that through processes of grower–worker accommodation and revision, workers have come to adapt their patterns of family life to labor market demands and growers have adapted the ways they organize labor markets to certain features of the populations they prefer; their preferences, a separate issue, stem from a variety of real and perceived worker characteristics (average physical size of individuals, reliability, productivity, docility, and so forth). These negotiations have established the general parameters of family life, household structures, and labor market behavior, within which some ethnic groups function more easily than others. Further influencing the behavior of groups in the farm labor market are those public and private organizations that attempt to ameliorate the worst of farmworker living and working conditions.

Farmworker Organizations and Programs in Immokalee

Farmworkers are among the most visibly ''serviced'' of populations. While other occupational groups, such as agricultural producers, may receive substantially larger government subsidies or access to proportionately more government programs, these tend to be more hidden from public scrutiny than the health-care, emergency food, housing, skill development, education, and other programs typically extended to migrant and seasonal agricultural workers. In Immokalee during the harvest season, crowds of migrant and seasonal farmworkers daily block the doorways of organizations such as the Coalition of Florida Farmworker Organizations, Inc. (COFFO), the Guadalupe Center, or Florida Rural Legal Services. These organizations dispense government emergency funds, run soup kitchens, provide job training, and offer free legal advice and assistance. The visibility of these agencies facilitates the spread of information about their services through Immokalee, leading farmworkers to incorporate the availability and range of services offered into their employment decisions, their behavior on the job, and their evaluation of Immokalee's living conditions. At the same time, their visibility underlies their often being understaffed and underfunded. And these programs function as subsidies to growers, providing workers the bare means to survive during times of unemployment and relieving growers of the responsibility of meeting workers' full cost-of-living requirements (of providing, in other words, a living wage). The costs of maintaining and reproducing what is a key factor of southern Florida agricultural production—labor—is thus transferred from the growers to the farmworkers themselves and to the federally and privately funded programs that help farmworkers meet their basic needs.

Use of services also facilitates the spread of information about documents needed to work and the various legal opportunities presented by immigration reform, resulting in a high level of sensitivity among immigrants about the need for specific kinds of documents. As such, legal status can become a factor in immigrants' access to public- and private-sector services. This tie between social services and legal status, further, has been solidified and legitimized by the use of some of these services to help illegals apply for political asylum or other legal statuses or to provide English classes to the newly documented. The importance of this tie is that farmworker services, already unevenly distributed over the farmworking population, have yet another criterion (i.e., legal status or documentation) for uneven distribution of services and a further cause of internal differentiation within the farm labor force. This provides more opportunity for farm labor contractors and growers to continue unscrupulous labor practices that worsen overall working conditions and pay scales in agriculture. For example, just as unequal power relations can develop based on gender or ethnicity, similar power disparities can develop based on the dependence of undocumented workers on *coyotes* (smugglers of immigrants) and farm labor contractors who know their workers are illegal and have restricted access to housing, legal assistance, and human-service programs. This differential access to social services is reflected in use patterns among the different groups we find in Immokalee. For all low-wage workers, the most commonly used social service is a reduced-price health clinic, used by over one-third of the households we interviewed, followed by food stamps (18.0 percent), legal services (16.3 percent), job training (11.2 percent), and subsidized housing (6.7 percent). Comparing family groups, lone-male and -female farmworkers seem the most different from the others, with far fewer receiving food stamps or utilizing job-training programs or legal services. This reflects the large number of undocumented or new immigrants in the group of lone-male and lone-female farmworkers.

In contrast to these public programs, Immokalee's private-sector programs that provide services to farmworkers often care little about the legal status of those they assist. Many of these are church or religious organizations and provide a wide range of survival or emergency assistance, support for child care and family educational needs, political asylum, safe havens for those fleeing domestic violence, counseling, spiritual support, and associated services. Similar services are provided by some public-sector programs, and, in practice, many organizations that receive public funds also extend assistance to illegal residents through other, private mechanisms. The *Immokalee Directory of Social Resources* lists eighteen public and private organizations whose primary or sole recipient population consists of low-income families and the working poor.

Of these, the service most widely used by farmworkers is Immigration Agricultural Worker's I.D., Inc., which issues the *tarjeta blanca* (white identification card).[9] Many farm labor contractors now require workers to present these cards before they are allowed to board their buses in the morning. The office, supported by local growers, serves both the Immokalee area and Hendry County; similar offices are located throughout southern Florida, serving major farmworker areas such as Belle Glade, Homestead, and Haines City. In Immokalee, the *tarjeta blanca* is a necessary prerequisite for access to the full range of agricultural job offers in the area. Not having a card, however, does not necessarily mean that one cannot find work. Noting the activity at El Centro in the early mornings, field observers reported that while many farm labor contractors stand at the doors of their buses and check workers' cards, others are less diligent about making sure workers are legal. In either case, the farm labor contractors usually know whether or not crew members are legal, hiring the illegals last and laying them off first. Before the 1989 freeze, for example, few farmworkers—legal or illegal—were out of work in Immokalee; after the freeze the only workers employed were legals.

In contrast to the Agricultural ID office is the employment (or job) service, the service probably least used by farmworkers. The primary reason for its failure to serve them is its rigidity in providing its primary services of collecting and disseminating labor market information and referring individuals to jobs. The paperwork involved in job referrals is sometimes so involved that migrant workers must wait days or even weeks to apply for a specific job, let alone begin work. Often migrants exist at the very margins of survival; a week's wait without work is enough to push them into homelessness or other forms of abject poverty. The Interstate Clearance System (ICS), the job service's system that, before recent changes, located jobs in other states for unemployed migrants, involved a particularly cumbersome series of forms, meetings, and referrals. In the past, when the local job service received an ICS order telling of work in another state, rather than passing that information along to potential workers, the office had the state and regional offices review the order to ensure that the firm requesting the workers had not violated wage and hour laws, would provide housing, and so on. This review process could take up to four weeks. In some instances, such as agricultural harvests, the work described in the ICS order may have lasted four to six weeks; by the time workers were able to respond, the jobs could have already been filled. An automated system recently installed to replace the ICS has not been in place long enough to evaluate its effectiveness.

We may contrast this extremely formalized system with the more informal way that migrants have come to meet most of their basic needs, that is, through social networks. Social networks are the building blocks of the social infrastructure of migration; they are, by all accounts, the most important and comprehensive feature of farmworkers' lives. Social networks may be based on kinship, friendship, common community of origin, ethnicity, national origin, common residence, or common job experiences. They tend to include both male and female members, old and young, who rely on one another for housing, transportation, financial assistance during crises, labor market information and job contracts, and emotional support. They are extremely flexible institutions that have arisen primarily in response to the uncertainties and difficulties of migrant and farmworking life. They are constantly changing and adapting, both growing and dissolving in response to labor market developments, crop failures, individuals' rites of passage, and so forth. They may become, alternately, impenetrable by new entrants, their members suspicious of outsiders, or open to new influences, new information, new services oriented toward migrants. They have become so efficient and flexible within the migrant way of life that they have often been used by farm labor contractors and employers to recruit new workers to packing houses and fields. As we note throughout this work, network recruitment—the recruitment of friends, kin, and the members of networks of current employees—has become the most common form of recruitment within low-wage labor markets, including and especially those staffed primarily or exclusively by migrant workers (see also Griffith 1993a).

Networks provide a model of organization and flexibility on which some service-delivery systems now in place have fashioned their own programs. Programs such as COFFO, the Guadalupe Center, and the Redlands Christian Migrant Association are the most successful because they provide a range of services that support migrants' networks. In contrast, programs that provide only a narrow, restricted, and rigid set of services have just limped along among the migrant population. Evidence of this is seen in farmworkers' use of employment service. Only 2.5 percent of the workers we interviewed freely volunteered that they would consider the job service as a place to find work; fully half of current and past farmworkers reported that they would not trust information that came from the job service about migrant destinations. While 19.1 percent of those interviewed—farmworkers and other low-wage workers—had had contact with the employment service, only 3.6 percent actually found a job through such channels, 1.1 percent were referred to a job that did not work out, and 14.4 percent were not referred to a job at all. The remaining 80.9 percent of workers interviewed had had no contact with the employment service at all. The lack of contact between the employment service and the larger body of farmworkers means that many of the protections of workers guaranteed by legislation protect only those farmworkers who file suit against growers.[10]

Despite the lack of communication between farmworkers and the employment service, farmworkers, through their networks, can and do find work outside agriculture. The two industries most likely to draw Immokalee farmworkers out of farmwork are construction and tourism. Many construction jobs consist of landscaping as well as cleaning up construction sites to prepare for the painting and other finishing crews (Burns 1993). The tourist industry requires chambermaids, janitors, restaurant help, bellhops, desk clerks (for English speakers), and so on. According to Hudson (1979):

> At the time Texas-Mexicans were moving into citrus harvesting, a considerable tourist trade was developing in Orlando around Disney World. This booming construction activity offered a marked increase in low skilled jobs in the construction industry. Many local harvest workers moved into these job opportunities. Consequently, the increase of Texas-Mexicans into the Florida harvest labor market was absorbed with little noticeable disruption of employment for local workers. (23–24)

While jobs in both the construction and tourist industries tend to pay as well as or higher than farmwork jobs, factors that seem to inhibit farmworkers from leaving farmwork are a lack of experience with nonagricultural working conditions, such as work schedules and different methods of supervision; transportation problems or costs, since most of these jobs are in Marco Island, Naples, or Fort Myers; and features of farmworking "society" that limit one's freedom in the labor market, such as access to a crew leader's or grower's housing, financial or affective indebtedness, and network ties (Table 2.2).

In the light of these figures, high annual exit rates from agriculture are understandable. Compared even with unskilled service and manufacturing jobs, farmwork tends to be less satisfying, to pay less, and to involve more frequent job changes (less job stability) through the year and from year to year. A more detailed examination of benefits by sectors of the economy illustrates the gap between farmwork and other work in low-income sectors of the economy in terms of desirability. If we assume a free market and its accompanying assumptions of maximization, free choice, and economic rationality, farmwork should not be able to compete, especially in a robust economy such as southern Florida's, with many opportunities in construction and tourism. This fact alone underscores the importance of network ties and other social relationships, power differentials between labor and capital (especially those maintained and enhanced by differences in legal and immigrant statuses), and other seemingly "noneconomic" factors in securing and organizing labor for farmwork. Simply, networks bind farmworkers to the agricultural labor mar-

TABLE 2.2 Job Satisfaction and Duration, Benefits, and Pay, by Economic Sector
(N = 196)

	Satisfied (%)	Plan to Stay in Current Occupation (%)	No Benefits (%)	Total Pay/Hour ($)	Months Worked	Number of Jobs/Year
Farmworker	32	60	79	4.56	10.8	3.2
Unskilled	26	59	87	4.41	10.8	3.5
Skilled	82	64	18	5.07	11.0	1.45
Agricultural service	33	33	67	4.59	10.2	3.33
Services/Manufacturing	57	71	41	6.98	11.57	1.49
Unskilled	53	70	51	6.20	11.51	1.62
Skilled	62	76	24	8.35	11.70	1.38
Job Outside the U.S.	40	50	83	3.40	11.50	2.5

Source: Immokalee survey data, 1989–90.

ket. These practices in the farm labor market are, moreover, diffusing into other sectors of the economy as farmworkers increasingly move between farmwork and other economic sectors, particularly, in southern Florida, construction and tourism. These practices, moreover, may underlie the low willingness of former farmworkers to return to farmwork. Under 10 percent of the former farmworkers we interviewed were willing to return to farmwork, and even fewer were willing to migrate.

The construction industry has always been a heavy employer of illegal aliens in unskilled and semiskilled positions, since many construction tasks are subcontracted to small firms who hire and pay workers daily. We learned of cases in Marco Island, for example, of unemployed farmworkers cleaning out buildings after the bulk of the crew had finished and before the more skilled finishing work (painting, wallpapering, etc.) began. In Indiantown, two and one-half hours northeast of Immokalee, Burns (1993) reports that Guatemalan workers were employed in golf course construction and landscaping, utilizing skills that drew on their subsistence-agricultural, peasant backgrounds of close, detailed attention to plant husbandry. Immigrants' backgrounds prepare them for work in the construction industry in other ways as well. Perhaps most important, as noted earlier, one of the principal goals of return migrants to Mexico and the Caribbean is to build a house. Usually this occurs over many years and involves building a house themselves, room by room, a task that gives them at least some experience with building tools and materials and hence some construction skills.

In addition to construction and tourism, the Immokalee area offers some opportunities for small-scale entrepreneurial activities that cater to farm labor migrants. These include such things as mobile food and ice cream stands and petty trading services, which assume importance in areas where many workers are living in isolated labor camps outside of Immokalee.

The Nature of Agricultural Work in Southwestern Florida

Winter vegetables and citrus dominate the cropping systems of Collier, Lee, and Hendry counties, although there are also ornamental horticulture operations such as gladiolas and nursery stock (Table 2.3).

Our survey revealed that nearly 60 percent of the farmworkers in Immokalee worked in tomatoes, 10.1 percent in peppers, and 9.3 percent in other vegetables, yet only 8.4 percent in citrus. The proportion of citrus workers should increase, however, along with the increased citrus acreage being

TABLE 2.3 Selected Features of Crops in Collier, Lee, and Hendry Counties, 1989–90

Crop	Acreage	Piece Rate	Pieces/Hour	Harvest Period
Citrus	80,510[a]	$ .45–.60/box	7.6	November–June
Tomato	18,400	$ .35–.40/box	11.0	December–April
Pepper	8,300	$ .40/bushel	8.75	October–April
Watermelon	6,500	$5.00/hour	n.a.[b]	January–April
Cucumber	4,450	n.d.[c]	n.d.	January–April
Squash	1,100	$ .35/bushel	9.6	January–March

Sources: Immokalee survey data, 1989–90; Florida Agricultural Statistics Service, 1991.

[a]Includes acreage in nonbearing trees.

[b]Not applicable.

[c]No data.

planted. Nevertheless, the heart of Immokalee's farmworking population consists of vegetable workers; like citrus workers in Polk County, many of the citrus workers in our study live in other, more settled communities as well as company labor camps outside of Immokalee.

In general, farms in southern Florida tend to be corporate-owned, often financed by out-of-state and, less often, foreign capital (e.g., Spanish capital in the sugarcane industry), and of relatively large acreages. During the study period, in southwestern Florida, 1,426 farms produced on 240,345 acres (168.54 acres per farm), generating receipts from sales of farm produce of $377 million. Monthly payrolls in agriculture are $14 million, compared with $21.9 million for tourism in the region, and monthly employment is 21,766, compared with tourist employment of 26,368 (*Florida Statistical Abstract* 1989). Agriculture's growth is causing increasing concern among southern Florida's urban populations, particularly as issues such as water quality and availability, environmental degradation, and agriculture's role in attracting new immigrants to Florida receive more media attention. In July 1993, environmentalists and representatives of southern Florida agriculture—notably sugar growers—agreed to initiate a program to clean up the Everglades.

The corporate presence in southern Florida agriculture is particularly relevant to the current study because, as we discuss in detail in the next chapter, the personnel policies of large corporate firms based in Immokalee affect labor issues in the labor demand regions of the north. For example, sensing the need to maintain the integrity of the migrant work unit, a personnel manager for one the largest growers in Florida said that he "arranges with growers in the north for the crew boss and team to stay together during the summer" (Florida. Collier County 1988), and that using this method yields a 90 percent return rate among family migrants and a 60 percent return rate among single males.

A second feature of southern Florida agriculture is the presence of H-2A workers in the sugarcane harvests around Belle Glade, Clewiston, Moorehead, South Bay, and the other communities on the southern shores of Lake Okeechobee. H-2A workers are legal aliens imported under the British West Indies Temporary Alien Labor Program, the program begun around the same time as the Bracero Program discussed in Chapter 1. In the past few years, citrus growers in Polk County have attempted to expand the legal-alien labor program into citrus, a move that has precipitated protest from Florida farmworkers (Barry 1990). No new legal-alien workers were hired, not because of the protests, but because of the freeze. Indeed, growers have historically been successful at gaining access to offshore workers in the H-2A program when such requests have been subjected to court scrutiny (Griffith 1986a). The alien-labor program has already expanded into tobacco and other harvests along the eastern seaboard. If this expansion signals a trend, in part stimulated by concern over the effects of the Immigration Reform and Control Act (IRCA), a growing dependence on H-2A workers would have severe consequences in the summar harvest areas. Two outcomes are possible. On one hand, if they discourage domestic farmworkers from taking jobs in H-2A-dominated harvests, as they have in the H-2A sugar and apple harvests, the supply of farmworkers to the summer harvests might increase as farmworkers who lost their jobs to legal-alien workers in Florida pour north in search of work. On the other hand, displaced farmworkers may leave the farm labor market altogether, which would constrict labor supplies to northern harvests. This latter scenario is more likely because, historically, interruptions in migrant itineraries have resulted in increased exits from agriculture, and the growers' association currently organizing the alien-labor programs has been actively involved in helping growers in the northern growing regions import legal-alien labor. North Carolina cucumber growers, for example, rely on the Florida Fruit and Vegetable Association to help them apply for legal-alien labor.

Most scholarly work on the farm labor market emphasizes tasks and labor processes associated with the harvest, since the concentrated labor needs at harvesttime overshadow those dispersed throughout the year (Fischer 1953; Thomas 1985). Nevertheless, a number of tasks in addition to harvesting take place, each of which influences the overall complexion and changes taking place in the farmworking population.

Producing tomatoes, for example, the largest crop in Collier County, involves preparing the ground with shovels, laying plastic, planting seedlings, transplanting the small plants, putting stakes in, and tying vines to the stakes. Tying vines, which pays by the foot, must be done a number of times before the harvest. After the bulk of the harvest, moreover, many farmworking households practice "pinhooking," a secondary harvest operation that entails independent contractors' buying the last of the tomatoes in the fields, harvesting them primarily with family labor or their own crews, using their own small trucks and boxes, and then selling them by the box in open markets in Immokalee and elsewhere. In the past few years, pinhooking has assumed a new importance as a form of disguised wage labor; U.S. growers historically have been able to circumvent regulations concerning documentation of legal status and laws designed to protect workers by creating various subcontracting agreements. We take up this issue in more depth in Chapter 10.

The variety of tasks in addition to the harvest reflect degrees of mobility within farm labor job hierarchies. They are important not so much because they imply greater employment alternatives or opportunities but because those who fill these jobs tend to be part of Immokalee's resident population. Data on monthly agricultural-worker levels through the year and from year to year in Collier County (Florida. Collier County 1988) indicate that around one in five workers remains employed in agriculture in Immokalee throughout the year. Many of these year-round farmworkers form the anchor households for those farmworkers who move between Florida, Mexico, and Texas, and the harvests of the North. At the same time, most of the year-round, low-wage, unskilled jobs in convenience stores and fast-food restaurants are filled by year-round residents. Renting rooms, garages, trailers, and just about any structure in one's yard to migrant farmworkers provides a good source of supplemental income for part of the year for families who have additional space.

Given rain days, freezes, low crop yields, and other features of the harvest that reduce the number of hours per day or days per week that they can be employed, farmworkers try to earn as much money as possible during the harvest. Underemployment is a chronic problem, occurring daily, weekly, monthly, and seasonally. As typically seen in Hollywood portrayals of farm life in America, the day begins before dawn, around 4:00 or 5:00 A.M., when Immokalee's central meeting places for farm labor contractors draw workers out of the neighborhoods. For those who find work, the workday can last from no longer than three to five hours to as many as nine or ten. The number of workdays in the week can fluctuate as well, from none to seven, depending on weather conditions; during the peak of the harvest period (December, before the freeze), it was reported that nearly everyone could find some work during the week.

While daily and weekly schedules are highly variable, seasonal schedules are less so. Farmworkers and labor contractors have precise knowledge about task succession within crops and the sequence of harvests in various regions, mixing, for example, peaches in Georgia with apples in Virginia followed by citrus in Florida. Although farmwork picks up in Immokalee around Thanksgiving and begins tapering off around Easter, some farmworkers work through the year. This trend is likely to continue as more citrus moves south and growers begin more diverse planting schedules and cropping strategies to hedge against devastating freezes, three of which occurred in Florida in the 1980s alone. Much of the planting/harvesting schedule is market- rather than weather-driven, so that with alternative market outlets (processing rather than fresh) it would be possible to vary planting and harvest seasons in southern Florida.

Workers' Relations with Farm Labor Contractors and Crew Dynamics

Several of the principal findings of our research directly pertain to the increasing use of labor intermediaries, farm labor contractors, in the farm labor market. In many ways, these contractors embody the central functions and the structure of the farm labor market as well as capture its range of impressions: from the "frontier" quality that seems to enliven Immokalee during the winter months to the rigid, structured patterns of living that characterize the controlled movement of crews from Immokalee into the northern harvests.

Farm labor contractors are present in virtually all components of the farm labor market. Even in firms and on farms that do not use farm labor contractors, their presence is felt indirectly, because of the heavy influence they exert over housing, working conditions, the mobilization of workers for recruitment and transport, and so forth, especially in places like Immokalee. To a great extent, farm labor contractor practices set the standards, establishing the floors for wages and working and living conditions. We found, in fact, that a farmworker's well-being was related to the presence or absence of a farm labor contractor in the worker's labor market behaviors.

We compared farmworkers who work directly for growers (N = 41; 55 percent) with those who are hired through farm labor contractors (N = 34;

45 percent), bringing to light some telling similarities and differences. Similar proportions of the two populations, around 80 percent, are legally authorized to work in the United States, and the average length of time in the country is around eight years for both groups. Using a farm labor contractor to get hired, it seems, is not a simple function of legal status or experience in the United States, despite the fact that many worker–farm labor contractor relationships begin with border crossings. That is, many farm labor contractors, particularly those who hire large numbers of Guatemalans, also smuggle illegal aliens across the border or have relations with smugglers.

Differences between the two populations emerge in housing, vehicle ownership, and the ability to speak English. Around 10 percent more of the farmworkers who use farm labor contractors live in shared housing than do those who do not use farm labor contractors. Substantially fewer of those who rely on farm labor contractors for work also rely on them for transportation: only 7.9 percent of those who use farm labor contractors own their own vehicles, compared with 41.4 percent of those who do not use farm labor contractors. Finally, fewer farmworkers using farm labor contractors speak English.

Each of these comparisons suggests that using a farm labor contractor involves establishing a relationship of dependence. Farmworkers who utilize farm labor contractors often rely on them not only for work but also for access to housing, transportation, and linguistic ability. Farm labor contracting is, in short, very much tied up with labor control. This dimension of farm labor contracting can be seen in the general features of the business as well as in specific cases involving farm labor contractor crews.

Farm labor contractors have been a part of many agricultural harvests of the eastern United States at least for the past twenty years, acting as crucial organizational and supervisory buffers between growers and the farmworking population. A farm labor contractor's crew might actually include a number of licensed contractors, each of whom occupies a different supervisory or support position in the crew. These other farm labor contractors are often referred to in the farmworker literature and in the community as crew leaders, field walkers, and foremen (Vandeman 1988). At the very least, farm labor contractors assemble a crew, enter into a verbal or written contract with a grower, make sure the crew accomplishes the necessary tasks, and see that crew members get paid. Beyond the simple task assignments, however, a number of relations may develop between farm labor contractors and crew members that might appear to be tangential to the business of accomplishing agricultural tasks. Usually it is in these tangential realms that the extraordinary behaviors occur: the abuses of authority, the acts of exploitation, the betrayals and abandonments, and the cross-country treks at costs more exorbitant than first-class air travel—all of which have become part of farmworker lore about farm labor contractors.

A case of Florida based Haitian migrants being recruited by a Fort Pierce crew leader illustrates not only crew dynamics but also the abuse some farmworkers receive from farm labor contractors working in concert with growers.

In July 1981, assembling a crew to take a Pennsylvania tomato harvest, an African American farm labor contractor named Willie Simmons sent farm labor contractors into Florida's inland cities to add to the workers living in his Fort Pierce labor camp. Simmons inherited the Pennsylvania contract from his father, who had since retired from farm labor contracting to run the labor camp's commissary. Simmons believed he would need over 200 farmworkers for the harvest but could count on only around 160 workers in his labor camp to make the trip. The workers living in his labor camp were African American, Mexican, and Haitian. Most of the farm labor contractors working for Simmons were African Americans, but earlier that summer two Haitians from central Florida communities supplied him with some crews of new immigrant Haitians; he directed them to recruit 56 more workers for the Pennsylvania migration. One of these Haitian farm labor contractors, Jeyune DuMonde, traveled to Belle Glade, where he was able to recruit a number of Haitian workers by showing them his farm labor contractor license and feeding them misinformation about the crops they would be working, the amounts of work, rates of pay, and so on.

Actually, DuMonde himself seemed to know little about the Pennsylvania farm. His relationship with Simmons was tenuous and in most cases mediated by one of three African American farm labor contractors also working for Simmons: Miller Davies, Elliot Williams, and Moses Frank. According to workers DuMonde recruited, who later filed suit against Simmons, over the next few weeks relations between the various farm labor contractors and the Haitian crew from Belle Glade, already strained by ethnic differences and by the sequence of joining the larger crew, became even further fragmented, eventually resulting in a fight in the Pennsylvania labor camp over amounts of work and discrimination between crews in terms of work allocations. The Haitians were forced out of the labor camp and stranded in rural Pennsylvania. The following passages, based on or taken directly from depositions, relate the events leading up to the Haitians' being fired and stranded.

DuMonde met L.V. [a Haitian, the plaintiff] walking down a street in Belle Glade. He told him he could work in Pennsylvania, making $2,000 to $3,000 picking cucumbers and then apples for four months. Later that week, DuMonde picked up. L.V. along with a group of L.V.'s family and friends, taking them from Belle Glade to Fort Pierce.

In Fort Pierce they stopped behind the house of Willie Simmons. They did not have money, but DuMonde told them they could sign a paper at a restaurant and pay him later. They did not eat. They slept in the bus and on the ground. The man who was given the paper about work conditions couldn't read. . . .

On August 1, they left for Pennsylvania; there were 212 people in four vehicles: three school buses and a van. The camp was ethnically diverse, including American blacks, Mexicans, Haitians, African American farm labor contractors working for Simmons drove the buses. Michel Fourtes, Willie Simmons's other Haitian crew leader, drove the van. In the van, they posted signs saying they would be picking tomatoes at forty cents a bucket. They also passed out flyers telling what Simmons's wife would be charging for meals, sandwiches, and hamburgers. People in the van got copies of these flyers, but not people in the buses. The flyer mentioned New York, but said nothing about Pennsylvania. Later, during testimony, one of the Haitian workers remarked, "This is the only written notice about the terms and conditions of employment I ever saw the entire time I worked with Simmons's crew."

On August 2, they arrived in Pennsylvania at the labor camp. A second group of workers under the supervision of one of Simmons's field walkers, Miller Davies, joined them as well, bringing a crew up from the peach harvests in South Carolina. After the crews arrived in Pennsylvania, Simmons divided the workers into smaller crews. "All the black Americans were in a single crew, with all the Mexicans in another crew and all the Haitians were in another crew. . . ."

According to one worker: "The camp was in bad condition, at least the portion where I stayed. The beds were broken. The drinking water had a mineral taste so that I bought bottled water for drinking. There was no hot water available at the camp and the bathrooms were filthy and frequently the toilets did not work properly. . . . Despite the promises made to myself and the others from South Carolina, there was not much work available for me in Pennsylvania. . . . I was only able to work two or three days a week because of the lack of work and the large size of Simmons's crew. I usually netted only about $50 to $90. I spent a good portion of this money at the camp commissary. The camp store was operated by Simmons's wife and sold meals at a high price, three dollars a meal, as well as selling soda (fifty cents a can) and beer to crew members."

During the first week, there was no work for the Haitian crews. The week of August 11, however, L.V. worked picking tomatoes on Tuesday from 11:00 A.M. to 5:00 P.M., without a break for lunch, and picked three hundred buckets. On Thursday, he worked from 11:00 A.M. to 6:00 P.M. Before they worked they told DuMonde the price, forty cents a bucket, was too low, but DuMonde said, "There is nothing I can do." Payday was Saturday. Between the time they arrived in Pennsylvania and the time they first got paid they had no money.

"While at the camp, Willie took them to the market," another worker testified.

"The shopkeeper gave him a paper to sign, in the presence of Willie, for the food for $17.00."

Over the next few days, work in the tomato fields became more and more sporadic. One of the Haitians testified that the grower wouldn't put them to work the week of August 5 through 10 because the market price was too low. Simmons contacted the grower, who said work would begin on or about August 5 or 6. He worked on August 11 and 13, but at other times could give them no work. Simmons and the field walkers then put the crews to work differently, working the African American and Mexican crews more than the Haitians. DuMonde complained that the Haitians weren't getting as much work as the others, which led to the fight.

"After two weeks in the camp without work, all the [Haitian] workers complained to Willie, and he told them he would fight with them (he put up his fists). . . . The discussion became heated. One of the African American foremen picked up a large rock and struck Jeyune [DuMonde] with it. A crowd of Haitian workers gathered around the scene of the attack on Jeyune. When Simmons saw this group, he drew a revolver and pointed it at myself and the other Haitian workers who had gathered at the scene. About five other foremen, including Miller Davies, also drew revolvers at the same time and aimed them at myself and the other Haitian workers."

This case illustrates the differences in vulnerability to farm labor contractor power among segments of the crew. Jeyune DuMonde's Haitian crew, recruited to the group last, is clearly the most susceptible to abuse and is the most abused. The African American and Mexican crews receive better housing and more work; the Haitians receive what is left over. This suggests that each of these segments of the workforce is subject to different qualities and forms of power.

Especially since illegal aliens have come to dominate the eastern U.S. harvests, farm labor contractorship in some crews has rested, in part, on the crew leader's knowledge of the labor market, experience and relations with growers, and means of transporting crews. Whether a farmworker works as an independent or as part of a crew depends on how these factors are combined in the systems of labor recruitment and task allocation. Crew leaders vary by the size and composition of their crews; by crew ethnicity; by the degree to which they specialize in crops, harvests, or regions; by the extent of control over their crews; and by the means of transportation and housing facilities at their disposal. As noted above in the segment on farmworkers' households, some crews consist of no more than six to eight related members, friends, or kin of the crew leader, while others are run by large farm labor contractors in charge of sixty to one hundred workers, with fleets of buses and trucks, all necessary harvesting equipment, and housing for at least a portion of their workforce. Most commonly, farm labor contractors maintain a "core" of workers who work with them from season to season and then recruit other workers as the need arises. In Immokalee, the core workers may live in the crew leader's neighborhood or labor camp, while the other workers may be recruited in the morning, often on a daily basis, at El Centro in South Immokalee.

We noted that the use of a crew leader of farm labor contractor by a farmworker directly influences the farmworkers's well-being or standard of living. What the worker trades for the labor intermediary's special access to the labor market, is his or her independence and the security and income such independence entails. We found that those working for farm labor contractors had "longest jobs" of shorter duration, and lower incomes, than those independent of farm labor contractors (Table 2.4).

The extreme difference in family income between the two groups suggests that those who use farm labor contractors either come from smaller, less complex households that have fewer individuals active in the labor force and belong to less complex networks or they simply earn less than those who do not use farm labor contractors. The reality lies between these observations: individually, those who use farm labor contractors earn less, and, collectively, they are distributed differently over the family and network types and immigrant statuses than are those who do not use farm labor contractors (Table 2.5).

TABLE 2.4 Workers Who Use Farm Labor Contractors (FLCs) and Workers Who Do Not, by Employment Record, Income, and Education

	Workers Who Use FLCs (N = 34)		Workers Who Do Not Use FLCs (N = 41)
Duration of longest job	3.8 months	$(p = .0016)^a$	6.2 months
Weekly pay at longest job	$ 169.73	$(p = .0326)^a$	$ 220.82
Annual family income	$5,786.00	$(p = .0029)^a$	$11,061.00
Number of jobs worked annually	3.7 jobs	$(p = .0472)^a$	3.0 jobs
Total months unemployed	1.4 months	$(p = .0983)$	0.7 months
Total months in farmwork	8.1 months	$(p = .0460)^a$	6.2 months
School grades completed	4.5 grades	$(p = .8103)$	4.7 grades
Percentage of income spent on housing	25.3%	$(p = .5500)$	22.5%

Sources: Immokalee survey data, 1989–90; current farmworker subsample.
[a]Statistically significant, analysis of variance.

Specifically, those workers who do not use farm labor contractors tend to be in more deeply embedded networks and more complex households, and are more often U.S.-born, than those who use farm labor contractors. As Chavez (1990) notes, strategies of residence, or the ways new immigrants arrange and rearrange their living arrangmenets, are the principal methods by which new immigrants resist the conditions of domination under which they find themselves. In this case, creative family strategies constitute ways of circumventing or reducing the power of labor intermediaries. Involvement in more complex households and more deeply embedded networks is indicated by the higher percentages of nuclear and extended households, lower percentages of lone-male/lone-female households, and higher percentages of native-born workers. Despite these differences, it is equally interesting that farm labor contractors are by no means overly selective regarding the legal, familial, or network profiles of their workers. This indicates the overall pervasiveness of farm labor contractors in the farm labor market.

Another point we can draw from comparing workers by their use of farm labor contractors is that workers who use farm labor contractors work in agricultural jobs for more months of the year and evidently work for shorter lengths of time in each job. These findings contribute to our observations about the structure of the farm labor force and the importance of farm labor contractors, and subcontracting relationships generally, in staffing harvests. Jobs of short duration in agriculture are generally harvest jobs, and the ability of farm labor contractors to locate, recruit, and organize workers for a series of harvests has become a fact of life of harvest enterprises. The difference between the two groups in terms of months per year in farmwork also reflects, again, the extensive farm labor contractor reliance on labor control: evidently, the power that farm labor contractors develop over their crews through housing, transportation, and cultural brokerage functions allows them to confine workers to the farm labor market. By contrast, independent workers are employed fewer months per year in agriculture because of the range of employment, informal economic, and other survival opportunities open to them, including unemployment benefits to the native-born and the legalized.

The similarities between the two groups are as telling as the differences. It is noteworthy that their members are virtually identical in terms of level of education and percentage of incomes spent on housing. Both groups come from low social strata and operate from positions of powerlessness relative to those who provide housing and education. Despite this similarity, those who have become independent of farm labor contractors have been able to reduce their powerlessness in some ways but have been unable to overcome disadvan-

TABLE 2.5 Family Type, Network Type, and Immigration Status by Use of Farm Labor Contractors

	Percent Who Use FLCs (N = 34)	Percent Who Do Not Use FLCs (N = 41)
Family type		
Lone male/lone female	62.2	38.1
Extended family	10.8	16.1
Nuclear family	13.5	31.0
Working couples	5.4	7.1
Single-woman household head	8.1	4.8
Other	—	2.4
Network type		
Traditional sending area	18.9	14.3
New sending area	56.8	50.0
Texas/Nuevo Leon	10.8	7.1
Bracero era	5.4	7.1
Legal U.S.-born	8.1	21.4
Immigration status[a]		
Section 210—SAW	39.5	21.4
Section 245—pre-1982	10.5	4.8
Refugee	7.9	16.7
Marriage, green card, family	10.6	11.9
Undocumented	18.4	19.0
U.S.-born	13.2	26.2

Source: Immokalee survey data, 1989–90; current farmworker subsample.

Note: Percentages may not total 100 because of rounding.

[a]Section 210 (SAW) refers to seasonal agricultural workers who were legalized under IRCA. They received temporary worker authorization if they could prove that they had worked for ninety days in agriculture in the previous three years. Section 245 is concerned with the "amnesty" immigrants, granted work authorization if they could prove they had lived in the United States since before 1982.

tages in other ways. In Immokalee, the premium put on housing has made this cost of living similar for everyone.

Our observations suggest that two key variables influencing crew size and composition, as well as the nature of farm labor contractorship, are housing and transportation. Clearly, farm labor contractors who operate labor camps are more likely to have a more stable workforce than those who recruit from places like El Centro, and those who have their own buses can assemble crews more readily than those who simply make arrangements to meet workers at the harvests.

Overall, access to the farm labor market is influenced and mediated by farm labor contractors, although there may be "layers" of mediation. Family members and friends represent farm labor contractors and new workers to one another, and there is a complex hierarchy, within crews, of field walkers, drivers, supervisors from the same ethnic background as workers, and so forth. Yet the presence of farm labor contractors in Florida and in the migrations out of Florida serves to influence general working conditions, labor relations, and other attributes of the agricultural job offer. This is particularly true in the area of labor recruitment.

Looking for Work in Immokalee

Locating jobs or keeping abreast of labor market information is a process dominated by one's relations with other farmworkers, friends and kin, and farm labor contractors. First, as is well known among students of migration, geographical mobility is often determined by previous contacts in an area: "pioneering" moves tend to be initiated in response to crisis, such as the devastating December 1989 freezes in Florida and Texas. Other kinds of crises we have encountered that seemed to stimulate pioneering job search behaviors were excessive abuse by a crew leader or grower, prolonged isolation and unemployment, terrorist activities in Central America, or some development that fundamentally changed the form and the reach of the farmworker's network (e.g., the death of a member). Changing immigration policy may also be considered a crisis of sorts, in that the passage of new laws seems to raise worker and crew leader consciousness concerning the need for documents. Attraction to Immokalee in particular, for those who have ties there or know about it through network ties, derives not only from the work available but also from its reputation as a place where new immigrants may be able to find papers. Acquiring legal authorization to work can stimulate job change as well, particularly to leave especially onerous working conditions. In his study of Indiantown, by contrast, Burns (1993) found that lack of work authorization served to restrict workers' movements out of known regions, for fear of deportation.

Outside of crisis situations, job search and job change behaviors combine network and labor market phenomena as well as legal-status issues. The specific region of the country and sector of the labor market with which farmworkers become familiar are in most cases guided by one's network ties: simply, people move to areas where they know other people and into jobs that are similar to those held by friends and kin. In some cases, the only person they know is a farm labor contractor, in which case the processes of job search and subsequent network building are usually mediated by that person. Whether moving with farm labor contractors or to meet friends and kin, the relations that develop expand because of the generally high degree of geographical mobility among farmworkers—between regions and crops inside the United States, between the United States and home villages for international migrants, and between counties or cities within regions. The ways in which workers' movements in the U.S. labor market are conditioned by network ties explain, in part, the lack of individual differences between migrant and nonmigrant farmworkers; network and family ties, in other words, influence economic behavior in general in the farm labor market, whether one migrates or not. Comparisons between farmworkers by whether or not they migrate reveal few differences. In our sample, the only noticeable difference we found was in terms of housing, with 81.8 percent of the migrants in shared housing compared with 68.5 percent of the nonmigrants. Improvements in housing, we suggest, thus reduce the propensity to migrate.

In case after case we have encountered such migration patterns as those of a Mexican worker and his relatives (Case 1) and of a Guatemalan lone male (Case 2).[11] Case 1 also chronicles a process of network building (Portes and Bach 1985; Massey et al. 1987; Portes and Börözc 1989).

Case 1. Juan Alier, a Mexican farmworker, moved between Mexico and Texas working in cotton harvests from 1951 to 1977. In 1977 he moved to Fort Myers for reasons unknown and began working in the pepper, tomato, and other vegetable harvests. He was the founding member of a household that currently has eleven members. His wife joined him in Fort Myers shortly after he arrived, and they established a more or less permanent home there. The following individuals, all the Aliers' children, then came to live with them in the following sequence (ages are those at time of arrival in the United States):

1978: a fourteen-year-old son.
1980: a twelve-year-old daughter, one of a pair of twins.
1980: a five-year-old son.
1985: the twin sister of the 1980 immigrant daughter.
1985: a nineteen-year-old son.
1986: a thirty-one-year-old daughter, with three of her children: two boys, aged thirteen and ten, and a girl of six.

All but one of the young sons work in a lumberyard in Fort Myers, while Alier, his wife, and all but one of the younger daughters work in a nursery. The youngest son, who came to the United States at age five and is now fourteen, is a student, as are his two nephews and his niece. The thirty-one-year-old daughter does not work outside the home but assumes most of the household and other duties associated with reproductive labor.

Case 2. Guillermo G. Vasquez, a Guatemalan farmworker, was a lone male at first migration to the United States and is so still today. He migrated to the United States first in September 1984, to Chandler High, Arizona. He stayed and worked there for fourteen months. In November 1985, he returned to Guatemala for the Christmas season, then returned to Chandler High in January 1986. After another year in Arizona, he returned to Guatemala, for the month of January 1987, returning to the United States to work again in February of the same year, this time to Fort Myers, Florida, instead of Arizona. After working around Fort Myers in the tomato and other vegetable harvests, he moved to Arcadia, Florida, in June 1988, and from then until 1989 moved around Florida with the same crew leader, working the tomato and other harvests.

Both of these cases demonstrate the great range of experience to which these highly mobile people are exposed, coming and going between countries, states, counties, and cities themselves or maintaining international and interstate connections by proxy. At the same time, however, their broad range of experience seems far more *geographical* than social or economic: within each setting their linkages and ties, whether with farm labor contractors or with families and friends, channel them toward the same or similar sectors of the labor market. The little pioneering that does go on, as in the case of Juan's eldest son's finding a job in a lumberyard, seems to result in more channeling of subsequent new entrants into the household or network.

Farmworker Attitudes About Work in Immokalee

Throughout this book we emphasize that farmworkers are less engaged in making choices about work based on income, working conditions, benefits, and so on, than they are in overcoming constraints, being pulled and pushed through the farm labor market, channeled and guided, and sometimes conned, duped, indebted, or coerced by force or the threat of deportation. Within this narrow range, however, they do make distinctions between jobs and components of jobs. They do attempt to make the most of their circumstances, and they do strive to be able to choose among alternatives, however impossible that may be.

What do farmworkers prefer? First, they seem to prefer security of employment over most other features of jobs, including pay. This preference, we may speculate, derives primarily from two features of the typical life circumstances of farmworkers: their jobs are seasonal in duration and unpredictable in terms of the size of the crop, number of workdays, number of hours a day, and so on; their household cash positions are generally at or below levels necessary for survival and reproduction. Farmworker preference for security of income, further, influences their relations with farm labor contractors, in that they can achieve greater security by establishing relations with a crew leader who has housing than with one who does not; farm labor contractors, in turn, have been able to convert this into a relationship of dependence not unlike the "patron–client" ties so common throughout Mexico (Wolf 1956; Lomnitz 1977). These ties may develop further with crises, such as a major freeze, that deepen the farmworker's dependence on the crew leader, similar to the way Lomnitz describes the emergence of *caciques* (native authorities) out of patron-client ties in a Mexican shantytown, a setting characterized by high levels of immigration of rural newcomers into the strange, urban economy of Mexico City.

> A shantytown patron expects loyalty from his clients in exchange for the access to scarce goods and services he provides. Thus a bricklayer foreman expects the cooperation of his gang or crew and may negotiate new jobs without consulting them. The tacit social contract between the foreman and his workers becomes an important economic resource for both parties. Reciprocity networks are the initial groups out of which such crews may develop, particularly since the male membership of a network tends to play the same trade. Thus, asymmetric patron-client relationships may grow out of symmetric reciprocal exchange networks. Full fledged *caciques* are found in the larger shantytowns of Mexico City. Their power tends to grow in proportion to their economic and social ascendancy over the settler. Subjectively speaking, an existing relationship of *confianza* [confidence] is converted into loyalty. At a higher level, political power of marginal population groups may be exchanged against patronage, which filters down to the individual settler in the form of jobs, land, water, and other scarce commodities. Reciprocity turns into redistribution, in which case the *cacique* or broker often retains the lion's share for himself. Such mechanisms of patrion-client relations often account for the effective articulation between reciprocity networks at the shantytown level and the urban industrial society at large. (Lomnitz 1977:202–3)

Finding a crew leader who is perceived to be good is, indeed, also a major consideration among farmworkers. What farmworkers expect from a good crew leader is exactly that range of services that extend into nonwork realms as housing, transportation for shopping, providing credit, and so on, as well as steady employment and fair and respectful treatment on the job.

Beyond security of employment and expectations regarding farm labor contractors, a principal farmworker concern seems to be one of dignity, of being treated with respect, like humans rather than animals in the fields. Dur-

ing a meeting for Guatemalan workers in Immokalee, organized to give Guatemalans an opportunity to voice complaints and learn of their legal rights, this
emerged as one of the main themes regarding working conditions. Translated,
edited, and summarized, the following concerns emerged from the meeting:

> The people who work for the labor contractors picking vegetables, mostly those
> who do not have immigration papers, are being exploited. Sometimes they get
> only $15 in cash a day working nine or ten hours. They do not have at the fields
> toilets, drinking water. They have to wash their hands in the ditches, with dirty
> and poisoned water. The Guatemalans are very shy to make their necessities
> [i.e., relieve themselves] in the fields in front of other people.
>
> We are being treated like animals. We do not have break time. The bosses allow
> us only fifteen minutes for lunch and are always mistreating us with words
> to work hard without any rest, picking tomatoes, cucumbers, peppers, and
> squashes.
>
> The grower pays $4 an hour to the workers, but the crew leader gives us only
> $3.35. We prefer being paid with the company's checks and not in cash by the
> contractor. In that way we can have the money we earn and the records for
> immigration and IRS purposes. (Camposeco field notes, October 16, 1989)

The sentiments expressed here, particularly the concern over treatment in
the fields, seem tied to similar desires of working for oneself, independent of
supervision, which is commonly expressed among pinhookers and farmworkers who are emerging as farm labor contractors themselves.

If job characteristics are open to any negotiation at all, farmworkers seem
to consider those issues more explicitly related to the job offer only after the
other issues—securing a job, stabilizing income, and gaining respect—have
been satisfied. It is only then that the job's characteristics become issues of
contention, only then that workers begin to protest wages and payment systems, field conditions, hours of work, pesticide use and abuse, and the extent
to which the job is physically taxing.

Conclusion

In Immokalee, new immigrants and old learn what is expected of them in the
labor market. The lessons they learn are more often than not harsh and relent-
less. Few of Immokalee's neighborhoods do not exhibit signs of poverty and
the struggles of the working poor. Yet the poverty rarely reeks of despair.
Immokalee's working poor may sometimes go without work or even without

food, but they continue to exhibit the drive and determination to find work and work hard. They are not an addicted, drunken, or even particularly dejected population, despite their material conditions of existence. Because of the labor surpluses in Immokalee, employers—whether growers or labor contractors— far too often take their workers' determination for granted, complaining about even the most minor instances of resistance to the authority and control of field bosses, foremen, landlords, and others.

The poverty of Immokalee's working poor is clearly tolerable to employers, perhaps even desirable for the message it sends to workers in general that severe want is no farther than a day's pay away. Employers need not harp on this point. So much of Immokalee's social and physical infrastructure reflects the essential character of the farm labor market that this lesson is driven home daily. Throughout the season, Immokalee's farmworkers learn how to crowd into substandard housing; how to establish symbiotic relations with farm labor contractors and Immokalee's permanent resident population; how to scavenge, beg, and find free food and shelter at one of the many social services or churches for the poor. One of their most valuable lessons occurs at the season's end, when they learn that either they or members of their households must leave this place of declining employment and move home to Mexico, Texas, Central America, or elsewhere, or migrate north with the crews.

Chapter 3

Migrant Workers on the Delmarva Peninsula

Maryland Tomato and Delaware Potato and Mixed-Vegetable Farms

At a hearing before the Commission on Agricultural Workers in September 1990, a woman testifying on behalf of North Carolina tobacco growers began her testimony by describing her relationship with seven workers who had worked alongside her and her husband on their farm over a number of years. The workers were Mexican Americans, based in Florida, and part of the group included a family of four with whom she and her husband had developed personal ties. Concerned for the family's welfare, she explained that she was unhappy that the family had to migrate to survive and hoped they would settle in her area. The couple's farm, however, could not provide the migrant family with work throughout the year. The woman embellished her account with details that emphasized how close the families had become.

> You don't hear about the producer taking his work crew and children to Show Biz Pizza to celebrate a child's birthday, sharing a garden together, going roller skating, going to the county fair, rushing a migrant child to the hospital for an allergic reaction to a bee sting, talking with teachers about a migrant child's progress in school, making numerous telephone calls to settle migrants' business affairs, setting up dental and doctor appointments, and in my situation, attending church together. Nor do you know about the customary barbecue to celebrate the end of the harvest before the migrants move on. (Commission on Agricultural Workers 1993c:369)

70

Florida farmworkers we interviewed often referred to similar ties they had developed with the families to whose farms they migrated.

During the testimony, however, this woman also told of helping six Mexican workers legalize under the seasonal agricultural workers (SAW) program, all of whom subsequently left their farm. The migrant family of four, who every year helped the growers recruit additional seasonal workers, had told her that it was becoming more difficult to recruit workers and that once they stopped migrating there very likely would be no one to follow them out of Florida: legalized workers there were beginning to work in construction and tourism. Labor supplies for agriculture were constricting, she claimed, expressing even more concern over the future and expecting to have to apply for H-2A (legal alien) workers within the next few seasons. "The 'H' in 'H-2A,' " she said, "stands for help" (Commission on Agricultural Workers 1993c:369).

The sentiments and fears expressed by this woman with regard to her workers are similar to those we encountered in our discussions with green-tomato growers in Maryland, and potato and fruit-and-vegetable growers in Delaware. It is common among growers in these areas to have developed, over years, personal relations with small families or networks of migrant workers who have been coming to their farms for many years and who have achieved a measure of familiarity with the grower and the grower's family. Similar to core or key personnel in other regions, these regular migrants often provide services as recruiters, locating other workers from their kinship and friendship networks in farm labor supply communities of Florida and Texas. And, as with the North Carolina grower's experience, growers on the Delmarva Peninsula also reported celebrating birthdays of migrant children and developing other emotional ties to the families who have worked for them over the years.

Familiar or fictive-kin workers like these, however, constitute only a small portion of the seasonal labor force on the peninsula. Because of this, Maryland and Delaware growers we interviewed also told of losing or expecting to lose workers to legalization and expressed the possibility that future losses might steer them toward the H-2A program. This combination of core employees supplemented by a large, less stable labor force derives from seasonal, structural, and market features of perishable-crop agriculture in the area. As the organization of the U.S. agricultural workplace becomes more formalized because of the increasing dominance of large corporate producers, traditional farm labor practices of the family farms, including the characteristic recruitment of migrant workers through informal family-based networks are likely to decline still further.

Perishable-Crop Agriculture on the Delmarva Peninsula

Irish Potatoes and Staked Tomatoes

The principal crops with high seasonal labor needs on the peninsula are Irish potatoes, staked green tomatoes, cucumbers, sweet corn, watermelons, apples, and peaches. For the entire peninsula, Irish potatoes are the most important crop in terms of acreage (over eight thousand acres in Delaware and another eight thousand to ten thousand acres along Virginia's Eastern Shore). Irish potatoes make up 62 percent of Delaware's fresh-market vegetable production, which is grown primarily for wholesale markets.

While potatoes dominate the peninsula's perishable-crop agriculture in Maryland, the over 570 acres of staked tomatoes attract enough migrant farmworkers to fill the largest labor camp on the peninsula (a camp in Somerset County with a capacity for seven hundred workers). These tomatoes, possessing the firm qualities that restaurants desire for handling, slicing, and presentation, are harvested and packed green to be ripened later with gas. Some staked tomatoes are grown for packing and shipping on Virginia's Eastern Shore as well, although in Delaware they cover only 60 to 70 acres and are grown primarily for sale at roadside markets.

Watermelons, Cantaloupe, and Mixed Vegetables

The watermelon, cantaloupe, and mixed-vegetable farms of southern Delaware market their produce at the Laurel Auction Block, a wholesale distribution point for the East Coast, and sell to the many produce stands and markets along Route 13 and the highways running east and west between the Washington, D.C.–Baltimore metropolis and the beaches of the Atlantic.

Labor is organized for the harvests that supply the auction block in an unusual way. The watermelon crews in particular tend to be specialized, professional contract crews that follow the watermelon harvests up the East Coast from Florida. These crews have their own trucks and equipment, arrange their own housing, and negotiate with individual growers about the crop, sometimes buying the crop from the grower and marketing it themselves or operating on a sharemarketing sort of arrangement and taking a percentage of the wholesale price. They are African American crews who have specialized in this operation over the years, occupying a creative and somewhat entrepreneurial niche in the farm labor market, similar to pinhookers and, in some cases, sharecroppers.[1] As such, they are among those groups of farmworkers whose operations may become "criminalized" either with closer government scrutiny or if and when they assume more prominence as subcontractors.

Other crews at the auction block negotiate with growers as sales are completed. At the auction block, buyers bid on a sample of produce, say, twenty-five cantaloupe. This sample represents a tractor-trailer load (forty thousand pounds) in terms of variety, size, appearance, and quality. Buyers with successful bids then send "their" crews out to harvest the melons, deducting the cost of the harvest from the grower's price. The crews consist of local and migrant African American workers and others who know the auction block system. Most have worked with frequent buyers at the auction block in past seasons. The block thus operates as a kind of "shape up," or street-corner labor market, for local, casual workers, like El Centro in Immokalee, running from July 20 through Labor Day. During the peak season (mid-August), twenty tractor-trailer loads may be sold on the block in a single day.

In Sussex County, home of the Laurel Auction Block, most growers have ten to twenty acres of watermelons; the largest producer grows around fifty acres. These are mixed farms, with small acreages of perishable crops and larger acreages devoted to grain and field crops (corn, barley, wheat, soybeans, etc.). Other crops sold at auction include cantaloupes and a variety of vegetables, most of which are ready for harvest around the same time. These small farm sizes and the labor arrangements that accompany the auction block allow Sussex County growers the "luxury" of relying almost exclusively on a local, native, predominantly African American labor force.

Delaware Potato and Fruit-and-Vegetable Farms

Potatoes and a variety of fruits and vegetables are the most labor-intensive crops in Delaware, as well as those requiring the most migrant and seasonal labor. Most potato farmers also grow a variety of grain crops, such as barley, wheat, soybeans, field corn, and hay; tasks associated with these crops have been almost entirely mechanized and require no more than family workers or the permanent, year-round labor attached to the farm. Personnel at the Virginia Employment Service and Delaware Department of Labor report, in fact, that a great deal of the acreage formerly devoted to potatoes on the Delmarva Peninsula has been converted to grain and field crops primarily due to labor supply constraints. On Virginia's Eastern Shore, for example, agricultural extension personnel report a drop in potato acreage from thirty thousand to eight thousand acres over the past fifteen years (Kenneth Annis, personal communication, 1990).

Fruit-and-vegetable farms tend to have a combination of two or more of the following: tomatoes, squash, pumpkins, carrots, peas, asparagus, sweet corn, cantaloupes, raspberries, peaches, apples, and plums. Complex operations sometimes combine a number of crops specifically because of labor-reliability problems; that is, additional, short-season crops may be added to the enterprise mix to keep workers busy during the slow seasons (down times) between major market crops. It is often during these times that growers have trouble keeping workers around. In labor supply communities, workers may be left to their own resources and can be counted on to return when work resumes, especially if they have their own housing and families in the area; in summer harvest regions such as Delaware, however, idle migrant workers may need to leave the farm to seek work elsewhere. Some of the growers we interviewed had had portions of their crews leave for places as far away as Michigan during a lull in work.

Both potato and fruit-and-vegetable farms rely heavily on migrant labor during the summer months. In the off-season, these farms tend to be run by family members and a small core of key employees. Most Delaware growers do their own packing, growing for primarily wholesale markets. The complexity of farms is reflected in the wide variety of fresh-market vegetables grown in the state (Table 3.1).

Although Delaware growers we interviewed conformed to the basic pattern of having a small core of workers supplemented by migrant crews, a number of Delaware growers are unique for their reliance on the employment service for recruiting workers. According to Delaware Department of Labor personnel, grower use of the employment service on the peninsula has declined from between seventy-five and one hundred job orders per season to the present twenty-five to thirty. Nevertheless, the employment service remains an important component in overall migrant labor recruitment. Even among those growers who do not rely on the employment service for recruiting, it has familiarized farm labor contractors and crews with the area, stimulated specific target migrations between Texas and Delaware and between Florida and Delaware, and contributed to the crew consolidation and labor pooling that has helped growers stabilize their workforces. Delaware Department of Labor officials estimate that fewer than half of the over sixteen hundred migrant workers in Delaware are recruited through the employment service, and yet it remains an influential method of recruitment.

Green-Tomato Production Patterns and Costs:
Somerset County, Maryland

Following the Delaware crops discussed above, particularly Irish potatoes, staked green tomatoes are the most important in terms of acreage and value.

TABLE 3.1 Delaware Fresh-Market Fruits and Vegetables, 1987–88

Crop	Acres Planted 1987	Acres Planted 1988	Acres Harvested 1987	Acres Harvested 1988	Per Acre Yield[a] 1987	Per Acre Yield[a] 1988	Total Production 1987	Total Production 1988	$/cwt.
Sweet corn	1,560	1,670	1,520	1,640	93	91	141,360	149,240	14.50
Watermelons	1,240	1,240	1,230	1,230	148	300	305,000	372,000	6.15
Cabbage	530	540	520	540	250	250	121,150	135,000	15.00
Spinach	210	230	210	230	55	31	11,500	7,130	46.20
Cantaloupes	225	200	215	200	124	95	26,750	19,000	15.10
Asparagus	320	320	320	290	14	13	4,600	3,850	88.00
Cauliflower	70	60	70	60	123	91	8,600	5,450	54.70
Tomatoes	70	70	70	60	197	120	13,800	7,080	20.30
Lima beans	40	35	40	25	35	34	1,380	850	50.30
Turnips	20	35	20	30	102	115	2,040	3,450	13.30
Sweet peppers	30	30	25	30	87	31	2,170	930	36.40
Green peas	30	20	25	15	43	40	1,075	600	31.30
Potatoes	8,000	8,400	8,000	8,400	210	215	1,680,000	1,806,000	9.35
Other vegetables[b]	890	830	865	740	—	—	69,740	56,780	—
Strawberries	90	90	90	90	34	62	3,040	5,580	38.40
Total	13,325	13,770	13,220	13,580	—	—	2,392,205	2,572,940	—

Source: Delaware Department of Agriculture, 1989.

[a]In bushels.

[b]Includes brussels sprouts, hot peppers, broccoli, pumpkins, squash, snap beans, sweet potatoes, greens, and cucumbers.

Southern Maryland and Virginia's Eastern Shore utilize the largest numbers of migrant and seasonal farmworkers on the peninsula for preparatory, harvest, and postharvest field-cleaning labor. Somerset County was chosen for our study because it includes large and small acreages of tomatoes, it typifies the tomato labor process, and it is the site of the largest labor camp on the Delmarva Peninsula. Furthermore, labor accounts for the greatest proportion of production costs in tomato production (about 48 percent), almost all of which is harvest costs (see Table. 3.2).

Growers we interviewed reported yields of around eight hundred to one thousand boxes per acre and reported that the lowest market price they could accept was between $3.00 and $5.00 per box, but that it was quite common to receive $6.00 to $8.00 per box. These prices vary with the season, with the yield (high yields create high supplies and force lower prices), and with the grade of tomato. If we adopt a conservative figure of nine hundred boxes per acre and $5.00 per box, gross receipts per acre would be $4,500, generating cash profits of just over $1,300 per acre.

Harvesting costs represent 44 percent of total production costs; harvest labor tasks require roughly ten times the labor of the preharvest and post-

TABLE 3.2 Representative Costs for Tomato Production
for Fresh Market in Maryland, 1989

Item	Cost/Acre
Nitrogen	$17.60
Mixed fertilizer	67.50
Lime	8.00
Transplants	600.00
Herbicide	4.00
Land rent	50.00
Plow	12.00
Disk and harrowing	20.00
Applying fertilizer and chemicals	36.00
Planting	100.00
Harvesting	1,410.00
Irrigation	56.00
Boxes (@ $.85)	680.00
Cultivation (two times)	9.00
Insecticide and fungicide	84.50
Interest	41.83
Total cash costs	3,196.43

Source: Maryland Department of Agriculture, 1989.

harvest tasks and tend to be associated with different methods of labor supervision and rates of pay (see Table 3.3). Additional, more specialized tasks tend
to be performed by the growers themselves, by foremen, or by skilled personnel and paid at somewhat higher hourly rates. Such tasks include marking off
the field for laying plastic; applying fertilizers, herbicides, and insecticides;
forming beds for transplants; and supervising operations.

Changes in the Population of Farmworkers

The peak labor demand months on the peninsula are July and August, although some migrants filter into the area as early as March and stay as late as
October. Among these longer-season workers are the reliable migrant families
who have been working for specific growers for years. According to local
employment service personnel, ministers, and personnel at other agencies that
provide services to migrants, migrant crews have been changing over the
years.

Before the 1970s, most of the migrant workers in the eastern United States
were African Americans, based either in Florida or in cities near the fruit and
vegetable farms where they were hired.

TABLE 3.3 Task, Seasons, and Pay Associated with Staked-Tomato Production, Delmarva Peninsula, 1989

Task	Season	Pay Rate	Pay Method
Laying plastic	March–April	$4.00	hourly
Transplanting	April–May	$4.00	hourly
Pruning and tying	May–July (4×)	$.35–$.40/100 ft.	piece
Harvest	July–August	$.40/bucket	piece
Cleanup	September	$4.00	hourly

Source: Reconstructed from interviews with growers.

> In Norfolk, Virginia [just south of the Delmarva Peninsula], for instance, it was customary during the 1920s for many large growers to hire ''row bosses'' who went to the Negro section of the city, stood on a street corner, and shouted ''Strawberry hands, Strawberry hands,'' to attract workers. When he had gotten as many as he wished, the ''row boss''—so called because in the field he assigns each worker to the row of berries or vegetables he is to pick—would take them back to the farm on a truck or a street car hired for the purpose, supervise them in the field for the day, and return them in the evening. The next morning, typically, the same performance would take place, and an entirely new group of workers would be hired. (Schwartz 1945:37)

Migrants who moved up from Florida either came with farm labor contractors directly from there or followed the harvests up from Florida, through Georgia and the Carolinas, and out onto the peninsula (Metzler 1955; Larson and Sharp 1960; Friedland and Nelkin 1971; Heppel 1983). These crews supplemented local workers, predominantly African Americans, Puerto Ricans, high school students, and women, who provided much of the field preparation, staking, and other labor prior to the harvests.[2]

Since the early 1970s, the migrant population, while still containing a number of African American crews from northern and central Florida, has included more Mexican and Mexican American workers from Florida and Texas, more Central Americans (primarily Guatemalans), and some Haitians. In Maryland, for example, we interviewed one grower who said he brought in the first Mexican family in 1973. Although they were initially suspicious, growers eventually realized how hard the Mexicans worked and came to prefer Mexican and Mexican American labor.[3] Again, this is evidence that the demographics of the workforce of the northern harvest regions changes with the demographics of Florida's farm labor force change.

During the late 1970s and early 1980s, the new immigrant Haitians were considered by growers to be highly preferred workers, and many believed them to be the answer to their labor supply problems. These hopes proved short-lived, however, as the Haitian crews that once migrated from southern Florida began to settle out of the farm labor force to work primarily in the numerous poultry-processing plants in the area. A study of poultry processing in the region (Griffith and Runsten 1988) confirms that Haitians have begun to work more in the poultry plants in the past eight to ten years. That study also reports some overlap between the farm and nonfarm labor markets in regions such as the Delmarva Peninsula, which we observed as well: some Haitians return to the fields for brief periods during the harvests, and some Haitian crews still migrate between Florida and the peninsula. Overall, however, the most notable ethnic change that has taken place in the area has been from a predominance of African Americans to a predominance of Mexicans and Mexican Americans. African American crews remain important on the peninsula, however, supplying crucial local seasonal and migrant labor to the potato and watermelon harvests, and to packing operations.

Along with ethnic changes, the peninsula has seen fluctuations in numbers of workers coming to the area. As we stress in many places throughout this book, estimating exact numbers of workers is difficult when dealing with transient and often somewhat invisible (because of the isolation of labor camps) populations. Nevertheless, expert informants at local employment offices, social-service agencies, ministries, and agricultural extension offices report that the migrant labor force dropped during the early 1980s, although later growth may have occurred because of increases in staked-tomato acreages.

Part of this drop, evidently, is due to more efficient crew consolidation measures by astute and seasoned farm labor contractors, who now keep their crews more active while they are on the peninsula, negotiating contracts with several growers instead of only one and thus operating their own sorts of labor-pooling services. This practice, which effects a leveling of labor demand, has emerged as a common strategy under conditions of labor shortage or perceived labor shortage.

A second reason for the decrease in migrants coming to the peninsula derives from reduced acreages of potatoes and the associated changing patterns of land use, from labor-intensive vegetable crops, which are more risky but more lucrative, to mechanized grain and soybean crops.[4] For the 1989 season, the Delmarva Rural Ministries, which deals most directly with the entire farm-worker population and hence probably has the most accurate count, estimated that there were between ten thousand and eleven thousand migrants on the peninsula (see Table 3.4).

TABLE 3.4 Migrant Population Served by the Delmarva Rural Ministries, by Ethnic Group, 1986–89[a]

Ethnic Group	1986	(%)	1987	(%)	1988	(%)	1989	(%)
Hispanic	3,719	(55)	3,866	(56)	3,711	(61)	4,487	(63)
African American	1,447	(21)	1,389	(20)	1,159	(19)	1,121	(16) ·
Haitian	1,330	(20)	1,182	(17)	806	(13)	772	(11)
Other[b]	244	(04)	453	(07)	357	(07)	701	(10)
Total	6,740	(100)	6,890	(100)	6,033	(100)	7,081	(100)

Source: Delmarva Rural Ministries.

[a]Delmarva Rural Ministries estimates that these figures represent 65 percent of the total population of migrant and seasonal farmworkers on the peninsula.

[b]Includes Southeast Asians.

Housing and Labor Camps

Housing for migrant workers in the Delmarva region tends to be of two types: grower-owned and -managed housing, consisting primarily of relatively isolated trailers, converted farmhouses, or other buildings; and labor camps controlled by corporations or growers' associations. Grower-owned housing usually holds crews of families and single migrants. These units tend to contain no more than twenty individuals and usually between eight and twelve, four or five of whom may be members of the same nuclear-extended family. By the designation ''nuclear-extended,'' we mean a typical nuclear family—an adult couple and their children—living and traveling with a few other single, related individuals, such as brothers, sisters, cousins. The labor camps housing these families tend to be at least as isolated as the grower's house and often within view of the grower's residence. They may sit near work and storage sheds, packing facilities, fields, and other centers of production on the farm. In these small labor camps live the ''fictive kin'' (returning migrant families and workers) who perform many of the pre- and postharvest tasks. In Delaware, labor camps such as this are also occupied by Florida- and Texas-based farm labor contractors and crews who have been recruited with the aid of the Delaware Department of Labor.

Proximity to the grower's house facilitates the development of close ties between the grower's children and the children of migrants, and helps growers monitor the behavior of their crews. It is not uncommon for relations between employers and employees to combine benevolence with labor control in this way. This has been documented in a variety of settings at different historical periods, ranging from colonial Sumatra (Stoler 1985) to Newfoundland fishing communities of the nineteenth century (Sider 1986) to seafood and poultry workers in the U.S. Southeast in the 1980s (Griffith 1993a).

On the entire peninsula, there are no more than four or five of the large growers' association/corporation labor camps. These tend to be used primarily by labor that comes into the region strictly for the harvest. They also tend to have a different character or "feel" than the smaller camps, more like institutional encampments than temporary homes-away-from-home. These camps house the most highly seasonal of Delmarva's workers, primarily the large numbers of crews brought in for the potato and tomato harvests. As noted earlier, the largest camp is the one in Somerset County, Maryland, housing around three hundred workers; the smaller of the growers' association camps, such as those near Exmore, on Virginia's Eastern Shore, house between seventy-five and two hundred workers.

Of course, those camps run by individual farmers for their fictive-kin workers are much smaller, usually housing under thirty people. That they are migrant labor camps is obvious from their appearance: clusters of concrete-block or tarpapered buildings, usually near Route 13 or other major thoroughfares, all of similar appearance, with cheap roofing, often a guard station at their entrances, and sometimes a commissary. They fluctuate between full and highly active to deserted, with a transitional period of moderate activity a week or two before harvest, during that time of year when growers start to become nervous about labor supplies. They contain accommodations for both migrant families and singles but tend to be dominated by single migrants and may move more toward singles accommodations in the future.

The types of housing available on the peninsula reflect the two major tiers of the labor force: fictive kin/reliable workers, who tend to occupy grower-owned housing and work a variety of crops and harvests for a longer season (e.g., April through September); and the highly seasonal, specialized harvest crews that tend to be recruited through farm labor contractors in Florida and Texas, sometimes through the employment service, or organized by corporate farms with packing and marketing interests in peninsula agriculture. The more detailed discussions of Delaware potato and fruit-and-vegetable farms and Maryland tomato operations show how these two tiers of the labor force combine to accomplish specific tasks on specific farms.

The Role of Farm Labor Contractors

Crews reunited through the employment service depend on farm labor contractors who have acquired reputations for being reliable. Such contractors usually are known by employment service personnel in either Florida or Texas and soon become known by employment service personnel in Delaware. They are of course registered with the Delaware Department of Labor and are insured, and otherwise perform their services in compliance with most regulations.

To become known as effective, farm labor contractors must go beyond simply bringing labor into the area and act as foremen and supervisors while they are in Delaware. Responsibilities in these roles include attending to the basic needs of workers by assigning rooms, for example, and monitoring activity in the designated, inspected labor camps; transporting workers between work sites and labor camps; ensuring that workers have access to food; addressing workers' complaints about working conditions; and making certain that enough workers remain in crews through the end of the harvest.

A common pattern among labor contractors seems to be one of recruiting most of their workers in Texas or Florida, making an intermediate stop in Georgia or the Carolinas to work in a harvest and pick up more crew members, and then bringing the crew to Delaware. Employment service personnel we interviewed believe that most workers recruited in the farm labor contractor's home region are probably legal, documented workers but that those recruited ''in-stream'' are less likely to possess valid documents. During the harvest, recruiting new workers and working to maintain current crew members tends to occupy much of the farm labor contractor's time.

The crews themselves are as varied as the mechanisms farm labor contractors use to assemble them. As in the supply communities and farm labor market in general, however, crews are internally differentiated by the nature of members' connections to the farm labor contractor and their attachment to the crew. Like the Haitian workers described in Chapter 2, those closer to the farm labor contractor by virtue of kinship or friendship ties and long association tend to receive favored treatment, getting work when it is available and being assigned the best accommodations in labor camps. Yet internal crew hierarchies are so variable and fluid that an accurate and representative characterization is difficult to formulate, except to say that when crews begin to approach or exceed twenty workers, the farm labor contractor usually designates other farm labor contractors, field walkers, or foremen as his or her employees.

In addition to crews that perform tasks associated primarily with the harvest, Delaware growers bring in family and single migrants under more direct arrangements to perform multiple tasks before and after the harvest. This two-tiered labor force—of long-season core workers/key personnel and short-season harvest crews—describes the structure of the labor force for green-tomato growers in Maryland as well as in Delaware. The ratio of harvest to preharvest labor is around ten to one.

Private corporate entities are more involved in organizing the staffing of the harvest in Maryland, however, than in Delaware, where use of the employment service and the Interstate Clearance System is greater. Both systems of organization, however, accomplish similar goals and indicate that harvests in perishable-crop agriculture have been growing increasingly formalized.

Corporate Production, Labor Recruitment, and Workplace Organization

Tomato production conforms to the two-tiered structure of the farm labor force on the peninsula but varies in the specific ways the harvest, as a separate enterprise from preparatory and postharvest labors, has been organized. Specifically, two multistate corporations that buy, pack, and ship the green tomatoes organize the largest harvests in Somerset County. Both corporations have tomato fields and packing operations in Immokalee, Florida, and other states in addition to those on the peninsula. Both have established partnerships with Somerset County growers. These partnerships operate in such a way that local growers supervise all the preparatory and postharvest tasks, while the corporate packers recruit labor for the harvests, drawing primarily on crews that staff their Florida fall and spring tomato harvests. They also recruit crews from states between Florida and Maryland and bring workers into the area for packing operations. One production manager we interviewed reported having a labor force of sixty to seventy workers for the preparatory work in tomatoes and a harvest labor force of between six hundred and seven hundred workers.

Like the Delaware growers who use the employment service, these corporations rely heavily on known farm labor contractors with whom they work in their Florida operations. Their relationship with local growers is mutually beneficial, although the control the corporations have maintained over the harvesting, packing, shipping, and marketing of the tomatoes clearly places them in the dominant position. Each of the two corporations has at least two key individuals who manage the crucial components of tomato production: a local grower who works with other local growers to see that the desirable production techniques are implemented and preparatory tasks are completed as required by the corporation, and a corporate personnel manager who contacts farm labor contractors for the harvest labor. These two individuals work in conjunction with one another, although the workers are recruited and set to tasks separately; the local growers recruit and house smaller crews on their own property, for pre- and postharvest tasks, while the corporation houses the harvest labor in the larger growers' association camp on Route 13.

Interaction Between Growers and Workers

It is usually with the pre- and postharvest workers that growers establish close personal ties of the kind described in the opening paragraphs of this chapter. These ties, moreover, usually serve additional and future recruitment and labor needs, as growers utilize current workers' networks to contact and hire new employees. According to the growers interviewed, the hiring and laying off of workers is more or less a continuous process between the spring and fall.

Willard McHenry employs on his farm one year-round worker and seventeen seasonal workers. The seasonal workers are differentiated along a number of lines and are completely separate from the crews that come in for the harvest. Five or six members of the crew come in only for a few tasks—harvesting melons, sweet corn, and so on—then migrate to Michigan, he thinks to the apple harvests there. The others stay with him six months and perform all the necessary work associated with preparation for the harvest: laying plastic, tying up the vines, and so on; harvesting other, smaller crops; then cleaning the field, pulling up stakes after the harvest.

All of his workers are "Spanish" and "most are family-oriented." About half bring family with them, and most of the time they all work except for those who care for the children, a job that rotates among the women until the county school opens its day-care facility for migrants. In addition to being differentiated from one another based on the length of time they stay with the McHenry operation every year, and based on family and single status, he has some who have been with him for years and others who come and go: a core, that is, who have been returning for seventeen years, and a turnover group, recruited each year into the operation by the core. "They know what I need and how many, and they bring them." The ones who have been coming back for seventeen years are from Immokalee.

He said they were "essential personnel" to his operation and so he treats them like essential personnel. Also he treats them like family, inviting them to birthday parties for his family, being invited to their parties in turn. He implied that he had a good reputation with the workers, saying that his labor camp is certified to hold twenty-seven and that he could fill it if he wanted to. He had no ideas about enhancing recruitment, simply saying he ran a good camp and he treated people well. He pays $.40 per hundred feet for pruning and tying. He uses no farm labor contractor. He, his son, and his wife supervise the group. He pays $4.00 an hour for hourly work, without any kind of bonus.

He used to use a farm labor contractor but got away from using one after a lawsuit that involved him, a farm labor contractor, underpayment or alleged underpayment, and no payment of Social Security. Actually, it was late payment that he confessed to, but he fought against it and won. This was three years ago. Between then and now, not only he, but all the other growers in the area here, either quit using farm labor contractors or have begun paying workers individually. Since he uses no farm labor contractor, one of the Spanish-speaking workers acts as a translator for him.

Buck Jones, like other growers in the area, claims to have been driven out of business by Legal Aid [public attorneys]. Around the mid-1970s, he had a dispute with "the company" over legal aid and joint responsibility for workers. "The company" refers to the partnership between Florida-based packer–shippers and a large local packer–shipper and grower association. The company wanted him to grow for them, so he wanted the packer to handle all the labor relations. But when Legal Aid came around, they said they would fight everyone and keep coming after them for one thing or another: Social Security, underpayment of wages, not having the farm labor contractor's registration number. The question he put to the company was: Who would be responsible? The company wouldn't take full responsibility, or couldn't, and so he felt he had better pull back on his operation.

Since then he has phased way back on his operation. Now he has a Latino group, which comes out of Pennsylvania, working for him, again with a kind of core group— the Mendotas, a mother and father who speak good English, another with them, as well as a daughter, age eleven, who doesn't work, and a single boy and two more singles who will soon come. The boy of the Mendota family works for them. The Mendotas are Mexicans, he said, who work for hourly wages some days and piecework the next. "It's up to them," he said, then told a story of a day they chose piecework because they wanted to get to Salisbury and knew they wouldn't be long in the field. One of the sons went into a training program to become a carpenter; Jones let him stay on in the housing rent-free when he was in training under the condition that he would stay and work the following year. He left, however, in March, just before Jones would have needed him.

His labor situation involves a kind of informal pooling: he "shares" his workers with two other growers, one of whom has a slightly larger operation than Jones's and has his own crew as well. He can always use them, which is what Jones wants. He has sporadic work for them from around April 2 to around Labor Day, but he can't work them every day and so goes to these other growers to keep them occupied. He sells to a roadside stand, with brokers from Connecticut and Pennsylvania coming through the months of August and July to buy his "pinks," similar to pinhookers.

They pass through the field, for the harvest, around four times; he plants a staggered crop so they bear in sequence. He needs to change hybrids or varieties every so often:

"Tomatoes don't like themselves," he said, explaining his crop rotation scheme of tomatoes–wheat/barley–soybeans–tomatoes. He follows tomatoes with other crops for three years prior to returning to tomatoes.

His family of workers brings in new workers for him. Part of the family has been with him for four years. He began using African Americans, then Haitians, who worked out well until, he said, they became Americanized. They started fighting among themselves; he was worried it would get to the press and they would make him seem like a villain. Now he has the Spanish-speaking/bilingual mix of family. He had two singles, both men, and one left for Mexico and told him he'd be back with his girlfriend, who also would work, but when he returned with her, she was too pregnant to work—had twins in the local hospital.

The "Mexican" family who works for him speaks good English, and their children speak fluently; they also recruit others, sometimes bringing workers Jones doesn't even need. They remain tied to a monolingual Spanish-speaking network after many years in Pennsylvania.

He quit using a farm labor contractor, though when he did use one he said the others "worshiped" the farm labor contractor. During that time he "hoped" the farm labor contractor treated them well. It seems he had to get away from using a farm labor contractor because of his concern over joint responsibility.

Now the Mexicans won't do anything separate from farmwork, such as mow the lawn, although he said they would do such odd jobs before. "They were afraid I would send them back to Mexico." He complained of the way they cared for his housing again and again in contexts such as these; when we suggested they could possibly establish some system whereby the grower and worker would share responsibility for the housing and standardize requirements, his response was that he wouldn't want to see them standardize things, because if they did that then he would have to improve his conditions as other growers improved theirs.

Concerning the employment service, he complained that they wanted to do things their own way: to control workers, placing them one day with him, another day with someone else, another with a restaurant in Ocean City. "They don't want specialized crews." He tried once to get a Filipino worker who had lived with Jones's family as a 4H "exchange" student, and the employment service said, "Let us find you a worker." Jones said, "They sent me a renegade from Texas who was wanted for armed robbery. The police asked all the neighbors about me, to see if I was the kind who would harbor a criminal." He never could get the Filipino again, whom he wanted to work in his dairy.

Only one Mexican ever expressed an interest in the dairy, but they didn't use him. Traditionally, the Latinos have not worked with the livestock.

He pays $4.00 an hour for hourly work, pays a little workers' compensation, no bonus, no benefits. They provide their own transportation to his place, and he deducts nothing for housing.

Faced with a labor shortage, he said he would just quit. From this he complained about the Mexicans becoming Americanized, saying how they used food stamps and free clinics.

Local labor is impossible to find, he said, for two reasons. First, they don't have to work. Second, they don't like the job. In this context, he told a story about an old African American woman who used to come by his place and tell him, "Plant some tomatoes or we won't have any work." Now they say, "Plant tomatoes. Go ahead. We'll eat 'em for you." (Griffith field notes, July 1990)

Not all operations conform to these patterns, nor all growers to these attitudes. Some growers we interviewed located and recruited new workers not with the aid of their key personnel but by virtue of their connection with the Florida-based corporation, which recommends farm labor contractors and crews to local growers. In any case, connections with Florida are crucial in the overall labor supply for tomato production; even workers who claim Texas as their home base usually have spent some time in the Florida harvests.

Other growers in the area operate independently of the partnerships, packing their own tomatoes in their own packing facilities. Notes from one such operation suggest that independence may be related to the size of one's operation.

Michael Berry claims close personal relationships with his workers, saying that if his workforce were to grow so large that the didn't know all of his workers' names, then he would be getting too large.

He has 30 acres of tomatoes and 60 acres of peppers, though at one time he grew 120 acres of tomatoes, also in the green-tomato harvest. He has his own packing operation, which he keeps running with all local labor—his mother's family, mainly, none of whom really need to work but do it as a favor to him. Other packers in the area have to import workers from Florida to pack.

Unlike Willard McHenry, Berry uses all single workers (or males who come without their families). He blames this on the health department—if they certify a dwelling for four people and he gets a family of five, he has to break them up. He has his own housing and doesn't use the Somerset/Winter Camp. He has eighty workers over the season, twenty more permanent. His seasonal workers come from "everywhere"— Tennessee, Florida, Texas. He recruits by "word of mouth." Two years ago, he had to fire a crew, and he went to a guy who works for Six "L" [a corporate farm based in Immokalee], who located a new crew. This new crew has been with him three or four years.

His season lasts from July 15 to September 15, and he maintains that the same people come back to work for him year after year. He said he has noticed that the quality of his workers has gone down in recent years. "The worker who can work at McDonald's and do as well as here has gone down. The cream of the crop, who can make nine or ten dollars doing piecework, is still here." The marginal worker isn't going to return.

Again, he made a distinction between core workers and others, the former being the skilled, productive, docile. When we asked him how much he paid his workers, he said, "We pay well." When I asked him about bonuses for his workers, he said, "Sure, they get bonuses. Or I call them benefits: hard crabs, pizza. A truck comes from the market and brings them fresh vegetables, watermelon, grapes." The workers provide their own transportation. He provides no transportation. He uses no farm labor contractors: "It's silly to pay a farm labor contractor to supervise when you do it yourself," he said.

Asked about potential labor shortages in the future, he said that the competition is growing stiffer all the time. He said the seafood houses are "hunting labor" and the McDonald's restaurants are soon to be bypassed by "even the phone company," who will train them to climb poles, he said. He has to fight for local help.

Who is his largest competitor for labor? "The government," he said. "Their entitlement programs. We have 14 percent unemployment, but you can't get them to come to work. A local packing house uses 125 workers. He got seventeen applications from locals and hired all of them. Only eight showed up for work." The packer had to import labor. (Griffith field notes, July 1990)

In addition to these arrangements, there exist informal labor pooling arrangements among smaller growers, as in Buck Jones's operation, and a number of pinhooking relationships between growers and small entrepreneurs. In the latter case, local food brokers buy from growers after the main harvest is over, picking the tomatoes themselves and transporting them to market. Some of this work is done by those who own and operate roadside markets for the tourist trade.

Conclusion

The Delmarva case illustrates a number of points regarding labor supplies to areas outside the traditional farmworker communities of Florida, Puerto Rico, Texas, and California. First, the connection with Florida is crucial, meaning that any development in Florida's labor profile will affect the quality and quantity of workers available for labor in the north. The demographics, socioeconomic status, and ethnicities of Florida labor supply communities tend to be replicated in the labor demand regions of the north. Clearly, this has been the case among Mexican and Mexican American workers, who migrated into Florida during the mid-1950s and later showed up on the peninsula.

Second, the peninsula reveals the two-tiered structure of the farm labor market and the relationship of that structure to the differential attachment of workers to specific peninsula farming operations: some workers, that is, develop closer relations with growers, growers' families, and growers' operations than others. The development of these ties is related to enhancing worker reliability, which remains a constant concern among growers and which accounts, in part, for the development of complex organizational forms to staff the harvests of the peninsula. This "formalization" of harvests in labor demand regions is closely linked to increasing corporate partnerships with family farmers in perishable-crop agriculture, to the growing use of farm labor contractors, and to concerns over labor shortages. Formalization is discussed in more detail in the final chapters. Here it is necessary to point out, however, that a central paradox we find in agriculture today is formalization accompanied by casualization, or workers organized for brief periods and with weak ties to any particular grower or firm.

As reported elsewhere in this book and in literature on farmwork (Friedland and Nelkin 1971; Foner and Napoli 1978; Griffith 1986a), growers on the Delmarva Peninsula are less concerned about having enough workers at the beginning of the harvest than about having workers remain through the harvest or between harvests (during down time). Worker reliability is foremost among their concerns.

Finally, our experiences on the Delmarva Peninsula suggest that joint efforts by Legal Aid, Delmarva Rural Ministries and Migrant Health Clinic, the Wage and Hour Division of the Employment Service, including OSHA (the federal Occupational Safety and Health Administration), and the health inspectors in charge of inspecting migrant housing have helped to improve farmworker working conditions. This grassroots or ad hoc coalition has been effective in upgrading recordkeeping by growers and is thereby effective in reducing the potential for farm labor contractors to under pay or otherwise abuse workers.

Chapter 4

Domestic Farmworkers in America's Heartland

Weslaco, Texas, and the Lower Rio Grande Valley

Midway between McAllen and Brownsville, in the lower Rio Grande Valley of Texas, Weslaco presents a paradigm case of a "traditional" farm labor supply community, where many families have developed a long tradition of migration north during the late spring and early summer months. Situated among a number of neighboring home-base communities for Texas migrant farmworkers, Donna (two miles east), Mercedes (two miles west), and Weslaco are the home communities for over half of the Texan families who travel every year to southwestern Michigan, the labor demand area featured in Chapter 5. Weslaco is also the subject of an ethnographic study, *Across the Tracks* (Rubel 1966), conducted in the 1960s, which provided us with a useful historical baseline.

We also chose Weslaco to study because it is a medium-sized town and less urbanized than McAllen and Harlingen. The urban centers of the valley are now dominated by retail trade and service industry employment. Because each valley community has distinctive links to distant labor demand areas, no particular town is entirely typical, but Weslaco is more representative of the overall texture of valley life than either the urban centers or some of the tiny hamlets such as Monte Alto, Elsa, and Edcouch. Weslaco is a town of about twenty-five thousand persons (Scott Barker, Weslaco Planning Department, personal communication 1989), one of the string of towns that runs from

Roma, in Starr County, one hundred miles along the lower Rio Grande Valley to Brownsville, near the mouth of the river. The once-distinct valley farming towns along U.S. Route 83 are quintessential victims of strip development, now merging together into a corridor linking several areas of urban development: McAllen, Harlingen, and Brownsville. To the south, along state highway 281, immediately along the U.S.–Mexico border, a string of less developed hamlets subsists on border-crossing tourists and locals, and to the north stretches yet another east–west string of small rural farming towns.

Like many other towns in rural America, Weslaco displays a strange mixture of old and new and of stagnation and development. The older highway, now called Business 83, running parallel to the original Missouri Pacific railroad, is lined with packing sheds, warehouses, auto repair shops, rundown motels, bowling alleys, and drive-in movies, vestiges of the prosperous aftermath of World War II. By contrast, along the south side of the new highway, Expressway 83, sit the familiar clusters of fast-food restaurants, the H.E.B. supermarket, and other aspiring new businesses such as a Ford dealership and a new motel complex. On the north side is the sprawling Haggar's plant, a "new" industry attracted to Weslaco by a surplus of Mexican and Chicana women who are willing to work for low wages as seamstresses (Fernández-Kelly 1983).

Geography in the lower Rio Grande Valley is important because it illuminates the interplay of invisible social and economic forces that constitute the framework in which people live their lives. The northern half of Weslaco, north of Business 83, was allocated by municipal ordinance to industrial complexes, Mexican and Chicano residences, and businesses, leaving the south side of the tracks for Anglos. For nearly fifty years, the northern part of town has been referred to as "Mexican Town." Understanding the residential geography of the lower Rio Grande Valley is crucial to understanding the dynamics of farm labor supply, because the extraordinary stability and endurance of the southern Texas migrant labor force is due, in large part, to cheap land and cheap housing.

One of the primary issues this study addresses is the extent to which a community such as Weslaco and, by implication, the lower Rio Grande Valley, will continue supplying workers to farm labor markets in the wake of immigration reform. In short, the Weslaco case helps us address the question, To what extent can agriculture rely on a truly domestic farm labor force, or will it need to replenish, more or less continually, the farm labor force with supplies of immigrant workers? Given the key role of network recruitment in the hiring of midwestern farm labor, traditional labor supply communities such as

Weslaco represent the "best-case" scenario for future farm labor recruitment. Communities that, compared with Weslaco, are economically, socially, and culturally less associated with farm labor provide less fertile ground for understanding future supplies of domestic farmworkers. Weslaco and the lower Rio Grande Valley also provide a means to examine the question whether rural areas with high unemployment and extreme poverty might provide a source of farm labor if wages and working conditions were to improve. Local unemployment in all sectors of the workforce climbed from a low of 12 percent in 1980 to a high of 20 percent in 1986. The annual unemployment rate for the last full year available was 17 percent (Texas. Department of Commerce 1990). Food stamp use in the valley is three times higher than in Texas as a whole (Texas. Department of Human Services 1990). Hidalgo County, where Weslaco is located, was in the lowest 2 percent of Texas counties in per capita income (Woods and Poole Economics 1990).

In analyzing labor supply, we explore the recent history of Weslaco, immigration patterns to the area, current demographic and socioeconomic changes, and the nature of the economic strategies that lead workers to move into seasonal or migrant farmwork.

Founded in 1920, Weslaco was carved out of the twelve thousand acres of the Llano Grande land grant purchased for two dollars an acre. Cheap homesites were marketed to midwesterners as part of the overall promotion of the area as "the Magic Valley." In a similar fashion, fifty years later, homesites were marketed to the Mexican immigrants moving into the valley in search of work.

Work, Housing, and Neighborhoods in Weslaco

The southern, once Anglo, area of town is now ethnically integrated but continues to have a distinct socioeconomic character as a high-income area. In the southern part of downtown Weslaco, ranch houses predominate, their expansive lawns adorned with crepe myrtle. At the southern outskirts, small, brick apartment buildings house those upwardly mobile couples who are not yet affluent. By contrast, the northern part of Weslaco—"across the tracks"—is densely populated, holding an average of thirteen homes per block. Tiny, brightly painted houses squeeze onto tiny lots. Most are built of old-fashioned lapped siding with asphalt-shingle roofs, battered screen doors, and low chain-link fencing. Some of the smallest and most decrepit of the houses are the homes of former farmworkers, now in their seventies and eighties. These homes are surrounded with dense and lavish home gardens. Most blocks have an alley running behind the houses, allowing easy access to backyards. Among the tiny houses are scattered a few larger homes, some of them two stories high. Although poor, unlike South Immokalee, these neighborhoods are in no sense a ghetto. They put forth a pleasant, family environment; some families have undertaken extensive remodeling and added rooms to the original homes of their parents. Many residents who built their own homes, or inherited them, have very low current incomes (under $12,000 a year), yet manage to live in a fair measure of comfort. The poorest of the downtown residents, other than the aging couples, widows, and widowers who own their homes, rent one of the side-by-side "apartments" in row houses where three or four units are stuck together. The neighborhoods are convivial, but the residents' firmest social ties are to their extended family, who may be dispersed throughout several neighboring towns or, in fact, throughout farmworking areas of the United States.

The main streets of Weslaco provide a thin skeleton of commercial development—a few small cafes, real-estate agents' offices, television repair shops, and such. The town library is magnificent but little frequented by residents of northern Weslaco. The neighborhoods, the real heart of Weslaco, remain isolated from the "official" downtown, butting up against packing sheds along the old railroad tracks. McManus Produce Company, the center of agricultural employment in Weslaco, on the eastern edge of town, has a parking lot often filled with over a hundred old cars, but other workers simply walk the five or ten minutes to work.

The areas between the officially recognized towns, the interstices of the lower Rio Grande Valley, are filled with *colonias.* These are unincorporated settlements, ranging in size from hamlets of ten or fifteen households to very large settlements with populations over a thousand. It is estimated that at least 450 *colonias* dot the valley. While some originally developed from settlements of farmworkers working for a local rancher, most were developed after World War II. Growth of the *colonias* peaked in the 1960s with the tremendous influx of post–Bracero Program green-card immigrants. These newly arriving immigrants settled in the *colonias* because they provided opportunities to buy, for almost no down payment and low monthly payments, small lots (*solares*) where they could build their own home. Even today, some of the lots farther from Weslaco can be purchased for as little as $100 down and around $100 a month. The availability of such affordable housing has become necessary for the working poor. In the farm labor story of Weslaco, the *colonias* are an important element because they make it possible for families who built their own homes in the 1960s to continue migrating north every year. An important dimension of this is that the *colonias* also provide some measure of housing reserve. Because, today, some lots in the *colonias* are fairly large, it is possible for families to allow their children or siblings to build additional houses on the original lots, enabling clusters of relatives to live near each other and form tight networks. The Puerto Rican case is similar to Weslaco in this regard; there, *parcelas* are government-sponsored housing-development projects designed to provide housing to workers displaced by the decline of sugar production. These lots are also large enough for more than a single nuclear family's housing needs, thus providing an infrastructural base for extended, anchor households from which migrating families or couples can leave and to which they can return.

In the community survey, we included nine *colonias* from the Weslaco sphere of influence. The older ones—Llano Grande, Agua Dulce, and Cuellar—lie southeast of town; Colonia Angela adjoins the southern edge of town, along with Colonia Seis (Expressway Heights). All of these are medium-sized gatherings of about one hundred households. To the southwest, Villa Verde, also an older *colonia,* is somewhat larger. Most of the *colonias* have a small, "mom-and-pop" store that serves as an informal hub for activity, although Villa Verde's store consists of a shack operating as a "drive-up" store. La Palma and Loma Alta, to the west, are somewhat newer *colonias,* is about to be swallowed up by Weslaco's northward expansion.

In recent decades, the *colonias* have received widespread attention, mostly because of rural development initiatives by the Ford Foundation in the 1970s. These initiatives focused attention on water supply problems, dirt streets, and flooding. The Texas legislature approved a $100 million bond issue to improve services in the *colonias,* and the U.S. Department of Health and Human Services has indicated it may provide a $5.5 million match. In November 1989, a Weslaco referendum that sought to annex the *colonias* to improve the infrastructure was defeated. Potential tax increases for ephemeral "improvements" such as streetlights seriously threatened the stability of many of the *colonias* residents.

Our study indicates that the *colonias* are not very different from other low-income neighborhoods of Weslaco. We identified several long-term, stable, migrant networks in the *colonias*, but the common perception that only farmworkers live in the *colonias* is false. A Texas Department of Human Services (1988) survey reported that 45 percent of the heads of households in *colonias* were employed in agriculture. Our survey found that 29 percent of its overall sample were current farmworkers and that migrant farmworkers also live outside *colonias*, throughout the low-income areas of Weslaco. Because of the low cost of housing in the *colonias*, however, the migrant networks of the *colonias* probably include families with the most stable migration patterns.

This reinforces our earlier observations that housing has played an important role in the lives of migrants in a variety of social and cultural contexts. Migrant sending regions in Mexico, Central America, and the Caribbean have seen the fruits of international and internal labor migrations converted first into new and expanded housing. Such is the case, as well, in Weslaco. The viability of farmwork as "career" among Weslaco's poorer residents rests on access to cheap housing. The average monthly cost of housing for current farmworkers in Weslaco was $47 per month. This is because more than half (54 percent) of the households of current farmworkers owned their homes and paid no rent. Another third of the current farmworkers lived in subsidized housing—the Weslaco Housing Authority Labor Camp, a large farmworker housing project. The highest rent paid by any of the current farmworkers was $225 per month. Overall, housing costs for current farmworkers averaged only 10 percent of total income. For the farmworker families who lived in the *colonias* and owned their homes (one-third of current farmworkers), it was possible to use periods of unemployment to maintain and repair housing. Even for the in-town families, home ownership had real benefits, allowing a great deal of "sweat equity" to be invested in repairing houses, adding on to them, or remodeling them. For those without access to free or low-cost housing themselves, the ability to live as part of an extended family is an important element in determining the viability of working as a farmworker, since having family in Weslaco allows one to live for next to nothing, making only appropriate contributions for taxes, repairs, utilities, and the like.

Like other rural areas, Weslaco's development has followed a checkerboard pattern. Interspersed with the traditional *colonias* are trailer parks populated by "snowbirds" or "winter Texans," retired couples from the North. There are approximately four thousand mobile-home spaces in the Weslaco area, and over fifty thousand in the entire valley. Ubiquitous middle-class subdivisions form part of the checkerboard. Not surprisingly, the development of Weslaco, like other parts of the valley, is now attracting a great deal of attention from professional planners and agencies responsible for land use. However, the area remains one of the last bastions of U.S. laissez-faire subdivision and home-building, to the relief of local residents.

Clearly, Weslaco and similar communities are not exclusively towns of migrant farmworkers. Yet migrant and seasonal farmworkers make up an important social and economic subpopulation. Our mapping of Weslaco and its surrounding *colonias* for sampling purposes indicates that the "low-income" neighborhoods (our sampling universe) make up about 80 percent of the town. Most, but not all, families residing in this area were, actually, low-income.

Overall Employment Prospects in Weslaco

In Weslaco, competition among workers for nonagricultural jobs is stiff, despite the fact that the available jobs are not very appealing in terms of wages or benefits. The overall valley labor market is weak because of the disastrous impact of peso devaluation on retail trade from Mexican shoppers, the impact of two successive freezes, and the overall weakness of the Texas oil economy. Weakness in these key sectors appears to have led to a general stagnation in the valley. Despite the weak economy and grim employment prospects, more than half of the heads of households in Weslaco (55 percent) refuse to consider farmwork at all as an employment option. These individuals are not rejecting farmwork by its reputation alone: fully 80 percent of those who will not consider farmwork have done it at some point in their lives. Only 2 percent of the noncurrent farmworkers said they were definitely planning to work in farmwork during the coming season, while an extraordinarily high proportion of Weslaco workers, slightly over one-quarter of the total low-income labor force (26 percent) felt that their physical condition would prevent them from doing farmwork. This reflects both a realistic assessment of the working conditions of farmwork and the fact that the population we sampled had a high proportion of older workers due to the "rest-and-retirement" function of migrant home bases such as Weslaco and the nonstandard demographic bulge resulting from heavy influx of young Bracero-era immigrant families in the 1950s and 1960s. Most former farmworkers who are now in other occupations (80 percent) have not done farmwork since 1985. Their access to farmwork would be severely limited by the fact that their network contacts have decayed over the interim.

Heads of household who were not currently in farmwork but were willing to consider farmwork at all made up 17 percent of the sample. Nevertheless, they did not consider it to be a leading employment option. Half of the 17 percent said it was not likely they would do farmwork, leaving only 9 percent for whom it was possible. However, a case-by-case review of potential farmworkers who stated they would (unenthusiastically) consider farmwork revealed that only 4 percent would be potential farmworkers, taking into account willingness to migrate and current earnings, wage expectations, and stability of employment.

Weslaco has a relatively diversified economy for a rural town, but nonagricultural employment is dominated by several large industries and employers. Our survey did not tabulate employment by employer, but the major employers include McManus Produce, which hires not only line workers but also forklift drivers, clerical workers, and others; Haggar's, Jordache, and Dickies, all of which hire seamstresses; and the Weslaco schools, which hire large numbers of janitors and aides from the neighborhoods we surveyed. Small, local cafes also provide an important source of employment for women, and carpentry and construction provide seasonal employment, which is highly desired among farmworkers. Like the rest of the country, Weslaco's service industries provide a growing source of jobs in banking, retail stores, and a variety of specialties. Family businesses such as small stores provide another source of employment. In a small but significant number of households (about 5 percent), a husband was working in a distant urban job (e.g., Houston or Corpus Christi). Finally, work in the informal economy is also an option— selling at the flea market, babysitting, or selling fruit at the side of the road.

Although employment options are limited, the labor force is quite stable. Nearly half (48 percent) of the heads of household had been in their current job for at least a year. However, over one-third (37 percent) of the heads of household had been unemployed at some point during the year; the unemployed include workers seasonally laid off who return to their regular jobs. Other workers, even those employed in jobs they liked very much, complained about seasonal slowdowns, furloughs, and unemployment.

Nonagricultural employment in Weslaco is much more stable and better paying than is farmwork. The average workweek is only slightly under thirty-nine hours, and the average pay is $4.87 per hour for the town as a whole. Forty percent of nonagricultural workers said they were very satisfied with their jobs, whereas only 25 percent of farmworkers were satisfied with their jobs. About 5 percent of nonagricultural workers were very dissatisfied with their current jobs, whereas 14 percent of the current farmworkers were. Benefits packages are not good at all. Slightly less than half (45 percent) of the nonagricultural jobs provide vacation pay, sick leave, or paid holidays, and 20 percent of survey respondents who were not current farmworkers reported they were not covered by unemployment insurance.

Contrary to surface appearances, the majority of the workforce (56 percent) does not work in agriculture. As noted, many of Weslaco's nonagricultural jobs are characterized by high levels of underemployment and seasonal layoffs. Nearly 20 percent of the households we visited contain unemployed household heads, and the average duration of Weslaco low-wage jobs is 8.5

months. Annual incomes reported averaged $11,767 with average weekly earnings of $188.

The group of nonagricultural workers experiencing the greatest economic hardship—female heads of household responsible for supporting several children—believed it very unlikely that they would do farmwork. Many were able, had farmwork experience, and were very willing to work. But for these mothers, who were renters, a major drawback to migrant farmwork was the disruption to their households and the economics of paying rent on a house in Weslaco while they migrated north, disrupting the lives of their children, even if their children were old enough not to need child care.

The female heads of households living as part of a subfamily in an extended family household were, perhaps, economically able to consider migration since they had a stable base. Nevertheless, it was not the customary thing to do. While women work extensively in farm labor, most work as young women with their parents, with their husbands, or, occasionally, with brothers, sisters, or family friends. Work in the packing sheds and clothes-manufacturing businesses provided women on their own with much more attractive options than farmwork, even when paid at the minimum wage and forced to work under pressure to maximize their production.

Analyses of labor supply based on macroeconomic data routinely underestimate the importance of social and personal concerns in the development of household economic strategies and individual decisions regarding employment options. The segment of the Weslaco labor force we focused on participates in a culture based on broadly shared values, a distinctive set of social interactions, and economic strategies characteristic of farm labor supply communities. Because participation in the farm labor force is so closely bound to the functioning of family and personal networks, it was necessary to look at economic interactions in a conceptual framework that extends beyond wage rates, benefits packages, and annual incomes. The widely recognized segmentation of the U.S. hired farm labor force is simply one facet of the segmentation of the social and economic fabric of the United States.

The low-income Mexican American neighborhoods of Weslaco, then, represent a social and cultural context quite distinct from the "mainstream" image of America. But Weslaco should be seen as an underappreciated social reality, not as a divergence. It is important to recognize that the United States, at the end of the twentieth century, is more culturally diverse than ever before and is witnessing the creation of more and more low-wage jobs and families and communities of the working poor. The neighborhoods we studied draw heavily on Mexican culture for their values, but they are distinctively American in many respects as well: in short, as bicultural as they are bilingual.

Housing and Households in Weslaco

The residents of the low-income neighborhoods of Weslaco are virtually all of Mexican origin. Unlike Parlier, California, and Immokalee, Florida, which are active immigration receiving areas, most of the heads of household in Weslaco—59 percent—are U.S.-born. These Mexican and U.S. influences manifest themselves most obviously in many of the younger residents' linguistic behaviors. During our interviews, we would ask survey respondents whether or not they wished to converse in Spanish or English. Many Weslaco residents responded by asking, "What am I speaking now?" or seemed confused by the question. Such responses derive from the truly bicultural and bilingual character of life in the valley for Mexican-Americans. Their use of "Tex-Mex," a language that freely mixes English and Spanish, reaffirms this in the everyday culture of ordinary talk.

While Spanish is the dominant language in Weslaco, spoken by 57 percent of household heads surveyed, many families in the valley are bilingual Spanish and English speakers, whether or not the household head's first language is Spanish. Over two-thirds of the teenagers (70 percent) speak English perfectly or well. Usually, they speak English or both languages with their friends. Valley society is more bilingual and bicultural than virtually any other area of the country. Media preferences reflect this, with radio audiences divided between rock, country-and-western, and the traditional Mexican music with its polka influences. Advertising and business transactions are usually conducted bilingually.

Educational level varies greatly among different groups. Although the mean educational level was seven years, the older workers who grew up in rural areas of Mexico have lower educational levels than those who are U.S.-born. Only 19 percent of the heads of household have a twelfth-grade education or higher. In contrast to patterns of high school noncompletion in most U.S. communities, Weslaco workers are much more likely to have dropped out of school before the end of elementary school (37 percent), or between sixth and ninth grades (40 percent). Current rates of high school completion, while still low, are increasing dramatically, however. A 1985–86 study of school attrition estimated a 48 percent dropout rate for Weslaco (Intellectual Development Research Association 1986), a rate not significantly different from those found throughout the valley. If previous estimates of 80 percent dropout rates for migrant students are accurate, the current valley dropout rate has decreased by one-third. Teenagers growing up in Weslaco today are probably no more limited in occupational mobility by language and education than are teenagers from other rural areas of the country.

One-third of the households (34 percent) are nuclear families with children. Another third of the households (35 percent) are extended families, usually with several generations living together. The balance of the households consist of couples with no children, including both younger couples and older couples who have no children at home. In contrast to the active immigrant receiving areas such as Immokalee and Parlier, Weslaco contains relatively few households (7 percent) with new-immigrant siblings, cousins, or other relatives. The common urban pattern of young adults living "on their own" in shared apartments is very uncommon in Weslaco, constituting only 2 percent of the sample. The rate of family dissolution is fairly high, however; 15 percent of the sample were female-headed households in which a divorced or separated mother was raising her children.

The Weslaco active labor force includes a core of workers who are employed in permanent or stable jobs. This group includes slightly over half (51 percent) of the heads of household who were employed during 1989. The rest of the workers employed during 1989 worked in more than one job or were unemployed part of the year. One-third of these workers (34 percent) had as their longest job during the year a job that lasted six months or less.

As is common among the working poor, many workers are at the margins of the labor market: we include here housewives, welfare mothers, the long-term unemployed, and the partially disabled. Just under one in five (18 percent) of the heads of household fall into this category. While some cannot be said to be "in" the labor force, others fall into that category of discouraged workers that is growing throughout the United States. Unable to find work at previous pay scales, unable to support families, or experiencing chronic unemployment and underemployment, such workers often move between a variety of informal economic activities and formal and informal social-support systems in an effort to maintain the barest level of survival. These workers, who did not report holding a "job" in 1989, may very well work informally or perform casual labor such as babysitting, cleaning neighbors' houses, "helping" relatives in farmwork, or repairing cars. Almost half (8 percent) reported some physical impairment that limited their ability to work but did not totally disable them. This suggests that in addition to moving between formal and informal social and economic support systems, these workers may also, throughout their lives, move through cycles of occupational injury and the therapy of family, friends, and community.

Just under one-fifth (19 percent) of the Weslaco labor force works primarily in farmwork. Nevertheless, the labor force maintains tenuous ties between agricultural and nonagricultural labor markets. In addition to the 19 percent, another 8 percent of the labor force whose primary occupation is nonagricultural actually did perform some farmwork in the year prior to the interview. Consequently, about 27 percent of the heads of household can be classified as "current" farmworkers. Employment in packing sheds is also important; although only 6 percent of the labor force worked primarily in packing, processing, or agricultural-support services in 1989, other workers, migrant farmworkers returning for the winter, and a few seamstresses supplemented their nonagricultural work with packing-shed employment. Almost all workers in Weslaco have some farmwork experience, however, with only 15 percent of the workforce never having worked in farmwork.

Forty-three percent of the heads of household are employed in nonagricultural jobs: 14 percent are unskilled service workers (grocery store checkers, security guards, waitresses, gas station attendants, janitors), 11 percent are unskilled workers in manufacturing (seamstresses, fork lift operators), 10 percent are skilled or semiskilled service workers (bookkeepers, teacher's aides, shipping clerks), and 8 percent are construction workers.

Although our survey included only low-income neighborhoods, 14 percent of the heads of household interviewed held supervisory or managerial jobs, were small-business proprietors, or were technical or professional employees. This reflects the fact that the "low-income" neighborhoods of Weslaco are well integrated socioeconomically. As such, they provide a hospitable environment not only for large numbers of very poor elderly residents and low-income working families with children but also for relatively well off families who grew up there and have lived in the neighborhood all their lives.

Like other valley communities and many rural American towns, Weslaco has become a "mixed" economy. Agriculture, while still important, is declining. This puts Weslaco in step with major trends in the U.S. workforce, paralleling the burgeoning of service industries and the decline of employment in natural-resource industries. Although wages and working conditions in nonagricultural occupations remain worse in the valley than in most other parts of the country, occupational mobility out of agriculture is not impossible.

In other important respects, reflecting its bicultural character, Weslaco is more like a Mexican village than a contemporary U.S. community. For example, casual employment based on a flexible network of mutual-aid relationships is widespread, softening the impact of underemployment. Secondly, Weslaco is a "rest-and-retirement" community for aging, former migrant farmworkers who manage to live in relative ease because they own their homes and because they are surrounded by a network of children and grand-children, even though they may not qualify for Social Security (Mines 1983).

Agricultural Labor in the Lower Rio Grande Valley

The lower Rio Grande Valley of Texas has a shorter agricultural history than California or Puerto Rico but not Florida. Citrus production was not begun until the 1920s and remained at fairly low levels until the period immediately before World War II (Hudson 1979). Production reached its highest levels immediately after World War II at about twenty-nine million boxes. Weslaco's development, like the rise of the lower Rio Grande Valley citrus and vegetable industry, stems from extensive marketing of "the Magic Valley" during the 1920s. Cheap land and easy credit spurred the initial subdivisions (similar to today's *colonias*) that led to the development of "Mexican Town."

Like the other areas of this study, Weslaco is a community whose entire story and culture is tied up with successive waves of immigrants, although in this case almost exclusively with Mexican–U.S. migration. The earliest waves of Mexican immigrants included railroad workers, as in other areas of the Southwest, yet an important incentive was the availability of extended-season work, consisting of winter work in citrus and vegetables, early-season work in Texas cotton, and midseason work on the migrant circuit (Briody 1987). Lower Rio Grande Valley workers migrated in-state to pick cotton as early as the 1880s, and midwestern states began to recruit Mexican workers from Texas by the 1920s (Mantejano 1987). In the 1940s, the Farm Labor Security Administration actively recruited Mexican workers, and Texas was an important area for employment of Bracero labor.

The lower Rio Grande Valley became a major supply for migrant workers because cheap land and winter work made it particularly attractive for Mexican immigrant families from central and northeastern Mexico to settle in the area. Decimation of cotton production in Mexico caused by the emergence of DDT-resistant pests is likely to have been a "push" factor for some migrants. This influx included immigrants from Mexico's core sending areas but also from the border cities. Elizabeth Briody (1987) notes that many families arriving in Texas from Reynosa or Matamoros were "stage migrants," having first migrated to urban employment on the Mexican side of the border. Our research indicates there was probably active recruitment of experienced citrus workers from southern Nuevo Leon. A relatively slow flow of "local" migrants from small ranches in northern Tamaulipas and Nuevo Leon has also persisted for many years.

The heyday of the Texas immigrant labor force can be recognized as lasting for about twenty-five years, from 1950 through 1975, a period we refer to as the Bracero era because the program facilitated migration and greatly increased flows. During many early years of the Bracero Program, however, low wages and incidents of abuse caused Mexican authorities to object to placing workers in Texas (Commission on Migratory Labor 1951). Later, Bracero workers were imported for cotton and other crops, and a high volume of green-card holders who were legalized after the program terminated benefited from an immigration policy that welcomed immigrant farm labor. One-quarter (26 percent) of our sample are green-card immigrants, while only 6 percent were legalized under IRCA (4 percent as pre-1982 immigrants, and 2 percent as SAWs).

Along with other sources, our survey indicates that the Texas migrant labor force is a rapidly dwindling population. Briody (1987) reports that the proportion of the labor force in agriculture in the valley declined from 42 percent of the total workforce in 1940 to 9 percent of the total workforce in 1980. The declining population of migrants reflects the impact of several factors that have made farm labor increasingly unattractive to residents of the lower Rio Grande Valley. Perhaps most important has been the loss of several key labor-intensive crops to mechanization—the most important being cotton and sugar beets. Before mechanization, these crops provided "bridges" between spring employment in the onion harvest and the midseason work in fruit and vegetable crops in the Pacific Northwest, California, and the Midwest. Sugar beets in particular were an important stimulant to migration to Colorado, Minnesota, Michigan, Ohio, and Indiana. Thus, the mechanization of the sugar beet harvest was a major contributing factor in the declining labor force of family migrants.

With a relatively continuous sequence of harvest tasks, "follow-the-crop" migration was a feasible and potentially lucrative strategy. One of our informants, describing the period, states that *troqueros* (farm labor contractors) would engage in a week or two of negotiations with neighbors to recruit enough workers to fill a truck, the final workers being recruited at a street-corner market in Weslaco. The *troquero* and truckload of workers would then depart for Colorado and Washington. Briody (1987) found that the number of months migrants spent away from home base peaked in 1965 at 6.6 months and declined afterward. A few of the older migrants in our sample, relying on long-term, stable contacts, continue to engage in follow-the-crop, or "horizontal," migration, which today includes key tasks such as sugar beet hoeing, but this is not prevalent.

In addition to reducing migration, mechanization of valley crops has also contributed to the decline of farmwork as an occupation in and around Weslaco and throughout the valley. The most important development has been the introduction of semimechanized loading for row crops, which has altered the character of the job by transferring more of the task from human to mechanical control. A former *troquero,* for example, argued that introduction of the conveyor belt in beets, carrots, onions, and carrots led many people to prefer migrating to local work. Aside from reducing the labor demand by a factor of about ten, the use of the conveyor belt has speeded up the pace of work, making it more demanding and reducing workers' earnings by shortening the work period.

A related factor in the decline of the southern Texas migrant labor force is that the circulating stream of Bracero-era immigrants was diminished as young Texas migrants married and moved to other areas on the migrant circuit. Survey information on the residence of the siblings of current Weslaco residents shows a significant proportion living along points on the migrant circuit—in Washington, Oregon, California, Michigan, and Ohio. This "horizontal" dispersion within the migrant network is an important dynamic relating to farm labor supply, since the extensive Texas migrant circuit of the 1960s and 1970s gave rise to subsidiary networks of Texans in Florida, California, and Washington. Our California study community of Parlier, for example, includes large numbers of families who were originally Texas migrants, some of whom remain in touch with relatives in the valley. The Texas migrant networks also reached east into southern Florida. Hudson (1979) reported that Texas migrants began to work in Florida citrus in the mid-1960s but that the largest influxes were after 1971–72. By 1975, when Hudson's study was finished, an estimated 60 percent of the Florida citrus harvest labor force was "Texan-Mexican," and today, as revealed by the community study of Immokalee, a number of farm labor contractors trace their family roots to Texas as well.

Migrant network dispersion also contributes to the gradual development of small communities of seasonal farmworkers. Some farm labor contractors and foremen in our southwestern Michigan study area were drawn from several Texas migrant families who had settled in the area. The "carrying capacity" of summer harvest communities is limited, however, by the amount of core, year-round farmwork jobs available, and the children of farmworkers growing up in these small communities are very likely to move into nonagricultural occupations.

Periodic freezes are yet another factor in diminishing the stream of migrants. Although many families committed to farmwork settle into stable patterns of migration, sudden inbalances of labor supply and demand push them out of farmwork. Freezes have decimated valley citrus in 1951, 1962, 1983, and 1989. This has resulted in labor market imbalances, with shorter periods of work in the crop that remains and lower total peak employment. While the citrus industry has some ability to rebound, the short interval between the 1983 and 1989 freezes in particular hurt the industry. It appears that the net result, as we have witnessed in central Florida as well, has been a steady decline in citrus production. The number of firms has declined as a result of both capital concentration and crop loss, with the number of citrus packing sheds falling from twenty-one to fifteen in the seven years before our study. At the same time, it has become more attractive to move citrus production "offshore," after the manner of other labor-intensive industries such as clothing and precision electronics. Griffin and Brand, a major agricultural producer, is reported to have relocated the production of citrus and other crops to Mexico. Finally, the difficulties in the citrus industry have also caused shifts in cropping patterns. Less labor-intensive crops, such as sugarcane, have become more popular, in the same way grain crops have displaced many vegetable crops throughout the northern states. In other crops, such as onions, semi-mechanization (e.g., the use of conveyer-belt loading of trucks just mentioned) has reduced labor demand.

On the heels of changes such as these, workers with an already low commitment to farmwork, many of whom are seriously underemployed, increase their resolve to move out of agriculture. Other farmworker families take advantage of subsidiary network ties, moving to other areas. Workers interviewed in January 1990, while waiting for freeze disaster assistance, said that other members of their families had left for the California grape harvests or for Florida to drive produce trucks. In both cases, network connections were important in making these moves.

The 1989 freeze was estimated to have affected about 4,000 citrus workers directly. Another 10,500 vegetable farmworkers lost an estimated two to three months of work, with no work until the onion harvest. These job losses multiplied through the loss of work in packing sheds. During the mid-April period of our community survey, at the height of the onion harvest, many workers reported that they were able to work only four to six hours a day for two or three days a week, resulting in a total farm labor income of around $30 a week. The official estimate by the Texas Department of Agriculture is that 17,579 jobs were lost. The impact of the 1989 freeze can be measured by comparing the unemployment rate for February and March 1990 with that for 1989. In February 1990, unemployment in Hidalgo County was 23.7 percent with 18.2 percent in the "normal" year of 1989; in March, unemployment had decreased to 21.4 percent, still about six points higher than the "normal" March unemployment rate of 15.7 percent (Texas Employment Commission 1990).

Overall, the interaction between the distinct factors of periodic freezes, increasing mechanization, the offshore movement of valley agriculture, and a shorter migrant season has served to make farmwork a declining occupation in the valley. The valley trends are not dissimilar from those throughout the state and the nation. In the years since World War II, Texas agriculture has declined by 40 percent, from 27.5 million harvested acres to 16.5 million harvested acres.

In addition to sporadic and sudden changes such as freezes and the technological breakthroughs of mechanization, two important long-term social trends are affecting valley migrants. First, the families of first-generation Mexican immigrants tended to be larger than those of later immigrants. As in many peasant economies, having more children resulted in more workers per family and improved family income. The U.S.-born children of the Bracero-era immigrants, having fewer children than their parents, have caused Weslaco to experience the demographic transition typical of industrializing Third World countries. In this case, however, the socioeconomic trigger for decreasing fertility was migration to a developed country and the changes such migration entails. Increases in education, female participation in the labor market, and movement from a natural-resource base to a service and information economy have all exerted downward pressures on fertility.

Second, along with educational levels, the occupational aspirations of teenagers and young adults are increasing. High school students who have entered the mainstream are not willing to consider farmwork very seriously, even if they have already had long-term farmwork experience. One young girl—an A student in ninth grade, one of eight siblings in a midwestern migrant family, who had worked since she was nine years old—summed it up as follows: "I'd work in farmwork if my parents needed me to do that to support them." Neither the interviewer nor the young girl believed this was going to be her only career option.

Even high school dropouts aspire to better things than farmwork. Vocational schools in the valley carry on a brisk trade; going to school to learn a trade is an option receiving serious consideration from many of the teenagers and young adults we interviewed who were still in farmwork.

Migrant farmworkers remain an important group in Weslaco and the *colonias,* but the group is aging and not reproducing itself. Furthermore, the paucity of winter agricultural work in the valley since 1983 has slowed the rate of new immigration of Mexican farmworkers to the area. New immigrant farmworkers have chosen, instead, to migrate directly to California and Florida. A further disincentive is that the strong, coherent, extended family networks in the valley, the surplus of local workers, and the reliance on labor contractors who have been tied into groups of family members and friends makes access to employment difficult for recent immigrants.

The lower Rio Grande Valley of Texas is the only major traditional farm labor supply area in the continental United States that consists predominantly of ''domestic'' workers. It shares certain characteristics with Puerto Rico, whose domestic farm labor force is also slowly leaving agriculture for other kinds of work as well as being reduced by aging and failure to reproduce itself. By contrast, Parlier and Immokalee are vibrant receiving areas for international migrants, representing the endpoints of international or ''transnational'' networks.

The valley's remaining domestic farm labor force thus represents a demographic bulge made up of early Mexican immigrants and their children. This group was able to pursue an economic strategy based on agricultural-labor migration with great success in the period 1950 to 1975. For a few, migrant farmwork continues to be a viable option, but the surpluses of immigrant farmworkers makes their participation in the farm labor force increasingly untenable. In part because of increasing mechanization-induced gaps in the migrant itineraries of Bracero-era Texas farmworkers during the 1980s, a partial ''vacuum'' developed in the labor market in the mid-1980s that made it easier for waves of new-immigrant workers to displace the Texas migrants. We see evidence of this displacement particularly in Washington and Oregon, where Texans now make up only a small proportion of the migrant labor pool. In the course of a few seasons, growers increased their reliance on cyclical migrants from Mexico who were able to meet their maintenance and reproductive costs because of lower costs of living in Mexico. This helped drive Texas migrants out of farmwork and into other occupations.

In the late 1970s and early 1980s, economic forces in Mexico were building up that would push large numbers of Mexicans northward to replace the Texas migrants who had begun to leave agriculture for new horizons. During the five to ten years before the immigration reform of the late 1980s, the strong streams of migration that in the 1970s had funneled rural Mexican peasants to work in urban areas of Mexico such as Mexico City and Monterey flowed steadily toward the United States, sending workers north once again into farmwork, the tattered welcome mat to the "golden door" of opportunity in America.

But the oasis of cheap housing and abundant work that beckoned Bracero-era immigrants in the 1960s and 1970s to the lower Rio Grande Valley no longer draws the new-immigrant farmworkers and low-wage workers. Bypassing the valley, new-immigrant workers head straight for the action: the receiving communities of southern Florida; the Central Valley of California; urban areas such as Los Angeles, Chicago, Houston, and Dallas. The valley, for them, is history, and like much history, the story of migrant farmworkers in the lower Rio Grande Valley has no real ending.

Weslaco's farmworker and low-wage working populations, like those of Immokalee and Parlier, are made up of subgroups that behave somewhat differently from one another in the labor market. Unlike Immokalee, however, Weslaco does not contain an ethnically heterogeneous working-poor population but instead is one that we classify primarily by the terms under which its members arrived in the United States, their experience, and their varying legal statuses.

Because Weslaco's farmworker population is aging, farmworkers we interviewed here are older than those in Immokalee and Parlier. The average age of heads of households working in farmwork is 43.6 years. Almost half of them (43 percent) immigrated to the United States to perform farmwork during the Bracero era or earlier. In those days, immigrating was often an informal process, especially given that for many years Mexican authorities had refused to place Bracero workers in Texas. One worker we interviewed who first worked in Texas in 1950 simply crossed the river and stopped at the first farm he found (about three miles north of the border), where he was hired to cut down cottonwood trees. Just a teenager at the time, he stayed on at this farm for more than ten years. Others worked in a variety of jobs, commonly migrating to California, Washington, Minnesota, and Illinois, states no longer among their migrant destinations. This group corresponds roughly to green-card workers, although some became citizens through marriage. These workers continue to work, along with their teenaged children, who still live at home. While teenaged children in many of the families work with their parents in the fields, they plan to leave farmwork as soon as they move out "on their own." Typical of this group is the Maldonado family.

Benito Maldonado, who is sixty-two, and his fifty-year-old wife, Elsa, continue to migrate to southwestern Michigan to pick cucumbers each year with their daughters, Teresa, age nineteen, and Estela, age fourteen. Of their six children, only one is committed to staying in farmwork. Three of the four oldest children graduated from high school and went into other lines of work. Teresa and Estela plan to do the same. Benito and Elsa Maldonado now travel north with Samuel, their son who dropped out of school and ended up in farmwork (although he liked office work better). They will keep on migrating to Michigan with Samuel and his wife until Estela graduates from high school. Then they will retire.

A second group of farmworkers are those who were legalized under the recent SAW and amnesty programs. Only 14 percent of the current farmworkers in Weslaco fall into this category. This small group is made up primarily of workers who have, in fact, worked in the United States since the late 1970s. The youngest of these post-Bracero workers in our sample is Filemon, a twenty-six-year-old farmworker who crossed the river from the border town of Rio Bravo as a teenager in 1980. Magdaleno Tamez, who first came to work in the U.S. in 1971 as a young man, but who did not settle on the U.S. side of the river until 1980, probably is more typical of this group.

With his wife and nine children, Tamez worked most of 1989 in Florida in a celery-packing house and in Tennessee picking pickle cucumbers. In recent years, the family has also migrated to southwestern Michigan and Indiana. He doesn't speak English well but, working with his wife, does rather well in farmwork, although he's dissatisfied with the farm labor contractor they travel with, who doesn't attend properly to his duties.

These workers, like the Bracero-era immigrants who immediately preceded them, are firmly committed to farmwork. They are the workers, however, most likely to criticize field-supervision techniques, as is suggested by Tamez's dissatisfaction with his crew leader. As such, they may be both the least desirable workers, to crew leaders, and the most likely to press for improvements in wages and working conditions. The fact that they achieved legal resident status only in the past few years belies the length of time they have lived in the valley and their experience with farmwork.

The third group of farmworkers—second-generation farmworkers who were raised in the valley—illustrate many of the reasons the farm labor supply in the United States is constantly being replenished with foreign labor. Despite the fact that the U.S.-born farmworkers who grew up in the valley are a diverse group, one characteristic most of them share is their uncertainty about their futures in farmwork. They do not particularly enjoy farmwork but feel they have few employment options and are for the most part resigned to the working conditions in farm labor. The members of this second generation of farmworkers are the children of farmworkers, usually families who managed to achieve some measure of stability in their migration patterns. Typical of these younger U.S.-born migrant families is the Flores family.

Francisco Flores, age thirty-one, is the son of a Bracero-era family of migrants who migrated to Arizona, California, and Oregon. Flores was born in Phoenix and began working in farmwork as a teenager, picking tomatoes with his family in California, but he has lived in the valley all his adult life. His parents say he never much liked school, but Flores says he had to quit school to work. In any case, he dropped out of high school after tenth grade. He married a girl from the valley, also from a migrant family. His three older sisters married farmworkers also. One lives in Oregon, one in Michigan, and one in the valley. His brother is also a farmworker.

For the past five years, Flores has migrated to southwestern Michigan with his parents, who stopped going to California and Oregon about ten years ago. In 1989, he worked in strawberries, blueberries, and tomatoes in Michigan. On his return to the valley, he worked in cabbage and melons. Unlike many migrants, he managed to work most of the year, but he never earned more than $4.00 an hour during the year. He and his wife have three young children, so they are the only wage earners. Their continuing life as migrants is possible, despite the family's low earnings, only because of help from food stamps, in-camp child care in Michigan, publicly subsidized housing, and access to low-cost health services at a migrant clinic. Their heavy reliance on such services underscores the extent to which public services, about which growers chronically complain, subsidize the costs of maintaining and reproducing an agricultural labor force.

The situation of nonmigrants is often worse than that of the successful migrants, as illustrated by the case of Rogelio Galvan.

Son of a Bracero-era farmworker who migrated to Indiana tomatoes, Michigan cucumbers, and western Texas cotton, Rogelio Galvan now works only in southern Texas. Although Galvan has cousins who are *troqueros,* giving him better access to work than some, he managed to work only six months in 1989. In January and February, when he worked in broccoli locally, he averaged only eighteen hours of work a week. By March he managed to find thirty-five hours of work a week in the onion harvest. He picked melons in May and June and went to Corpus Christi, two hundred miles north, for a few months of truck driving. He doesn't know how much he made during the year, or even during any single week, because his hours varied so much. Although Galvan is thirty-one, he is already in ill health. He has gone deaf in one ear from repeated ear infections and has chronic back pain. He and his wife are separated; Galvan's cousin, who works with him often, is also divorced and helps him a great deal as his growing deafness and illiteracy make it hard for him to organize his life. His cousin feels it's not worth migrating unless you have a wife and children to work with you; that is why he and Galvan go no farther than Corpus Christi. After being unemployed in August and September last year, Galvan went to Minnesota to live with his brother for a while. He went to vocational school for two months there, but that didn't work out. He'd like to leave farmwork, but his lack of English and of education, and his ill health make it very unlikely he'll be able to leave.

Finally, several of the "current" 1989 U.S.-born farmworkers differ from those described above only by the more casual nature of their attachment to farmwork. They tend to drift in and out of the farm labor force. Members of this group had already left farmwork when we interviewed them in 1990. Their work histories included a mixture of farmwork and nonagricultural work or sometimes supervisory or skilled work in the fields. This group is diverse yet characterized by fairly unsuccessful employment histories. They tend to be disenchanted with their lack of occupational opportunities and options. Farmwork is, for them, an employment option of last resort but, unfortunately, an option they must often choose.

Jaime Montoya, a farmworker who had packed tomatoes and cucumbers in Michigan and melons in the valley, was placed by an employment-training program in a janitorial job that he liked because "it wasn't in the fields," but he was planning to leave because it paid only minimum wage.

Miguel Zamora, a local chile picker, moved into a factory job but grew bored with the work.

Jose Barajas, who had worked as an assistant *mayordomo* [crew leader] in Florida tomatoes, returned to Weslaco in late 1989 after the company where he had worked for the previous fourteen years closed down. He was working as a security guard when we interviewed him but liked neither the hours nor the pay.

Juana Alonso, a separated mother of three children who had worked as a ticket taker for years in Florida, came home to Weslaco to live with her parents because her access to her estranged husband's network of job connections was not effective once they separated—an example of network dissolution that receives too little attention in the social-scientific literature on networks. She has been out of work for six months; she is, in short, a "discouraged" worker.

Javier Bustamante, the only farmworker in our sample whose job was found through the job service, went to North Carolina to work in tobacco at a job with steady work and good housing but still was not sure if he would continue in farmwork. Although he planned to return to North Carolina, he did not like being so far from the valley and did not like tobacco work. He was looking for work in construction so he could leave farmwork.

Even with effective support services, this group's attachment to farmwork is uncertain. It would require powerful incentives to increase their commitment to farmwork and would be equally difficult to address the constraints that prevent their participation (e.g., caring for elderly relatives, child-care responsibilities, lack of transportation). Questions remain relating to the productivity and "quality" of a labor pool that considers farmwork its employment of last resort. Still, those who have recently left or plan to leave farmwork represent an important subgroup of displaced domestic workers who have difficulty keeping up with changes in the farm labor market because of their tenuous connection to it. There is little to suggest, however, that growers will adopt a strategy of retaining these farmworkers through improvements in work stability, housing, and working conditions as long as they have access to new-immigrant workers. Domestic farmworkers' jobs could be "saved," but the long-term benefits of such a policy are unclear, given that this group is not deeply attached to farmwork jobs.

In any case, such developments are not likely given current trends in the industry. The alternative to importing cheap labor, of course, is exporting capital and technology to areas with cheaper labor costs. Seeking to reduce labor costs, southern Texas agricultural production has begun to move to Mexico and Latin America like other offshore producers. In the context of industrial policy, the southern Texas group of domestic farmworkers is clearly a group of displaced workers; yet unlike the workers displaced from unionized, high-paying manufacturing jobs with extensive fringe benefits, these workers have little stake in remaining in their jobs.

Work Patterns of Current Farmworkers in the Lower Rio Grande Valley

Slightly over half (54 percent) of the current farm labor force of the lower Rio Grande Valley consists of migrants. Migrant destinations for our sample included Michigan, Ohio, Indiana, Tennessee, Missouri, Iowa, North Dakota, Minnesota, Florida, North Carolina, Vermont, and Washington. The earliest migrants to leave the lower Rio Grande Valley depart in late March for asparagus in Washington or in April for asparagus in Michigan. The next wave of departures is in late April or early May for families going to the strawberry harvest in Michigan. In 1990, we observed that many families made plans to leave the week after Easter, an important holiday in the community, but other families do not leave until later. The main migrant exodus is in May for midwestern migrants, some of whom go first to Missouri or Tennessee, some of whom go directly north to Michigan, Ohio, or Indiana. The peak of summer harvest work is in July and August. Some families return to the valley as early as September, but others work a late crop such as apples and return only in late October or early November.

Farmworker households in our sample included several families of Florida migrants (10 percent) who spent their winters in Florida. These families did not migrate to Florida but lived there regularly. They are part of the dispersed "horizontal" Texas–Florida network and had returned to their hometown of Weslaco only because of various personal crises and family commitments. While in Florida, they combined work in citrus and tomatoes, working quite steadily until late spring (since the Florida peak season is winter). The midwestern migrants we interviewed preferred work in the packing sheds to work in winter crops, but some did do field work in the valley. Others rested during the winter or held seasonal, nonagricultural jobs that dovetailed with farmwork. Examples of this pattern include a migrant family who operated a small store in a *colonia* during the winter, a school bus driver who migrated north after school closed, and several winter construction workers.

Work in the valley consists of four main crop tasks: fall and early-winter harvest of cucumbers and peppers; winter harvest of broccoli, cauliflower, cabbage, and carrots; the spring onion harvest; and late-spring melons. Packing-shed, trucking, and other agriculture-related work are important sources of income, short-term and sporadic like the field work tasks but usually providing slightly more stability than actual harvest or thinning tasks. The farmworkers who worked only in the valley, instead of migrating, worked in melons in May and June but often were unemployed during the middle of the summer. Our sample included only one worker who detasseled corn, but we were told demand for this summer work is increasing because of the increasing production of seed corn in the valley. Those who worked in the valley were much more likely to be casual workers than migrants. For example, the mean time spent in farmwork by nonmigrants (4.7 months) was much lower than the mean time spent by migrants (6.4 months). The stable, year-round valley workers we interviewed were older Bracero-era workers who had worked their way into steadier nursery employment.

These work patterns, we noted earlier, depend heavily on ideal weather. Massive winter and spring unemployment followed the December 1989 freeze in the valley. In mid-January, farmworkers waited in line for ten to twelve hours outside state offices applying for freeze assistance. The *Harlingen Valley Morning Star* estimated that 10,500 workers were out of work in the valley, the result of the loss of 50 percent of the cabbage, 100 percent of the broccoli, 90 percent of the celery, and 100 percent of the lettuce crops. We estimate that 1,500 workers in the Weslaco area applied for freeze assistance. Total crop losses in the valley were estimated at $138 million, $48.7 million in vegetables and $46.8 million in citrus, $34.2 million in "noncitrus perennials," mostly aloe vera, and $8.3 million in nursery production.

A crisis like this illuminates the essential features of complex social processes. During this period of hardship, some desperate workers attempted to activate old network contacts and go to California or Washington early in search of work, indicating what we take to be the most essential of survival mechanisms in farmwork: networks and migration. Others simply devoted themselves to making ends meet. Onions suffered a 15 to 30 percent loss, which may have contributed to the widespread unemployment we observed in April, where at peak harvest few workers had more than thirty hours of work a week. Although the winter of 1989–90 was an unusually bad year for Texas farmworkers, our work histories, which covered January–April 1989 (the year before the freeze) indicate that winter underemployment is very common.

Sharp fluctuations in availability of work, caused by increases in the flow of recent immigrants, drops in demand due to freeze or drought, or mechanization, pump dedicated farmworkers out of the farm labor market by increasing the risks of underemployment beyond acceptable levels. The most common choices made by workers who are pushed out of farmwork include setting time aside to go to trade school; setting up one's own small business; accepting highly casual, local, nonagricultural work; drifting between informal employment and social services; and "retiring" by relying more on the support of relatives if one is an older worker.

Current Farmworkers' Employment, Unemployment, and Earnings

The yearly earnings of Weslaco "current" farmworkers (workers who had done some farmwork in 1989) are very low, with a mean of $5,396. Reported yearly family incomes are only slightly higher, $6,547. These earnings are very low even for Weslaco—55 percent of the mean family income in the community survey. Since the mean household size is 4.5 persons, farmworker household earnings are less than half the poverty level. The sample includes both local valley farmworkers, among whom hourly pay is prevalent, and migrant farmworkers, among whom piecework is prevalent. Two-thirds of the farmworkers interviewed reported they were paid hourly wages and only one-third were paid piecework. Mean weekly earnings level was $138.

Farmworkers' low earnings stem not only from low wage rates but also from underemployment. Seasonal unemployment combines with fluctuations in hours per day and hours per week to make underemployment an ever-present feature of the farm labor market. Over half of the farmworker heads of households (57 percent) reported they had worked in one job during the previous year where their daily earnings were less than $25. Although minimum-wage violations exist in piecework jobs, the cause of these low earnings was most likely to be short days. During any given month, because of the lack of work, approximately one-fifth of the Weslaco farm labor force is earning less than minimum wage (Table 4.1).

The possibility of being underemployed during any given week is very high, especially during the midsummer months, when many Weslaco farm-workers migrate north for work. The uneven distribution of working hours is an important element in farmworkers' economic strategies. We found that, typically, farmworkers maximize their access to available work, attempting to

TABLE 4.1 Mean Hours Farmworkers Worked per Week by Month, 1990 (N = 28)

Month	Percent Employed		
	<40 Hours	40 Hours	>40 Hours
January	56%	21%	23%
February	50	50	0
March	66	25	8
April	47	20	33
May	41	35	24
June	27	47	26
July	54	36	9
August	56	22	22
September	20	20	60
October	44	22	33
November	56	33	11
December	40	40	20

Source: Weslaco household head survey, 1989–90 (see Appendix).
Note: Percentages may not total 100 because of rounding.

move from the underemployed group to the overemployed group. Such access is difficult, though, because two to three times as many workers are underemployed as are overemployed.

Because underemployment is such a high-probability risk for Weslaco farmworkers, they place great emphasis on avoiding that risk, which, they recognize, has more of an impact on their economic welfare than does the exact rate of hourly earnings they receive. The variance from the worst wage offer to the best wage offer in any given farm labor market is much less than the expected variance in hours worked per day and per week. In Weslaco, the spread between the worst job offer in the labor market and the best offer in a given crop task will result in a difference of about $40 in earnings per week ($1.00 per hour differential times forty hours). In an assessment of the desirability of different wage offers, this gain or loss due to wage rate must be compared with the likelihood of being underemployed for more than ten hours per week ($4.00 per hour times ten hours) for the duration of the job. This concern over the possibility of underemployment explains, in large measure, the desirability of working in certain crops, such as pickle cucumbers, which last relatively long and provide steady work, in contrast to working in other crops, such as onions, which are usually associated with short workdays and short workweeks. Thus, farmworkers weighing job opportunities give at least as much weight to amount of work as they do to pay rate. Moreover, in piecework employment, it is not clear exactly what earnings will be, since they vary by the condition of the crop. This means that it is especially important to access jobs with employers who are most likely to provide a stable flow of work or, at least, in a crop that provides adequate work.

The algebra of decreasing the risk of underemployment, then, justifies a number of ''expenditures'' that farmworkers make—compromises, commitments, and buying into networks of reciprocity, all of which are seen as investments in strengthening one's network to increase employment stability.[1] The very high likelihood of underemployment among Weslaco farmworkers also serves to explain the importance of informal networks of relatives and acquaintances who can be counted on to help cope with uneven cash flows, short-term loans, or deferred payment for critical needs like rent. For workers whose economic well-being rests on farmwork, financial crises are not a result of bad planning but inability to solve cash-flow problems through planning. The strong links that workers develop to farm labor contractors or favored employers suggest effective risk management.

Even with these social-resource-based measures against underemployment, both unemployment and underemployment remain common. The ''average farmworker'' in our Weslaco sample worked 6.6 months in farmwork during 1989, supplementing this farmwork employment with 2.8 months of nonagricultural employment. There is a great deal of variation in ''mixes'' of farmwork, processing work, and other work. Migrants are more attached to farmwork, while nonmigrants are more often casual workers supplementing nonagricultural employment.

Current farmworkers' longest duration of unemployment was 11.4 weeks. This does not include weeks of partial employment or time spent moving from one job within the harvest to another. We emphasize that it is the seasonality of farmwork that ensures farmworkers' poverty more than do low wages. Only 29 percent of the workers surveyed received unemployment insurance. Those who did received $69 per week on the average, adding an estimated $700 to their annual income (given the waiting period for receipt of unemployment insurance). The sample of unemployed farmworkers is too small to give a definitive profile of reasons for not receiving unemployment insurance. The surveys indicate, however, that lack of coverage by the employer is a significant reason. Other workers were not available for work because they were ill or injured or family responsibilities kept them from working. Despite this, over half of the farmworkers (54 percent) said that, at one point during the previous year, they had wanted to work but couldn't because no work was available. Our analysis of the relationship between Weslaco respondents' plans to do farmwork in the coming season and the amount of current work shows that the number of months worked in the previous year is well correlated ($p < .01$) with future plans, suggesting that farmworkers base their future estimations on past realities.

Standard employment benefits such as vacation pay, sick pay, and holiday pay have never been a prevalent part of the employment picture for Weslaco's farmworkers. Such standard benefits therefore play little or no role in employment decisions. However, Weslaco farmworkers do consider housing, transportation, and other common attributes of farm labor jobs similar to the way union workers may perceive benefits. One-fifth of the current farmworkers, for example, had access to the typical farmwork ''benefit'' of the ability to borrow money from a farm labor contractor or employer.

Generally poor earnings, the high incidence of underemployment, and the lack of benefits all take their toll on the farm labor market's ability to retain workers. Examining workers' previous five years of employment, we attempted to determine the extent of occupational migration in and out of farmwork from one year to the next. Comparing current primary work with previous work history, we found that half of the current farmworkers have worked only in farmwork and packing work for the five-year period. The other half have mixed farmwork and other work over the entire five-year period. Only 4 percent of the current farmworkers had not done agriculture during the preceding five years. Specific "mixes" of farmwork and nonfarmwork vary greatly. Close to half the current Weslaco farmworkers (40 percent) supplemented farm employment with another job, in construction, packing sheds, or some other sort of unskilled service or manufacturing job. While in Weslaco, migrants were relatively more successful than nonmigrants in combining farmwork and other employment, achieving a mean 9.8 months of employment in 1989, in contrast to the 8.2 months worked by nonmigrants. The lower levels of seasonal unemployment among migrants also stems from their slightly higher levels of employment in packing sheds and agricultural-support jobs (1.1 months vs. .75 months). Thus, nearly half of Weslaco's farm labor force, moving between agricultural and nonagricultural jobs, is likely to leave agriculture altogether in a crisis such as the 1989 freeze. The attrition of farmworkers is enhanced across generations. While the current Weslaco farm labor force consists of a steadily decreasing number of aging immigrants from the 1950s and 1960s, their children are leaving the farm labor force in even greater numbers. The perennial farmworker dream of a better life for one's children is a reality for many U.S.-born Mexican Americans, now moving into a wide range of professional, technical, and service occupations that provide greater employment stability and offer less harsh working conditions than farmwork.

Farmworkers's children who dropped out of school and married into new migrant networks continue in farmwork, but each year their numbers dwindle. Their parents' dreams that they would, with better education, move into easier and better-paid jobs than farmwork may not be a current reality for them, yet it is a strongly held and continuing aspiration. They seek other options wherever they can, drawing on ever-increasing network ties to siblings, cousins, and others who work outside of agriculture, as they did previously for their agricultural jobs.

Virtually all of Weslaco's current farmworkers are the children of farmworkers; 93 percent reported that one or both parents worked in agriculture. More than one-third have brothers or sisters working in farmwork in another state, providing the basis of a quite far-flung network. At the same time, more than half of the current farmworkers (57 percent) reported they were the only one of their brothers and sisters doing farmwork. This conforms to our other observations that the children of domestic farmworkers tend not to perceive farmwork as a viable career option. While many of the children of current farmworkers work in the fields, work experience as teenagers does not predispose them to continuing in farmwork once they leave high school. Neither they nor their parents want them to continue in farmwork. One measure of the potential of Weslaco as a farm labor supply source is that 72 percent of the heads of households interviewed had fathers who worked in farmwork. Yet since only 29 percent of the labor force is currently working in farmwork, the multigeneration propagation of farmworker networks is weakening. To assess the degree to which traditional migrant networks currently function, we examined the question of siblings in farmwork. Again, as just noted, slightly under one-third (30 percent) of the Weslaco household heads, including current farmworkers, had at least one brother in farmwork; 12 percent had at least one sister in farmwork. This indicates a weakening of the formerly strong networks that characterized earlier generations of migrant farmworkers, particularly when we compare Weslaco with traditional Mexican sending communities that have a culture of *nortenizacion* (that is, of looking to the United States as a source of jobs and income); these communities possess networks sufficient to continually replenish the U.S. farm labor supply.

Migrant networks, however, are complex, and some of the structural characteristics of network processes continue to elude us. We do not yet definitively know, for example, how long unused network contacts might remain functional. Nor do we know the "critical mass" needed for an effective network. What does seem to be the case is that structural changes (decreasing family size, dispersion of networks, multigenerational farmworker contacts, ability to marry into neighboring migrant networks) go hand in hand with changes in cultural, personal, and work values. Weslaco's networks are clearly weakening, but we do not yet understand whether they will subside in a linear fashion as farmworkers no longer saturate the community or whether they will collapse rapidly.

These observations suggest that the farm labor force—similar to other low-wage labor forces dominated by immigrant labor—is less likely to reproduce itself through natural means than through social processes such as continued immigration from underdeveloped regions. Family connections and network linkages with long-term employers or farm labor contractors are key elements in current farmworkers' employment strategies. Above all else, these social mechanisms give farmworkers access to the most stable possible farmwork employment as well as other nonagricultural work. This is because many nonagricultural jobs in the valley have assumed some of the characteristics of the farm labor market (e.g., hiring through personal contacts, no fringe benefits, seasonal layoffs).

Overall, farmwork is desirable for workers who have difficulty marketing their skills in the nonagricultural labor market because of lack of education, ability to speak English, or vocational skills. It also provides a means to maximize household earnings by allowing almost all members in the family to work. Low educational level, and lack of ability to speak English, themselves closely correlated, are also important determinants of willingness to do farmwork in the future ($p > .01$). By contrast, immigration status is not significantly correlated with commitment to farmwork. The valley presents employment alternatives to farmwork for immigrant workers willing to work for low wages. The most recent immigrants gravitate toward restaurant work, sewing, and housekeeping. While surveys generally are not a good means to examine participation in informal or "underground" economic transactions, our ethnographic work suggests that this is an important part of personal planning for all low-wage workers in Weslaco. Just as access to housing is a critical element in life as a farmworker, so is access to informal networks of family or friends who can provide credit and child care. Successful delivery of support services designed to meet the pressing needs of farmworkers needs to copy the efficiency and flexibility of these informal systems. Unlike current bureaucracies, whether public or private, these informal networks can respond rapidly to emergencies, facilitate daily life, and connect job seekers with fleeting job opportunities.

Publicly Funded Services for Farmworkers

As noted previously, the population we surveyed in Weslaco consists almost entirely of low-income nuclear- and extended-family households. Unlike the majority of new-immigrant farmworkers in Parlier and Immokalee, current farmworker families in Weslaco rely heavily on several publicly funded services. The most widely used program is the food stamp program, which was used by 79 percent of the farmworker families but by only 47 percent of the other low-income families. Other major services that affect farmworkers' welfare were migrant-health-program clinics (used by 54 percent of the households) and publicly subsidized housing (36 percent). During the winter of 1989–90, Disaster Unemployment Assistance was an important program for unemployed farmworkers. Valleywide, slightly over seventeen thousand farmworkers applied for assistance, and slightly over fifteen thousand applications were approved—an approval rate of 88 percent. According to the Texas Employment Commission, total benefit payouts were $10,822,247, an average of eight weeks of unemployment insurance per eligible worker.

Use of educational services was lower than use of the major social-service programs, but was still a significant support service for farmworkers seeking to move into new occupations. One-quarter had gone to ESL or GED classes, and 10 percent had participated in a job-training program. Also, contact with the Texas Employment Commission was relatively high, partially as a result of seasonal unemployment among Weslaco farmworkers. One-third of the farmworker heads of household had visited the employment commission during the year, but only 10 percent had been referred to jobs.

Nonwage sources of economic support—including unemployment insurance, food stamps, subsidized housing, reduced-price health care, and the Women, Infants, and Children program—provide an important contribution to the welfare of Weslaco's farmworkers, all of whom fall into the category of the working poor. Farmworkers' use of such income-transfer programs is higher than that of the low-income population overall because farmworkers experience higher levels of seasonal unemployment and have much lower annual incomes. A very important complement to this winter support in Texas is the network of social services provided to migrants in northern, summer harvest states. These services maximize family members' ability to work during the limited time the peak harvest season lasts. Key services provided in the labor demand area of southwestern Michigan, for example, include migrant Headstart programs, in-camp child care and summer educational programs for children, and night school during the school year for high school students. By facilitating women's and teenagers' labor force participation, these programs, as well as providing valuable educational services, also augment family incomes.

Conclusion

The similarities between Weslaco of the 1950s and 1960s and Immokalee and Parlier today are striking. When Weslaco was an active receiving immigrant community, it possessed some of the same structural characteristics now found in Immokalee and Parlier—the street-corner labor markets; the preponderance of young, single workers; and a central role for farm labor contractors in recruiting workers and organizing the workplace. This suggests that the traditional farm labor supply towns occupy different structural positions in international farm labor demand and supply networks. Such a "structural" view of the dynamics of farm labor networks suggests the following process. Initially, lone-male pioneers, supported by informal but monetarized networks, dominate migrant streams. They are followed by their wives, who are developing their own networks based on extended-family relationships, and begin to rely less on the mediation of farm labor contractors. Finally, their children, whose levels of education and cultural outlooks are rapidly changing, move into the mainstream of the society, and the networks begin to contract once again, unless replenished by an ongoing flow of immigrants. These dynamics of network expansion and contraction are, presumably, sensitive to "push" factors in international migration, and to such other factors as the structure of the farm labor market, immigration policy, the efficacy of programs designed to increase social equity or occupational mobility, and the degree to which nonagricultural industries develop specialized adaptions to preferentially hire immigrant workers.

The era of Texas-based migrant family workers then can be seen as the result of a unique combination of historical factors—an initial influx of pioneering lone-male immigrants, followed by a generous legalization program, and the availability (prior to mechanization) of an extended migrant itinerary of multiple harvests. The decline of Texas family migrants as part of the U.S. farm labor force stems from the network's tremendous success in dispersing Texas migrants throughout the United States, the impressive—if not entirely adequate—efforts to educate and integrate the children of newly arrived immigrants into U.S. society, changes in northern farm labor markets (such as the replacement of Texas farmworkers by Mixtec workers in Washington apple harvests), and a dramatic contraction of the availability of farmwork in the lower Rio Grande Valley, altering migrant and seasonal itineraries forever.

The stable patterns of Texas family migration probably cannot be reproduced under current conditions. One significant difference in the 1990s is that the increasing unevenness of farm labor demand makes the "mature" stage of family migrants more difficult to achieve. The best strategy for dealing with a risky farm labor market is for the household head to migrate alone, adapting to a farm labor market that increasingly selects for single-male workers. Family migration provides payoffs only when there is a fair measure of employment stability or job guarantees, as in cases where families and networks of farmworkers can develop close, fictive-kin relations with growers. Related to this, current selective pressures appear to favor more cyclical migration and less settling out of nuclear- and extended-family households than were common during the post-Bracero period. The weakening of migrant family itineraries favors a Mexico-based, long-distance commuting labor force.

The situation of Weslaco, the lower Rio Grande Valley, and southern Texas may be most illuminating in that it requires us to examine more critically the coherence of federal, state, and local policies regarding low-wage labor. Continued protection of a segmented farm labor market results in a labor force characterized by workers adapting to substandard working conditions. Inevitably, public funding must be provided to close the gap between workers' earnings and the minimum survival level for U.S. families. In short, their wages must be subsidized, by state welfare programs or by the farmworkers' families or, most likely, by a combination of the two within what we call, in Chapter 10, the labor reserve model. In this sense, the disappearance of Texas migrant family workers is simply another facet of a process of occupational migration that results in a growing and vital bicultural labor force of Mexican workers with relatively good access to a wide range of low-wage occupations. However, a cause for growing concern is that young adults entering the work-force are not receiving access to employment opportunities that meet their aspirations and are not obtaining reasonable economic returns for their educa-tion, weakening their attachment to the labor force. There is some evi-dence—an incipient youth gang problem and the appearance of multigenera-tional welfare households, for example—that because of chronic structural unemployment, a rural underclass with little attachment to the labor force may be replacing the prior generation of working poor.

Chapter 5

Labor Demand in Southwestern Michigan

Last Bastion of the Family Farm

Agricultural production in this part of the Midwest is a paradigm case of the romantic American myth—the farm owned and operated by an extended family of independent-minded entrepreneurs. Virtually all of the small towns in the area have a special 1950s look to them, as do the winding roads, and the roadside cafes—the look of vintage movies—and a firmly entrenched ethic of hard work, well-tended farms, and immaculate yards. This romantic American myth fails to note that the area has, at least since the 1930s, relied heavily on migrant workers—African Americans emigrating from the South; whites from Arkansas and Appalachia; and finally Mexicans, who combined work in southwestern Michigan with work in Minnesota sugar beets. The backdrop to the white farmhouses and red barns is one closely associated with the 1960s—Texas-based migrant families working side by side in the fields, returning in the evenings to camps of shacks and, now, trailers, clustered around a communal shower and water spigot. This is the core of American agriculture: on one hand, seemingly unchanged since World War II; on the other, accepting the inevitability of a variety of social and economic changes.

It also exemplifies the central paradox of contemporary farm labor: while Mexican migrant workers travel one or two thousand miles from Texas, Florida, and Mexico to work in summer jobs, unemployment in neighboring communities is well over 10 percent. Several farmers interviewed had, in the past, attempted to recruit African American day-haul workers from Benton Harbor with little success.

Southwestern Michigan began to rely on Mexican migrant workers from southern Texas toward the end of the Bracero era in the mid 1960s. That reliance continues, but in recent years more Florida-based migrants, most of whom are recent Mexican immigrants, have entered the southwestern Michigan labor force. This trend will likely continue as Florida agriculture continues to expand and Texas agriculture continues to decline.

This study focuses on the link between southwestern Michigan and the Donna–Weslaco–Mercedes area of the lower Rio Grande Valley. This link is particularly strong, since an estimated 55 percent of the lower Rio Grande Valley migrants in southwestern Michigan are from one of these towns. Yet the southwestern Michigan labor market is also very strongly linked to sending communities in southern and central Florida and international migration networks in Mexico, specifically the core sending areas of Guanajuato, Michoacán, and Zacatecas, as well as the "new" sending area of Guerrero.

"Southwestern Michigan" refers to an area bordering the western shore of Lake Michigan, consisting of Berrien, Van Buren, and Cass counties. The three-county area is defined as much by climate, agricultural production, and organizational parameters as by political boundaries. The area has an extraordinary diversity of crops, produced primarily on medium-sized family farms, the leading crops being apples, cucumbers, tomatoes, strawberries, blueberries, cherries, and asparagus. There is also significant production of other fruit (e.g., peaches, plums), vegetables (e.g., bell peppers), and nursery stock. The concentration of fruit, vegetable, and horticultural production is a function both of climate and market pressures. Early-spring temperatures are moderated by Lake Michigan. Early-season crops are planted nearer the lakeside, while midseason crops, like cucumbers and tomatoes, are planted farther inland. Chicago, one hundred miles to the west, provides a large regional market for fresh produce; surely this proximity has been responsible for the area's long history and continued success as a fruit-and-vegetable producing region (Schwartz 1945). Many farms combine wholesale marketing to brokers or cooperative marketing associations with roadside retail sales.

Through corporate interests, Michigan produce is also sold on the national market. Pickle producers sell cucumbers to Vlasic and Heinz; a few pack and market their own pickles. Processing tomatoes are also sold to Heinz. A small number of large, local shippers such as DeBruyn Produce, VanBuren County Fruit Exchange, and Greg Orchards and Produce actively market virtually all significant crops. Production concentrated in this small area makes Michigan the leading national producer of pickling cucumbers and blueberries, the fourth-largest producer of processing tomatoes, and the sixth-largest producer of strawberries. Production of apples, which extends along Lake Michigan from Ottawa and Kent counties south to Van Buren and Berrien counties, makes Michigan the nation's third-largest producer. There is a similar cropping pattern in asparagus, where Michigan is the third-largest producer. These crops create a demand for approximately twenty thousand migrant workers. The early-season labor force of asparagus cutters and late-season labor force of apple pickers in central Michigan (Oceana, Ottawa, and Kent counties) consist in part of workers who have worked midseason in the southwestern part of the state. Consequently, these workers make up about half of Michigan's migrant labor force. As in other areas of the Midwest, islands of labor-intensive "truck farming" or fruit, vegetable, and horticultural production are interspersed with standard, highly mechanized production of corn, sorghum, and soybeans.

The main crop competing for migrant labor is corn detassling in Indiana. When the U.S. auto industry was stronger, there was a robust flow of workers to Detroit and other, smaller, manufacturing centers. That flow has weakened, and now meat packing is one of the main nonagricultural industries migrants can enter as they leave agriculture (Stull, Broadway, and Griffith, in press). But after two generations of migration from Texas to Michigan, there is a growing community of settled-out migrants. The main streets of small towns such as Hartford and Berrien Springs now have Mexican grocery stores, and posters for *bailes* (dances) appear on phone poles along with notices of garage sales and the 4-H Club.

The migrant labor force working in southwestern Michigan is believed by many observers to consist primarily of domestic workers (i.e., "green-card" immigrants and their children) based in Texas or Mexico. We cannot confirm this view. The southwestern Michigan labor force includes a rapidly increasing proportion of recently documented (e.g., SAWs) and undocumented immigrants. The composition of the labor force changes throughout the summer with successive waves of migrants. The migrant labor force is still predominantly Texan, but a growing number of Florida-based migrants are actually international migrants from Mexico. Most of these international migrants appear to belong to networks from Mexico's core sending areas (predominantly Guanajuato, Zacatecas, Michoacán, Nuevo Leon, and Tamaulipas), and they entered the United States through Texas, though they did not remain in southern Texas since there was little winter work there. Guatemalans from Florida do not seem to have identified Michigan as a work destination yet. We estimate that about 60 percent of the labor force consists of domestic U.S. workers from Texas (the labor supply profiled in the Weslaco community study), while the remaining 40 percent are Florida workers (the labor supply profiled in the Immokalee case study).

Farmers and service providers in the region demonstrate a firm commitment to respond seriously to farm labor issues. The services provided to migrants by state, local, and charitable organizations are responsive to newly emerging problems, well attuned to seasonal migration patterns, and committed to a long-term strategy for improving the living conditions of migrants. The state operates an underfunded, but popular, program to rehabilitate and improve the decaying stock of migrant housing. There is strong support for migrant Headstart, migrant education, and housing initiatives. Local farmers regularly manage their own farm operations directly and take decisive action to recruit and retain a productive labor force. Working conditions are among the best in the country in terms of work stability, yet housing and pay rates are among the worst. This reflects, perhaps, farmers' recognition that farmworkers are at least as interested in the stability of employment as in working conditions and pay.

While the Michigan migrant labor force was probably never quite as much a domestic labor force as it has been depicted, the thirty-year dominance of a Texas labor force (from around 1955 to 1985) is currently eroding and being replenished with an increasing flow of recent immigrants. This is similar to other cases of new immigrants both replacing and displacing old labor forces in a variety of industries, including food processing and manufacturing (Griffith 1987, 1993a; Lamphere 1992).

Labor and Labor Processes: Small Family and Large Corporate Farms

There are between 200 and 225 agricultural producers in southwestern Michigan who grow labor-intensive crops relying on migrant workers. Most produce multiple crops. Because of the unique soil and climate requirements of blueberries, blueberry farms are specialized and mostly clustered geographically. Asparagus production is also geographically clustered, but some asparagus is grown by the small multicrop farmers. The "typical" labor-intensive farm in southwestern Michigan has a combination of tree fruit and vegetables (e.g., strawberries, cucumbers, cherries, peaches, and apples). Depending on the particular cropping profile, the farm will have an early-season, full-season, or late-season labor demand. Key early-season crops (April to mid-June) are asparagus and strawberries, while the key midseason crops are cucumbers and tomatoes (July and August), followed by a late season of apples (September and October). Other tree fruit (e.g., peaches and plums) and vegetables are midseason.

The typical farm is operated by family members who directly supervise workers. Many of these farms are multigeneration farms managed jointly by an older couple, their children, and in-laws. Yet there are also several very large operations. The largest of these reputedly has over twenty thousand acres in production. There are limits to the number of workers any family member can supervise, so the larger operations, characteristically, turn to farm labor contractors for worker recruitment and supervision. Pickling cucumbers, a leading crop in the area, are produced by a few very large producers who specialize in them and by smaller producers who combine them with other crops.

In general, there is a ratio of one supervisor to thirty or forty workers, regardless of whether the supervisor is a farmer himself, a core (permanent) employee, or a farm labor contractor. Farmers and farm labor contractors, in turn, rely on assistant supervisors or lead workers for additional supervisory tasks. Local mores strongly emphasize ''well-run'' farms and good worker supervision. Several farmers spoke very approvingly of a neighbor fortunate enough to have four sons who were all good farm managers, allowing his family to manage a great deal of acreage without relying on farm labor contractors. Labor management often changes substantially when farm operations are handed over from older farmers to their children, resulting in either improved or worse management. Farmers who are less skilled labor managers are regarded with tolerance and amused disapproval. There is also widespread disapproval of overexpansion that leads to heavy reliance on farm labor contractors, who are generally believed to be bad supervisors. One farmer vehemently referred to farm labor contractors as ''leeches.'' Farmers who use farm labor contractors to meet spot shortages do not brag about it. Supervision arrangements vary a great deal in response to varying crop demand profiles, complexity of tasks, and length of work season. Nursery operations, for example, appear to have higher supervisor-to-worker ratios than some short-season crops such as strawberries.

In the family farms, it is common for wives to manage the books and for husbands to supervise operations. The level of administrative competence varies widely. We observed one overworked housewife making payroll on a card table on the back porch, with grossly inadequate documentation of withholding and hours worked (to provide an audit trail for minimum-wage compliance). A long line of migrant workers waited in the rain as she struggled through her paperwork. Less than a mile away, one of her neighbors used an online accounting system developed and marketed by the Michigan State University extension service to monitor all aspects of farm operations.

Most harvest tasks are paid on some sort of piecework basis, although units, payment rates, and specific structuring of payment schemes (e.g., bonuses) vary from farmer to farmer. Tasks such as hoeing, machine operations such as tractor driving, or mechanized harvesting of cherries, which are difficult to link to productivity, are paid hourly wages, usually the minimum but sometimes up to $.70 per hour over the minimum. Work in cucumbers is often paid on a sharecropping basis—50 percent of crop revenue. Farm labor contractors and crew leaders are paid a fee calculated as a markup on the wages of their crews. While they are, legally, "farm labor contractors," they are, in other respects, supervisors working directly for agricultural employers. Other locally hired supervisors and operations personnel are paid hourly wages. Fringe benefits are virtually nonexistent, in both farmwork and the packing houses. Housing is considered the most important noncash benefit provided to migrant workers, but travel advances are also sometimes used as a means of worker recruitment. Many growers also provide (and sometimes forgive) loans for family emergencies.

Labor management concerns revolve around constructing or accessing a stable, motivated labor force. Labor recruitment rests in large measure on the amount of work farmers say is available and their follow-through in making the commitment a reality. Several farmers interviewed stated that one of their prime considerations in crop diversification was to have a full range of "complementary crops" to provide a constant flow of work for their labor force. While marketing considerations also enter into crop diversification, almost all of the farmers interviewed had explicit strategies to retain workers throughout the season. Cucumber production, which provides work during July and August, is an especially important bridge for farmers with early-season strawberries and late-season apples.

There appears to be a particular complementarity between retail operations and efforts to retain a stable, productive labor force. Retail operations entail both some measure of crop diversification (to provide a wide range of produce) and require high-quality workers (to produce attractive produce). Retail operations appear to allow an adequate profit margin to pay premium wages. One successful retailer paid approximately 30 percent above the mean wage, as well as providing top-quality housing to retain a stable labor force; he was very happy with his current profitability and optimistic about the future. Another large retailer, who was in a fortunate location next to an interstate highway, provided the best housing we saw in the region and had an extremely stable labor force, despite paying only average wages.

Migrant workers, farm labor contractors, and farmers are all extremely sensitive to the amount of work made available. During our interviews, several different farmers' main current concerns were providing enough work for workers "so they wouldn't leave." Farmers felt that providing enough work for migrants was both a duty and a practical necessity. Typically, the "fill-in" work consisted of hoeing at an hourly wage if weather or crop production provided only part-day work. The concern was real: one worker who felt it had been a very slow week in strawberries told us that he planned, immediately after lunch, to go to the job service to see what else was available. Another strategy for smoothing the flow of work was to refer workers to jobs with neighbors who had complementary crops; several farmers noted that they'd prefer to have their workers find fill-in jobs nearby than to leave for good. Farm labor contractors also worried about flow of work and negotiated explicit arrangements with the farmers whose camps they were using about the sorts of fill-in work the farmers could provide for their crews (including who they could work for). Thus, while farm labor contractors are tied to "primary" farmers whose camps they use, supplemental fill-in work is a regular feature of their business strategy. We found this "pooling" of labor among farmers in Maryland as well (see Chapter 3).

Most farmers rely on extended-family networks as their primary means of worker recruitment. There is often some turnover within the family network, however. Children remain in Texas some summers; pregnant wives may also stay behind. One year, some brothers from a family may come to Michigan; another year, others will. The ties between the family networks and farmers often endure for decades or generations, however, replicating the fictive-kin relations reported in Chapter 3.

Growers with less satisfactory network arrangements (i.e., a network too small to fill their total labor needs) also hire walk-in workers or use the job service office in Hartford to meet their needs. The employment services does match temporarily unemployed workers with farmers experiencing spot shortages, but the bulk of these placements are at high-turnover farms. This is because low-turnover farms are worked by members of stable networks. Experienced migrant workers feel that the farmers frequently hiring through the employment service are those with inferior supervisory skills. Poor supervision, in turn, results in high labor turnover and a psychologically less appealing job offer. Thus, seeking and accepting a job service referral is, in some respects, an employment strategy of last resort.

The Michigan agricultural workplace is strongly permeated by *caciquismo* (bossism), informal but highly structured relationships in which workers are tightly bound to farm labor contractors, a farmer's core worker who recruited them, or to the farmer himself by bonds of duty, loyalty, and reciprocal obligation. Again, this is similar to the fictive-kin relationships we discovered on the Delmarva Peninsula. The positive aspect of this type of relationship is its stability and its "social security." At the same time, workers in such relationships are susceptible to the currents and eddies of favoritism and paternalism. These relations inhibit workers from changing jobs midseason. When workers do quit, it is often in an explosive context, as when they have been cheated, treated unfairly or improperly (e.g., being cursed at), or provided with too little work. Less clear-cut maltreatment (e.g., a poor housing assignment or inferior wage rates) is more likely to result in the worker shopping around, making new arrangements for the following year, and simply not returning to the former, inferior employer.[1]

Many workers interviewed felt that poor workplace organization was a common failing of farmers and an important reason to look for other work. Workers and growers concur in the need to organize work in order to maximize productivity (and, consequently, workers' piecework earnings). Epitomizing this shared value, one outspoken *mayordoma* for a farm labor contractor told us with some indignation of having to threaten a farmer by saying that she was going to have the crew go work at a neighboring farm because he was slowing up her crew by not providing enough boxes to dump cucumbers in. The farmer, with some ill humor, complied and provided more boxes.

This example illustrates the initiative of workers to keep productivity high. At its extreme, this drive can result in workers assuming some control over the disposition of the crop itself, as in the case of sharecropping, common in Michigan in the pickling-cucumber harvest. From the worker's perspective, sharecropping is attractive because each family is assigned its "own" block of cucumbers, decreasing conflicts among pickers and allowing easy work assignments. From the farmer's perspective, sharecropping is attractive because pickers are motivated to maximize the crop value (by hoeing and weeding better and managing the tradeoff of pickle grade and weight skillfully) and because it minimizes cash-flow problems. Sharecropping families arrive early (to cultivate their plots) and have no income during the first part of their stay in Michigan. Thus, they qualify for Aid to Families with Dependent Children and food stamps until the harvest comes in, externalizing a portion of the crop production costs. Miriam Wells's (1987, 1990) work on sharecropping has also shown that it can be a beneficial arrangement for farmworkers, despite its reputation as being exploitative.

While workers benefit by maximizing both social-service revenue and harvest payments through sharecropping, it is not always an entirely benevolent arrangement. As with pinhookers in Florida, sharecropping can simply be disguised wage labor that relieves growers of much responsibility for complying with labor laws or that growers exploit by other means. For example, there were reports that some Michigan farmers sought access to the sharecroppers' revenue stream from social services by charging workers rent for early-season housing although, traditionally, migrant housing has been provided at no cost.

Housing and Recruitment: Family Workers or Lone-Male Workers?

Housing in southwestern Michigan, inadequate to accommodate the peak migrant labor force, assumes a key role in recruitment and labor control. Family workers are particularly responsive to housing opportunities and keep in touch with farmers during the winter regarding the number of workers needed and the timing of workers' arrival. While lone-male migrants also need to find housing, flexibility in housing them is greater, and they tend to be more willing to make do with substandard housing.

Migrant-housing regulations specify a minimum amount of housing footage per person. Such regulations unwittingly discriminate against family migrants, especially those with young children. Widespread violations of the housing-footage requirements occur by mutual agreement among workers and farmers, since highly productive younger couples with children too young to work might occupy "too much" space if the regulations were followed. Most farmers we interviewed were torn between labor strategies based on recruitment of family workers and minimizing housing costs by building housing for lone-male workers. As with sharecropping relationships, the benefit of hiring family workers is labor stability and the potential for them to supervise each other; in this context, farmers can draw on the inherent authority kinship bestows upon older family members to keep younger family members reliable and productive workers (see also Griffith 1987).

The demand for farmworker housing in Michigan reflects, to some degree, the availability of housing in the sending regions. During the freeze of December 1989, many younger Weslaco families attempted to make arrangements to migrate to Michigan before work became available so they could gain access to free housing. This occurred not only in Michigan asparagus but also in Washington asparagus and California grapes. In fact, these arrangements were not very feasible because migrant housing is not certified for occupancy so early in the spring. In addition, early-season crops in Michigan were delayed by cold weather, so early arrivals had virtually no work. Thus, the Texas freeze probably had a significant impact on availability of early-season labor in Michigan, highlighting how sensitive the balance of midwestern labor supply and demand is to factors unrelated to local wage offers, benefits, or working conditions. Similar relationships exist between Florida migrant sending communities and labor demand regions of the North and have been well documented in relationships between Mexico and the United States as well (Goldring 1990; Massey et al. 1987).

In addition to housing, other factors influencing migration to Michigan are mechanization and the changing nature of the market for fresh fruits and vegetables. Before the historic mechanization of cotton and sugar beets (see Chapter 1), families combined work in Minnesota sugar beets or in cherries in the Grand Traverse area of northern Michigan with work in southwestern Michigan. Since the mechanization of sugar beets and cherries, there has been a shift toward a more fragmented farm labor market, with Texas migrants going only to southwestern Michigan or some other midwestern destination. Many migrant flows have assumed this more targeted character, similar to the patterns of directed, highly organized migrations such as those in government-sponsored programs (e.g., the Bracero Program). The exception appears to be the migration pattern of crews of lone males during the latter part of the harvest season. Crews arriving in Michigan apples included those leaving corn detassling in Iowa and others leaving vegetables on the eastern seaboard.

Additionally, the demand for fresh produce is rapidly increasing nationally, and Michigan appears to be involved in very effective marketing efforts. With successful marketing of blueberries in the national market, demand for harvest workers is expected to increase. Blueberries do not require as much skill to pick as other crops, are not as time sensitive, and are considered ideal for less productive workers such as older women and children. Many blueberry producers have no housing, however, so their labor supply depends on successfully recruiting day-haul workers from neighboring towns (including local African Americans) or stemming the exit of family workers from Michigan agriculture. Some Anglos from Appalachia still come north for the blueberry harvest but no longer work in crops that have been ''Latinized.''[2]

Organization of Work and Labor Force Stability

To understand southwestern Michigan agricultural labor demand one must recognize the interplay of three key elements: a workplace based on family organization, the importance of housing in labor recruitment, and heavy grower reliance on family supervision. The case of southwestern Michigan suggests that labor force stability and volatility are two sides of the same coin. Because the production unit is so small, the labor force is potentially quite volatile; on the other hand, there is a strong organizational emphasis on labor stability. The norm is for migrant families to return year after year to the same job, until family circumstances change (e.g., children leave school and perhaps marry; couples are divorced or leave farmwork altogether). To reduce volatility, labor recruitment efforts have focused on stability of employment and inducing ''professional'' migrant families to return to the best-managed farms indefinitely. This illustrates the dynamic connections between family formation and the organization of work.

Three of the four families we interviewed in Weslaco who migrated to Michigan had returned to the same farmer for more than ten years. Those who had changed jobs had adequate knowledge of the labor market and local networks to secure similar permanent ties with other growers. For example, one set of workers who changed their working arrangements did so only after their farm labor contractor retired because of heart trouble. Not surprisingly, southwestern Michigan is the only one of the farm labor markets we studied in which old age was a leading reason for leaving an employer. Again, this contributes to the image of the career migrant farmworker in Texas and Michigan, a career made possible, in part, by both detailed attention to job stability and income stability on the part of farmers in Michigan and low-cost housing in Texas. While the exodus of teenaged children who leave home to go to college, to nonagricultural work, or to be married also increases the likelihood that older workers will cease to migrate, the Bracero-era families are, in some cases, so large and the youngest children born so late that the family can endure a good deal of attrition and still be a viable migrant work group.

Like the relationship between farmers and workers on the Delmarva Peninsula, an almost feudal paternalism links many small Michigan farmers to migrant workers. For example, one Michigan farmer ran a migrant camp widely recognized as one of the best in the area. He and his wife considered the workers and their children ''like family,'' sending Christmas and graduation cards and generally paying attention to the personal lives of workers. Growers who follow this pattern, recognizing the importance of treating workers like people, generally invoked the notion of "dignity" in their response. At the same time, this farmer was known to run a "tight" camp, because he was intolerant of drinking, messiness, and loud noise and made all camp residents sign a contract that outlined a long list of rules and regulations. His neighbors and former workers in Texas and throughout Van Buren and Berrien counties held him up as an exemplary employer. When the camp was closed because of his ill health, he helped his workers find work with neighboring farmers. The neighbors were eager to hire these workers because they constituted a stable, largely self-supervising labor force of family workers.

This sort of individual responsibility was not universal. When some older farmers retired and their children sought to "rationalize" their labor relations and increase productivity, most of their workers quit. Supposedly modern or "rational" forms of work organization often clash with the flexible and some-times seemingly "dysfunctional" arrangements that are crucial to the func-tioning of network recruitment. We interviewed, for example, a sixty-seven-year-old, low-earning worker who was included in a work crew because her nephew had asked her to find some good workers from her neighborhood in Texas. While she could not keep up with the couple she had recruited, she needed to work since she was a widow with no social security. Hiring and housing a marginal worker was, in this case, part of the price the farmer needed to pay to tap into the network. While, ideally, this elderly woman should not have been working at hard labor, the functioning of the network allowed her access to work that she could never have obtained on her own.

The Crop Succession in Southwestern Michigan

The succession of harvest labor demands from early-season crops in May and June, through midseason crops in July and August, to late-season crops in September and October is the basic structural feature of Michigan labor de-mand and has important consequences for wage and benefit offers.

Strawberries are picked from late May through June. Some families com-bine work in the strawberry harvest with work in asparagus.[3] Other families arrive only in time for the strawberry crop. The harvest appears to be domi-nated by family workers. Harvest work in strawberries is usually paid at a rate of $1.60 per carrier, or tray of eight quarts, for processing berries and $2.00 per carrier for fresh-pack berries, making the piece rate $.20 to $.25 a quart. This rate has barely kept up with inflation. There appears to be little variation in piece rates. Growers report that worker productivity varies by as much as

200 percent, but we believe this is an exaggeration. Actual earnings in the strawberry harvest probably vary from $3.00 per hour for marginal workers to $5.00 for excellent workers—a range of "only" 170 percent, with a mean close to the minimum wage. Neither workers nor farmers could say with certainty what workers' hourly earnings actually were, since they fluctuate according to weather. Strawberries are highly climate sensitive. They cannot be picked when it is hot and they mature slowly in the cold. In June 1990, for example, workers experienced serious problems because of short days and lack of work. Several workers were making $10 to $15 a day, in large measure because of short days. The strawberries are usually packed in the field, and workers are paid hourly wages for this task. Furthermore, future wage increases are not likely, given the low profitability of this crop.[4]

Because strawberries are an early crop, strawberry workers' bargaining position in the harvest is almost always weak. Early employment in the North is at a premium for migrants, allowing them to lengthen their total summer employment and giving them access to housing allocated on a first-come, first-served basis.

In summary, how workers respond to wage rates and working conditions in strawberries derives not only from strawberry-harvest conditions and the critical timing of work but also from variables such as family composition (e.g., having children willing to work) and alternative means of obtaining housing to work in midseason crops.

Pickles are the leading midseason crop in southwestern Michigan, usually harvested from early July through the end of August, or mid September, depending on the weather. As is common with processed-fruit-and-vegetable production throughout the United States (Commission on Agricultural Workers 1993a:35), the pickling-cucumber market is dominated by two large, corporate food-processing firms. Only one local firm brines and markets its own pickles. Pickle cucumbers are grown in combination with other crops (e.g., strawberries, apples) as a midseason crop, but several family corporations specialize in large pickle operations of around eight hundred acres each.

Because pickles are graded, it is very important for there to be an uninterrupted supply of labor since the pickles rapidly become oversized. A standard approach in the pickle harvest is to pick through the field or plot over a cycle of three days so that each vine will be harvested once every three days. Some of the large, specialized farms plant half of producing acreage to mature slightly ahead of the other half to smooth demand for harvest labor.

We noted earlier that pickling cucumbers are often produced under sharecropping arrangements. Sharecropping lends itself particularly well to fairly large family units, typically a couple with two or three teenaged children who work with them. A typical sharecropping plot is about five acres, a ratio of about one worker per one or two acres. Growers view this organization of work as desirable because it makes a work unit, the family, responsible for the quality of harvest work. By contrast, harvest work driven purely by piece-work rates involves a tradeoff between harvest speed and damage to cucumber vines (which reduces yield). Sharecropping also provides an incentive to work hard at the hourly task of hoeing.

The standard piece-rate wage for pickles in 1990 was $.50 per bucket ($1.00 per bushel). Almost all of the wage rates fall in the $.45 to $.55 per bucket range. In the case of sharecropping, the sharecropper is given 50 per-cent of the price of the crop. In the large pickle-producing operations, it is common for wives and family members to sort and pack pickles, being paid an hourly rate, usually $4.00 per hour. Although physically demanding, earn-ings from picking cucumbers can be quite good, with extremely productive workers making up to $8.00 per hour and the poorest workers earning mini-mum wage.

Large pickle-farming operations cannot recruit workers the same way oper-ators of small farms do. Network labor recruitment reaches an upper limit of twenty or thirty workers as the lead "recruiter" exhausts the pool of willing family members. The two main alternatives or supplements to network recruit-ment are use of farm labor contractors and grower-coordinated movement of a labor force via a "migrant itinerary" of one or more crop production loca-tions. Typical of the farm labor contractor approach is the strategy of one pickle farm, growing eight hundred acres of pickle cucumbers. Some workers, recruited through extended family networks, have worked for the farm for many years (in one case for three generations). This set of extended family networks is supplemented by three farm labor contractors, two who bring crews from Texas and one who brings a crew from Florida. The crews include some extended family networks but, essentially, have aggregated several dif-ferent family networks into one ad hoc group of workers. Thus, approximately 70 to 80 percent of the peak-season labor force consists of crews of forty to sixty persons each, and the balance are directly hired workers from Bracero-era networks. While the composition of each crew changes over the years, the farm labor contractors have had very long relationships with the farm, working for it for somewhere between twenty and thirty years. This strategy reflects the core and peripheral workers typical of the farm labor market.

An alternative labor strategy is the one used by another pickle farm, which farms eight hundred acres of pickle cucumbers in southwestern Michigan and a similar acreage in central Missouri. A staggered harvest schedule permits some of the 350 to 450 migrant workers to move from the first pickle harvest in Missouri in June to the Michigan harvest, and then return to a second harvest in Missouri. The manager estimates that as many as 150 workers (about 40 percent of his labor force) rotate between the two farms. This extended "migrant itinerary" provides migrant employees with an unusually long and stable amount of employment, making work at this particular pickle farm attractive, despite average wages and housing.[5]

Another large producer coordinates its Michigan pickle harvest with citrus and strawberry work in Florida. Although this pickle farm's housing is among the worst in the area, it experiences little difficulty in recruiting workers. The workers we interviewed, who were lone males from Guanajuato and Sinaloa currently living in Florida, were pleased with the employment stability this arrangement afforded them.

Sharecropping has received regulatory attention because it may be a means to circumvent labor laws, especially minimum-wage standards. However, a Seventh Circuit Court of Appeals decision has held that sharecropping can be a bona fide contractual relationship (if a written contract is prepared), removing from the employer responsibility for unemployment insurance and workers' compensation. Thus, sharecropping "saves" farmers around 15 percent in fringe benefits for workers. Because sharecropper families experience such economic hardships in the month or two they cultivate plots before the crop comes in, some farmers provide them with loans to make the arrangement more attractive. Support for sharecropping is so strong among both farmers and migrant families that the Farm Labor Organizing Committee even allowed it as a payment means in a three-year contract with Vlasic. The benefits and entrepreneurial nature of sharecropping have been documented by Miriam Wells (1987, 1990) in California and the Midwest. Wells argues that the two primary models of sharecropping relations—complementary and coercive—characterize different regions, crops, and periods in U.S. agriculture.

Mechanical harvesting of cucumbers is technologically possible, but its use has fluctuated over the past decade because of several factors. At its peak, an estimated 60 percent of the crop was harvested mechanically, but this has dropped to less than 35 percent today. Mechanical harvesting results in lower quality and yield (a 55 percent reduction) as well as high capital-investment costs (about $150,000), which must be balanced against the lower operating (harvest labor) costs (a reduction of 90 percent). Problems of mechanical harvesting include damage to the cucumber pickles, dirt, and incomplete picking of small pickles. These disadvantages would appear to have doomed the technology, yet it has been retained as an option to counter efforts to unionize pickle workers, a threat that has had an unduly high political profile in the area. For the foreseeable future, it is likely that hand harvesting of cucumbers will prevail.

Other important midseason crops include peaches, tomatoes, and blueberries. Blueberries and tomatoes are produced on specialized farms. Tomato harvest work is paid by piece rate. There are two separate rates, one for pink (immature) tomatoes and one for red (ripe) tomatoes for processing. As with cucumbers, the piece-rate wages for tomatoes allow highly productive workers to earn $6.00 to $9.00 per hour. Several growers specialize in tomato production; but the market has been erratic because of competition with Ohio and Indiana farmers. There was a good deal of negative sentiment about the difficulties of contracting with the large processing companies who make the market for processing tomatoes. Other fresh vegetables such as broccoli and peppers are also grown, but none is particularly prominent, and on the eastern edge of the study region grapes are grown, but without high labor demands.

Blueberries are concentrated in southern Allegan County. The blueberry labor force is unique in that it includes ''drive-in'' workers who are Anglo or African American. Most workers earn only the minimum wage for working in blueberries, and while it is possible to make as much as $6.00 per hour, blueberry work is not highly favored by migrant workers. The peak season is August, but the harvest continues until the first frost. Because blueberry acreage is increasing, housing is recognized as a problem.

Apple plantings are extensive in southwestern Michigan, although the heart of apple production lies about one hundred miles to the north. The apple harvest generally lasts about six weeks, beginning in late August or early September and ending in early to mid-October. Some early varieties ripen in August. These varieties compete more for labor with other crops than the late varieties do, but labor supply problems are associated with late-harvest apples also. If the weather delays the harvest, there may be a gap between the end of the cucumber harvest and the beginning of the apple harvest, and workers may then return to their home bases. New plantings of apples will be primarily semidwarf varieties, leading to a decrease in demand for labor. Currently, however, the area is still dominated by large, older trees.

As is common in late-season crops across the country, an important aspect of labor demand in apples is to have enough to finish the harvest. Because the area relies so extensively on Texas migrant family workers, teenagers' school needs present a problem for adequate labor supply. Families combined teenagers' dual involvement in school and farmwork in a number of ways. Some teenagers returned to Texas, to live with relatives who were not staying for apples. One teenager was even sent home to Texas by plane to begin school again. These arrangements, of course, depend on a social infrastructure of friends and kin in Texas who can care for children while the parents remain in Michigan. Others stayed with their parents, attending night school in Michigan.

Harvest costs appear to make up a much smaller proportion of total production costs in apples than in any of the other labor-intensive crops in the area. Apple picking is very strenuous work, but it is done by both men and women. It is also relatively dangerous, with a workers' compensation rate ($9.24 per $100) about three times higher than the rate for vegetable workers. During 1989 and 1990, the piece rates for apple picking were mostly in the range of $9.00 to $10.00 per eighteen-bushel box. At this rate, good workers could earn about $7.00 per hour. Marginal workers earned around minimum wage. Bonuses ranged from $1.00 to $1.50 per box for completing the harvest, meaning that workers who did not complete the harvest could earn only 85 to 90 percent of the $10.00-a-box rate. There are numerous reports of exploitation based on the bonus system, all revolving around schemes to avoid paying out the end-of-harvest bonus to workers. Reports included accounts of workers harassed so they would leave early and arbitrary changes in the date given as ''the end of the harvest.''

Because of the need for quality picking in some varieties of apples, farmers with these varieties paid a good deal above the standard piece rate. One retail sales farmer (whose labor strategy was explicitly focused on paying premium wages to recruit and keep experienced, high-quality workers) paid $13.00 per box for fresh-pack apples; another paid $12.00 per box to slow pickers down in early, easily bruised varieties such as McIntosh. The same farmer paid only $6.00 per box for juice apples.[6]

The farm labor contractor we interviewed who worked extensively in apples was based in Michigan and engaged in a great deal of in-stream worker recruitment, tapping into an eclectic range of networks—Texans from Houston, Michoacán workers recruited out of Chicago, San Luis Potosí workers, Jalisco workers, and recently immigrated SAWs from Immokalee, Fort Myers, and Ruskin in Florida. The end result of this recruiting strategy was a crew composed almost entirely of lone-male workers. By contrast, few of the lone-male cucumber workers stayed for apples. The combined factors of late-season harvest, relative unattractiveness to family workers, working in the cold, and the risk of injury in ladder work are likely to make apples an indicator crop, showing the first signs of farm labor shortages. At the time of our visit to Michigan in early September, there were some spot shortages that were being filled with workers arriving in the area after finishing corn detasseling. On the other hand, one of the large apple farmers we talked to had an extraordinarily stable traditional network of workers based in Brownsville, Texas. Workers in this network constantly recruited extended family members from the Tamaulipas side of the Rio Grande. All in all, the apple-harvest labor force is a great deal more varied than that of any of the other crops.

Migrant Housing

The licensed migrant camp capacity for the study area of southwestern Michigan is about nine thousand, a capacity representing about half of the estimated migrant population working in the area. Unlicensed housing (less than five persons occupancy) may provide a small amount of additional capacity. Yet it is difficult to estimate the exact migrant-housing shortfall since it is not clear what proportion of the twenty thousand migrants estimated to work in the area are actually present during the August peak season, how reliable the estimates made by state workers are, what the mix of lone-male worker and family workers is, or to what extent the shortfall is made up by families sharing overcrowded housing. Despite these uncertainties, the housing shortfall is serious, and housing tends to be filled well beyond licensed capacity. Housing thus becomes an instrument of labor control, eclipsing other characteristics of job offers.

The shortage of housing, coupled with state regulations requiring one hundred square feet of living space per person, generates disincentives toward hiring families with young children. The cost of housing a couple with two young children is double the cost of housing four single workers. In screening prospective workers, farmers estimate the "worker yield" for any given family unit, as in the days when New England mills advertised for family workers (Gordon, Edwards, and Reich 1982; Lamphere 1987). Older couples whose children are teenagers represent a very different situation since the "worker yield" is very high. Another problem related to housing regulations and family workers is that the available units may not fit the family unit. This problem poses a serious constraint, for example, on job service efforts to find housing for job applicants in cases where prospective and qualified workers have "too many" children. When a family judged to be stable and hardworking can almost fit into a unit legally, they are usually shoehorned into the housing.

Nevertheless, the overall result of housing shortages and minimum-space requirements for migrant housing is to favor lone-male workers, most of whom are Mexico-based migrants. The few young, Texas-based families who have decided to follow their families' footsteps into migrant labor will, inevitably, be shoved out of the labor market in the near future or, at best, be confined to competing in the "premium" sector of the farm labor market where farmers are willing to trade off higher housing-related labor costs for worker stability and productivity.

Almost all migrant workers and their families live in privately owned camps operated by farmers for whom they work or a farm labor contractor who is "given" the camp to operate for the farmer. Particularly favored workers or farm labor contractors live in detached houses owned by the farmer. The discrepancy between housing for the general workforce and housing for preferred workers reflects a bifurcation within many firms' workforces between core and marginal workers. Core workers are those whom farmers encourage to return year after year, regarding them as fictive kin, while marginal workers are those who attach themselves to the operation under less binding terms. Favored workers' houses are not, technically, licensed camps, since they house fewer than five persons.

The housing units in migrant camps consist of shacks, houses, or used trailers. The shacks are mostly quite old, built in the 1960s for Bracero-era immigrants. The houses may well be older but are sometimes in better condition. Overall, the housing stock is dilapidated. Over the past five years (1985–90), about 30 percent of southwestern Michigan's migrant camps have had some rehabilitation of housing or new construction, but, this pace of improvement is inadequate. Another third of the housing is substandard.

The "typical" migrant camp houses forty to fifty persons, but camps vary tremendously in size. Small camps of three or four units are common. These small camps seem to function especially well since they often consist of groups of an extended family or neighbors and since the camp population (fifteen to twenty persons) is manageable. The typical, or medium-sized, camp has ten to fifteen trailers or shacks (fifty to sixty persons), communal showers, and some sort of recreation area. By the time a camp reaches this size, it is virtually inevitable that the surroundings begin to decay, with packed soil, puddled water, a high noise level, and a fairly constant stream of cars coming and going. The largest of the camps (with up to two hundred residents) are similar to military settlements, consisting of row upon row of shacks or trailers. These large camps are more likely to be dominated by lone males, since the farmers with this size operation have already exceeded the scope of family networks. Again, this illustrates the dynamic that exists between social structure and infrastructure (housing and acreage) in the farm labor market. Large camps vary in quality of housing from good to appalling bad. Of the six camps in the area licensed for over one hundred persons, two were in excellent shape and one was widely acknowledged to be the worst in Van Buren County.

In recent years, secondhand trailers have become popular as replacement housing for decaying shacks. The trailers tend to be better insulated than older houses or shacks and often have standard plumbing, but they get terribly hot during the day, and families find them more inconvenient to live in than do lone males. They also decay rapidly. Rain water puddles on their flat roofs and drips into the insulation, causing the wall veneer to balloon and fall apart. Trailers also cost more than standard construction to repair. Despite this, the initial capital investment in purchasing a trailer is $2,000 to $3,000, or approximately $400 to $500 per worker housed.

With government subsidies, growers may provide more durable and long-lasting housing than this. An example was a small camp consisting of four motel-style attached family units built in 1989 by a farmer, who, after years of frustration with "drive-in" workers, decided to build his own migrant housing. This was considered a model of new construction by the state housing technician. The units had standard plumbing, including a bathroom with shower. They were small but extremely well designed, providing housing arrangements somewhat better than a medium-priced motel. The farmer had cut costs by buying used windows and by modifying plans developed by the cooperative extension service. His construction cost was about $6,000 per unit, with a cost-match of $2,000 by the state migrant housing authority, his net cost was $4,000 per unit.

While these costs may seem a reasonable business expense, many growers continue to save money by allowing housing to deteriorate to substandard levels. Clearly, farmers' reluctance to invest in construction or in rehabilitation of dilapidated housing insures profits by favoring undercapitalized operations. One large farming operation runs one of the most flagrantly dilapidated camps, consisting of two rows of shacks with hanging doors, few windows, and hard-packed mud yards and parking spaces, housing over 150 workers. We were informed that the firm had a five-year plan to invest over $300,000 in replacing the shacks with trailers, but this is not a major expenditure for a corporation with a payroll of at least $50,000 a week. Another medium-sized camp, some of whose houses are owned by the same large firm and others by its leading competitors, regularly witnesses standing water and bins of reeking garbage, their odors permeating the camp. Finally, another of the growers in the area was convicted in the summer of 1990 of housing violations stemming from 1985 conditions. The judgment details a long history of substandard housing conditions at several different camps for the ten years prior to 1985. Five years after the case, we observed housing conditions in two of the camps in question that, if not technically in violation of the law, certainly violated the spirit of the law, which was intended to secure clean, "decent" housing for migrants.

Michigan's migrant-housing law and associated regulations are fairly thoughtful and progressive yet include an unfortunate loophole (Sec. 12414) that dilutes all housing regulation. The loophole provides for issuance of "temporary" licenses for camp operation pending correction of violations discovered in the initial preseason inspection. Because of housing inspectors' workload, many camps that were cited for violations were not reinspected to determine compliance before the season ended. Thus, "temporary" licensing allows continuing violations, undercutting other program incentives (the housing-rehabilitation and construction grants program) that might move the agricultural community toward wholesale migrant housing rehabilitation and construction. Several farmers noted with bitterness the unfairness of investing in housing while neighbors easily ignored housing laws.

The broad range of housing styles and conditions available to southwestern Michigan's migrant workers is common in any rural setting that imports large numbers of migrant farmworkers. On one hand, decent housing can be provided to workers, and upgrading housing is a primary concern of many farmers. On the other hand, the largest farming operations in the area, rather than providing leadership in achieving improved industry housing standards, provide compelling evidence of corporate irresponsibility. Michigan's migrant-housing regulations appear to have failed both practically and politically to avoid the pitfalls of "OSHA-type" regulation—the promulgation of detailed technical standards that are difficult to enforce. The level of technical detail in the law (e.g., one linear foot of closet space per child under 12) has led to bitter hostility on the part of all farmers, both those who comply with the regulations and those who do not, while, at the same time, highly visible footdraggers continue to operate with impunity.

Michigan's migrant-housing law provides a "carrot-and-stick" approach to migrant housing, entrusting the Department of Public Health with authority to enforce regulations and provide incentives to improve migrant housing. While the enforcement situation is depressing (but not atypical), the migrant-housing grant program represents a promising initiative. The rehabilitation and construction grants program provides state matching funds for 50 percent of the cost of rehabilitating existing migrant housing or building new housing.

Each project is capped at $10,000, but farmers can, in principle, be funded for one project per year for successive years. The housing staff for Region I (corresponding closely to our study area) estimated that about five hundred housing units had been rehabilitated since 1985. There is, however, a waiting list of fifteen hundred units in Region I (which includes about half of the state's migrant housing), since the grant program is funded at only $400,000 a year for the entire state. The program's popularity stems, in part, from streamlined grant compliance procedures (submission of auditable accounting of construction/rehabilitation expenditures) and from providing a means for housing staff and farmers to work together to meet regulatory standards. Housing staff estimated that the actual leverage exerted by the state funds was in the order of 2.30 private dollars for every 1.00 dollar of public-sector grant support, although funding up to a one-to-one match is technically feasible. The program design and implementation deserves national attention, but the low level of funding severely limits the program's ability to stimulate private-sector investment in migrant housing.

Sunrise Apartments, outside Keeler, is the only public migrant camp in the area. It contains twenty low-income rental units, half of which are two-bedroom, the other half of which are three-bedroom units. It is operated by a community-based, nonprofit organization governed by a coalition of farmers, civic leaders, and migrant advocates. The motel-style unit is well designed, well managed, and widely respected as a model project. Unfortunately, with a housing capacity of 140 persons, the project meets less than 1 percent of total migrant housing needs for the area. The group is attempting to move forward with another project, but the process is slow and frustrating.

The availability of public housing for migrant workers has important practical and policy implications for the southwestern Michigan labor market, since workers who live in public housing are not tied to a single farmer. A substantial public-housing capacity would improve competition within the labor market, since farmers would have to bid for workers who were unfettered by obligations arising from housing arrangements. It is unlikely that these dynamic effects on wage rates will occur, given current attitudes regarding public-sector spending.

The Role of Farm Labor Contractors in Southwestern Michigan

Farm labor contractors play an important role in the southwestern Michigan by providing labor regularly to some of the largest producers and providing workers to meet spot labor shortages for other farmers. Farm labor contractors supply labor on the basis of a markup on standard piecework wages paid to workers. The markups were low, in the 10 to 15 percent range. Several farmers we interviewed were adamant about paying workers directly because they felt that otherwise farm labor contractors would take cuts from the workers' pay.

The farm labor contractors we interviewed specialized in one type of crop (e.g., row crops or tree fruit) for practical reasons. In each case, the farm labor contractors had a "main" farmer/client they worked for who provided the bulk of the work for them and their crew. The tree-fruit farm labor contractor said his workers do not like "stoop labor," while the row-crop farm labor contractor said her workers do not like to work on ladders. This stereotyping reflects, in part, differing recruitment emphases: the tree-fruit supervisor used mainly lone-male workers, while the row-crop supervisor used mainly family workers. While they specialize in crops, farm labor contractors sometimes actively attempted to secure fill-in work in other crops for their workers during slow periods or, at least, "allowed" their workers to work in another crop (e.g., blueberries during a lull in July before cucumbers). The least experienced farm labor contractors needed to rely on the job service at times to find work for their crews.

To be a farm labor contractor, it is necessary to have one or several migrant camps to house one's crew or crews. Two of the farm labor contractors we knew of had one camp only, two had two camps, and one had four camps. Getting a good camp is a key recruiting tool. Farm labor contractors appear to be involved in a great deal of mediation between farmers and workers, mediation related to housing, pressuring farmers to make repairs (but not always succeeding) and trying to convince workers to resign themselves to shortcomings of the housing (but not always succeeding). This reflects the ambiguous position of farm labor contractors—on growers' sides for some issues and workers' sides for others.

Since the camps are privately owned, they are supplied by the "main" farmer. One farm labor contractor, a bright and aggressive businessman, was exploring the possibility of buying land and building his own migrant camp. Farm labor contractors are responsible for living conditions at their camps, although repair work is done by maintenance men directly employed by the farmer. Not surprisingly, farm labor contractors were impatient at the slowness of the farmers' maintenance people and self-righteous in complaining about vandalism.

Beyond housing, farm labor contractors' primary responsibilities are recruitment and supervision. We interviewed farm labor contractors based in

Florida, Texas, and in southwestern Michigan. The majority of farm labor contractors we heard of were, however, from the lower Rio Grande Valley. The local farm labor contractor we interviewed was originally from Weslaco and had settled in Michigan with his family in the early 1970s. Each of the farm labor contractors interviewed had somewhat different recruitment strategies and management styles. Each was responsible for about 100 workers (perhaps 125 to 150 persons, including dependents). The farm labor contractors were energetic and aggressive entrepreneurs, managing a constant barrage of problems and working very long hours. They were bright and knew their business well. Since they were paid a markup on each crew member's piecework-based wages, they were very interested in maximizing workers' productivity. Their earnings were in the order of $20,000 to $50,000 per season, although the higher-earning farm labor contractors' income included the work of family members.

Most farm labor contractors began as farmworkers themselves and worked their way up (see also Griffith and Camposeco 1993). A typical example was a successful farm labor contractor who got into farmwork because another *troquero* (farm labor contractor) singled him out to be an assistant farm labor contractor and more or less apprenticed him, giving him increasing responsibility over the years. He, in turn, apprenticed his sister, who became a farm labor contractor on her own several years back.

The only female farm labor contractor we interviewed began working as a farm labor contractor with her three brothers, working in beets in the late 1960s, then in corn detasseling, and then in oranges. She first came to Michigan with another farm labor contractor who was not part of her family. The farm labor contractors we interviewed all had a great deal of experience, having been farm labor contractors for ten to fifteen years. Other well-known local farm labor contractors had worked for twenty to thirty years in their positions.

Like family farming, farm labor contracting is a family occupation; one farm labor contractor we interviewed employed her husband and son as her main lieutenants; another relied on his wife; and a third outfit consisted of a father and son. Several other farm labor contractors we were told about were brothers. One of the problems identified by farm worker advocates is that farm labor contractors convicted of violations under MSPA (Migrant and Seasonal Agricultural Workers Protection Act) often turn their businesses over to spouses, children, or siblings. A similar practice involves the nominal ownership by farm labor contractors' family members of labor camps in the farm labor supply communities. Thus the contractors are participating in the process associated with housing workers without exposing themselves to MSPA regulations.

In Michigan, farm labor contractors, like farmers, feel a strong sense of responsibility for their workers. While this sense of responsibility is not entirely altruistic, it is a strongly expressed sentiment. As one farm labor contractor put it, *"Yo trato bien a la gente porque yo sin gente, no soy nadie"* (I treat people well, because, without people, I'm no one). However, this concern extends only to good workers. A good worker is one who likes to work hard ten hours a day and who "pays attention," not one who "drags their legs," who is lazy. Good workers are treated well; "lazy" or troublesome workers are not. Good workers are given the most stable jobs; "bad" workers are given the worst jobs.

The farm labor contractors from Texas and Florida give crew members loans for travel advances, car repairs, and for emergencies. Not surprisingly (given the cash outflow of "helping out" even five to ten families), they are not enthusiastic about this role but consider it to come with the turf, because even the best workers are likely to be in a weak financial condition when it is time to migrate north.

An important consequence of MSPA, in Michigan and elsewhere, is that its success in mandating insurance coverage for farm labor contractors has put all of them out of the transportation business or has driven them underground. All farm labor contractors we interviewed were adamant that the insurance costs were too high so they did not, themselves, transport workers to Michigan. Instead, they led a caravan of workers with cars. Having to rely on workers with their own transportation reduces a farm labor contractor's power over the crew members' mobility.

The farm labor contractors we interviewed, while understanding the functioning of extended family networks and operating extensively within the networks of their home-base communities, did not rely heavily on network recruitment. This is because the strong allegiances within family networks can threaten their own control and ability to manage workers. Both the Texas and Florida farm labor contractors said that the main way they hired people was through people coming by their houses asking for work. While some family groups may work with a farm labor contractor for ten to fifteen years, worker turnover does not particularly bother farm labor contractors, since they are well placed to recruit more workers from chronically underemployed communities. While farmers might be tempted to negotiate with potential workers from a position of weakness because of worries about possible labor shortages, farm labor contractors were supremely self-confident that they could get more workers if needed. Farm labor contractors' prominence in their home-towns allows them to screen workers fairly effectively, hiring the most promising and productive.

The single Michigan-based farm labor contractor we encountered recruited entirely in-stream and specialized in hiring more recently immigrated Mexican workers. He preferred to hire lone-male workers, feeling that they worked harder, were easier to house, and complained less. He did not keep in touch with workers over the winter.

We also observed several less experienced farm labor contractors with crews made up entirely of recent immigrants. These farm labor contractors contacted the job service for workers because they had not been able to line up enough on their own. The experienced farm labor contractors we interviewed complained some about defecting assistants who felt they "knew it all" and decided to go into the farm labor contractor business on their own.[7] Given the importance of connections with farmers in securing access to housing, and given the general distrust farmers have for farm labor contractors, new farm labor contractors who are not sponsored by a relative have a difficult time making the step up from leading a crew of ten to fifteen workers into large-scale labor contracting.

Services to Migrants

Michigan has a well-developed network of human-service agencies providing support for migrant farmworkers. Important services in the southwestern Michigan area address health care, education, legal assistance, advocacy, employment assistance, and general assistance (e.g., Aid to Families with Dependent Children).[8] These services bear directly on labor market issues. From the perspective of family workers, child-care educational services are crucial because they allow adults and teenagers to be free of child-care responsibilities and to work full-time. Clinics providing good primary health care are well located and accessible. About one-quarter of the migrant population appears to use food stamps.

The service agencies are well adapted to the seasonal patterns of migration. Most hire bilingual staff on a seasonal basis. Often, the seasonal workers hired to work with migrants are former or current migrants. Different agency staff's knowledge of the area and ability to relate to farmworkers varied substantially, however, and we observed examples of both excellent and very bad service delivery.

Michigan's migrant services are coordinated both at the local level and statewide. The three regional migrant-resource council meetings we observed exchanged a great deal of information oriented toward interagency problem solving rather than the pro forma "show and tell" that characterizes many human-service coordinating groups' activity. The effectiveness of the councils seems to stem from the fact that advocates, service agencies, and regulatory agencies are all represented. Thus, immediate, individual problems surfaced easily, and the technical expertise to resolve questions was easily at hand.

The councils are committed to conflict resolution and long-range planning. The director of the Michigan Office of Migrant Resources is very active and attends most of the regional meetings, promoting interagency linkages; the result is an unusually "seamless" information and referral network. The Michigan Migrant Legal Action Project has a clear set of priorities, avoids adversarial stances outside of court, and appears to have a high degree of success in negotiating and informally lobbying for improvements in housing and working conditions. Meanwhile, it has also won several important legal decisions on behalf of farmworkers. All in all, the Michigan service-delivery system appears to be a model one.

The migrant-services network is an important structural element in meeting labor market demand because it maximizes the labor force participation of an existing pool of migrant labor by providing services that allow them to accept low-paying jobs. In this sense, of course, it operates as a subsidy to growers. Such a subsidy, however, is not without hidden costs to growers as well, since the migrant-services network also provides an efficient and well-organized forum for addressing workers' rights issues. For example, the night school for migrant teenagers allows about three hundred teenage workers to remain in Michigan rather than return to Texas at the beginning of the school year. The "yield" of additional labor for the apple harvest generated by this service amounts to somewhere around one hundred thousand worker-hours in September and October. While beneficial in the short term to growers, it is likely that the increased education of family members will contribute to their leaving farmwork or questioning practices within farmwork.

Conclusion

Southwestern Michigan is a labor market with a relatively stable migrant labor force. Provision of housing, recruitment through extended-family networks, serious efforts to smooth the labor demand curve, and effective delivery of a wide range of useful services have allowed most employers to develop a productive workforce with minimum turnover. What turnover there is consists mainly of ''natural'' background turnover as teenagers complete school, marry, and move into new careers, and as older workers retire to Texas. Yet the stability of the labor force is now threatened by deteriorating migrant-housing stock and slow efforts at rehabilitation. The labor problems that do exist, predictably, are concentrated among the poor labor managers who pay lower wages and have the worst working conditions.

As is common throughout the United States, Michigan's pool of migrant family workers is dwindling (Commission on Agricultural Workers 1993a). The children and grandchildren of the Braceros who emigrated from Mexico to Texas in 1950–70 are less and less likely to continue in farmwork. Rising housing costs in the lower Rio Grande Valley and dwindling amounts of winter work there make the specialized adaptation of Texan migrants increasingly unfeasible. The mechanization of some northern harvest crops such as cherries and sugar beets and a succession of devastating freezes have decreased the amount of work available in the typical migrant itinerary. The 1988 midwestern drought also squeezed some migrant families out of farmwork for good. Slow improvements in the dropout rate in the Texas secondary school system, where traditionally 80 to 90 percent of migrant high school students did not graduate, slowly diminishes the pool of young adults who become migrant farmworkers because their access to other occupations is blocked. At the same time, the increasing availability of immigrant workers makes it economically unattractive for many farmers to build family housing when housing for lone males is so much cheaper.

Given current conditions, we expect the southwestern Michigan (and the entire midwestern) labor market to be increasingly dominated by lone-male migrants from Mexico. In the short run, the Michigan labor market may become stratified into ''premium'' jobs filled by U.S.-born and legally authorized family workers and ''casual'' jobs filled by recent, lone-male immigrants. In the long term, however, the main question is not whether there will be a shift to an immigrant labor force but how rapidly this shift will occur.

Chapter 6

Offshore Citizens as a Supply of Farm Labor

El Maní and Sabalos, Mayagüez, Puerto Rico

Of the four labor supply communities in our study, Mayagüez, Puerto Rico, is the most different from the others, primarily because the island's economy and society, as well as specific features of its population, have been more consciously "constructed" by patterns of government expenditure and industry–government partnerships than have those of any of the other communities. This characteristic of Puerto Rico carries over into the ways Puerto Ricans have established communities on the U.S. mainland and have subsequently supplied agricultural and industrial labor markets with workers. Yet in the distinctiveness of the Puerto Rican experience in U.S. agriculture, we can locate many of the principles on which the labor markets of the working poor rest: ethnic succession, the relationship between legal status and workplace discipline, and the influence of housing—especially government-subsidized housing—on labor supplies.

Unlike Mexicans, Guatemalans, Jamaicans, Haitians, Dominicans, and others who migrate from culturally and linguistically distinct regions into the U.S. labor markets, Puerto Ricans do so as U.S. citizens. This legal status grants them free access to the labor market, to social-service agencies, and to generally well established Puerto Rican communities. They remain, however, "second-class citizens," utilized as workers primarily in low-income sectors of the economy, politically members of a commonwealth rather than a state,

151

represented in Congress by a nonvoting representative, not included in federal income taxing, and not allowed to vote in national elections except as residents of states on the mainland (Picó 1986; Borjas and Tienda 1987). Thus, while the terms of their incorporation into the U.S. economy and society—as "Hispanics," "minorities," and culturally distinct people from an "exotic" place—have been similar to new immigrants' experiences, the legal and historical dimensions of their incorporation remain fundamentally different. This has characterized the way they have been utilized as farmworkers throughout the East and Midwest since first becoming citizens.

By nearly all accounts, Puerto Rico's role in U.S. farm labor has been declining steadily since the early 1970s. Once a major exporter of farm labor, a number of factors have contributed to this decline. As will be seen in Chapter 7, however, Puerto Rican workers remain crucial to a variety of agricultural labor processes, occupying key positions on farms as supervisors, foremen, labor recruiters, and cultural and linguisitc information brokers. Nevertheless, statistics on government-sponsored migration from the island to the mainland indicate that Puerto Ricans have been playing a smaller role in U.S. farm labor over the past twenty years, dropping from a peak of 18,884 in 1970 to 5,639 in 1975, 3,580 in 1980, and 2,541 in 1987 (Puerto Rican Departamento de Trabajo 1987). The populations, housing projects, settlement patterns, and economic-development initiatives of the municipality of Mayagüez, on the island's western shore, help explain the central features of this decline, which have been driven by both the supply and the demand sides of the labor market.

Especially since the early 1970s, a variety of economic and cultural changes have taken place in Puerto Rico that, seen together, discourage Puerto Ricans from seeking work in U.S. agriculture. The most important development on the island to have dampened Puerto Rican farm labor migration has been the decline of the plantation system and the concomitant rise in employment in manufacturing, tourism, and service occupations. Fewer Puerto Ricans are coming from agricultural backgrounds and fewer, in particular, suffer from the uneven income and seasonal shifts in employment that once accompanied working in sugarcane, tobacco, coffee, and other tropical agricultural harvests. Fewer Puerto Ricans, therefore, are familiar with farmwork or consider it a viable employment alternative.

Second, accompanying the decline of plantation agriculture were a variety of social programs designed to retrain and reorient individuals whose agricultural jobs were disappearing, to prepare them for future job displacement and to quiet potentially revolutionary unrest coming from the rural areas as sugarcane workers experienced the disintegration of their ways of life (Mintz 1956;

Steward et al. 1956; Buitrago Ortiz 1973). One particularly relevant consequence of the emphasis on social-services solutions to shifting economic trends has been the Puerto Rican government's attention to housing. Two types of subsidized housing schemes—low-income housing projects, *caserios,* and self-help housing, *parcelas*—succeeded in resettling urban and rural populations and further attaching workers to the island in the same way the provision of adequate housing in Immokalee seems to have discouraged long-distance farm labor migration.

Third, Puerto Ricans have become increasingly conscious of their minority status and sensitive to being treated as second-class citizens in the United States, the Caribbean, and the global economy. In terms of the present study, the legal or policy manifestation of these sentiments was the passage of Public Law 87, which prevents active private recruitment of Puerto Ricans by mainland firms (whether agricultural or industrial) without the participation of the local department of labor as well as guarantees of explicit work contracts, terms of employment, and earnings.

Mayagüez in the International Division of Labor

Mayagüez is a municipality of one hundred thousand, dominated by a small central city of approximately eighty-three thousand people on the southwestern coast of Puerto Rico. Composed of mostly rural barrios, or territorial units, the population is concentrated in the coastal barrios of Pueblo (town), Sabalos, and Algarrobo, and the unit east of Pueblo, the barrio of Miradero. Like many Puerto Ricans, the people of Mayagüez trace their identity to the growth of plantation and hacienda agriculture in the nineteenth century, which set the stage for Puerto Ricans to become active participants in an increasingly integrated world economy.

The first settlement was located on the margins of the Yagüez River, close to the shore of Mayagüez Bay, in 1760. Agricultural development in the region was based on the cultivation of sugarcane, coffee, and minor crops. While sugarcane production, aided by slavery, dominated the first half of the nineteenth century, coffee production became dominant in the second half of the nineteenth century due to the expansion of haciendas in the highlands. During this period, protective and repressive laws were passed to force the landless laborers and peasant population to work for the coffee planters. By the end of the nineteenth century, the Mayagüez economy was dominated by coffee and sugarcane cultivation and production (processing), and the city had developed a booming harbor second only to San Juan Harbor in commodity handling and commerce.

Toward the end of the nineteenth century, with the U.S. economy and politics beginning to dominate Puerto Rico, Mayagüez began a new path of social development. Still an important regional harbor and sugarcane and coffee producer, the municipality was located between two large central mills, one in Guanica, to the south, and a second in Coloso, to the north. The United States took advantage of Mayagüez as a centrally located commercial port, and U.S. investors sponsored the growth of formerly artisanal or cottage industry economic activities, such as cigar making and needlework, recruiting a large number of women (adult and children) into the labor force. Mayagüez became one of the key centers for the garment industry in Puerto Rico. The needlework industry's need to profit from lower salaries or piecework payment systems led businessmen to establish the sweatshop system, subcontracting with local shop owners in San Juan and Mayagüez, some of whom were women.

The sweatshop remained the physical context of the "garment" or needlework sector on the southwestern coast, with the main shops in Mayagüez either opening sweatshops or subcontracting piecework to households throughout the region, using word of mouth, newspapers, and radio to offer "jobs." Piecework; labor conditions at the workplace; exploitation of children, women, men, and household labor; and low wagers became the major complaints of a discontented labor force in the 1930s, which led to strikes and boycotts throughout the island. In Mayagüez, labor unrest occurred at the urban sweatshops of the needlework industry, at the Coloso and Guanica central sugarcane mills, and at the Mayagüez harbor (Taller de Formacíon Política 1982, 1988).

Relations between labor and capital stabilized in the 1940s. The decade of transition was tainted by the economic changes of the post–World War Two period, however, and the needlework capital abandoned Mayagüez for Taiwan and the Philippines, in search of lower salaries and lower production costs. At the same time, sugarcane production was on the brink of its demise, rendering much agricultural land idle, and other plots became the setting of the new urban expansion. In keeping with the regional pattern, Mayagüez lost population in the 1950s; nearly four thousand left the municipality, most likely to migrate to the northeastern cities of the United States, when the demise of sugarcane production and the flight of the needlework industry loomed large in the household economy.

From 1940 to 1970, the Puerto Rican economy increased the number of industrial jobs to 103,500 but lost 230,000 jobs in agriculture, service work, and the needlework industry (Pratts 1987:61). In this context, the Common-wealth of Puerto Rico, created in 1952, started its economic development program known as Operation Bootstrap, which oriented the island economy toward industrialization and the expansion of the service sector, driven in part by tax breaks given to corporations based in the continental United States.

The manufacturing sector in Mayagüez, represented by seventy-nine estab-lishments, now accounts for the majority of the municipality's employees (U.S. Census data excludes government employees), with 12,776 employees and the largest payroll, followed by the retail trade and services. Most (7,020 employees) of the labor force in manufacturing is involved in processing food and kindred products, of which seafood processing (e.g., StarKist Tuna) ac-counts for the largest share. Apparel and textiles follow with 4,334 employees. Other industries, including pharmaceuticals and electronics, hire a relatively small number of employees.

Home to a large campus of the University of Puerto Rico, a small campus of a private university, and five other private colleges and technical schools, the city has become, to a large extent, a university town serving nearly fifteen thousand students from the region and a large percentage from other munici-palities on the island, including the San Juan metroplex.

A large floating (migrant) population, a growing industrial-labor popula-tion, and the educational and service employees have stimulated the urban growth of the city into middle-class subdivisions surrounding the urban cen-ter, as well as a number of shopping centers, improved transportation, and modern health, schooling, and communications services.

Compared with the rest of the island, Mayagüez's industrial and economic growth has been slow. While other urban centers and large towns have experi-enced rapid growth of high-tech pharmaceutical and electronic industries and the service sector, Mayagüez has remained tied to the food-processing and garment industries. Notwithstanding, the city has grown in terms of small businesses, services, and as a government regional center serving the popula-tion of the rural barrios and nearby municipalities. It was Mayagüez's reputa-tion as a government center that led us to select it for closer analysis, since the employment service there has been active in farm labor placement.

Although Mayagüez was the municipality chosen for this study, our data collection focused on two settlements recognized by officials of the Puerto Rico Department of Labor as "sending communities" of migrant workers to the United States. These are the public housing of Sabalos (which includes both new and old housing projects—Sabalos Nuevo and Sabalos Viejo, re-spectively), south of the urban area, and the *parcela* El Maní, to the north.

Puerto Rico's high rate of unemployment, long tradition of agricultural work, and pervasive poverty would appear to provide a major supply of potential farmworkers. Yet this has not been the case, either from the *parcelas* or the *caserios*. Although some farm labor recruitment continues, the low levels of participation in farmwork of residents of Sabalos and El Maní conform to our observations that fewer and fewer low-income households are considering farmwork an employment alternative.

The selection of Sabalos Nuevo, Sabalos Viejo, and El Maní for data collection in this study was based on our knowledge of the housing programs discussed above (e.g., *parcelas*), which were designed to relocate and concentrate rural working families in order to provide services and create a target workforce. Our investigations were also based on local information from the Puerto Rico Department of Labor. As in Immokalee and the other supply communities, we were interested primarily in identifying low-wage working populations who were familiar with farmwork, but we encountered very few current farmworkers and only a handful of former farmworkers in each settlement. Thus, our Puerto Rican study focuses primarily on the population of "potential" farmworkers and the social, economic, and cultural factors that make them largely unavailable for work in U.S. agriculture. We supplement this information with data from a life-history project conducted in Puerto Rico from 1987 to 1989.[1]

Housing and Labor Market Behavior in Mayagüez

Both types of housing units, public housing (*residenciales* or *caserios*) and the self-help *parcelas,* are provided by the government to the urban and rural poor. Since the 1930s, the government has supported the construction of low-income homes for the urban poor who live in the slums and shantytowns. In the 1940s, according to the mandates of the Land Law (*Ley de Tierras*), the poor were relocated from those "unhealthy" and "filthy" areas in which they lived, mainly in the coastal areas near the "unproductive" and "smelly" mangrove forests and wetlands that needed to be filled to serve the interest of agriculture and urban expansion. The law was developed mainly to provide landless rural workers with homes and a piece of land to live on and cultivate, or a housing unit in a building (see Steward et al. 1956). García Passalacqua and Heine (1983) outline the history of these housing units and place them in the context of the local political economy.

Haitian women, tomato harvest, Homestead, Florida. © *1982 Ken Light*

Picking tomatoes in Homestead, Florida, 1938

Break in the field, Rio Grande Valley, Texas. © *1979 Ken Light*

Carrot worker in Edinburg, Texas, 1937

Farmworker with 50-pound onion sack (60 cents a sack), Imperial Valley, California.
© *1984 Ken Light*

Puerto Rican sugar cane worker, 1940

Grape picker, Napa Valley, California. © *1984 Ken Light*

Washing up, migrant camp, Hood River, Oregon. © 1980 Ken Light

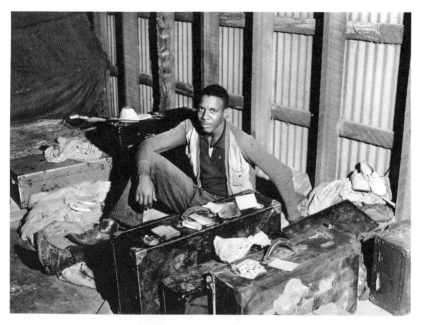

Living quarters of migrant agricultural workers in attic, North Carolina, summer 1938

Florida migrant woman in North Carolina, summer 1938

Farmworkers in their car, green onion field, Salt River Valley, Arizona, 1938

Migrant worker with child, cherry orchard, Sunnyside, Washington. © *1980 Ken Light*

Picking cherries in Berrien County, Michigan, 1937

[The *parcelas* were] a result of the first "wave" of projects designed by the ruling PPD [Popular Democratic party] in the forties and fifties to deal with Puerto Rico's housing problems. Rather than [aiming] at providing needy families with a ready-made apartment or single-family home, the low-cost *parcelas* program proceeded on the basis of the governmental transfer of land parcels to qualifying individuals. The houses were built by the owners through a variety of self-help projects, which relied on some government-provided materials, the work of friends and neighbors and other such inputs. The government provided a minimal infrastructure in the form of roads and utilities but, by and large, the *parcelas* are the product of the residents' own efforts and community work—the outcome of both individual and collective attempts to resolve a densely populated island's serious housing problem. The result is a *Gemeinschaft* of private home owners who, whatever their other problems may be, share pride of a place marked by strong community bonds. (21–22)

In contrast, the *caserios,* similar in appearance to inner-city housing projects on the mainland, represent a

"modern" response to the island's housing problem. With a basic design of two- and three-story walk-ups lumped together in a more or less haphazard fashion, they embody everything that is wrong with Puerto Rico's urban development: fully functional but extremely inhospitable collections of concrete boxes with which few dwellers can identify, let alone be proud of. (22)

Caserio residents, by definition, do not own the public housing they live in, whereas *parceleros* were totally involved in building their houses. Moreover, the common policy of "graduating" residents whose incomes reach certain levels, increasing their rents along with their incomes, has had the perverse effect of increasing the turnover of potential "community pillars." These policies put a premium on staying unemployed; working in cash-only odd jobs, called *chiripas*; or engaging in informal or illegal economic activities (García Passalacqua and Heine 1983: 22).

For the rural landless workers, from which the pool of migrant workers is drawn, the only way to get housing was to move to the urban centers or to San Juan and construct a house in the bordering shantytowns, where they would be close to potential jobs or in a better place from which to migrate to the mainland. Government efforts to eliminate the shantytowns led to the development of public-housing projects at the margins of the San Juan metroplex, where the population remained relatively isolated from job opportunities. The relocation process uprooted and dispersed people accustomed to living in communities and aggravated the problems of adaptation to the new housing, which the people opposed politically (Ramirez 1978; Safa 1984). In contrast, the *parcela* became a partial solution for landless rural workers, as well as for the urban poor who lived in shantytowns.

In Mayagüez since 1950, population pressure has led to the construction of a number of public-housing projects, such as Sabalos, designed to relocate nearly eight thousand urban residents considered to be living in unhealthy urban slums and shantytowns. Although the easy availability of low-cost housing has removed some of the incentive for Puerto Ricans to migrate to the mainland, the institutionalization of island–mainland migration patterns and the existence of well-established Puerto Rican communities in Chicago and the Northeast continue to draw workers to the mainland, some of whom work in agriculture.

Sabalos Nuevo and Sabalos Viejo lie at the fringe of the urban sprawl of Mayagüez, a few meters off the major road. The projects consist of fifty-seven buildings with a total of 440 residential units. Next to the projects is the urban *barriada* (a small group of houses of the poor working classes) called Nadal, which is connected to Sabalos by a pedestrian bridge. Nadal is a small *barriada* of seventy-one houses, highly concentrated and positioned in a haphazard fashion, and connected by narrow and winding roads, which leads municipal observers to describe it as having a "disorganized" housing design. Most houses are one-story units built of wood, hooked up to deteriorating cesspools. There are neither private nor public phones.

The base of the stairway of the pedestrian bridge, along with two bars at the edge of Nadal, is where most migrant workers meet to exchange information and to interact with friends. Drinking plays a major role in their social interaction. As early as 7:30 in the morning, with beers in their hands or small bottles of rum strategically placed (to avoid police detection) on the steps or underneath the stairway, these farmworkers meet at the corner. This corner is a main area for farmworkers' interaction. One of the crew leaders for Sunny Slopes Farms, a South Carolina peach farm, lives in Nadal. This corner provides the informal setting where he meets, informally interviews, and recruits workers into the South Carolina peach orchards. Most of the farmworkers he recruits are from public housing. The recruitment process is simple: once he has identified a group of farmworkers worthy of recommending, he "sends them" to the Departamento de Trabajo (DT) to fill out papers. The DT then forwards these papers to the Glassboro Services Association of New Jersey, which recruits Puerto Rican workers for agricultural operations throughout the eastern United States. In one study (Amendola, Griffith, and Gunter 1993), researchers found that Sunny Slopes Farms had, in line with other agricultural producers along the East Coast, begun shifting from Puerto Rican to Mexican

labor, both in its fields and packing houses. Similar shifts have been documented on Pennsylvania mushroom farms and in the New Jersey nurseries
(see Smith 1992; Garcia 1993; Chapter 7, this volume).

The *caserios* themselves do not have any stores or bars and, therefore,
buying groceries and most other social interaction are done in town or in the
small stores and bars across the road. The *caserios* do have a community
center, a Headstart center, and a basketball court. A recent report by the Census Office of the Municipality of Mayagüez (OCM) shows that the residents
of Sabalos suffer from health problems caused by flooding of a nearby creek
and the sewer, poor building and area maintenance, and drug addiction (including a large number of children sniffing ''thinner''), and the school dropout rate is high. The high incidence of drug addiction has contributed to the
perceived rise in the number of robberies in the *caserios*. In the residents'
view, according to the report, the government responses to their claims is
''too slow.''

To solve these problems and to increase educational and job opportunities,
the government has developed a coordination program office called RED
(Dedicated Network of Resources), which combines several agencies. There
is an office of RED in Sabalos. Information from the OCM also indicated that
unemployment is a pervasive problem in the *caserio*. Of the 103 informants
they interviewed, 86 percent were unemployed. Of course, many of the ''unemployed'' work in the informal sectors of the economy or are placed into
agriculture on the mainland through links between labor intermediaries in
New Jersey and the DT. Thus, out of these come former farmworkers like
Cholo Dominguez:

Currently thirty-seven years old, Dominguez has migrated to the U.S. mainland on and
off over the past two decades, first taking jobs in agriculture and later moving into the
transportation sector in New York City, working as a mechanic for the city's bus service. For each of his jobs in agriculture, unlike most of the farmworkers in today's
labor market, Dominguez secured contracts before leaving the island and fulfilled the
terms of his contracts. He sought farmwork because of a short-term financial crisis,
during a time when he could not find work in the formal or informal sectors of Puerto
Rico's economy at the wages he desired. He stated: ''In Puerto Rico they don't pay
us what we are worth. We can earn more. We have more benefits working with the
Americans.''

Dominguez describes his experience working on farms on the U.S. mainland in
much more favorable terms than many other farmworkers do. At the farm, he enjoyed
his work. He was supervised by American and Italian American bosses, treated well,
and provided with medical attention when he was ill. He was paid $3.45 per hour (in

the early 1970s) and worked with Dominicans, Mexicans, and Cubans, reporting no tensions between these groups. He picked grapes in 1970 in Churchill, Connecticut, and picked apples in 1972 in Glassboro, New Jersey.

Despite his favorable comments about his work, Dominguez moved out of agriculture after the 1972 season. Since 1972 he has worked as a mechanic both in Puerto Rico and in New York, moving back and forth as ties of family and economic crises dictated, mentioning his mother's concern for his welfare as a major reason for his periodic returns to the island and financial reasons for his migration to the mainland.

Dominguez's case highlights some of the key features of Puerto Rican migration to the mainland. First, he had advantages enjoyed by few farmworkers we encountered in the other labor supply communities: contracts that guarantee wages and working conditions, for example; established labor intermediaries that routinely deal with the state (i.e., Glassboro Services); and satisfactory working conditions and labor relations with his bosses. Second, he first migrated at a young age, only seventeen, and moved out of agriculture into the transportation sector before he turned twenty. Third, his migrations between Puerto Rico and the mainland were frequent, performed with relative ease because of his legal status, and as much responses to his family circumstances as to economic survival. All these factors reflect the wider opportunities for Puerto Ricans—as opposed to, say, Mexicans—in the labor markets of the mainland and the informal economies of the island. We cannot emphasize enough the role housing has played in creating an environment where migration and economic behaviors like Dominguez's are possible.

El Maní is a *parcela* with one block bordering the shoreline. Two kilometers north is another *parcela*. Slightly less than a kilometer south of El Maní are the tuna canneries and several garment factories. The ocean lies to the west, and to the east are the wetlands. Adjacent to the southern row of houses of El Maní is a *comunidad de rescate,* a group of nearly twenty-five squatters' houses settled on private land without permits or ownership.

El Maní has nearly 470 *parcelas,* or plots of land, in which there are 916 residential and business units. Houses in the *parcela* are almost all built of wood and cement or cement blocks. Most are one-story units. In contrast to the *caserios,* the *parcela* has a wide array of small stores including bars, cafeterias, a bakery, grocery stores, hardware stores, fish houses, a fish-landing center, and others. El Maní has a large baseball park, a school, and a number of churches of different denominations to serve the population. Like the other *parcelas* around the island, El Maní is a neighborhood of a variety of housing styles built up over long periods of time. While its growth was both encouraged and subsidized by government expenditures, it does not have any of the "public-housing" flavor of Sabalos or the *caserios*. Many of its lots have become family hearths, housing three generations in much the same manner that the *colonias* of Weslaco have become centers of reproduction and social security.

Another feature El Maní shares with the *colonias* of Weslaco is that it provides a secure base from which Puerto Ricans can enter the farm labor force. Combined with legal status, this access to housing gives Puerto Ricans—like Chicano children of Weslaco farmworkers—an increased ability to reject poor job offers in the farm labor market and to protest working conditions or wages once they have been hired.

The State's Role in Farmworker Recruitment

Puerto Ricans are uniquely protected in the farm labor market, as long as they enter farmwork with the help of the state (i.e., the DT). The DT provides placement assistance to prospective Puerto Rican farmworkers, recruiting workers for mainland farms, arranging labor contracts, and discouraging both "walk-ons" of Puerto Ricans onto mainland farms (who are not covered by contracts) and direct recruitment of Puerto Rican farmworkers by mainland growers. Mayagüez hosts a DT district office that services rural and urban neighborhoods throughout the municipality and western portion of the island. The office provides information on available job opportunities on farms, fills out applications, requests the appropriate documents (ID card, health certificate, penal record), and connects the pool of laborers with the locally certified recruiters from the major farm labor recruiting companies and growers, such as the Garden State Association and Glassboro Services. The DT negotiates labor conditions and salaries with these companies and provides information to farmworkers about their rights and obligations as migrant workers. The DT is actively engaged in the promotion of farmwork among the local population, not only referring them to jobs, but also obtaining unemployment benefits for farmworkers once their seasonal work ends.

Despite these efforts, only a fraction of the residents of Sabalos and El Maní utilize DT services. While nearly one fourth (24.6 percent) of the heads of household surveyed had some connection with the DT, only 8.7 percent were actually placed in employment as a result of that contact. Although these figures are low, they are somewhat higher than the figures for the use of the employment service is Weslaco, Parlier, and Immokalee. This reflects the active, though ambitious, public-sector involvement in the recruitment of Puerto Ricans into mainland agriculture.

As noted earlier, the number of workers migrating under the DT contracts reached an all-time high in 1968, when nearly 23,000 farmworkers were placed in mainland agriculture. By 1972, the number had dropped to 11,900 and by 1987 the number had fallen to under 3,000. An important development during this period was the massive transfer of federal funds into the Puerto Rican economy and the expansion of the government, which was on the road to becoming a major employer (see Pratts 1987). Government employment and reliance on transfer payments (welfare) compete with migrant farmwork for the annual schedules of Puerto Ricans.

DT officials believe a host of factors were responsible for the decrease in willingness to migrate. These include poor working conditions in the fields and workers' abandoning field work to move to other rural areas and suburbs to look for other jobs. During this period, the DT was under fire for "allowing Puerto Rican migrants to live and work in 'inhuman' conditions" (Parilla 1973: 6), and, under pressure from farmworkers' organizations, the commonwealth government adopted an aggressive stance toward the farmers. In some ways this new advocacy backfired. Instead of forcing growers to improve working conditions and raise wages, it seems to have resulted in growers' either hiring Puerto Ricans outside of contracts (i.e., walk-ons) or switching from Puerto Rico to Mexico, Haiti, and other sources for their workers. According to the DT's estimates, thousands of laborers migrated without the intervention of DT contracts. A federal circuit court of appeals declared that Law 87 cannot force growers to sign contracts or agreements with the DT unless growers recruit in Puerto Rico; nor does it require them to provide work guarantees to the workers they hire.

Farmers and companies do recruit workers without signing contracts. Enticed by promises of better working conditions, these laborers migrate without the involvement of the DT. Farmers send them plane tickets and provide other incentives, and they maintain close relations with the laborers, relationships that often stand for many years.

The medical examination required to migrate presents another problem with respect to DT recruitment. By law, potential farmworkers must obtain a health certificate from the Migrant Health Program, but an unspecified number do not pass the exam due to illness, incapacitation, alcoholism, or drug abuse. These potential farmworkers often have little choice but to leave the island without the protection of a DT contract.

Events on the mainland as well as in Puerto Rico have contributed to the demise of officially sponsored migration. In the New Jersey case study (Chapter 7), which focuses on nursery industry labor demand, we discuss employers' growing preference for Mexican and Central American workers over Puerto Ricans. At the same time, highly publicized incidents have undermined Puerto Rican farmworkers' interest in mainland farmwork. In 1978, for example, in an attempt to staff H-2A-dominated harvests in West Virginia and Virginia, the U.S. Department of Labor imported Puerto Ricans at the same time the Jamaican H-2A workers arrived. This led to a standoff between the U.S. Department of Labor and local apple producers after growers refused to hire Puerto Rican workers. During the time the Puerto Ricans remained in the apple-growing region, they had to be housed in local Holiday Inns at government expense, were given no work, and were eventually sent back to Puerto Rico. This incident generated cynicism and mistrust among Puerto Rican farmworkers as well as among Department of Labor personnel about officially sponsored "enhanced recruitment."

For 1990, the DT estimated it would place an all-time low of less than two thousand farmworkers. This has been further influenced by the growing supply of more vulnerable, less vocal, and less protected Mexican and other immigrant workers. The dilemma faced by the DT is not unlike the dilemma faced by the entire Interstate Clearance System, where attempts to enforce worker-oriented regulations result in the system being bypassed.

Migration to mainland farms constitutes only one of a set of economic and overall life strategies available to Puerto Rican workers. As in home-base areas on the mainland that have traditionally supplied migrant farmworkers to upstream harvests, increasing levels of education and nonagricultural industrial production in Puerto Rico have contributed to the decreasing interest in migrant farmwork. We noted earlier that Mayagüez is, in many respects, a college town, having had college-educational opportunities since early this century. The campus of the University of Puerto Rico at Mayagüez, founded in 1908 and developed around the federal agricultural experiment station, became an agricultural and mechanical college serving the island, thus providing educational opportunities to the local youth. This campus offered limited opportunities, oriented toward those groups with access, time, and resources for the completion of a high school education. By contrast, the InterAmerican University of San German offered a college education to rural workers, farmers, peasants, and their offspring as long as they could pay for their education in cash or by working in the construction of buildings or running the college farm.

Despite this access, college education remained a possibility for only a few until late in the 1970s, when the availability of Pell Grants allowed most Puerto Ricans, due to their income level, to receive a college education. The supply of money for education stimulated the growth of the handful of private universities on the island, and they increased their size, number of campuses, "regional" colleges, and numbers of students. Other universities, technical colleges, and schools also appeared. With less stringent admission standards than the commonwealth university, college education became a universal possibility, providing opportunities for everyone to move up the social and occupational ladder of Puerto Rican society as well as raising expectations among those who achieved even a small measure of education (see Pratts 1987: 90–93).

In keeping with the emphasis on education, the Mayagüez area has the High School Equivalency Program (HEP) for school dropouts from farmworkers' households. This program provides participants with classes, tutorial services, counseling, and preparation for the high school equivalency test given by the Commonwealth Department of Education. This federally funded program also prepares students to take the College Board Entrance Examination. In the Mayagüez area, the InterAmerican University runs the program, and a high number of HEP graduates enter the university as well as other private universities and technical schools. The paradox of this program in terms of farm labor is that it encourages one member of a household to engage in farmwork so that all other members gain access to the program. Younger members of households, as in Weslaco, are thus less likely to enter the farm labor force during any time of their lives.

Agricultural Work in Western Puerto Rico

Sugarcane cultivation and production had dominated the coastal plain in Puerto Rico since early in the nineteenth century and continued well into this century. When the sugarcane markets collapsed and sugarcane cultivation turned less profitable, land on the coastal plain gave way to industrial development. At the same time, the real-estate market and the construction industry recruited labor from other sectors of the economy, including agriculture.

In the 1960s, the government created the Sugar Cane Corporation to subsidize cultivation, harvest, and processing of sugarcane. The government still subsidizes a large number of sugarcane workers, who remained employed thanks to the massive transfer of funds into a decaying industry. But as the mills slowly closed, a number of agricultural workers were left unemployed.

The demise and decline of the industry and its capacity to absorb labor has been accompanied by an apparent decline in the number of migrant farmworkers. It is plausible to contend that those workers simply left agriculture for other employment opportunities in the service or industrial sector.

Coffee is still an important crop and one that has an urgent need for harvest workers. But finding adequate farm labor even to meet Puerto Rico's local needs is a difficult task for the DT. The DT is even trying to get permits for laborers from the Dominican Republic, or to entice the youth to harvest coffee. But work on U.S. farms competes with local needs, according to a DT official, because of overlapping schedules (see figure).

| FEB MAR APR MAY JUN JUL AUG SEPT OCT NOV DEC JAN |

U.S. farmwork   >>
Coffee (lowlands)   >>>>>>>>>>>>>>>>
Coffee (highlands)   >>>>>>>>>>>>>>>>>>>>
Zafra (sugar cane) >>>>>>>>>>>>>>>>

Figure 6.1 Seasonal Pattern of Puerto Rican Farmworkers

Very few U.S.-bound migrants work in the coffee or sugarcane harvest after their return from the United States, mainly because they would lose their unemployment benefits. Instead, they do *chiripas* in the "informal" economy: they fish, work in construction, help relatives, and do other activities that are not officially accounted for.

In describing the farmworker families of the 1940s, Elena Padilla (1956) mentions that most of them consisted of married men who made great effort and sacrifice, leaving their wives and children back home while migrating seasonally (in Steward et al. 1956). Farmworkers interviewed in Sabalos do not conform to that pattern. The Mayagüez farmworkers we interviewed were men of different ages who were, for the most part, either never married or divorced and who were living with their mothers, siblings, and other relatives, who may include fathers; only a few were married or living with a woman. A portion of them had been married or had children, but consistently they were young men or bachelors who could afford to migrate because they had no family of their own. The following two cases exemplify the differences between former farmworkers, who came from households similar to those described by Padilla, and those we encountered in the field in the late 1980s.

Born in 1918, Roberto Rolón married at the age of sixteen and began a family that eventually grew to nine people, including his wife and seven children, forcing him to undertake a diverse economic strategy that included small-scale, petty-commodity production (fishing), odd jobs, and work on the U.S. mainland and on the island. Thus, Rolón has a long and detailed work history that is divided among mainland and Puerto Rican jobs and *chiripas*. Initially working in the sugarcane fields, from 1938 to 1954 (ages twenty to thirty-six), he was a cane cutter. Beginning in 1954, however, he began working in the United States six months out of every year, first in Michigan, then in Pennsylvania, and later in Connecticut. During this time, he would return to Puerto Rico and spend six months fishing, then the other six months working in U.S. agriculture. Beginning in 1965, he came back to the island for good, landing a job with the public-works department (highway construction) that lasted until 1971. After this he worked for two years in construction in Rio Piedras, securing this job through his brother. Thereafter, with skills he developed in the construction industry, he worked *chiripas* as a mason, whenever asked.

Rolón's occupational history is not atypical for workers of his generation. The transition from Puerto Rican cane cutter to marginal laborer has been documented in a number of studies (e.g., Mintz 1956; Steward et al. 1956; Griffith, Valdés Pizzini, and Johnson 1992). Also, Rolón's ability to secure a construction job in the public sector during the 1960s attests to the importance of public spending in altering migrant pathways. His case differs significantly, however, from that of Luis Angel.

Like Rolón, Luis Angel married young but, as yet, has no children and relies much more heavily on his father and mother than did Rolón. He and his young wife live with Angel's parents and younger brother and sister in a small, half-wooden, half-brick house that has seen recent additions to its living space. While the front room of the house—a kitchen and living room—and one of the bedrooms were built out of brick and concrete, other rooms made of wood have the appearance of being built onto this main structure later. Adding rooms to accommodate additional family members brought into the household through marriage is a common feature of *parcelas* throughout Puerto Rico.

The area surrounding Angel's house also bears the marks of small-scale producer activities. Like Rolón, Angel fishes with his father but also keeps pigs in a small pen behind the house and tends a small garden. The household also receives food stamps.

Angel's work history begins, not like Rolón's in the cane fields of Puerto Rico, but on highway construction, with a job secured through political patronage. He took a vacation in 1987, traveling to the United States to visit a family member and found a job there—through ties to other Puerto Ricans he met—picking tomatoes and cucumbers and weeding around cabbages in New York. He reported enjoying this work but worked only for a month. He thought he might do the same thing again in the future, but he wasn't certain.

While back on the island, he is able to continue working for the highway department even though he has also become extremely active in his father's fishing operation, which was financed by a combination of government loans (following hurricanes Frederick and David) and by an occupational-injury suit filed by his father.

Clearly, Angel's decision to enter the U.S. agricultural workforce did not derive from desperate need. He simply moved into farmwork as a convenient way to make a little money while on vacation. Clearly, too, his behavior is more indicative of the current state of Puerto Ricans' participation in farmwork than Rolón's is.

The Effects of Industrial Development on Farm Labor Supply

Industries providing local employment for low-skilled workers have also had an important impact on the Mayagüez region. The high labor cost of tuna processing in the California plants led the companies to leave that state and look for cheap labor alternatives in the Pacific and in the Caribbean. In 1960, StarKist Caribbean started to operate a processing plant employing three hundred people in Mayagüez, close to El Maní. Twenty years later, the tuna-canning industry was responsible for nearly five thousand jobs, a large payroll, and fringe benefits for employees. Such economic clout impacted the local economy and gave the processing plants a limitless bargaining power with the government and local commercial and industrial interests. These interests cannot tolerate the idea, often expressed by the canneries' management, of the canneries moving to the Dominican Republic or the Pacific due to increasing production costs.

The canneries hire large numbers of unskilled laborers from the area. Increases in job opportunities at the canneries have had the effect of reducing the available pool of farmworkers. Since they now have jobs nearby, they can avoid migrating and facing the harsh living and working conditions of the "concentration camps," as the local farmworkers describe U.S. farm operations. El Maní was considered to be an important source of labor, one of the most prominent in the district. It was difficult to locate "migrants" in El Maní, since most people were working in the tuna-processing plants. Daily and weekly wages reported by Mayagüez respondents are, in fact, higher than those available in most U.S. farmwork. The wage expectations of workers potentially willing to consider farmwork are also quite high, reflecting the influence of prevailing wages in low-skilled work.

Other industrial operations, which include various pharmaceutical plants, garment factories, commercial houses, and the government (which has the fastest employee growth rate on the island), offer opportunities that divert rural workers from continuing in farmwork. Mayagüez also presents broad opportunities for work in the informal sector for street vendors, "helpers" to other workers, and domestic help.

The above discussion suggests, in broad terms, the transformation of a local as well as insular economy in a way that is likely to forever undermine Puerto Rico's status as a labor supply region for U.S. agriculture. Puerto Ricans of the 1990s live in a social and economic environment that is qualitatively different from the environment that once made the island a source of highly preferred farmworkers. Don Taso, the Puerto Rican sugarcane worker made famous in Sidney Mintz's *Workers in the Cane,* has been succeeded by workers who engage in a more multifaceted economic existence that may include farmwork but also—as Luis Angel's case illustrates—includes a range of survival strategies based on government programs and activities in the informal sector of the economy. While Puerto Rico remains a society with persistent high levels of unemployment, underemployment, and various indexes of poverty, specific features of the Puerto Rican social and cultural environments bind families to a "transnational" Puerto Rican community—on the island and the mainland—that has been gradually severing its ties with the U.S. agricultural labor market.

About half of those we interviewed were, when we interviewed them, employed; another 10 to 12 percent had been in the labor force but were unemployed at the time of the interview. While few current migrants were in the sample, 29 percent of those interviewed were former farmworkers. This reflects the fact that Puerto Rico was once a major supplier of agricultural workers to the U.S. mainland and that many of the people living in housing developments such as the *caserios* and the *parcelas* are familiar with individuals who have participated in the farm labor market at one time in their lives. Most commonly, workers we interviewed, if employed, worked in unskilled or semiskilled positions, with 44.7 percent of the heads of households so employed and 22.2 percent of the spouses (N = 117). Around 5 percent of the household heads reported being self-employed, suggesting they work in *chiripas.* An extremely large proportion of both household heads (44.9 percent) and spouses (73.6 percent) reported being unemployed.

Underemployment is also fairly extensive: the average number of hours worked per week was thirty-six. At $35.10, however, the mean daily pay is as high as in the U.S. labor supply communities. Spouses of the heads of household were less well paid, earning an average of $28.66 per day and working a mean of thirty hours per week. They were not likely to migrate to the United States, however, because the farm labor force is dominated by men and because family migration would entail their husbands' losing their employment in Puerto Rico. All in all, 5.5 percent of the jobs held longest by head-of-household respondents were on the U.S. mainland, and 9 percent of the jobs held longest by spouses were on the mainland (since they were more often unemployed on their return to Puerto Rico).

To repeat, slightly more than 5 percent of the respondents fell into the "casual" employment category; at least another 10 percent of the unemployed were also involved in casual labor. Many of these people perform what Puerto Ricans refer to as *chiripas,* which, as noted, may be loosely translated as "odd jobs." *Chiripas* imply more than simple odd jobs, however, calling to mind small-scale, entrepreneurial economic activities such as street vending or crafts production. These generate modest incomes yet contribute to household cash flows in an underground economic context in which earnings are not figured into the formulas that determine amounts of public assistance for the household. Usually these activities involve undervaluing household labor, taking advantage of specialized economic and ecological niches, recycling junked materials, and drawing upon the skills and resources of most or all members of the household (Long and Richardson 1977). An example of this comes from an interview with a teenaged boy cooking and selling tamalelike snacks near a beach on weekends. The snacks were made with pumpkin and a kind of fish larvae that live in the small rivers near Arecibo on the northern coast. The boy said that he and his father fished the larvae out of the rivers with mosquito netting early in the morning while his mother and sisters cooked and mashed the pumpkin paste, later stirring in the fish larvae. They portioned the mixture into individual servings about the size of a hot dog, wrapped them in banana leaves, and stored them in small coolers. Alongside the road approaching the beach, the boy cooked the snacks immediately before selling them, for $1.25 apiece, over a "grill" made from an old barrel and a flat metal sheet. Working only two days a week, the family earned between $200 and $250 a week from this trade.

Besides *chiripas,* access to housing, and a wide variety of public-assistance programs, other factors that undermine farm labor migration to the mainland are qualitative factors about farmwork in relation to other jobs or even unemployment. Comparisons with data from Immokalee, where most of the low-wage labor force performs farmwork, reveal some interesting differences between Puerto Ricans and Immokalee residents regarding benefits and levels of job satisfaction. In Mayagüez, in their longest recent jobs, fully 41.2 percent of the survey respondents were covered by health insurance, 62.1 percent were covered by unemployment insurance, and 66.7 percent were covered by workers' compensation, compared with 22.5 percent, 24.7 percent, and 35.2 percent, respectively, in Immokalee. Mayagüez respondents also expressed higher levels of job satisfaction than did Immokalee residents.

In addition to these differences, Puerto Ricans we interviewed reported liking or disliking jobs for reasons related to quality of supervision or general worker treatment rather than pay more often than did Immokalee workers. This could be construed to suggest a more holistic approach to employment, in contrast to the "target-earning" outlooks of many immigrant workers (Portes and Bach 1985).

The recent work experience of survey respondents supports the observation that fewer Puerto Ricans are entering the agricultural labor force, while more are working in the unskilled service and manufacturing sectors. That many of these jobs are staffed primarily by women (e.g., garments and electronics) may be seen in the higher proportions of *working* spouses who cluster in these kinds of positions.

Conclusion

In many places in this work, we point out that government and informal support systems available to farmworkers constitute a subsidy to growers, allowing large pools of surplus workers to maintain themselves during times of unemployment and underemployment. We cannot claim this observation as our own; indeed, numerous social scientists have observed that low-wage working populations, by means of their own resources along with government programs, are able to meet many of their own maintenance and reproductive costs. This reduces pressure on employers to provide them with health or pension plans or even with wages sufficient to meet costs of living (Burawoy 1976; Bonilla and Campos 1981; Portes and Walton 1981; Griffith 1985, 1993a). This arrangement is particularly beneficial to employers where reproductive and productive labor are separated through labor migration between rich and poor nations or regions, as in Mexican–U.S. migration and migration between the Bantustans and the white-dominated cities in South Africa (Burawoy 1976; Portes and Bach 1985).

The social-science literature on this issue tends to emphasize the benefits that accrue to employers from these arrangements. There is, however, another way to consider these support systems, a way that conforms, in fact, to employers' perceptions of these programs and to the intentions of legislators who authorized bills establishing free clinics, social programs, and other services that help workers meet maintenance and reproductive costs. At the same time that these "social safety nets" constitute subsidies to employers, they empower workers by giving them the means to reject wage and working-condition packages and still survive.

The level at which formal support systems maintain families is often one of bare survival, "chosen" as an alternative to low-wage labor with the knowledge that it will involve hardships such as crowded housing, little or no disposable income, dependence on family members, and associated emotional burdens. Nevertheless, when workers combine public assistance with informal support systems and diversified survival strategies, they assume better positions in relation to the labor market and thus achieve more power relative to capital. The power achieved by these means is limited, however, under conditions where employers have been able simply to move on to other sources for workers. Unaccompanied by the enforcement of immigration laws, the power these programs offer workers does not enable them to force employers to upgrade working conditions, stabilize wages by guaranteeing work, or otherwise improve the job packages agriculture has to offer.

The development of Puerto Rico has involved constructing a progressively more multifaceted social infrastructure capable of meeting the basic needs of Puerto Ricans. Housing, food, health, and education are all within reach of the population, allowing Puerto Ricans to subsist at poverty levels or to move among casual employment, underemployment, and unemployment with relative ease. Included in these survival strategies is working in the informal sector. The Puerto Rican economy still contains a multitude of "niches" for small-scale entrepreneurs—for example, the *chiripas* described above, small-scale fishing, and peasant farming. At the same time, Puerto Rico's Operation Bootstrap development continues to match wage workers with unskilled and semiskilled industrial instead of agricultural jobs, allowing them to find work in Puerto Rico and on the mainland that, though often low-paying, has none of the insecurities of agricultural labor.

Despite its high unemployment and the presence of a large Spanish-speaking labor force only a generation removed from an economy that rested very heavily on agriculture, Puerto Rico does not represent a significant supply of agricultural labor under current conditions. Its long tradition of supplying migrant workers to the eastern seaboard will evidently soon be over.

Chapter 7

A Labor Force in Transition

Farmworkers in the New Jersey Nursery Industry

The factors outlined in the previous chapter, undermining the reproduction of a Puerto Rican farm labor force in the eastern United States, are reflected in the changing composition of the workforce of New Jersey's nurseries. As in the low-wage labor markets of New York, Connecticut, and Chicago, Puerto Ricans have been incorporated into New Jersey agriculture through many public and private means: they have been recruited under the auspices of government-monitored migration and job placement programs; through "spontaneous," network-based flows into the region from Puerto Rico; through large-scale recruitment by growers' associations; and through individual growers, using as means of recruitment kinship and friendship ties linking current and past workers to potential workers in Puerto Rican municipalities and rural barrios.

Despite deep ties between the two regions, Puerto Ricans, especially in the past ten to twelve years, have been making up smaller proportions of the farm labor force, a phenomenon that has been observed in the Pennsylvania mushroom industry as well as in New Jersey (Smith 1992). One index of the decline of Puerto Ricans in New Jersey agriculture has been the reduced role of Glassboro Services Association, an organization in southern New Jersey that, since 1946, has been bringing Puerto Ricans into the region primarily for vegetable harvests. At one time the association imported 12,000 Puerto Ricans for work in New Jersey agriculture, yet for the 1989 season it imported only 2,500 Puerto Ricans. Similarly, its grower membership (those growers who regularly use the association for labor recruiting), once 1,200 strong, today consists of only around 250 growers. The geographical range over which Glassboro provides its services, too, has shrunk from several states to just New Jersey and a single peach grower in South Carolina. While many growers formerly with the association have simply begun recruiting Puerto Ricans directly, avoiding fees paid to Glassboro for its brokerage services, others have dropped out of the association because they have been tapping into other labor pools and using other labor intermediaries.

In place of Puerto Ricans, New Jersey growers have been hiring Mexicans, Central Americans, and Southeast Asians, as well as mechanizing some operations. Many of the new labor pools have been tapped by crew leaders who operate out of Philadelphia (Pfeffer 1992), while other workers have come into New Jersey agriculture as part of the growing Mexican/Central American presence along the eastern seaboard (Papademetriou et al. 1989).

The ethnic changes taking place in New Jersey agriculture have accompanied changes in labor union activity among Puerto Ricans, changes in working conditions (primarily housing), and changes in the ways specific firms' workforces have been internally segmented. These changes have occurred at a time of increasing demand for nursery products and pressures on the industry to succumb to urban growth by selling off acreage, recombining proportions of operations devoted to greenhouse or field stock production, and relocating either within the state or to other states. The industry remains robust, however, and continues to maintain historically high levels of labor demand, combining seasonal, subcontracted workers with permanent, year-round employees.

Characteristics of the Nursery Industry

The New Jersey nursery industry was large and well organized enough by the early part of this century to establish, in 1915, its own growers' association. The industry contains two sectors: field nurseries and container, or greenhouse, nurseries. Field operations require more land to grow nursery stock, primarily ornamental bushes and trees. Container nurseries specialize in smaller plants that can be grown in containers in greenhouses. Many nurseries in New Jersey combine the two operations.

According to nurserymen, field nursery operations have the longest history, while container operations have been in New Jersey only for the past twenty to twenty-five years. Since the early 1900s, the nursery industry has grown to become the state's number-one agricultural sector in terms of sales, accounting for 31 percent of all cash receipts from agriculture. This compares with under 20 percent from each of the following: vegetables (17 percent), horses (14 percent), fruits and berries (11 percent), field crops (10 percent), dairy products (9 percent), poultry and eggs (5 percent), and cattle and hogs (3 percent) (New Jersey. Department of Agriculture 1988: 83).

Of the 980 nursery operations in the state in 1984, 46.6 percent had annual gross cash receipts of $100,000 or more, 17.9 percent had $250,000 or more, and 5.0 percent had over $1,000,000. Sales of vegetables during the same year were only 37.5 percent of nursery sales, and since 1984 the nursery industry has remained the leader in New Jersey agriculture. These high receipts, however, must be considered in the light of higher average production costs in nursery operations than in most other agricultural sectors. On average, their production expenses were about twice the average for all farms in the state: $88,430 for nurseries, compared with $42,920 per year for all farms. The average production expenses of nurseries were about the same as those of fruit and nut farms ($75,981) but were higher than those of vegetable farms ($51,108). These average expenses were exceeded only by dairy farms ($10,422 per farm).

Reliance on hired farm labor appears to have contributed to the high average level of production expenses on horticultural farms. About 31 percent of all farms in New Jersey hire labor, while over 40 percent of nurseries hire workers. Nursery operations pay more for the workers they hire, on average, as well: of those farms that hire workers, nearly 42 percent of all nursery operations in the state had hired-labor expenses of $25,000 or more, compared with 35 percent of vegetable farms and 32 percent of fruit and nut farms. Average hired-labor expenses are $74,523 for nurseries, over twice the average for all farms and over 35 percent higher than fruit and nut operations (U.S. Department of Commerce 1987).

In 1984, most nurseries (59 percent) were individually owned, 10 percent were partnerships, and the remaining third (32 percent) were corporate owned. Since 1984, industry concentration has increased slightly, with average acreage per operation growing while the number of farms has decreased.[1] The latest statistics (1987) estimate that 961 nurseries grow 14,510 acres of nursery stock and produce more-specialized products inside, using 12.7 million square feet of greenhouse space (New Jersey Association of Nurserymen 1984; New Jersey. Department of Agriculture 1988). The general contours of the distribution of farms and types of products reflect, primarily a combination of history and proximity to urban markets. Those closer to Newark, New York City, Trenton, and Philadelphia, in the northern and central portions of the state, tend to specialize more in landscape and retail/greenhouse work than in field operations, while those farther south and more distant from large metropolitan areas devote more time, labor, and space to field production of wholesale nursery stock. All regions of the state produce wholesale, retail, landscaping, and other products (usually specialized labor and materials for construction projects). The northern region derives 35 percent of its sales from landscaping, 33 percent from wholesale, 27 percent from retail, and 5 percent from other sources. Comparable figures for the central region are 30 percent, 23 percent, 43 percent, and 4 percent, respectively; those for the southern region are 12 percent, 23 percent, 64 percent, and 1 percent, respectively (New Jersey Association of Nurserymen 1984).[2]

This distribution reflects densities of types of operations and their associated labor needs. We noted above that the industry is divided into primarily field operations and primarily container operations, although many firms combine the two to keep workers employed throughout the year and to reduce seasonal peaks in labor demand. Field operations tend to require heavier and more seasonal labor inputs than do container operations; in these operations, shrubs, trees, and other ornamentals are planted in fields for later uprooting, bagging, and shipment. By contrast, container industry operations perform most of their tasks inside heated and unheated greenhouses, consisting of more planting, shaping, caring for, and transplanting ornamentals in containers and less heavy digging, lifting, and other physically taxing tasks. In the landscaping components of the industry, jobs consist of deploying workers to construction sites to lay sod or plant shrubs and trees.

According to the most recent survey, the industry as a whole employs 1,152 (12 percent) unpaid family members, 4,836 (51 percent) full-time workers, and 3,550 (37 percent) part-time workers, whose combined wages exceed $52 million per year. It is unclear whether or not statistics collected by the industry include contract digging crews, however, which are factored into the production process differently than hired workers are.

The industry's busy seasons occur between March and June and again between August and October. During these times, the composition of work crews and recruiting methods assume their most complex dimensions. Field operations, in particular, require highly variable labor inputs throughout the year, with peak seasons driven primarily by market considerations. Field industry products tend to be sold for landscape construction, including private architectural and landscaping firms and municipalities. Most of the demand for these products coincides with the beginning (spring) or end (fall) of construction/landscaping projects. These are the digging seasons, when young but sometimes large trees and shrubs are uprooted, bagged, and shipped. Digging season is to nurseries what the harvest is to fruit and vegetable producers: what Lloyd Fischer (1953) once described as an entirely separate enterprise, out of which emerge the most creative labor management techniques. Many operations keep workers employed between peak seasons, during the slower summer months in particular, to stabilize their workforces; others maintain skeleton crews throughout the year, supplementing year-round workers with contracted crews or day-haul workers during the busy seasons. Patterns of work organization, supervision, recruitment, and other features of the labor process vary considerably from operation to operation, however. They are influenced by such factors as availability, cost, and condition of housing on and off the farm; markets for products and associated profitability of the firm; relations with core employees and their network ties with other potential workers; individual management styles; and levels of mechanization.

Composition of the Labor Force

Tasks at nurseries differ according to the particular firm's specific mix of field, container, landscaping, and other specialized operations. Many firms combine all operations, sometimes performing different operations in different parts of the state and integrating them at the corporate office level, if not at the level of the labor force. The number of workers needed is not a function of the size of the operation; instead, the number and type of workers (seasonal, year-round, contract, those who punch the time-clock, etc.) needed depends on the product mix of the enterprise, corresponding markets for those products, and the services provided by the firm (Table 7.1) This is particularly true in greenhouse or container and landscape operations. The most highly seasonal and labor-intensive operation we encountered (no. 5 in Table 7.1) was primarily a landscaping firm, operating its nursery strictly to supply perennials to its landscape jobs. Other container operations, however, utilize only family labor or have stable workforces, their tasks evenly distributed over the year. Most problems of coordinating labor demand and supply occur in the industry's field component.

Field tasks tend to be the heaviest, most difficult of tasks in the nursery, consisting of transplanting young shrubs and trees, weeding, pruning, digging, tying roots and bagging, and loading the finished products onto trucks. These tasks tend to be dirtier than container or landscaping tasks, involve prolonged exposure to the sun (as is typically the case with farmwork), and are consid-

TABLE 7.1 Selected Characteristics of Study Nurseries

Nursery	Type[a]	Size[b]	Labor Force	Ethnicity of Workers	Hourly Wage
1	C	50 a. 160 a.	30–37	Mexican	$4.00–8.00
2	C/F	1.5M sq. ft.	50	Puerto Rican	$6.50–10.00
3	F	35 a.	10	Local	$4.50–6.25
4	F	270 a.	15	Mexican	$4.50–5.25
5	L/F	10 a.	250	Puerto Rican, Mexican	$6.50–8.00
6	F/C	175 a.	8–19	Puerto Rican, Mexican, Asian	$4.25–10.00
7	C/F	320 a.	25–45	Mexican, Puerto Rican	$4.00–6.50
8	F	2,000 a.	40	Puerto Rican, Mexican	$7.00–8.00
9	F	83 a.	1–8	Puerto Rican	—
10	C	2.25M sq. ft.	25–65	Asian	$6.50–9.50
11	F/C	51 a.	5	Puerto Rican, Mexican	$5.25–6.50
12	C	0.15M sq. ft.	29	Local, Puerto Rican	$4.00–5.00
13	F	200 a.	18	Puerto Rican	$4.00–6.00
14	F/C	3,000 a.	100–260	Local, Mexican, Asian	—

[a]F = field; C = container; L = landscaping.

[b]Greenhouse area is usually expressed in millions of square feet.

cred, with one or two exceptions, unskilled labor. There are, however, a few tasks in field operations that growers perceive to require special skills, such as chemical application, operation of machinery, and some of the more specialized digging tasks.

Field nursery work, for the most part, is hourly wage work, paying starting wages of between minimum wage and $5.00 per hour, compared with $3.85 per hour, typically, for work in the vegetable harvests of southern New Jersey (1989 minimum wage). Some operations pay more, even up to $15.00 per hour, although such high rates tend to be confined to longtime employees. Some tasks, such as digging up large trees and preparing them for shipment by balling up the roots, are paid by the piece—rates are, however, highly variable, depending on the size and variety of tree or shrub being uprooted.

Given these features of field nursery production—difficult, heavy work; unskilled tasks; low wages relative to high costs of living and seasonal labor inputs—this component of the industry suffers from high labor turnover. It is thus in the context of field tasks that New Jersey nurseries marshal their most complex and creative labor recruiting and task allocation strategies.

Labor Recruitment: Core and Peak-Season Employees

The labor processes of New Jersey nurseries vary, principally, by the extent of their internal segmentation. From the extent of internal segmentation derive other concrete features of a firm's labor process: benefit packages, whether or not workers are provided housing, relations between workers and growers, mechanization, scheduling, and propensity to experiment with new products to stabilize or reorganize work on the farm.

The distinction between core and peripheral workers, as noted in other labor demand regions, applies to New Jersey nurseries as well. Virtually all farms have core employees: steady, permanent, year-round, reliable workers who have become central to the operation as foremen or supervisors, "jacks-of-all-trades," trainers, and managers or assistant managers. This group of individuals may consist of the nursery owner's family workers, longtime hired employees, or, most commonly, combinations of family workers and reliable hired hands. We found very little task specialization among this component of the workforce. They have learned most of the operation's tasks; tend to be fairly well paid; sometimes have their housing subsidized by the grower; are often covered by pension, health, and related benefit packages; and are characterized by nurserymen as possessing initiative and being "part of the team." Furthermore, core groups of employees tend not to be hierarchically structured: which member of the group "leads," organizes, directs, and supervises the group depends on the specific task at hand and the skill of the member in terms of that task. Three examples illustrate the relatively unspecialized and crucial character the workforce's core.

Case 1. The nursery employs only one foreman. The few distinctions between workers include those between high school boys specializing in heavy fieldwork and retired women concentrating on sorting operations. Within these groups, "everyone has to do everything." The operator uses workers flexibly because the forty different varieties [of plants] produced on the farm demand different work schedules and workers often have to be shifted from one task to another. Most work is unspecialized and unskilled, requiring little training. Workers are taught the minimum necessary to do simple tasks such as digging, transplanting, sorting, and loading.

Case 2. There is little in the way of a hierarchy among workers on this farm. There are no foremen. Key people are those who are most skilled in various aspects of the operation.

Case 3. About twelve years ago, the operator decided to close the labor camp and stop using migrant workers. Occasionally a local high school or college kid works on the farm, and this works out reasonably well. However, the core workforce consists of three Puerto Ricans who, formerly migrant workers on the farm, settled in the area with their families. When the operator decided to close his labor camp twelve years ago, he decided to do what he could to keep his best workers. They were the three that he has working with him now. He offered to turn the labor camp into a home for one of them and his family. This man is now his foreman. Turning the labor camp into a family home ended regulatory scrutiny from the Department of Labor and led to a reduction in maintenance problems as well. The worker maintains the house himself, but the operator pays for any materials he needs to keep the house up. The structure is a long cinder-block building that looks quite modern and well kept from the outside. The other two core workers, one of which is the foreman's brother, live in nearby towns, Mount Holly and Pemberton. They live there with their families as well. The families supplement the basic three-man crew and bring the regular workforce up to a total of eight. The women workers do not participate in tree digging. Contract diggers are brought in to assist with this work. However, all other work on the farm is completed by these three Puerto Rican families. The female members of these families typically do not come to work until after the digging is complete and begin to work when the planting on new crops begins. They are also involved in all of the crop maintenance operations that continue on for the remainder of the season. (Pfeffer field notes, March 1990)

While initiative, reliability, flexibility, and loyalty to the firm are common descriptors for core employees, these workers also contribute to the shaping of the labor process in important ways. First, core employees often recruit new workers into the nursery through kinship and friendship networks. Second, they usually train and supervise new workers and work alongside the contracted crews that perform specialized digging operations. Third, as part of their roles as labor recruiters, they provide cultural and linguistic brokerage services between nursery owners and migrant or seasonal workers. This last function is especially characteristic of Puerto Ricans; many of them began as migrant workers in nursery operations, coming to New Jersey as lone males seasonally every year, and subsequently developed close enough material and emotional ties with nursery owners to settle in New Jersey, bringing their families with them from Puerto Rico.

The Role of Puerto Rican Workers

Nine of the fourteen New Jersey firms contacted use Puerto Rican workers;[3] anecdotal information further suggests that the Puerto Rican role in the nursery industry has been one of providing workers to the industry's core.

Case 4. The operators have come to rely primarily on Puerto Ricans from Trenton as their core workforce. They have been very successful in holding onto these workers in recent years. For example, ten of the Puerto Ricans have worked for the company for five years. There is little turnover within this core workforce. Several are foremen. The main foreman of the firm comes from this group, earning $15 an hour. This man is a key figure in labor recruitment as well, bringing workers with him from Trenton. The same is true of another foreman. Some of the Puerto Ricans that provide transportation charge the others for this service. Most of these Puerto Ricans live in Trenton year-round, and the firm provides no housing for them.

Case 5. This nursery was established in 1954. In the early years, the firm harvested trees in the wild and relied mostly on Polish immigrants living in the area and Canadian Indians. The Canadian Indians are still around, but they work as contract diggers throughout the area. As the firm became an established nursery, it began to rely on Puerto Rican migrant workers. Some of these workers have been with the nursery for as many as fifteen years. Many of these men are key people, and all are the most experienced diggers on the farm. Beyond the key people the nursery has had, and continues to have, however, there are problems getting laborers at the right time, especially at the onset of the harvest in March. Despite these problems, the firm continues to rely on informal recruitment mechanisms to find workers. The workers are put in contact with the nursery through kinship and community connections.

Case 6. The farm was established in 1952, and the operator grew up on this operation. While he was growing up, the farm relied on local workers of various racial and ethnic backgrounds. The majority of this workforce was African American. Both men and women worked on the nursery. In these years he recalls few labor problems and little labor turnover. Many employees had been with the nursery for many years. He gave examples of particular individuals who had been with the firm for thirteen and twenty years. Of course, other workers had come and gone, but the problem of labor turnover came to a head about one year ago. Until that time, the nursery relied exclusively on local workers. The labor problems experienced here were almost completely related to the employment of young males, whether white or African American. Many of these young workers were involved in drugs or other criminal activity. One of the workers was arrested last year for selling illegal weapons. Through all these problems the farm was able to hold onto a nucleus of about five to seven reliable workers, mostly local Puerto Ricans. These Puerto Ricans had been coming to work on the farm since about 1982. Currently, the labor situation has stabilized. The main reason for this stability is the arrival of Mexican workers about two years ago. First a few workers came, and then more joined them. Typically one Mexican was hired, and then later he would bring three or four more with him. These workers came from Mexico on their own and arrived on this farm on their own. They just showed up asking for work. These Mexican workers were added to the core workforce of local Puerto Ricans. Since the addition of the Mexicans to the workforce, the operator no longer advertises in local newspapers for workers. (Pfeffer field notes, July 1989)

Like longtime Mexican American and Chicano workers in the West and Midwest, who have also assumed key personnel positions (along with becoming crew leaders, pinhookers, and sharecroppers), the Puerto Rican core personnel in the New Jersey nursery industry constitute an aging workforce, one that may eventually be replaced by Mexican workers settling out of the migrant stream in New Jersey.

Workplace organization varies a great deal among different nurseries in New Jersey, perhaps reflecting the fact that it is a relatively isolated farm labor market where there has, of necessity, been a great deal of improvisation as nursery operators experimented with different strategies for meeting their labor needs. The least internally differentiated forms of workplace organization are those that hire no workers beyond the core employees, maintaining a small workforce of five to fifteen individuals and reorganizing tasks and product mixes so that work is evenly distributed over the year. Usually these operations provide workers' housing or help them establish housing, pay them well, and so on.

Beyond those that use only, or primarily, a core workforce, New Jersey nurseries have become differentiated from one another in terms of their labor processes. Most farms supplement core workers during the spring and fall seasons. Some hire migrant workers, others seasonal local workers, and others contract crews based in Philadelphia or other cities of Pennsylvania and New Jersey. As noted earlier, Mexicans, Central Americans, and Southeast Asians have been making inroads into the industry, generally at the expense of Puerto Rican and local African American workers.

Most complex are those operations that, in addition to core workers, utilize migrant workers between May and November and even more highly seasonal contract digging crews for specialized labor inputs during extreme peaks in market demand. This creates three "internal" labor markets: core workers, migrant workers, and contract workers. We refer to nurseries with these segmented labor forces as the most complex of operations because they draw upon a number of labor pools, utilize a range of recruiting strategies, and segment the labor force by allocating tasks to different crews, paying each crew differently, and varying wage-and-benefit packages by the workers' positions in crews and crews' positions in the production process. Drawing upon a number of labor pools implies, furthermore, that the workforce will be heterogeneous in terms of ethnicity; workers' legal status; whether workers are lone migrants, family migrants, or settled local people; and so forth. This heterogeneity becomes, then, a source of further differentiation within the labor force and a mechanism by which internal labor markets are maintained.

Avion Nurseries (pseudonym) coordinates groups of workers, with a number of internal pay, benefit, ethnic, supervisory, and other distinctions within and between groups. In short, the operation has a complex approach to labor recruitment and management, referring to itself as a "personnel-oriented company." Workers are divided into three categories:

1. Time-clock employees (80 to 120 workers). These are salaried and hourly core workers who are more or less year-round workers. Ninety percent are hourly workers.
2. Contract crews that are "truly seasonal" (around 80 workers in two crews). One of the crews has 15 to 35 workers, working from March or April through the summer into November (eight months), and the other crew has anywhere from 20 to 55 workers and works "almost year-round." These contract crews are primarily Cambodian crew leaders with Cambodian/Guatemalan crews, coming from Philadelphia daily. The Guatemalans had been taking up a larger proportion of these crews over time, but they were cyclical migrants and temporary laborers who might stay around only one season or so, not long enough to learn any of the skilled jobs on the nursery grounds or move onto the time clock.
3. Contract digging crews. These include a number of crews of 3 to 5 or up to 15 people, professional diggers who work for piecework and have been in the business for years. They tend to be skilled at digging and consist of a mix of ethnic groups: African Americans, Puerto Ricans, Cambodians, whites; usually the crew leader brings a crew of his or her ethnic group. These crews, combined, total around 80 workers.

Of these three groups, the second seems the most interesting in terms of changes and experiments in the labor process. Cambodian crew leaders who assemble these crews have been selected more and more Guatemalans over the years, selecting for a reliable workforce. Cambodian workers will be on the grounds in great numbers, but not necessarily from day to day. They seem to be involved in a number of other businesses, informal economic activities, and social services, and they are less reliable on a day-to-day basis. In addition to the Cambodians, another branch of the nursery negotiates directly with the Puerto Rican government to get a group of Puerto Rican workers. These workers live in a dorm, so the company has some experience with providing housing, which has influenced its ideas about addressing future labor problems. The branch we visited, however, has tried to operate without a dorm (Griffith field notes, June 1990).

Housing

One option personnel managers of Avion Nurseries have only just begun to
explore is that of providing housing for workers. Despite the fact that other
farms owned by the same parent company provide housing, this farm has been
slow in providing it because housing carries an additional set of problems
(mortgages, inspections, taxes, safety, insurance, etc.). Nevertheless, some
New Jersey nurseries provide housing for their workers; one we visited was in
the process of expanding, buying other farms in the area, and using the farmhouses on those farms to house more of its workforce.

Housing has become one of the cornerstones of labor recruitment and re-
tention for one of the largest nurseries in the northeastern United States. Although not in New Jersey, this operation is nonetheless important because of
its size, its proximity to New Jersey, its reputation among nurserymen, and
the way in which Mexican workers came to totally replace, from one year to
the next, a Puerto Rican workforce after the nursery had relied on them for
twenty-five years.

Old Gold Nursery is a three-thousand-acre field nursery that, last summer, officials at
the Puerto Rican Department of Labor described as having the most abysmal living
conditions on the mainland. Obviously this was before recent improvements, because
the labor camp is now clean and exemplary. The male dormitory contains either four
or eight bunks and lockers, along with the migrants' personal belongings like small
televisions. More impressive were a number of three-bedroom "homes" for migrant
families; these cost between $28,000 and $34,000. They are less than one year old.
Much more than the addition of this family housing has changed in the past year,
however: for twenty-five years, until just this year, the operation hired nearly a fully
Puerto Rican workforce, but this year it changed to Mexicans hired out of Arizona and
Texas (SAW workers). This is an "experiment" project, said the Mexican supervisor
in charge of the workers. The company had a high turnover, dropping from 150 to 72
or 74 workers between last March and now. Some are coming back, though, and those
that last through the season will serve as the core of good workers—the owner will
rely on them to recruit family and friends to get a full contingent. The season lasts
from March to December, with particularly busy times during the spring (March
through May) and fall (September through November). (Griffith field notes, July 1989)

Between the least and most complex firms described above lie those that,
in addition to their core workers, utilize seasonal, usually migrant, workers
during their busy season and through the summer months. Formerly, these
migrant workers were recruited either through Glassboro Services out of

Puerto Rico or from local populations. Today, increasingly, these segments of the labor force are made up primarily of lone-male migrants from Mexico, who come to New Jersey from California or Florida, usually with some farm-work experience as well as with some experience with the labor market in general.

Adaptations to Labor Problems

We can identify at least three adaptations to labor problems in New Jersey nurseries. Each of these is associated with different product mixes, labor management strategies, firm sizes, and market niches. Within each of the adaptations, moreover, we find variations and labor management experiments as problems of labor supply, productivity, and reliability occur.

Corporate adaptation. A corporate operation typically has three groups of workers. The most important segment consists of a core of permanent, hourly or salaried workers who constitute between 10 and 30 percent of the workforce and to whom the firm provides fairly comprehensive benefit packages, including health insurance, paid vacations, and pensions, as well as bonus and other incentive programs. The second and third groups of workers consist of sub-contracted crews that work in the nursery for varying lengths of time. They are differentiated from the core workforce by the fact that they are paid less, receive no benefits, and are considered seasonal employees, and they are differentiated from each in two ways: the second group works during more of the year than the third, while the third group consists of more specialized workers.

Family corporate adaptation. The core of the family corporate operation consists not of time-clock employees but of unpaid family workers and paid fictive kin/longtime hired hands. How much of the work is done by this core varies from operation to operation. While the paid core workers in these operations may not receive elaborate benefit packages, they often benefit from personal or patron-client ties to family workers. Housing and end-of-season or annual bonuses often constitute major components of the total wage offer to these employees. These workers are supplemented by a second group of workers composed of local seasonal and migrant workers, often recruited from the networks of the key fictive-kin employees but generally recruited through a variety of mechanisms, including labor contractors and associations such as Glassboro Services.

Family farm adaptation. Family farm operations have only the core employees of family and fictive-kin workers, hiring supplemental workers individually (as opposed to using crews or labor contractors) and episodically.

Within each of these operations, we encountered various strategies designed to enhance worker loyalty to the family or firm, all of which sometimes further internally differentiate the workforce as well as locate and allow firms to take advantage of different levels of individual initiative and productivity within the workforce. Most commonly, firms offered various incentives, and bonuses to seasonal and year-round workers. Bonuses for seasonal workers, common in perishable-crop agriculture of northern labor demand regions, were designed primarily to keep workers around through the end of the season. Benefits and other incentives for year-round workers were usually tied to profit margins, rewarding workers when the firm was doing well. The use of bonuses, in general, seems to be associated with operations with high profit margins, such as those that sell specialty trees and other products to architectural firms and municipal construction/landscaping projects. The use of bonuses tied to profits varies according to nursery owners' and operators' general attitudes about worker productivity and the nature of their reliance on core workers.

Managers overwhelmingly reported that initiative—someone willing to learn more about the operation and then think and act without being told what to do next—was the most desirable trait a worker could have. Those managers who took the time to recognize and reward initiative, moreover, generally reported fewer labor problems than those who held generally dim views of their workers. These observations are supported by industrial sociological lore as well as social-scientific work on underlying reasons workers might behave as though they were stupid or lacking initiative. A large body of literature, much of it written as a critical response to F. W. Taylor's *Principles of Scientific Management,* published in 1911, suggests that workers mistreated by employers, whether through attitude or pay, will respond with feigned ignorance, dissimulation, evident laziness, and other minor protests that James Scott (1985) calls ''everyday forms of resistance.''

Hiring from Preferred Ethnic Networks

Agricultural employers are inclined to theorize about the work habits of their current and former employees, often comparing workers in terms of the ''work ethics'' of their ethnic group. In any sector of the economy with as high turnover as the farm labor market, employers often have no choice but to ''experiment'' with workers from different ethnic backgrounds and socioeconomic conditions; frequent comparisons among these groups, in terms of how well they "fit" with the employer's business, is inevitable. At the same time, employers must deal with the workers' and their own preconceived notions of ethnicity, nationality, gender, age, and other attributes (Griffith 1987).

In such a context, workers and growers learn from one another about how to behave and what to expect at work and beyond the work setting (e.g., in housing); this learning is a process of negotiation that reflects power differentials between employers and workers. The tendency in these settings is for the least empowered workers (those without legal documents, who have no access to government programs, and who are isolated) to set the standard against which other workers are judged. Certain kinds of workers, in other words, "spoil" employers, who respond by modifying their notions of the work ethic in terms of the work habits of these workers.

In this process, employers began to associate the preferred work ethic with specific attributes of workers that extend well beyond actual initiative on the job or output per hour to include family type, language, skin color, attitude, and so forth. This may explain why so few New Jersey nurserymen described productivity in terms of output per hour, as well as why it is so common for smaller-nursery owners to attempt to develop close personal ties with workers and subsequently to utilize those ties to acquire more workers from the network of the extended family or village network of the preferred workers.

Restructuring the Flow of Work

A common means to bond workers to a specific operation is to reorganize work routines and production schedules to keep workers employed through the year rather than as seasonal employees. This strategy is not as useful for field nurseries as it is for container nurseries, since the former have marked seasonal fluctuations in work that cannot be any more evenly distributed over the year. Expanding a field nursery by building greenhouse space and moving into container operations, however, is one means of keeping workers employed for longer portions of the year.

Recruitment Through Extended Family Networks

Developing close personal ties with workers is an important recruitment strategy. This is the preferred strategy of smaller operations, field nurseries, and operations that are operated by older, less well educated individuals. In this respect, field nurseries form a distinct subgroup within the industry, being more established than the container industry. The container industry is a post–World War II phenomenon, whereas some field nurseries are one hundred years old. Operators of field nurseries tend to be less educated and innovative than those in the container business. The success of this personal network strategy seems to depend a great deal on the personality of the operator and his or her ability to develop a good relationship with workers. One of the key ingredients appears to be the ability and willingness of the operator to give qualified workers a degree of responsibility in the operation.

More than just the personality of the operator is involved in making close personal ties work. Some degree of profitability of the nursery is also demanded. Nurserymen who paid for the transportation of their seasonal employees to and from their winter homes were the most successful in attracting qualified workers year after year. The ability and willingness to provide comfortable housing for workers is also an important ingredient in making this strategy work. Those that have successfully implemented this strategy have held onto their workers for many years. Often workers from the same family come to work on the farm generation after generation.

Use of Contract Workers

Finally, as noted earlier, a labor recruitment strategy of increasing importance in the nursery business is the use of contract labor. This strategy is especially popular on field nurseries during the spring harvest season, when nursery stock is dug out of the ground. This work is particularly hot, dirty, and heavy. During digging time the regular nursery workforce is supplemented with a contract workforce that is paid a piece rate; the peak labor demand is during the completion of the operation. Few of the regular workers on the nurseries are paid on a strictly piece-rate basis, but some regular workers do receive a bonus for digging. Contract workers are also important to some of the container nurseries. Contract workers in these nurseries appear to be paid an hourly rate but are not eligible for the benefits paid to regular workers.

Conclusion

The recruitment and labor management successes of the New Jersey nursery industry demonstrate that motivated agricultural employers can respond creatively and effectively when a traditional source of labor such as the Puerto Rican migrant stream begins to decrease. The New Jersey nursery industry is particularly interesting in that its labor strategies involve more tiers and types of workers than is usual in most other agricultural operations. At the same time, the recruitment incentives provided by the industry more commonly consist of multiple features—not only housing or bonuses or benefits but a combination of incentives—than do those in most other agricultural areas.

New Jersey nursery operators' experience with Puerto Rican migrants appears to have given them an appreciation of the dynamics of a workplace organized on the basis of network interactions, which may occur between either family workers or crews of single workers used to organized modes of cooperative work. The industry's extensive reliance on core workers who recruit, supervise, and organize much of the day-to-day operations suggests that, more than many agricultural employers, New Jersey nursery operators recognize the utility of informal modes of workplace organization. The special incentives such as housing, profit-sharing bonuses, and health insurance that are provided by some employers indicate that their recognition of core workers' value is genuine.

The case of the New Jersey nursery industry strongly suggests that an improved package of wages, housing, and benefits can be paid for by the productivity of the premium workers it attracts, given the reality that the extraordinarily strenuous work involved (particularly in field digging) is very difficult to manage and conduct successfully with workers who are not motivated. To some extent, New Jersey's response to a shortage of able, willing, and qualified local workers has been facilitated as new pioneering migrants from Mexico discover New Jersey.

While the New Jersey nursery industry has had demonstrable success in adapting to the dwindling stream of Puerto Rican migrants, nursery owners and personnel managers have discovered, at the same time, that the incentives that worked when recruiting Puerto Ricans do not work well for local nonimmigrant workers. This suggests that improved wages and working conditions, and enhanced recruitment, will have a strong impact in stabilizing worker turnover, increasing worker productivity, and making more effective use of a limited pool of workers willing to do strenuous agricultural work. Yet it also implies that even these improved conditions will not yield a workforce of U.S.-born workers.

Chapter 8

Northward out of Mexico

Migration Networks and Farm Labor Supply in Parlier, California

Parlier, California, has a long, well-documented history as an agricultural-labor supply area. Like Immokalee and Weslaco, its history is closely linked to international migration. Despite its unique social history, Parlier is a paradigm for understanding the historical, economic, and social forces that have shaped the rural towns in agricultural areas along the Pacific Coast, throughout California's Central Valley, in Oregon, and in central Washington.

Situated about seventeen miles southeast of Fresno, the fertile Central Valley, Parlier is one settlement among several small agricultural towns east of Highway 99, the main north-south artery. It has an estimated population of eight thousand, and like the neighboring towns of Sanger, Reedley, Orange Cove, and Dinuba, it has an economy firmly rooted in agriculture. Parlier fits the romantic stereotype of the small, rural farm town: acquaintances wave at each other; cafe owners know patrons by name. Yet Parlier is a neighborhood in a global village, less insular than the lonely midwestern plains towns most Americans think of as "farming communities." The town's principal languages are Spanish and the Tex-Mex hybrid. Over three-quarters of its residents were born in Mexico; those who were not are the children of Mexican immigrants. Parlier straddles an area within a set of overlapping migrant networks, successfully spanning two cultures. Its function as a clearinghouse for migrant farm labor dominates the town's life. Tree-lined streets give it a suburban look, but the commuters who populate Parlier are not stockbrokers or lawyers but migrant farmworkers coming north from Mexico, traveling several thousands of miles in search of work. Around dinnertime, you are likely to see them: young or middle-aged men walking home along the railroad tracks with small bags of groceries to cook on small hotplates or old stoves. They have no cars. Their lives are defined largely by long days of work and the return to crowded rooms. The more settled, long-term residents of Parlier run the stores, laundromats, health-care facilities, and other businesses that serve the cyclical migrants. Because the migrant stream flows continually, Parlier's social reality is firmly and inextricably rooted in Mexico.

Through its young people, Parlier also has some connection with mainstream America. After school, the teenaged sons and daughters of farmworkers sweep into their local hangout—the Pizza Pirate—to gossip, order French fries and soda pop, and play video games. Unlike their parents, they prefer to speak English.[1] Their clothes, their aspirations, and their personal values are mainstream American. Their play, their socializing, so unlike the seriousness of their contemporaries in Mexico, prepares them for life in the "information economy" of the United States.

People in Parlier are generally neighborly. Overcrowded housing creates some conflicts, but city government has moved aggressively and creatively to solve the problem. Parlier has twice the amount of low-income housing of a California city such as San Francisco. And although it appears to have an undeveloped infrastructure, its quality of life is probably superior to that of some communities that appear more "developed."

Nonetheless, Parlier is a poor town. Substandard living conditions are prevalent, although little of the housing is as bad as the worst housing in Weslaco or Immokalee. The only coin telephone on the main street usually attracts a long line. The homes of long-term residents have telephones, but not the crowded households where recent migrants accumulate. Data from the 1980 Census, for example, show that most residents were unemployed for at least three months during the previous year and that about a third of the town lived below the poverty level.

This part of California, the "Eastside" area of the San Joaquin Valley, is quite densely populated. At the same time, it is used for extremely intensive agriculture. Toward the eastern edge of the valley, abutting the Sierra foothills, orange groves predominate, but these give way to grapes, nectarines, and peaches in the Parlier area. The town's history, politics, and development can be largely understood in terms of the major inputs to agricultural production—land ownership, cheap water, and cheap labor.

Parlier has something of a barbell shape, consisting of a cluster of population known as La Colonia, and "downtown" Parlier, a cluster about a mile

farther east, along a major east-west thoroughfare called Manning Avenue. As
in the past, La Colonia today houses large numbers of recently arrived immigrants who have come to do farmwork. Before dawn, the neighborhood is
crisscrossed by the vans of *raiteros* (drivers who sell rides to farmworkers).
In a rural version of the urban street-corner labor market, labor contractors
stop in front of the houses of recent arrivals to round out their crews.

Along Manning Avenue, a small cafe, one auto repair shop, a used-car
dealership, and an apartment complex constitute the first smudges of urban
sprawl. In the middle of town, north of Manning Avenue, the town remains
quiet and old-fashioned. On one of the rare clear days, after a spring rain, one
can see the Sierras close at hand; in the more common smoggy heat of a 100-
degree summer day, the houses are cooled by closely planted trees. Apartment
houses dot the area, all the result of the town's efforts to build enough affordable housing, efforts that appear doomed to lag behind the ongoing influx of
farmworkers.

In the middle of town, bordering the old railroad tracks and packing sheds,
is a narrow strip of park with picnic tables under cedar trees, where *mayordomos* (supervisors), farm labor contractors, and farmworkers gather daily.
On the south side of the street, across from the strip of park, lie Parlier's
downtown businesses, including small Mexican restaurants, a defunct movie
theater, a videocassette rental service, grocery stores, a real-estate agent/no-
tary public, and a jewelry store. Around the corner is the laundromat. To the
north of the park lies Parlier High School. The main street is quieter than in
the past, now that the city council has banned the cantinas. Although the
restaurants can serve better, Parlier is not quite as wild on Saturday night as
some farmworker towns are.

Parlier is a town of contrasts. It presents an image of life in twenty first
century California: an optimistic, vibrant town with a multicultural population
that is dynamic and hard-working. But it is confronting immensely difficult
economic problems, buffeted by the forces of an emerging global economy.

Waves of Immigrants

Parlier presents a microcosm of California farm labor history. Tremendous
changes have followed successive waves of immigrants, first from the Midwest, in the late nineteenth century, and then, in order, from China, Japan, the
Philippines, and Mexico. Midwestern farmers who flowed into the area were
spurred by the free land made available by the Homestead Act of 1862. The

town's founder, I. N. Parlier, initially homesteaded 160 acres and later purchased an additional 600 acres from the railroad. Along with other Anglo immigrants, Parlier established small, family wheat and livestock farms, selling their produce to a local market. But the growing use of railroads for a rapidly expanding national agricultural market made wheat production unprofitable. Improved freight service more fully integrated the region into national markets, and local farmers sought to produce more cash crops. By the 1890s, formation of a cooperative water district made the move to labor-intensive agriculture possible.

The intensive-agricultural production of the growing raisin industry made the recruitment and maintenance of a large surplus labor force of farmworkers in the 1890s an important element of business strategy. The first immigrant farmworkers in the Parlier area were Chinese, moving into agriculture after the construction of the railroads ended in 1869 (Massey et al. 1987). By the early 1890s, however, the initial welcome extended to Chinese immigrants had turned to virulent opposition. Residents claimed there was "unequal competition" by "Mongolians," who were an "inferior race outside the boundaries of social equality—a very stench in the nostrils of well-bred people" (*Selma Irrigator* 1882).

Recruitment of Japanese farm laborers began in the 1880s to meet the labor needs of the sugar beet industry. It was estimated shortly after the turn of the century that about 60 percent of the farm labor force of Fresno County was Japanese. The native reaction to the Japanese followed a pattern similar to the Chinese experience, except that the subsequent manifestation of racism appeared when Japanese farm laborers began operating their own small farms (McWilliams 1939). Beginning in the 1920s, successive, increasingly discriminatory, anti-Japanese laws were passed. Nevertheless, Japanese became important landowners in and around Parlier. For example, Henry Kubo, president of the powerful Nisei Growers' League, was born in Parlier.

Local growers began to rely on Mexican labor after World War I, and Mexican immigration increased because of "push" factors of economic dislocation during the chaotic period following the 1910 Mexican Revolution and "pull" factors including the demand for labor to replace "Orientals." Mexican migrant families who worked initially as "follow-the-crop" workers began to settle in Parlier in the early 1920s. During this period, the area of Parlier called La Colonia was first established as a migrant labor camp. By 1930, the composition of California's farm labor force had changed so that more than half of California's hired farmworkers were Mexican, with only about 20 percent Japanese and another 20 percent Filipino. These trends proved short-lived. During the depression years, nativist sentiment again turned, but this time against Mexicans. Widespread "repatriation" of Mexican farmworkers (including some who were U.S. citizens) occurred throughout the state. In Parlier, vigilante committees were organized to enforce nativist policies, and the Mexicans who remained lived in constant fear. However, California agriculture's historical reliance on surplus labor and repression of labor-organizing efforts—particularly effective among Japanese hired workers and labor contractors—led to renewed enthusiasm for Mexican farmworkers. During World War II, new "labor shortages" laid the foundation for establishment of the postwar Bracero program. Mexican settlement in La Colonia and Parlier boomed during the postwar period.

Understanding the nature of Parlier as a farm labor supply community requires, primarily, understanding the history of Mexican migration northward. The Mexican networks most heavily represented in our sample originate in the states of Guanajuato, Jalisco, and Michoacán. Many older, settled residents of Parlier left this core area, an area of intense recruitment, during the period of the Bracero Program (although they did not come to Parlier at that time). When the Bracero Program ended in 1964, many of these individuals returned to the United States illegally, and some simply never returned to their home communities in Mexico. In time they applied for and received permanent residency status, brought wives and children, and settled in the United States. Their sons and daughters now refer to themselves as Chicanos, run the local political machinery, own homes and rentals, and own a major portion of local businesses. Today they are not, by and large, employed in agricultural labor, nor do their children aspire to careers in agriculture. Nevertheless, the migrant pathways they forged are those by which newly arriving farmworkers continue to arrive in Parlier.

Temporary migration from Mexico to the United States has been a common phenomenon since 1884, the year the railroad link from Mexico City to El Paso, Texas, was established. The pattern of temporary migration to Arizona, Montana, and other western states was affected by the 1910 revolution, the upheavals that followed, and the prolonged struggle over land reform. In time, with the accelerating demands of an ever-increasing population, the numbers of temporary migrants rose. As population pressure increased, so did movement across the border. It is not difficult to imagine that the tide of movement from central Mexico, moving through Texas, would bring in its wake an increased movement from the border states of Nuevo Leon and Tamaulipas.

For some time afterward, these migrants were able to find employment in the Rio Grande Valley communities of Donna, Weslaco, Mercedes, San Benito, and others; yet the same pressures that forced them to seek work in Texas forced them eventually to search for work in Washington, Oregon, and eventually California. The Valley communities became the staging area, and Parlier became the receiving community, for migrants who today have become either settled residents or cyclical migrants. The history of the Jaramillo family exemplifies this flow.

Martin Jaramillo was born on a small ranch in Jalisco, during the turbulent postrevolution period. He first came to the United States to work in 1944 as a migrant; by 1947 he had settled in the United States, and he became a permanent green-card resident in 1953. After working some years in the lower Rio Grande Valley (including Weslaco), he settled in Parlier in 1963. Like other green-card workers, he has remained strongly attached to farmwork throughout his life. During his last year of farmwork, at age seventy-six, Jaramillo pruned fruit trees and picked nectarines, peaches, plums, lemons, and oranges. He now supports himself, his wife, and one grown daughter by housing unaccompanied male migrants.

Parlier attracts two different streams of migrants from Mexico. The first consists of migrants who come directly from sending communities in Mexico. The second is made up of migrants who move first into the lower Rio Grande Valley, where they work for a while, and then settle in Parlier. According to an excellent social history of Parlier (Trujillo 1975), there were migrants from both the lower Rio Grande Valley and the Winter Garden areas of southern Texas. Our interviews suggest, however, that Starr County (e.g., Rio Grande City) and the Winter Garden area (e.g., Del Rio) were less important sending regions than the lower Rio Grande Valley, particularly Hidalgo and Cameron counties.

An important element in the migration during the Bracero and post-Bracero period was mechanization. As cotton and sugar beets were mechanized, for example, some Texas-based midwestern migrants managed to settle out in areas such as Parlier, where jobs in other crops (e.g., grapes and peaches) were still available for a good portion of the year. A review of the history of lower Rio Grande Valley citrus production suggests that periodic freezes "pumped" migrants into the Texas-California migrant stream (Hudson 1979). Martin Jaramillo, for example, arrived in Parlier the year after the 1962 freeze in Texas, which lowered citrus production from 5,000,000 to 110,000 boxes.

Housing in Parlier

Like the other towns in our study, Parlier is characterized by "supersaturated" housing—living arrangements that may involve a number of different personal and economic relationships but that all result in extremely crowded living conditions. The average farmworker household size in Parlier is 7.3 persons.

Virtually all of Parlier is residential. Both old Parlier and La Colonia are compact, densely settled areas. Newly constructed homes, if not added onto the fringes of Parlier, are squeezed into open spaces in town. Downtown Parlier is an area of forty blocks, and La Colonia is made up of another thirty blocks. While much of the housing stock consists of unattached houses, there are several old buildings whose rooms are rented out to recent arrivals, backs of stores used for living quarters, and several motel-style complexes of dilapidated rooms next to each other. Garages, bedrooms, storage sheds, and tool sheds are also rented out to recent immigrants and their families. One house, for example, has nine outbuildings used as rooms or apartments. At one edge of town, a piece of property with three houses has had as many as forty workers living there. The several downtown buildings in which rooms are rented out have from five to fifteen units each. We estimate the downtown area of Parlier to include, therefore, well over a hundred rooms, most without heating or cooking facilities and sharing a common bathroom and shower.

Many houses that were originally single-family dwellings now house multiple families, with bedrooms occupied by relatives or rented out to boarders. The garage behind one of these is rented out during peak season to twenty to twenty-five workers who shower in a combined shower and bathroom behind the garage. In other cases, single-family dwellings are rented out to groups of lone males; at the peak of the harvest season, the overflow spills out into the neighboring vineyard.

The prices exacted for the worst of the crowded housing arrangements are up to $25 per week per renter. Thus, for example, a single-family house occupied by seven workers generates $700 per month rent. It is interesting that the $25 per week rate (for a room) is exactly the same one observed on the East Coast in Immokalee. Such a finding suggests that this figure is most likely pegged more to farmworker wages than to landlord costs. The availability of weekly rental arrangements is essential for workers living well below the poverty level, as few could accumulate the "capital" for the standard first and last months of rent. However, long-term residents of Parlier, more established, report paying rents as low as $200 per month.

Competition for housing is intense, and access to housing is a key element in every worker's or family's economic strategy. As might be expected, recently arrived immigrants have the least access to housing and live under the worst conditions when they do find housing. Access to housing is closely tied to work. In the two-bedroom house shared by a crew of seven workers, the "normal" rent of $700 per month is lowered to $14 per week per person ($395 per month) during periods when there is no work. The "housing benefit" of $11 per week provided by the labor contractor is a crucial element in keeping his crew attached to him. During periods of no work, the crew is allowed to simply accrue the rent. When work begins again, the accumulated rent is deducted directly from their checks.

From the farm labor contractor/landlord perspective, the arrangement is lucrative and beneficial as a labor control mechanism. By extending credit to his workers and decreasing an exorbitant rent to a more reasonable rent during slow months, the contractor both maintains a reserve labor force and keeps his rental housing fully occupied. The "benefit" of reduced rent is funded simply by not charging the most traffic will bear for a short period of time. His risk in extending credit is minimized by his ability to withhold rent due from his workers' paychecks and the loyalty he has secured. From the worker perspective, the rent is no higher than they would pay other landlords who might, in fact, throw them out if they ran short of cash during bad weather, injury, or a family crisis.

Another example of the close link between housing and work is illustrated in the budget of a recently immigrated Oaxacan who pays $100 per week into a pool of money shared by the household of lone males with whom he lives. The $100 payment covers not only rent but also food and transportation to work. This total subsistence package makes up about 40 to 50 percent of his weekly earnings.

Yet another example is that of a boardinghouse operator who charges $60 per week for room and board. The advantage of living at his house is that several labor contractors frequently call or stop by to look for workers who round out their crews. If no labor contractors come, the boardinghouse operator makes a special effort to secure employment for his boarders. For example, when a worker living at his house is unemployed, the owner calls acquaintances who are *mayordomos* to find work. While unfamiliar in the American workplace, this combination of support services—housing, food, and job search, combined with free check cashing—is an extremely attractive package to recently arrived immigrants with no cars, no bank accounts, and few job contacts.

Rental income is an important revenue source for Parlier homeowners and is potentially quite lucrative. The elderly man who rents out his garage to a large number of workers is able to gross up to $2,000 per month from this practice. At the same time, the main house that he, his wife, and a young daughter occupy is owned by another daughter who charges him no rent.

An important element in the housing stock of Parlier is public housing. The Parlier Housing Authority operates 50 "conventional" units of single-family housing and 130 units of the Migrant Farm Labor camp. Additional developments include La Paz Villa, an apartment complex of 81 units owned and operated by the National Farmworker Service Center, and the Orchard Apartments, a complex of 40 units financed by the Farmers Home Administration. These units of publicly funded housing represent approximately 25 percent of the total housing stock of Parlier (if we include rooms as single housing units).

Public housing in Parlier is extremely attractive. At the Parlier Plaza, for example, low-income families rent two-bedroom units for $366 to $395 per month. Rents at La Paz Villa, at $325 for two-bedroom units and $425 for four-bedroom units, are even more attractive. Unfortunately, only a relatively small portion of Parlier residents (17 percent of survey respondents) reported receiving "reduced-price" rents.

The Parlier Migrant Farm Labor camp (which is actually an apartment complex) is a somewhat different situation. Like other public labor camps in California, eligibility for residence requires proof that the applicant has migrated more than fifty miles and is a bona fide farmworker. The camp consists of two- and three-bedroom units each with a living room, kitchen, and bath, and equipped with a stove, refrigerator, and furniture, including beds and mattresses. The camp is largely occupied by migrant families from the lower Rio Grande Valley. A two-bedroom unit rents for $3.00 a day, with monthly rentals around $90. Hence, the competition for these units is intense. Camp services also include free day care for two- to five-year-old children and infants. Yet because slots for infant and day-care services are very limited, some older children care for younger siblings. An elected tenants' council meets monthly to resolve problems and decide on a variety of issues, including the camp's opening date for the following year.

Project guidelines allow for preferential rentals to former occupants who meet the eligibility guidelines (migrancy, income, legal immigration status). About 90 percent of the units are reoccupied each year by migrants from the former year. With the very low turnover, about ten units are "raffled off" to applicants each year. The effective "value" of the migrant camp to a migrant family of six persons is in the order of $400 to $500 per month, in comparison to "market rates." For a family of three workers (a couple and a teenager), the "value" of access to migrant camp housing is equivalent to about $1.00

an hour in wages, or 20 percent of their earning power. It is not surprising, then, that housing is one of the most important factors in stability of the flow of migrants.

Availability of housing appears to be the key factor that limits the "carrying capacity" of Parlier and the available labor supply. Because of the December 1989 freeze in the lower Rio Grande Valley, migrant workers began calling the Parlier migrant camp in February 1990, seeking to come early to California. Presumably they were prepared to do any work that was available, even though it is well known that March is the month of lowest labor demand.

While specific arrangements for housing in Parlier differ from those in other farm labor supply communities, in most cases the local area's ability to increase farm labor supply rests on either the availability of housing or a labor force willing to occupy ever more crowded dwellings. In each case, housing demand is so great that a substantial number of living arrangements are substandard, illegal, or both. Access to even substandard housing is a powerful labor recruitment tool, limited only by the housing provider's ingenuity and daring. In one case, neighbors who complained that workers were using backyards as toilets were either threatened by landlords or ignored.

As noted earlier, Parlier city government has given top priority to the housing problem and approached it with great creativity. While the complicated financing arrangements are beyond the scope of this study, approximately 90 percent of the Parlier Redevelopment Agency revenue for the past five years has gone to housing development, drawing on a variety of funding sources (e.g., Farmers Home Administration, local tax revenues).

Transportation

Parlier has no public transportation. Consequently, transportation has become nearly as closely linked to employment as housing has. Long-term local residents rely on private vehicles for transportation to work and a variety of services not available in town. Texas migrants also tend to own vehicles. Since most families (local and migrant) own only one vehicle, however, coordination with family, relatives, and friends is required for all family members to work.

Transportation problems of recent immigrants are met mostly by the system of *raiteros*, coworkers, or crew chiefs who charge for rides to work. The going rate is $4.00 a day. Not all *raiteros* are licensed, and for those without licenses the line between costsharing among coworkers and being in business is thin. There is some concern among farmworkers that the going rate will rise to $5.00 a day, as it already has with some van owners.

As noted, transportation is often linked to work arrangements. In Esteban Murillo's crew household, the *raitero* also happens to be the crew's *mayordomo*, working for Esteban yet using his position to earn money for himself on the side. Of the seven workers in the household, only two have cars. Julian Zamora, one of the workers with his own car, was the only one in the house to leave the Murillo crew for part of the year. Interestingly enough, because of his car Julian was able to supplement his farmwork income during slow periods with temporary jobs in construction, equipment maintenance, and poultry.

It appears that the *raitero* system, like the housing system, has achieved an elegant balance between greed and altruism. At standard rates, a *raitero* providing six workers rides grosses about $600 a month (double or triple the payments and operating expenses of a van), while the day cash payment of $4 (or weekly payment of $20) is manageable for most workers. If an individual worker were to seek to buy a car he or she would be looking at an outlay in the neighborhood of $800 to $1,000, in addition to the costs of a loan. Operating the car would then require the worker to go through the difficult process of securing a driver's license and to pay insurance. Alternatively, the worker could risk being stopped by police and cited for multiple violations. For the Murillo household of single men, the combination of job placement, housing, transportation, and credit "services" provides a net of control as powerful as the classic examples of crew control exerted by labor contractors in the East Coast migrant stream.

The California characteristic of linking transportation and work, in contrast to the classical eastern horror stories of abandoning crews far from home, generally relies not on coercion but on a strategy of mimicking the mutualism of traditional Mexican systems of *compadrazgo* (ritual co-parenthood). Such a strategy may also constitute a disguise, for there are accounts of *mayordomos* who will not employ workers unless they ride with them (and pay the usual rate for the ride). Lack of transportation, coupled with lack of a telephone, compound the difficulties of the job search and have important structural implications in labor market segmentation, since drivers can separate crews by vehicles as well as tasks, positions in hierarchies, rooms, and so forth.

Transportation also affects decisions to migrate. Rides to Washington cost between about $125 and $150, to Idaho, about $150. As with local *raiteros*, the transaction has aspects of cost sharing and aspects of business. One *rait-*

ero, for example, bought a van and covered the gas with $1,000 generated by transporting eight workers north. In Washington, he sold the van and came home on a bus. The high cost of rides to the Pacific Northwest suggests that transportation advances (or grower-provided transportation) could both be economically feasible and serve as a significant recruitment incentive.

Public Services

Some publicly funded services are important to community life in Parlier. Low-income housing programs are the most visible single service in Parlier. As important for the migrant population, however, is the multiservice migrant health clinic operated by United Health Centers of the San Joaquin Valley. Slightly over a quarter of the survey respondents (26 percent) reported making use of reduced-price health services, compared with 17 percent for public housing. Emergency food and shelter have been mentioned by several respondents.

Adult-education programs providing general education degree (GED) or English as a second language (ESL) classes are also important to the community. Almost one-fifth of the heads of household (19 percent) had taken ESL, math, or GED classes. Use of the Aid to Families with Dependent Children (AFDC) and food stamp programs appears to be moderate, with 10 percent of households reporting some reliance on food stamps during the previous year and 13 percent reporting use of the Women, Infants, and Children (WIC) program.

The child care provided by the migrant camp is an important element in the economic strategies of migrants from Texas because it frees all adults in the family to work. Increased child care would improve the summer-school program participation of children who otherwise must take care of younger siblings and free mothers who currently have to remain home with children.

While recently immigrated workers are aware of emergency services, including medical care, but are not aware of even those other services for which they are eligible, long-term residents are generally aware of the full range of services and find them to be of moderate importance in their economic strategies.

Parlier as a Northern Destination in an International Migration Network

Like other transnational communities in the western United States, Parlier is composed primarily of immigrants. This is reflected in the ethnic affiliations of farmworker heads of household. Three-fourths (74 percent) of our survey respondents described themselves as Mexicanos, 17 percent as Mexican Americans or Chicanos, and 9 percent as Mixtecos. Only 7 percent of the current worker heads of households were U.S.-born. However, the 10 percent of foreign-born Mexican Americans, similar to U.S.-born Mexican Americans, include Texas-based migrants and those who came to the United States at an early age. The immigrants reflect the increasingly heterogeneous character of the farm labor market with regard to ethnicity and region of origin. Parlier's farmworker community includes immigrants from both "traditional" migration networks in the states of Michoacán, Guanajuato, Jalisco, and San Luis Potosi (44 percent) and from "new" migration networks in the states of Colima, Guerrero, Oaxaca, and urban centers such as Mexico, D.F., and Pachuca, Hidalgo (39 percent—$N = 115$). Though they are not represented in the survey, Parlier also includes a small number of Guatemalan immigrants.

Important village-based networks feeding immigrants to Parlier include Santiago Naranjas and San Juan Mixtepec, in Oaxaca; Monte Alegre and Tres Palos, in Guerrero; and Colima, in Colima, among the new networks. Sending villages in the traditional networks include Tangancicuaro and J. Mugica, in Michoacán; Teocaltiche and Jalostitlan, in Jalisco; and Guarapo and Leon, in Guanajuato. The networks of Texas-based migrants coming to work in Parlier during the summer are also strongly binational, with links to Dr. Cos, Las Aldamas, and Linares, in Nuevo Leon.

Two important issues concern the origin and formation of "new" networks. Massey et al. (1987), Cornelius et al. (1982), Mines and Martin (1983), and other migration researchers have emphasized that many of the traditional migration networks originated in the chaotic period after the Mexican Revolution. Recent work by these same researchers, along with our findings, however, indicate that the economic problems experienced by Mexico during the 1980s also influenced the size and composition of current migration flows. Kearney and Nagengast (1981) have linked emigration from the Oaxacan highlands to ecological factors in home-village areas, including increased soil erosion, and to the development of labor-intensive agriculture in Sinaloa and Baja California. These two areas have provided staging areas for Mixtec immigration into California agriculture. Not surprisingly, much Mexican-based agricultural production is done by or in partnership with firms that also produce in California and the U.S. Southwest; these corporate linkages at the managerial level facilitate experimenting with Mexican labor from different areas within Mexico before encouraging their migration to the United States.

Our ethnographic work revealed that the fathers of several of the very recent Oaxacan immigrants had been in the United States during the Bracero period, while other Oaxacan migrants were the children of parents born in Oaxaca who had left the Mixtec region to go to an urban area within Mexico. Confronted with a decaying urban labor market, these sons of domestic Mexican migrants apparently tapped into the fund of knowledge about migration from their parents' home villages to guide them northward. As noted in contemporary research (Runsten 1993; Zabin et al. 1993), members of one of the Mixtec-speaking, extended-family networks in Parlier, for example, came to the United States by way of Sinaloa. Other members had previous experience migrating within Mexico as well, to sugarcane and vegetable-producing areas. While children of Bracero-era migrants and sons of Mixtec urban migrants have the advantage of well-developed family and village support networks, some first-time, non-Mixtec Oaxacans have only rudimentary awareness of areas in the western United States with concentrations of fellow Oaxaquenos.

The Guerrero networks have linked Parlier and Guerrero since 1973, but the group is differentiated internally by village of origin. Five years ago, a newer group of migrants from Guerrero arrived in the United States. Among the Parlier survey respondents from the state of Guerrero, 47 percent arrived only within the last year. All of the Guerrero migrants are living in households of unaccompanied males include not only *campesinos* (peasants) but also workers with nonagricultural work histories.

Although Guerrero and Oaxaca have not been major sending areas for U.S.-bound migrants, they have, since the 1960s, experienced strong out-migration to Mexico, D.F., and other urban areas. The urban experience, occupational background, and educational levels of the recently arrived immigrants to Parlier from both states suggest that the stagnation of urban job growth and the economic development of rural communities have played major roles in diverting the rural to urban migration streams from their destinations in Mexico northward toward the United States.

Among the foreign-born household heads interviewed ($N = 114$), the largest proportions arrived during the 1970s (33 percent) and since the mid-1980s (32 percent), with only 15 percent arriving before 1970 and the remainder arriving during the 1980–85 period. Recent migration to Parlier appears to include a growing proportion of workers who have migrated fairly extensively—within Mexico, between Mexico and the United States, or both—before arriving in Parlier. This includes rural-to-urban migration in both the United States and Mexico. This pattern contrasts with the ''one-to-one'' correspondences between rural farmworker ''sending areas'' in Mexico and farm labor demand areas in the United States documented in studies such as *Return to Aztlan* (Massey et al. 1987), although there is also immigration via these mature international networks. The increasing geographical mobility of the farm labor force coming into Parlier may signal the growth of a population whose members incorporate frequent migration to a number of locations into their lifetime employment strategies. Each of their movements, moreover, leaves a residue. The growth of transnational networks and communities, with ties in a number of regions, villages, and cities throughout North America, is both a symptom and result of this broader process.

Almost half of the heads of households interviewed in Parlier (43 percent) return regularly to Mexico. Since 1986, cyclical migrants who achieved legal status as seasonal agricultural workers (SAWs) can return to their home villages without having to pay fees to *coyotes* for crossing the border. Also, now that they can legally enter Mexico with vehicles purchased in the United States, they can easily provide relatives with transportation to the border; their undocumented relatives have to pay *coyotes* only for the actual border crossing.

In large part because of the seasonal nature of farmwork, cyclical migrants are even more heavily represented in the farm labor force than in the Parlier community as a whole, making up more than half (54 percent) of the heads of household who are current farmworkers. Among the cyclical migrants in Parlier are two distinct groups of equal size: young, pioneering migrants who are coming north for the first or second time, and older migrants who have settled into a seasonal pattern of migrating north for work and returning to home villages during the off-season.

International migration from the Mexican sending states of Jalisco, Zacatecas, Michoacán, and Guanajuato has been going on for some one hundred years. In his work on Tlacuitapa, Las Animas, and Gomez Farias, Cornelius (forthcoming) discusses that long tradition. His conclusions support research by Mines and Anzaldúa (1982), Massey et al. (1987), Alarcón (1988), Goldring (1990), Kearney and Nagengast (1981), and others. The flow of migrant workers to the United States from these areas was only briefly broken during the depression of the 1930s and then increased during the 1940s and 1950s. Like other central Mexican migrants, individuals from these communities were enthusiastic participants in the Bracero Program. Large numbers of households had as many as three generations of individuals who had migrated to the United States for work.

Migration to the United States and the remittance of U.S. dollars have allowed individuals to realize goals in Mexico such as the creation and maintenance of small-scale, family-run operations that include homes, family-owned businesses, and small (even if inefficient) plots of land. Researchers on the region concur that the result has been a continuous and increasing flow of migrants to the United States from these communities, the Immigration Reform and Control Act (IRCA) notwithstanding, and an increasing dependence on dollars in the local economies. Following Michael Burawoy's (1976) comparative work on Mexico and South Africa, several researchers have underscored the importance of Mexico as a labor reserve. Alarcón (1988) refers to the phenomenon as "nortenizacion" and suggests that it causes communities to become nurseries for reproducing laborers for U.S. labor demand markets. Rouse (1988:7) suggests that Aguililla has become a "nursing home for wage-laborers in the United States"; Mines observes that Las Animas fulfills a similar role. Like the Aguilillans, migrants in Parlier from these west central communities have established various outposts in the United States. A description of their arrival in Parlier and the surrounding area illustrates how such outposts become established.

Like Rouse's informants, west central Mexican interviewees stay in Parlier for varying lengths of time. Those who have chosen to stay maintain contact with the communities they left; even those who may have left some time ago generally return to their home community for occasional visits. In early writings, Cornelius has suggested that the migration of whole families is indicative of permanent migration "regardless of destination" (Cornelius 1976:11). Yet during the course of our investigations in Parlier, we found that the migration of *female* household members is most likely to result in the establishment of the "outposts" but does not necessarily imply permanent migration or settlement. Other factors, including access to or purchase of stable housing and access to permanent employment, also influence settlement. The following case demonstrates the ways in which networks create linkages among a variety of locations in the United States while remaining anchored in a single Mexican village.

Some of the first migrants from Guarapo to Parlier were the Gonzalez brothers. In the mist of the Mexican Revolution in 1914, four brothers, Pedro, Jose Luis, Manuel, and Armando Gonzalez, made their way to the United States.

Pedro and Manuel returned to Guarapo between 1928 and 1930, leaving two of their brothers—Jose Luis and Armando—behind in Fresno County. These two brothers both married and remained in Sanger (a short distance from Parlier) with their families. Back in Guarapo, Pedro married Carmen Romero. Their first child, Consuelo, was born in 1930. Her birth was followed by the birth of Agustina ("Guti") in 1931, Maria de

Los Angeles in 1932, Rodrigo in 1934, Domingo in 1936, and Alfonso in 1940. During
the same period, other networks of migrants from Guarapo took root in Santa Ana and
Sacramento.

Rodrigo and Domingo, two of Pedro's sons, came to the United States for the first
time in 1956 as Braceros working on ninety-day contracts. Shortly afterward, in 1961,
at the age of thirty, Pedro's daughter Guti came to the United States. With her was a
female first cousin, Lourdes Espinoza. She applied for a tourist visa at the El Paso,
Texas, border and was given a three-month permit. The two women traveled to Watsonville, California, where Lourdes had two nieces. The original plan was to spend two
weeks with her nieces. After remaining in Watsonville for a while, however, Guti
found work in Los Angeles as a housekeeper. She lived in Hollywood at the time. She
says she got the job by applying at an employment agency. Later, Guti was able to
help other immigrants to get jobs as housekeepers also. Guti married in Los Angeles
and had a son, but after several years she left her husband and came to stay with her
uncle Armando, who had remained in Fresno when Guti's father moved back to Mexico. It was then that Guti began to work in farmwork—work she did for over two
decades. This was a full-time, year-round job with a Japanese, family-owned agricultural firm. Although she is now retired from farmwork, she supplements her income
by taking in boarders and providing them with meals, a role she played even while she
was still working full-time in farmwork. She also babysits for her son and daughter-
in-law's young child. Neither her son nor his wife work in farmwork.

Guti's youngest brother, Alfonso, came to the United States for the first time in
1966, when he was twenty-six. According to Alfonso, when he arrived, his uncles, Jose
Luis and Armando, were still living in Sanger. Like his sister, he carried his uncle's
addresses with him when he came to California. A *coyote* charged $300 to transport
him from Tijuana to Sanger. On that first trip, Alfonso says he was in Fresno County
for only one or two weeks and returned to Guarapo. He worked in the table-grape
harvest and remembers being paid $1.65 per hour. He returned to California the next
year, making his way to Riverside, where he worked for three or four months harvesting oranges. He then left Riverside to come to Parlier. About a year after Alfonso's
arrival, Guti married Nico Calabretta, a U.S.-born citizen of Italian descent whose
sister and Guti had worked together in Los Angeles. Nico was employed with the
Immigration and Naturalization Service. Guti and Nico were married in May, and by
July she had received her permanent resident-alien card. Soon afterward, with Nico's
help, Alfonso Gonzalez and his older brothers, Domingo and Rodrigo, were able to
secure either border-crossing cards or visitor's permits to cross the border. In 1968,
when Alfonso and his brothers came north again, they came to the homes of their
uncles, who had in the meantime moved from Sanger to Parlier. However, they eventually went to live in the camps provided by the growers. He explains that in those days,
mayordomos often came to the labor camps at the ranches looking for workers.

Ever since his arrival in Parlier, Alfonso has worked there for long periods of time,
spending as many as nine to eleven months of the year in Parlier and then returning to

Guarapo. On only two occasions has he stayed in California through the winter. Since he dislikes the weather in the winter, he usually leaves once the grape harvest is over. Alfonso is a wanderer and in 1983 went to Houston, where he did landscaping work ("en las yardas") for two months because no agricultural work was available in Texas. He returned shortly thereafter to Mexico. He states that he went to Houston with a *coyote*. He learned about the *coyote* through *guias*, middlemen who provide that kind of information in Guarapo.

In 1984, Alfonso went to Washington State with a number of workers from Parlier in a pickup truck and worked in Wenatchee and another town in the apple harvests. They returned in time for the fruit-tree thinning. In 1986 he made a return trip to Washington "con uno de las Zacatecas." Once there, they went first to Juan Lucas's home, a man originally from Guarapo who has been living in Washington since 1985 with his U.S.-born wife and two children.

Alfonso continues the yearly pattern of migration back and forth from Guarapo to Parlier. His sons, daughters, and nephews have settled in Parlier for most of the year and return to Guarapo only when emergencies arise or on occasional holiday visits. Because Alfonso's children and nephews live in Parlier, he has no difficulty finding a place to stay when he comes north. And since he has been migrating to Parlier for so long, he has no difficulty finding employment when he returns. Currently, Alfonso is working for Remick Farms, where his nephew, Gilberto Gonzales, is employed. Gilberto has secured work for all of his brothers and at least one of his cousins at Remick, forming part of a year-round crew.

Following these pioneer immigrants have been successive waves of more recent immigrants. In 1978, Gilberto, great-nephew of the original pioneers to Parlier, arrived at the home of his aunt Guti. Until his marriage to a woman who was born in Parlier, Gilberto, with other newly arrived workers, lived in a room built behind the garage.

Gilberto was followed by a brother, Miguel, seven years later, in 1985, and eventually, in 1986, two more brothers came north. By this time, Gilberto and his wife had purchased a house and could provide a place for his brothers to live. A cousin of Gilberto's arrived in 1990 and moved into his house. Gilberto has been able to secure jobs for his brothers and the cousin on the ranch where he is a permanent, year-round employee. Four brothers from this particular family are now living and working in Parlier, although older migrants from Guarapo continue the year cycle of returning to Parlier and then home to Guarapo for the winter when work slows down. Today, individuals with ancestral ties to Guarapeños living in the Sacramento area own their own landscaping businesses in which they employ recently arrived Guarapeños. Others living in the area are employed in the service sector. Communication is still vital among Guarapeños living in each of the nodes of this large network, allowing recently arrived Guarapeño migrants a number of employment options.

Three sons and three daughters of Alfonso Gonzalez are now living and working in Parlier. Two of the youngest daughters are newcomers, having left Guarapo, where they were born and raised. The $600 cost of transporting them from the border at

Tijuana to Parlier was borne by their older siblings, already established in Parlier. Both went to live with their Aunt Guti, as their predecessors had done before them. The eldest, age twenty-one, quickly secured a false work permit and is now employed in a packing house. The youngest is having more difficulty securing a job because of her age.

The Gonzalez case illustrates a number of the essential features of migration and the development of transnational communities. From the migration of a small group of brothers in the early part of this century, today the Gonzalez family has developed the social, cultural, linguistic, and physical infrastructures to accommodate the easy movement of family members between Parlier and Guarapo. Guti Gonzalez's and the other women's roles in this process have been particularly interesting. While the single-male migrants of the Gonzalez family tended to move back and forth, it took Pedro's two brothers' marriages and their niece's migration to lend stability and predictability to the family's migration. Guti's arrival and subsequent marriage secured a foothold in Parlier that, though previously established by her married uncles, had not served as central a role as Guti's household. With the exception of her uncle Armando's role, Guti's migration was achieved largely in the company of women and through female network ties. Once established, or anchored, in Parlier, Guti's household, now both household and rooming house, allowed other members of the Gonzalez family to migrate into Parlier and move out into other regions, jobs, and sectors of the labor market. The close connection between Guarapo and Parlier remains, however, and links the two communities in a migration stream that spans generations and draws on lateral as well as lineal kinship ties.

Many of today's immigrants from Mexican cities have some history of migration within Mexico before coming to Parlier. Such people, while indistinguishable from other young, unaccompanied men working in farmwork, have virtually no experience as farmworkers. While they may be employed by labor contractors or growers alongside workers from *campesino* backgrounds in Mexico, they are hired primarily because of their willingness and ability to adapt to a workplace dominated by immigrants, not because of their ability or skill as farmworkers.

Based on our survey, migrants from the state of Guerrero make up the largest proportion of recently arrived, undocumented immigrants to Parlier. Almost half (47 percent) of our respondents from Guerrero have arrived only within the last year, and all are living in households of lone males. In addition, some are not native speakers of Spanish, although no amount of coaxing would elicit their native language.

Like the immigrants from urban areas in Mexico, the rural Oaxacan interviewees have extensive domestic migration histories and experience. Transnational migration began for some as early as 1979, although they did not migrate first to California. Immigrants from Oaxaca informed us that their fathers had come to the United States during what they refer to as the period of *las contrataciones* (the Bracero period). Unlike migrants from central Mexican states, however, they did not immediately reenter the United States illegally following the end of the Bracero Program. For many Oaxacans, the termination of the program initiated a search in the Mexican interior for labor demand areas. The tremendous economic pressure of the initial peso devaluation in 1975, however, forced them to enter the United States, going first to Oregon and eventually to California in search of work.

Like the newest migrants from Guerrero, many of the new immigrants from Oaxaca speak Spanish only as a second language or not at all. Increasing numbers of Mixtec-speaking migrants are entering United States agricultural-labor markets and contributing to the development of a body of literature on so-called new sending communities (Zabin et al. 1993). The migration of Mixtec-speaking migrants and other indigenous peoples from both southern Mexico and Guatemala is seen as a contemporary manifestation of the ethnic replacement that has characterized farm labor throughout the United States.

Mixtec-speaking migrants in Parlier, coming to the area since 1979, are not the newest arrivals; others came whose fathers did not precede them, and most of the Oaxacan influx is recent. Thirteen percent of the respondents from Oaxaca first came to the United States less than one year ago, and the mean number of years in the United States for Oaxacan migrants we interviewed was two. The low mean is a result of the large influx of newly arrived Oaxacans taking advantage of established Oaxacan networks. As in the case of Guti Gonzalez, established Oaxacan networks center around households containing women who are related to a variety of consanguineal and affinal male kin. As is typical, however, more recent arrivals live in households of lone-male migrants. This is not surprising, since new sending areas have not yet established the mature California support networks so evident in our material on the Gonzalez family. Recent immigrants from Oaxaca have arrived in Parlier because *coyotes* informed them that other Oaxacans live there and that they would find work. Many of the new arrivals among the Oaxacans are relatively well educated, have little or no agricultural work experience, speak no indigenous languages, and see themselves as distinct from the Mixtecs. By contrast, the Mixtecs have more migration experience, more farmwork experience, and better job contacts. By distancing themselves from the more established Mixtec networks, these newest Latino arrivals from Oaxaca are forced to rely instead on labor contractors and informal providers of services. The following case of the emigration of a single community in Oaxaca demonstrates the ways in which the indigenous Oaxaquenos have been able to secure firm positions in the farm labor market.

Like so many other west central Mexican workers, many Oaxacan migrants in Parlier trace their migratory paths back to the Bracero Program. Many of their fathers had preceded them to California. Before that, most had migrated within Mexico in search of work. Javier Lopez recalls that when individuals from his Oaxacan hometown—Santiago Naranjas—wanted to register for the Bracero program they had to travel to Huajuapan de Leon. There were roads to Santiago Naranjas, but no buses passed through. They could walk to nearby towns and take buses into Mexico City, where they could register for the program. Some of these workers first found work in the cotton harvests of Sinaloa, Mexico. Those who worked hardest in cotton would be given the opportunity to sign up for the Bracero contracts.

When the Bracero Program ended, individuals from Santiago Naranjas traveled to areas inside Mexico, looking for work. They worked in the sugarcane harvest and in the *jitomate* (tomato), corn, and jicama harvests.

At that time, *mayordomos* from the sugarcane harvesting area would come to towns in Oaxaca to recruit workers. Many of those *mayordomos* were originally from Santiago Naranjas but had gone to work in sugarcane sometime earlier and had earned a position of trust with their employers. According to Teodoro Valle, these *mayordomos* were paid to take workers back to the sugarcane harvest.

The newest Oaxacan migrants we interviewed came first to Oregon. For example, in 1968, at age fourteen, Javier Lopez, our key informant, went to Navajoa, Sonora, where he worked in a taco stand for three years. He first came to Navajoa with an older brother who had been working there for two years before bringing Javier north with him. The older brother had gone to Navajoa because he had a friend living there already. This was the first trip Javier had made out of Santiago Naranjas. When he arrived in Sonora, he says he did not speak Spanish well. He states also that there were very few Oaxaquenos there when they arrived.

The next year Lopez went north again, this time to Campo Mula in Sinaloa with another brother, Rafael (now deceased), and a friend, Timoteo Garcia. They walked from Campo Victoria to downtown Culiacan, Sinaloa. After this, Lopez found his way north to San Quintin, in Baja California, where he worked in tomatoes during the entire decade of the 1970s. Finally, in 1979 he traveled to Hillsboro, Oregon, a town "discovered" by a close friend of his, Gonzalo Varela, who had first gone there the year before. Varela and Lopez had first met in the Mexican tomato fields when they were teenagers. Eventually, Lopez had become the supervisor of a tomato-picking crew, and Varela had worked under him as a crate packer.

After finishing the strawberry harvest in Oregon, Lopez went to Selma, California, and Varela went to Washington for the apple harvest. Lopez came to Fresno County through his contact with Samuel Luevanos, a worker he had met in the Hillsboro camp. They went there and were hired, although at the time, Lopez says, most of the workers at the Selma ranch were from Michoacán.

When Varela and Lopez first arrived in 1979, the occupants of the camp in Hillsboro were "familias de Tejas, de la area de McAllen" [Texas families from McAllen]. By 1981, the occupants were all lone-male Oaxacans from their village network.

Another of the workers on that first trip of Oaxacans from Santiago Naranjas to Oregon was Teodoro Valle. Valle's path northward begin in 1966 when he, like Lopez, had gone to Culiacan. From there he went to Navajoa to work for his uncle. He worked there for six months. His uncle owned three taco stands at the time. Valle worked selling tacos.

In Culiacan, Valle earned the money to make the trip to Oregon. With his half-sister, Tomasa, he left on March 20, 1979, but they were deported shortly after crossing the border. They reentered with the help of a man who charged them $100 each for the trip. He drove without even stopping for riders to go to the bathroom. He provided no food. He also required all of them to lie down the entire trip. Upon arrival he demanded payment. When they eventually arrived in Oregon, in mid-June, the strawberry harvest was almost finished. Tomasa and Teodoro went to the same camp. They stayed for the strawberry, caneberry, and cucumber harvests. In 1981, Teodoro went to a camp in Gresham, Oregon, with a friend, Gerardo. In 1982, Teodoro finally went to the "Campo Azul" in Hillsboro, where he works now. He notes that when he arrived most of the workers were from Guerrero and Jalisco, and very few were from Oaxaca. They worked through the cucumber harvest and left Oregon for Parlier, searching for Teodoro Valle's uncle, Rodolfo Dominguez, who was living in Parlier. Dominguez had come to California during the Bracero period and, according to his son, worked somewhere in California, picking lemons and harvesting lettuce. He was also among those individuals who later left Santiago Naranjas to go both to Veracruz and Cuautla, Morelos, to work in the sugarcane harvest and tomato harvest once the Bracero Program was terminated.

Sometime between 1970 and 1972, Dominguez began traveling to Sinaloa and Sonora to work. It was not until 1975 that he began to enter the United States once again, as an illegal worker. By 1979, he was known by other migrants from Santiago Naranjas to be living and working in Parlier.

In 1979 and in 1980, when Tomasa Valle went to Oregon to work in the strawberry, raspberry, and cucumber harvests, she didn't like the work because the pay was too low. She decided to remain in Parlier during the early part of the summer. However, all the male members of the household have maintained a pattern of returning to Hillsboro for the strawberry harvest, beginning in June and staying until the end of the cucumber harvest (July or early August). They return to Parlier for the raisin-grape harvest.

Along with other members of her household, in 1989 Tomasa Valle was employed in agricultural work for most of the year. During January she pruned and tied grapevines. No work was available in February. In March she thinned tree fruit. In April she thinned grapes and in May began picking peaches. In June she harvested bell peppers, returning to tree-fruit harvesting in July. In August, September, and until the tenth of October, she worked the raisin harvest. Through the year she worked only in the Parlier area. There was no work for her in November, and she collected unemployment compensation. In December, she returned to vine pruning.

The workers from Santiago Naranjas—Javier Lopez, and Tomasa and Teodoro Valle, their friends, and other relatives—have now established a household of both nuclear- and extended-family members and friends. As in the Gonzalez case, the household circulates around the earliest arriving female, Tomasa, who maintains a two-room cabin in Parlier and stays in the area throughout the year.

Although Tomasa Valle recently became employment authorized through the SAW program, many Oaxacan migrants were forced to return to their home villages or could not convince their home-village authorities to release them from their village obligations (or "cargos") and therefore were not able to apply for SAW permits or amnesty. Nevertheless, Oaxacans still travel to Oregon and to Parlier, whether legally or illegally, facilitated by Valle and her household.

All members of Tomasa Valle's household and Oaxacans we interviewed from Santiago Naranjas are full-time agricultural workers. Almost all make the trip to Hillsboro for two months of the year, return to Parlier and surrounding communities for the raisin-grape harvest, and make the trip to Oaxaca when that season is over. Tomasa Valle is the exception, staying all year in Parlier and supplementing her unemployment compensation checks with housekeeping jobs for local residents. Most of her extended household returns to the established northern outpost in Parlier for the start of vine pruning in December.

The Oaxacan migration into Parlier seems to be much more of a secondary migration, after internal migration in Mexico, than the primary migration described for the Gonzalez family. Clearly, however, similar processes drew Oaxaqueños into Parlier: the Bracero Program; increasing road and rail development; and greater involvement of *mayordomos*, *coyotes*, and other labor intermediaries. Most interesting, however, is again the important role women immigrants play in anchoring networks to regions and stabilizing migrations. Despite other contrasts, this characteristic describes migration from other communities in the United States and the borderlands into Parlier as well.

For example, the migrant network connecting the lower Rio Grande Valley to Parlier is a very mature, stable one that covers two to three generations of migrant farmworkers. This network appears to have become established to supply labor to the Texas citrus industry. Sending communities for current migrants are the same ones that migrants left in the 1950s.

The Texas/Nuevo Leon (borderlands) networks in Parlier can be divided into two groups. The first, coming from the border states of Nuevo Leon, Chihuahua, and Tamaulipas, began arriving in Parlier in the late 1940s and early 1950s. Individuals who left Montemorelos, Los Medinas, and Reynosa, Nuevo Leon, apparently arrived in Texas and became part of the stream of migrants moving to Oregon, Washington, and California, a migration facilitated extensively by *troqueros*.

The second group was brought to Parlier as children, worked as part of migrant households, and eventually settled in Parlier. They are among the least likely to be working in agriculture today. Those who remained in agriculture are employed as year-round, full-time employees, but most are employed in blue-collar jobs in construction and as skilled technicians. Their children and grandchildren are no longer working in agriculture. The case that follows demonstrates, however, that the two groups are not entirely distinct from one another; instead, the first group laid the social groundwork for the second group to seek work outside of agriculture. The case of the Valdez-Campos family shows this process occurring over three generations.

The evolution of a network that has its inception in Montemorelos, Nuevo Leon, is best seen through the experience of Leonardo Valdez, who retired to Weslaco after many years of living and working in other areas.

Born on May 23, 1906, in Montemorelos, Valdez first entered the United States, without papers, in 1926, a period of accelerated migration from Mexico. All that time, he was working at home as a *mediero*, a sharecropper. He says he began working at age fourteen, as his family was poor. The first year he arrived, he describes the area around Weslaco as consisting of small, twenty- to forty-acre tracts owned by firms just beginning agricultural production. According to Valdez, it was not until 1930 that more agriculture was visible, namely, cotton, corn, and winter vegetables. He says that work was available in cotton harvesting, which paid by the pound, from the early 1930s until 1958. Hourly wages and piece rates at the time were low. He recalls that in 1926 hourly wages were $.15 per hour and a normal workday consisted of ten hours. In 1950, hourly wages were $.25; in 1956, $.70.

From his initial entry into the United States until 1955, when he applied and received a permanent-resident permit, Valdez lived in Reynosa and crossed the border to "el valle" to work in seasonal harvests. His wife and children remained in Nuevo Leon. In Reynosa, he worked on a ranch that produced carrots, beets, and cotton on irrigated land.

During the 1950s and 1960s, according to Valdez, an abundance of work was available to agricultural workers in Texas. During the winter, work was available in vegetable harvests. Many workers were employed in the harvest, and much of the work was done by hand.

In 1956, already middle-aged, Valdez went to Washington State for the first time to harvest asparagus. At that time, *troqueros* cruised the main street of Weslaco to recruit casual workers but also made arrangements with neighbors to go north. Valdez paid $30 for the ride to Washington and the contact with an employer. Workers were paid a piece rate amounting to $.03 a pound.

Valdez worked in hops production during the decade of the 1950s because, he said, apple-harvest work was not given to Mexican workers. Anglo workers picked apples.

The same year that Valdez went to Washington, his daughter Abigail married Jesus Campos, a young man born in 1930 in Cerritos, San Luis Potosi. At age fourteen, Campos had left Cerritos and gone to Progreso, a Texas bordertown about twenty miles east of Reynosa. He worked in Texas exclusively until 1956, when he made his first trip to Washington with Valdez. Like his father-in-law, Campos continued to go to Washington State. After several seasons, a friend encouraged him to stop in Parlier on the way home to Texas. The friend had an aunt living in Parlier with whom they could stay. Campos states that in those days finding work in Parlier was not difficult. Ranch owners put up signs announcing the availability of jobs. He found a job quickly and decided he liked the town. Soon after he settled in Parlier, his father-in-law arrived with his sons (his first wife was now deceased) and stayed for seasonal work, adding Parlier to his migrant itinerary. Valdez and his sons continued this migration pattern until his sons married. One married and stayed in Parlier, and the other married and stayed in Washington.

In 1960, Campos brought his wife from Texas and settled in Parlier. He has worked for the same firm for twenty-eight years and is a permanent, year-round employee. His children do not work in agriculture, although as teenagers all except one worked on farms. Two of the four children attended Fresno State University and completed degrees, and a son has made the military a career. Campos's youngest daughter is attending a local junior college.

Valdez remarried and had two daughters, both of whom attended Pan American University. Now a very elderly but spry retired man, he has settled in Weslaco. None of Valdez's or Campos's children expects that their own children will ever work in agriculture.

Again, linkages among friends, kinfolk, and friends' kinfolk are the medium by which immigrants from Nuevo Leon move into other harvests and eventually choose the locations in which they settle. And once again, in this case it was a connection with a female relative—a friend's aunt—that led Valdez's son-in-law to Parlier, where he settled, brought Valdez, and raised his children.

A second group of migrants from Texas originally came from the border state of Nuevo Leon. Seventy-five percent of the respondents giving Nuevo Leon as their community of origin live in the Parlier Migrant Center. The mean year of arrival for heads of household and their spouses from Nuevo Leon is 1971. Of the U.S.-born migrants and their spouses and children, 62 percent were born in Texas, and most of the rest in California. The U.S.-born workers who migrate regularly between Texas and Parlier constitute one of the few groups of domestic workers in the agricultural labor force. Adult children, part of extended households of these families, are more likely to be employed in agriculture than others of their generation.

The provision of low-cost housing, including utilities and child care, replicates the pattern utilized throughout the California migrant housing system. The availability of this particular housing has encouraged and perpetuated whole-family migration, but, unlike other migrating family units, those living in the camp are even today viewed as outsiders by residents of Parlier. Stories of welfare fraud, laziness, and unemployment among residents of the camp abound. In Parlier, residents preface derogatory remarks by referring to the Migrant Center as "el campito" and residents of the center as "los del campito."

Residents of the camp are committed agricultural workers. Their employers insist that they work every day for the 180 days they are in the camp, showing the same strong relationship between work and housing in the farm labor market in Parlier that was reported for the labor demand regions of the north. Interviews in the camp indicate that almost all heads of household and their spouses are employed in agriculture during the time they are in the camp. With the exception of two women we interviewed, all spouses are employed in agriculture, often working in the same crews with their husbands. The case of the Hernandez family, presented below, exemplifies those who occupy the camp. Their access to camp housing, year after year, allows them to provide a basis for other relatives' entry into the community and the agricultural work around Parlier.

Trino Hernandez was born in Miguel Alerman, Tamaulipas, in 1962 but has spent twenty-eight of his twenty-nine years in the United States, traveling with his parents and siblings throughout Texas, Oregon, Washington, and California as a migrant agricultural worker. His wife, Rosalia, was born in Fresno. When the Migrant Center opened again this year, Trino, Rosalia, and their three children returned to the unit they had lived in last year. With them came Rosalia's sister, Victoria; her husband, Santiago; and their three children.

Trino Hernandez is now driving a truck hauling raisins from the dehydrator in Selma to the packing house in Fresno. Throughout the season, he will haul raisins from Madera, Caruthers, and other communities within a one-hundred-mile radius of Fresno. He has been driving a truck, putting in fifty or more hours a week, for the last five years. He likes the work and has no interest in changing jobs. After the season, he will return to Weslaco, Texas, with his family and draw unemployment compensation. He has been guaranteed that he will be retired when he returns next year.

For most of the time they are in Parlier, Rosalia Hernandez works in a packing house until raisin-grape harvest begins; then she moves into the fields to pick grapes. Her sister and brother-in-law arrive in Parlier earlier and begin their seasonal round with fruit thinning. After they move in with Trino and Rosalia, they begin the fruit-harvest work and stay until the end of the raisin-grape harvest. Santiago and Victoria will return to his home community of Ixtlan, Jalisco, until March of the following year.

Trino's parents live in the Migrant Center and continue to work in agriculture. He also has three sisters. Two of his sisters are married and are also living in the camp with their families, who are also employed in agriculture.

Network Connections Between Parlier and Other U.S. Locations

Because Fresno County is the site of some of the most intensive agriculture in California and the nation, Parlier does not lose many workers to emigration. As is evident from the case histories above, however, lone males and others migrate north to Washington and Oregon during temporary troughs in the central California harvest season; there, they work in the early asparagus and cherry harvests and the late apple harvest. In Parlier, as in the other farm labor communities described in this volume, access to free or low-cost housing accommodations appears to be a crucial element in a farmworker family's willingness to migrate. Two-thirds (65 percent) of the workers who migrated from Parlier to another labor demand area went to a work site where employers provided housing. One group of unaccompanied Mixteco males, who migrated to Hillsboro, Oregon, for the berry harvest, went in part because the employer-provided housing allowed them each to save twenty-five dollars a week in rent, although there was little work available when they first arrived and, later in the season, there was a large surplus of workers competing for a limited number of jobs.

The diffusion of migrants throughout the labor-intensive agricultural areas of the United States is facilitated by the existence of "switchboard" households of unaccompanied male migrants—unrelated migrants from distinct migration networks who end up living together in a crowded household and exchanging information regarding jobs, working conditions, wages, means of transport, labor contractors, and so forth. One typical household of this type in our Parlier sample included several workers recruited from the ranks of urban workers in Los Angeles because of growing concern by an established labor contractor about availability of workers following the 1986 changes in immigration laws. Unemployment insurance data shows that Los Angeles–based workers, many of whom were relatively "casual" farmworkers with the bulk of their earnings in nonagricultural employment, were an important element in the farm labor force in California even before immigration reform (Martin 1989). Our observations suggest that the intensity of such urban-to-rural migration flows may increase as urban immigrant receiving areas, like rural ones, experience surpluses of workers.

The composition of a "switchboard household" of lone males recruited by one labor contractor suggests an excellent alternative to established, "mature" networks of extended family members. Such households are composed of a much more "chaotic" and weaker set of network relations. The household of Los Angeles migrants includes a young worker who has recently lived almost equally in Fresno County and Pachuca, Hidalgo; another recently immigrated young worker from Colima who initially migrated to Los Angeles to work in construction; a teenaged worker who came from urban Mexico directly to Parlier in 1989 via relatives in Los Angeles; a worker permanently residing in Parlier; a long-term cyclical migrant from Jalisco who had worked in manufacturing in Los Angeles before moving into farmwork; and an emigrant from urban central Mexico who came to the United States after working as a street vendor in Tijuana. There are no family relations among them, unlike most of the other networks described previously. In contrast to the households of unaccompanied workers from a single village who share a single, common fund of knowledge, each resident of diverse households such as this one can provide new information on migration destinations and working conditions to his *compañeros*.

The Regional Agricultural Labor Market

The regional labor market in which Parlier is situated includes primarily Tulare and Fresno counties, although there is some spillover of workers into Kern County to the south, and Madera County to the north. The Fresno area, the "heart" of the San Joaquin Valley, is the center of agriculture in California. For many years Fresno County was the number-one agricultural county in the

United States, with total agricultural sales of $2.6 billion in 1989. Fresno agriculture has been intensive ever since irrigation systems were developed in the late nineteenth century. Fresno is also a major regional manufacturing and service center, however, with heavy manufacturing, light manufacturing, and a wide range of agricultural-support-service firms.

A historical division exists between the eastern and western sides of the valley. Lying below the foothills of the Sierra Nevada, the eastern side was traversed by various rivers that flow northwest toward San Francisco Bay. In part because the gold rush took place in the Sierra foothills and in part because of the availability of water, railroad lines were built along the eastern side, stimulating the growth of family farms and small towns. The western side of the valley remained little more than desert until the government subsidized irrigation works after World War II. Now the western side is characterized by large farms growing field crops, tomatoes, melons, and vegetables, with few impoverished towns sprinkled here and there. The eastern side around Fresno is still characterized by a diverse farm structure and grows mostly fruits, such as grapes, peaches, nectarines, plums, and citrus. The east side is also more densely settled than the west, with medium-sized towns such as Sanger, Reedley, Orange Cove, Dinuba, Cutler, and Orosi, and slightly smaller towns such as Parlier and Del Rey. Running diagonally from northwest to southeast is an urbanized strip along Highway 99. The agricultural towns of Fowler, Selma, and Kingsburg are diversifying rapidly. East-side communities, while still rural in character, are being affected by Fresno's growth, becoming its suburbs.

Parlier sits in the middle of a highly developed agriculture of tree fruit and vines, probably the largest contiguous area of intensive fruit horticulture in the world. One can drive for many miles in any direction from Parlier and see only orchards and vineyards. The labor intensity of these operations has not changed much in the past century. Although this area has experienced extreme need for seasonal agricultural labor, it has always been characterized by producers who, for a variety of reasons, failed to participate in government-sponsored labor programs. Area growers have therefore always pushed for liberal immigration policies, continually relying on new waves of immigrant workers.

Because the land around the city of Fresno was settled early on by homesteaders and others who bought small parcels of land from the railroad, there were no huge expanses of land held in single farms in and around Parlier. Yet the passage of time has been accompanied by the steady concentration of landholdings. Thus, while many thousands of grape and fruit growers from around Parlier, a relatively small number account for most of the production.

The exception to this is raisins, where some five thousand growers of all sizes survive, many through off-farm work activity.

Land concentration has lately become more pronounced, in part because of financial stress and in part because of the aging of the farm-family population. The average age of farmers in California is about sixty-two, and many who live on relatively small acreages sell out when they retire. For-sale signs dot the countryside. Some properties are bought by new, part-time farmers escaping to the country, but most are bought by the larger diversified operations. Packing-house owners in the area, in need of additional acreage to expand their range of marketable fruits, for example, are driving some of the concentration. One owner said that he used to have fifty small growers who sold him their fruit, but he has bought out all but a few over the years. An overview of the major labor-intensive crops in the central California area of the study appears in Table 8.1.

Aggregate seasonal demand for labor consists of the sum of demand for the different crops (Table 8.2). The July peak labor demand of 96,060 hired workers is more than 250 percent of the March trough demand of 38,120 workers—the underlying structural factor leading to both the very high levels of seasonal unemployment and the high summer influx of migrants. Since the production schedule for each crop is affected differently by weather and

TABLE 8.1 Major Labor-intensive Crops, Fresno and Tulare Counties

Crop	Acres Harvested	Production Value (millions)
Almonds	40,383	$74.8
Broccoli	9,700	31.2
Cantaloupes	38,300	57.7
Garlic	12,700	37.0
Kiwifruit	1,856	12.6
Lemons	5,698	27.0
Lettuce	17,810	81.9
Oranges	94,626	524.5
Nectarines	20,454	125.5
Peaches	17,995	95.7
Plums	34,362	137.4
Raisins	201,258	406.0
Table grapes	31,698	182.9
Wine grapes	48,950	55.5
Tomatoes	6,010	34.5

Source: California Agricultural Statistics Service, 1989 (based on County Agricultural Commissioners' Reports for 1987).

TABLE 8.2 Agricultural Workers Hired in Fresno and Tulare
Counties, by Month, 1989

Month	Fresno County	Tulare County
January	33,320	24,180
February	25,930	27,880
March	16,840	21,280
April	19,470	24,200
May	28,980	30,650
June	41,640	37,640
July	54,210	41,850
August	52,210	36,770
September	48,620	41,280
October	23,070	35,610
November	21,330	24,480
December	22,760	23,840

Source: California Employment Development Department Report 881-M, February 1990.

marketing considerations, the likelihood of spot labor shortages increases in areas with multiple labor-intensive crops. For example, the end of the nectarine, peach, and plum harvests overlaps with the beginning of the grape harvest.

The crop task for which spot labor shortages have been most frequently reported, the raisin harvest, not only competes with the end of the tree-fruit harvest, it also has unusually low wages for work that is unpleasant relative to other agricultural tasks. A profit squeeze in the raisin market in the early 1980s put a number of growers out of business, simultaneously lowering wages and piecework rates; the latter fell from $.16 to $.10–$.12 per tray (about a 30 percent drop). The wage depression is so serious that a 1988 wage survey found some workers earning about 15 percent below the minimum wage (California. Economic Development Department 1988). Wages in 1989 returned only to the previous rate of $.16 per tray, although, adjusted for inflation, the rate should be $.25 per tray. The survey found hourly earnings to range from $3.63 per hour to $11.13 per hour, in a relationship only very poorly correlated with piece rates offered and a generally chaotic labor process, including the appearance of workers who had not been hired but who joined in picking with crews in the hope that they could continue working (and be paid).

Farmworkers interviewed in Parlier worked in a relatively narrow range of crops and tasks. Peak demand for labor appears to begin in late May, with the harvest of tree fruit (nectarines, peaches, and plums) and continues through the harvesting of grapes (table, wine, and raisin) until the collection of the "rolled trays" (sun-dried raisins wrapped in paper). Current farmworkers observe that the amount of work available in any given task is decreasing yearly because of competition among growing surpluses of workers. The agricultural-labor demand in the area cannot be represented as consisting primarily of demand for harvest labor. Availability of labor for a wide range of pre- and postharvest tasks is also an important component of labor market demand.

Field tasks do not exhaust the inventory of demand for agricultural labor. A wide range of agricultural-support occupations complement field tasks, including sorters, packers, checkers, loaders, truckdrivers, labor contractors, equipment salespersons, repair persons, bookkeepers, and so on. Processing-plant and packing-shed labor is of particular importance, since these jobs are sex-segregated and a leading source of income for women workers (see Ruiz 1987).

Demand for supervisors at a variety of levels is very important, and the quality of supervision varies greatly, leading to numerous labor management problems. Quality of supervision and workplace organization are widely recognized to be important elements in worker productivity and business profitability. Consequently, concerns about supervision are important parts of growers' personnel-management strategy, whether that strategy consists of simply hiring a labor contractor or conducting extensive in-house staff training. Perhaps because of the high demand for supervisors, women occupy supervisory roles in some operations, although some field tasks (e.g., pruning) remain sex-segregated.

Meeting labor demand in this region, with its wide variety of labor-intensive crops, mix of very large and very small producers, and differing labor recruitment and managing strategies, is not a simple business of getting pickers into the fields. Instead, it is a complex proposition involving year-round planning, coordination, and a variety of tradeoffs. To appreciate this complexity, the remainder of this section reviews in greater depth the labor demand in the specific crops that dominate the Parlier area.

While the principal crop of the area is grapes, increasing plantings of stone fruit have been made. Peach acreage increased by 66 percent, plums by 71 percent, and nectarines by 80 percent. The improved ability of California to export such fruit has improved its profitability, and there is a slow evolution in the Parlier area from grapes toward fruit orchards. In Madera, Fresno, and Tulare counties in 1987, there were a total of 72,811 bearing acres of freestone peaches, plums, and nectarines.

The labor process in these three fruits is similar. Trees are pruned in December and January, thinned during a three-week period in April and May, and harvested from May to September. While these tasks are done by seasonal workers, other agricultural practices are performed by year-round employees. Fresno County Cooperative Extension personnel estimate that seasonal labor requirements for peaches and plums are around 360 to 380 person-hours per acre. During 1970–80, therefore, the expansion in acreage in the three-county area has added over 11.5 million person-hours to the labor demand profile.

These figures show the difficulty of expanding seasonal crops. If we assume that all the thinning must be done in three weeks' time and that seasonal workers were employed sixty hours a week over a three-week period, then an additional 15,757 workers were needed just to thin the increased acreage. If we assume that the harvesting could be done over three months, then only 5,320 full-time workers (sixty hours per week times twelve weeks) would be needed to meet additional harvesting needs, and 7,100 full-time workers for a two-month pruning season. Depending on how farms mix these tasks, then, the additional acreage would create labor demand for between 15,000 and 20,000 workers.

The labor management practices of the stone fruit growers in the Parlier area reflect the seasonality of production. There are approximately one hundred shippers of stone fruit in the region, with most packing houses scattered throughout the small towns and others located on farms. Parlier itself has three principal packing houses, with several more on surrounding farms. As reported in previous chapters, there are distinct tiers to the agricultural labor force in Parlier, with different groups of workers enjoying differential access to more preferred, less seasonal, and higher-paying jobs. A typical strategy is to employ a core labor force of local, settled workers, supplemented by a six-month seasonal labor force, which in turn is supplemented with peak-season workers in thinning and harvesting. For example, one firm employed in the field twenty locals year-round, another thirty locals for most of the year, and about a hundred cyclical migrants from Mexico for six months, starting with the thinning season in April. This directly hired labor force (as opposed to labor hired through contractors) was then supplemented by contract labor at the peaks of thinning and harvesting, with contractors providing another hundred or more workers. Workers hired by the firm are thus employed continuously for at least six months, and as the firm expands it expands both this directly hired labor force and its demand for contract labor.

An integrated firm such as this also expands its packing-house employment, which was about seventy workers at the time of the interview. Fruit-packing jobs are seen as desirable employment by the settled population of

Parlier. Historically, packing houses have been staffed by women (Ruiz 1987), and Parlier is no different: most of these jobs are taken by local women or by female cyclical migrants whose husbands usually work in the orchards.

Another ranch operated with thirty year-round workers, hired thirty to forty more for the six-month season, and then supplemented this workforce with a contractor who provided a hundred or more workers at the peaks. The proportion of contract to directly hired labor varies according to the particular mix of varieties and crops and to the extent the firm desires to hire its own workers or to minimize its responsibility to provide steady work for its labor force. Some of the larger firms have taken to using contractors for almost everything that has a seasonal nature to it, including providing packing-house crews.

The growth of many of these grower–shippers gives them the opportunity to spread work out through the year by planting varieties that fill in periods of down time. Nevertheless, certain tasks and harvests create seasonal spikes of labor demand that have been exacerbated by increases in producing acreage. It is these peaks that create the need for an excess supply of labor and that the firms have resolved by turning to farm labor contractors. The contractors are then faced with the task of stringing together enough jobs to be able to hold a labor force from the spring through the grape harvest in September. Because this is the daunting challenge that firms are unwilling to confront themselves, contractors must usually endure high rates of turnover as workers leave to find enough work.

One of the local farm leaders has hundred-acre fruit-and-vegetable farm outside Parlier where the family hires about twenty workers on a year-round basis. They claim to use no seasonal labor. They are able to provide ten months of work to their employees through complementary cropping and then have a woodlot where the workers can cut and sell firewood during the other two months. This is a clear demonstration that the pattern of seasonality can be at least partially overcome by a conscious effort to smooth labor demand. It is not clear, however, that it could be done on the scale of the larger grower–shippers, and it certainly could not be done if absolute short-run profitability is the sole criterion for planting decisions.

The Fresno area has been the world's principal raisin-grape producer since before the turn of the century. This continues to be the case, but the grapes grown for this purpose, the Thompson seedless, can also be used to mix in wine or can be shipped fresh as table grapes. The agricultural practices employed differ slightly according to end use, but the possibility of alternative markets to siphon off overproduction has been important in sustaining the growth of the industry.[2]

Generalized overplanting of grapes occurred in California in the 1970s, fueled in part by tax shelter arrangements. Several markets that sustained this overplanting declined, particularly the bulk wine and wine cooler markets, which lessened the ability of raisin growers to divert their grapes into wine, as a 1983 law decreased the percentage of varietal wine that could be accounted for by such blending grapes as Thompsons. As Nuckton, Heppel, and others have noted, this led to a crisis in 1983, when the largest raisin crop ever was delivered to packers as the Thompson seedless share of the wine crush fell from between 20 and 25 percent to 12 percent. As a result, raisin growers' average returns fell from an average of $1,204 per ton in 1979–82 to $590 per ton in 1983. This in turn led to a fall in raisin vineyard values from $10,840 per acre in 1982 to $6,850 per acre in 1984 (Nuckton 1985) and to $4,000 per acre in 1986 (Heppel and Amendola 1992). A large number of growers thus faced foreclosure.

From the point of view of the labor market, this scenario had an important consequence. On the one hand, there was a significant expansion of grape acreage, which required more workers. In particular, the expansion of raisin grapes and their increasing use as raisins and not as wine meant that the peak labor demand in the raisin harvest in late August and September was exacerbated. On the other hand, the extreme financial pressure on growers in the mid-1980s led to downward pressure on wages. Thus, the Fresno area needed more workers willing to work at lower wages, at a variety of tasks.

For raisins, labor demand ranges from a low of 24.3 person-hours per acre during the first few months of the year to a high of 57 person-hours per acre during September, with few tasks that need to be done during the rest of the year. Wine grapes, too, have peak periods for pruning in December through February, leaf removal in May, and harvesting in August and September, requiring 20 to 30 person-hours per acre for each of these tasks. By contrast, table-grape labor needs are more evenly distributed over the year yet still need high labor inputs during the summer months.

There is a growing demand for workers to remove leaves to allow more sun to reach wine grapes. This is a relatively labor-intensive practice that has created demand at a fairly slow time of the year. Because pruning can be done over a several-month period in the winter, it is really only the harvest that creates labor supply problems.

The wine-grape harvest is accomplished by hand-cutting grapes into picking pans, which are in turn dumped into a gondola pulled through the field. Crews of three to six workers are used for a one-ton gondola, and larger crews for five- to six-ton gondolas. The crews are paid piece rate jointly by the gondola. This is considered a good job by the workers.

The raisin-grape harvest begins late in August, with most of the fruit picked during the first two weeks of September. Bunches of grapes are cut into pans, which are in turn dumped onto paper trays and spread over the paper to dry. Workers are usually given individual rows to harvest and are paid according to the number of trays. This is considered a bad job by the workers because it requires a great deal of bending to spread out the grapes and because it is relatively dirty. Piece rates are such that it requires extremely hard work to make significant amounts of money, but traditionally a large amount of work has been available over a short period of time. Workers have often dealt with this by bringing their families to help them pick, which has further depressed wages.

If we assume that people work sixty hours per week for four weeks on the raisins (although some work seventy or more, and the time period of the raisin harvest varies), then the industry needs 39,071 workers just to get the fruit on the ground. If we assume that half the raisins harvested in that month also must be turned and rolled within the same time period, then at seventeen hours per acre, an additional 1,992,630 person-hours are required, or the equivalent of 8,303 additional workers. This is a total of 47,374 workers. The industry estimates that 55,000 workers are needed, which is the equivalent of saying that all the raisin grapes must be picked, turned, rolled, and boxed within one month with people working sixty hours per week.

The increase in raisin acreage of 40,860 between 1976 and 1985 translated into an increased demand for 9,700 additional workers under the same assumptions. Thus, the industry faced a 25 percent increase in labor need at the harvest at the same time as the increased acreage was leading to financial disaster. Financial crisis coupled with labor surpluses caused piece rates to be cut by $.04 per tray between 1983 and 1984. Thus, piece rates in raisins are about $.15 to $.16 per tray, as they were ten years ago. In real terms, this has meant a significant loss of income to farm workers through inflation. This situation depended on continuing influxes of new immigrant workers and others willing to put their families to work to meet the labor demand needs of employers.

Is it any wonder that, as noted earlier, Fresno-area growers have supported immigration policies that allow easy migration between Mexico and the United States? The highly seasonal nature of raisins and other Fresno-area crops has contributed to the flooding of the entire agricultural labor market in California. If fifty thousand workers are needed to harvest raisins, then surely sixty thousand or more were at work in late August in Fresno in 1990. The short crop was harvested in record time, and workers interviewed expressed bitterness in their inability to get sufficient work. Many had been idle for some weeks waiting for the harvest to start, only to find that they were able to work for only a couple of weeks, and that there were usually too many workers in the fields. As several told us, you had to work like the devil or you would get two-thirds of the way down your row only to find someone had finished his and was coming at you.

Technological change has not improved this situation. Indeed, there has been no discernible mechanization in fresh stone fruit, apart from the use of mowers to prune the tops of some large orchards. The only change in the harvest has been the introduction of bags instead of buckets for picking. This change was made to lower the bruising of fruit and did little to improve the productivity of labor, although the bags are somewhat more convenient and less cumbersome. Growers interviewed had no expectations of technological changes.

The mechanization of the wine-grape harvest has proceeded gradually for twenty years. Perhaps 30 percent in the Fresno area is now mechanized. Such mechanization reduces harvest labor demand from about forty hours per acre to five and so has a significant effect. Table-grape harvesting and field packing require tremendous care, heavily dependent on hand-pickers to maintain high-quality fruit, and there are no prospects for mechanization. Raisin-grape harvesting can, however, be done by machine. Our participation in the 1990 mechanical harvesting tour in the Fresno area demonstrated this convincingly. One grower in particular has been developing a machine for many years, and it appeared to work well. However, the tour also demonstrated that mechanization is not imminent, as workers at some of the ranches told us that the machines had not even been used this year, since labor was abundant and it was simpler (and perhaps less costly) to harvest by hand. Thus, labor surpluses and low wages in raisins discourage mechanization.

Many of the tasks that follow the harvest may be mechanized. Several simple and relatively inexpensive machines have been demonstrated to turn and pick up raisins off continuous tray rolls. Growers are often concerned to pick up raisins in a hurry if rains come. Also, many workers leave after the harvest, and it sometimes becomes difficult to obtain workers quickly in late September. These tasks are estimated to require seventeen hours per acre of seasonal labor, and with mechanization probably no seasonal workers would be required. This would be a significant reduction in labor demand, but it would also serve to increase the seasonality of the already highly seasonal raisin harvest.

Fresno-Tulare-Madera County Farm Labor Market Dynamics

Despite dire predictions that with immigration reform America's food would rot in the fields as legalized farmworkers left agriculture, labor supply and demand in central California increased significantly because of expanded production. While the trend in stone fruit appears to be toward a smoother labor demand curve with slightly less fluctuation, the sharp demand spikes associated with the raisin harvest continue to pose a real concern to local producers. Given fluctuations in demand, one of the most interesting of our findings is the degree to which informal networking modulates the constantly shifting balance of labor supply and demand and buffers agricultural producers and the whole system against destabilizing forces.

Serious problems for workers and genuine concerns for agricultural producers remain that could be mitigated by deliberate efforts to improve the efficiency with which the available labor force is utilized. What this study reveals is that the central California farm labor market is affected not so much by "surface-level" changes in the social and economic framework as by more slowly acting, deep-level forces—the evolution of migration networks; the changing face of what is now a hemispheric, if not global, agricultural economy; long-term demographic and social changes in American culture and the immigrant population; and the development of the local economy and infrastructure, particularly housing.

Unfortunately, these forces seem to have evolved beyond the point of relying on a domestic labor force to harvest America's crops. The employment and earnings of current farmworkers suggest that farmwork is much too unpredictable to interest many currently unemployed local workers or workers in other low-wage occupations. Even those who are familiar with farmwork, willing to work long hours in physical labor, and tied into networks allowing them access to agricultural employment seem uninterested in entering the farm labor force.

Workers currently employed in farmwork are primarily those who came to the United States to work in agriculture and who have done so since their arrival. Survey data on farmworker earnings indicate that local workers' disdain for farmwork reflects, in part, the fact that farmwork does not represent a viable economic strategy except for persons who have explicit and effective

social strategies for surviving well below the poverty level. Many of those
workers who have made the adaptations to allow them to remain in farmwork
(e.g., cyclical migration, securing access to low-cost housing in the migrant
camp, supplementing their income by selling services to other workers) are
strongly attached to farmwork. Because of this poverty, labor force participation is very high, with virtually all able persons over thirteen years of age
working at some point during the year. Without retirement benefits, furthermore, older adults continue to work as their health permits.

Data for Parlier and the communities discussed in this study indicate that
seasonal unemployment and the risk of underemployment even during peak
harvest season are the main factors underlying farmworkers' poverty. The key
problem workers face is securing enough hours of work each day and maximizing the number of days of work during the peak season. This is a consistent
problem, although the off-season troughs of low labor demand in Fresno and
Tulare counties are less extreme than in some other areas (e.g., southern
Texas).

In Parlier, 37 percent of the current farmworkers reported having held at
least one farmwork job during the year that resulted in subminimum daily
earnings (i.e., less than eight hours at the minimum wage). In some cases, the
subminimum daily earnings resulted from a piece-rate wage that did not yield
a minimum hourly wage, but the majority of low daily earnings stemmed from
short workdays. Workers were underemployed even during peak season, with
one-fifth (19 percent) reporting that they had at least one week during peak
season in which they could not work a full week; a similar proportion (20
percent) reported at least one day in which their earnings fell below the minimum because of short hours.[3]

Overall, our data indicate that current farmworkers in Parlier have a mean
of 7.1 months of farmwork employment per year. Our questionnaire did not,
however, adequately capture the full extent of unemployment in moving from
one job to another, in short workweeks, or in short workdays. Our observations suggest that this figure overestimates the actual amount of work farmworkers have available. This is, also, an average, which does not reflect the
variability that exists between workers in the farm labor market. Reported
earnings, for example, varied significantly for different groups of Parlier farmworkers. Unaccompanied males had a mean annual income of $4,005. Ex-
tended-family households had mean annual family incomes of $10,835, while
nuclear-family households had the highest earnings, with a mean annual income of $11,716. As these data indicate, the welfare of farmworker house-
holds rests on the existence of multiple wage earners for each family. All the

subgroups of current farmworkers in Parlier fall below the federal poverty guidelines, after comparing mean family income to mean family size. Of course, the adequacy of family income to meet each family's basic economic needs varies according to family expenses, especially housing expenses. Moreover, again, the averages do not fully reflect the variance in family size and individual family earnings.

Policy emphasis on low hourly wage rates has obscured the more critical issues of employment security and low annual incomes relative to costs of living. The peak-season mean weekly earnings of current farmworkers in Parlier is 125 percent of the weekly earnings of a full-time, minimum-wage worker, yet the annual earnings of an unaccompanied male worker are about 45 percent of the earnings of the same minimum-wage worker's annual earnings. It is not surprising, therefore, that key concerns in farmworkers' economic strategies involve managing the inherent insecurity of farm labor employment. The priority given to employment security also explains workers' extensive noneconomic investments in networking activities to improve the stability of their employment, reflected in network recruitment.

Labor Recruitment and Management

Employers who rely on network recruitment invest substantial effort in these same informal social activities, such as visits to friends and relatives in sending villages. Employers' recruitment aids that mitigate the inherent employment instability of farmwork (e.g., loans, free housing, emergency assistance) appear to be cheaper to provide than wage increases. By allowing farmworkers to survive such misfortunes as illness, injury, broken vehicles, or no work because of bad weather, these ''benefits'' give the impression that farmwork job offers are capable of sustaining and reproducing a population of workers. Such ''benefits'' have all but replaced those fought for by unions during California's turbulent labor history.

Fresno County, and Parlier in particular, have historically been at the center of union influence, but, through the 1980s, union contracts in agriculture declined precipitously. United Farm Workers statewide contracts have decreased to fifteen thousand jobs and a membership of 22,800. A corollary of union decline has been an increase in farm labor contracting. More than three-quarters (78 percent) of the farmworkers interviewed in Parlier had worked for a farm labor contractor at least once during the preceding year.

Farm labor contractors are increasing in importance in the local agricultural

labor market. Wages paid by farm labor contractors almost tripled in the period from 1978 through 1987, rising from slightly over $150 million to about
$430 million statewide. Fresno County is, if anything, even more reliant on
labor contractors than other areas of the state are. This is in part because of
changing immigration and other laws, which make it feasible for growers to
pass some of the paperwork and other regulatory responsibilities from their
own operations onto the shoulders of farm labor contractors. Also, the increase in labor contracting is a result of long-term changes in the agricultural
workplace that are occurring nationwide, especially greater reliance on specialized and general agricultural-service firms. Don Villarejo's (1988) tabula-
tion of third-quarter 1987 wages paid on fruit-and-vegetable farms by employer type shows that 35 percent of wages were paid by farm labor
contractors. A later report indicates that 42 percent of agricultural employers
used "labor market middlemen" during 1988 (Martin and Taylor 1990). Finally, studies conducted for the Commission on Agricultural Workers (1993b)
found farm labor contracting to be a crucial component of labor supply and
supervision in the California tomato and citrus industries (Zabin et al.
1992:49–53; Mason, Alverado, and Riley 1993:82). Reliance on general farm
management services is also on the rise.

Farm labor contractors occupy an important niche in the farm labor market,
moving workers from one crop task or location to another—a difficult proposition in a labor market in which each agricultural employer is competing not
only with fellow employers seeking workers for similar tasks but also competing with other crop tasks. By filling this role, farm labor contractors "stabilize" farm labor. At the same time, the cost of stabilization is surplus labor,
a reserve pool of workers, constantly replenished through immigration. The
increasing control of farm labor employment by labor contractors significantly
constrains the "free-market" flow of workers to employers who hire workers
directly.

As with other trends in the farm labor market, the move by agricultural
employers away from paperwork and the associated liabilities related to compliance with a variety of labor laws and regulations appears part of ongoing
structural change in the labor market. The job package provided by a labor
contractor, for a surcharge of about 15 percent of wages and benefits, includes
administrative services, paperwork associated with regulations, labor recruitment, and worker training and supervision.

Farm and Nonfarm Work in Parlier

Almost everyone in Parlier (89 percent of the respondents) has done farmwork
at some point. Almost two-thirds of the respondents (63 percent) performed

some farmwork in the year we conducted the survey. Only 44 percent, however, listed farmwork as the most extensive work they had done during the previous year. Another 7 percent had held a job in agriculture-related work such as packing or processing as their longest job during the year. Because our spouse and teenager interviews included a higher proportion of respondents who are housewives and students who were not working or seeking work, the proportion of heads of household who are current farmworkers is even higher than in the overall labor pool—72 percent.

Work histories show that almost half of the current farmworkers are strongly committed to farmwork—33 percent of all the heads of household had worked only in farmwork over the five-year period. A slightly larger proportion (39 percent) had mixed farmwork with nonfarmwork employment. Leading nonagricultural occupations for heads of household are work in unskilled janitorial, restaurant, and domestic work (7 percent); construction (6 percent); unskilled manufacturing (3 percent); and other unskilled services (3 percent). Another 4 percent of the heads of household held technical or managerial jobs, or were the proprietors of their own businesses.

Reflecting the high turnover rates in the farm labor force, nearly one-third (31 percent) of the respondents said they were definitely not planning to do farmwork in the coming season or thought it would be very unlikely. Another 63 percent said they were very likely or certain to do farmwork. Only 6 percent were uncertain. These proportions changed when we examined subgroups of workers. Nearly all (88 percent) workers legalized as special agricultural workers (SAWs) said they were definitely or very likely going to work in farmwork in the coming season, while less than a quarter (22 percent) of U.S.-born workers were definitely or likely to do farmwork. While this suggests that SAWs in Parlier are not moving out of agriculture in the catastrophic scenario that had concerned agricultural interests, they are very gradually building the skills, contacts, and experience needed to improve their employment stability, either by leaving farmwork or by moving upward into positions as core workers, foremen, or labor contractors.

An overwhelming majority (84 percent) of the current farmworkers we interviewed in Parlier are very likely to remain in farmwork in the near term. This may be related to their legal status, as slightly over one-third (36 percent) of the current farmworkers surveyed in Parlier are undocumented immigrants. Another third (35 percent) are SAWs or pre-1982 immigrants who were legalized under the 1987 immigration reforms. The remaining third of the labor force consists of green-card workers and U.S.-born workers. Only 6 percent of the current farmworkers said they would not consider farmwork in the coming season. Of the respondents who were not currently farmworkers, about one-

third (34 percent) were willing to consider doing farmwork. Yet after review-
ing this pool of potential farmworkers case by case, it became evident that
this willingness does not equate to a reliable employment-authorized pool of
farm labor. More than half of the noncurrent farmworkers willing to do farmwork were not employment-authorized. Another third were older workers or
had a physical ailment likely to affect their ability to work.

Among the youth, the case against farmwork was far more clearly stated.
None of the teenagers not currently doing farmwork was willing to consider
working in farmwork. The continuing participation in the farm labor market
of Parlier teenagers who are currently farmworkers is related in large part to
their parents' requiring them to be part of a family work group. In contrast,
the group of teenagers expressing some interest in continuing in farmwork
were from the Texas-based migrant families. The case study in Weslaco indicates that for the southern Texas teenagers key factors related to continued
participation in the farm labor force include whether they complete high
school, family constellation, and marriage into a migrant family with extensive network connections.

The data from Parlier and the other communities discussed in this volume
suggest that "new" supplies of farmworkers are not likely to come from the
ranks of employment-authorized domestic workers. The findings do, however,
reveal an important asymmetry in the balance between "potential exits" and
"potential entrants." The group of potential exits, current farmworkers considering leaving farmwork, is much larger than the group of potential entrants
and is much more likely to respond to improvements in wages or working
conditions. Developments that might reduce exit rates include, for example,
improvements in unemployment insurance support for underemployed farmworkers and farmworkers who are unemployed for very short durations, programs designed to facilitate the upward movement of field workers into increasingly responsible supervisory positions, and collaboration between the
public and private sectors to improve the availability of free housing for migrants. Achieving such improvements, however, requires greater appreciation
of the relation between workforce stability and productivity than is evident on
today's farms.

New and Old Networks in Parlier

The case material presented above shows that recent arrivals from villages
with well-established traditions of migration can rely on an extended-family

network built by previous generations for housing, transportation, and job contacts. By contrast, recent immigrants from new sending networks may have access to a village "fund of knowledge" about types of crops and places in the United States, but little more. We consider it significant that the group of migrants to Parlier who live entirely in an unaccompanied male households are the Guerrerenses, since they come from a new sending region in Mexico.

In Parlier, as in Immokalee, well-developed market mechanisms have grown up to provide recent arrivals with the barest of support services they need to survive in the United States. This constitutes an "artificial" support network. While these artificial networks replicate many features of the more "natural" village-, ethnic-, or family-based networks, they differ from natural networks along such lines as their close correspondence to labor demand, the length of time they offer support, the bare survival nature of the support, and the fact that their reproduction does not depend on demographic processes. In Parlier, the key elements in this support network are landlords who provide access to crowded housing in the "dormitory" households occupied by unaccompanied males, the *mayordomos* and labor contractors who engage in "drive-by" hiring, and the *raiteros* who provide workers with transportation to the fields. We do not have detailed information on credit transactions, but moneylending is also important in artificial support networks.

An important aspect of artificial support networks is that, to a certain extent, they mimic traditional Mexican institutions of reciprocity among extended family and neighbors (e.g., *compadrazgo*). At the same time, they allow recently immigrated workers to function fairly effectively in a culture and labor market they know little about. The standard $25-per-week fee for a place to sleep in a crowded living room, garage, or backyard monetarizes informal traditions of hospitality and expense sharing; the standard $4 per day for rides to work monetarizes cost sharing for transportation; and the provision of credit by labor market intermediaries such as *mayordomos* and labor contractors is a longstanding feature of Mexican labor recruitment by *enganchadores*. The drive-by labor market in Parlier, where labor contractors and *mayordomos* visit crowded households of unaccompanied males to recruit workers, functions very effectively for workers who know little about the labor market. At the same time, the functioning of this drive-by labor market or the similar street-corner labor market requires a surplus of workers without the family contacts others use to secure employment.

The cost of crowded housing and transportation, the essential ingredients for recent immigrants to participate in the farm labor market, amount to $55 to $60 per week, approximately one-quarter of the average unaccompanied male farmworkers' mean earnings of $215 per week during the peak season. Taking into account the fact that the overhead costs of housing and food continue even when work is slow or nonexistent, the food, shelter, and transportation costs of unaccompanied males may well approach 50 percent of their earnings.

In addition, the artificial networks available to unaccompanied males provide less security than networks of extended-family members; on the other hand, unaccompanied male workers can tolerate higher levels of uncertainty than migrant families can. Security in the unaccompanied-male networks stems primarily from the ability to share housing costs, the exchange of information, and mutual support in deciding to take risky courses of action (e.g., to leave town in search of work in another area) and in negotiating with employers and foremen. The artificial support networks in the Parlier labor market play a critical role in supporting the continued migration of cyclical migrants, most of them unaccompanied males who return home to their village each year, and in making the pioneering migration of newcomers a great deal less risky than if they were forced to develop their own job contacts.

Recruitment of farm labor relies so heavily on the extended family or village and the artificial network support systems that working in farmwork requires that potential farmworkers know and successfully function within "the rules of the game" of these systems. This aspect of the "working conditions" of farmwork is, in large measure, one of the most important barriers segmenting the current farm labor market from many other portions of the U.S. labor market.

Long-Term Demographic and Social Changes Affecting Farm Labor Supply

In Parlier, a long-term demographic change is under way that will have significant consequences for farm labor supply. The second and third generations of Mexican-Americans, the children and grandchildren of Bracero-era green-card immigrants, are very different from the older generation and, perhaps, from each other. If the farm labor force were not constantly replenished with new immigrants, under current conditions, we could expect a steady decline in the pool of farm labor available to local agricultural employers. Among the pool of potential farmworkers, the groups most strongly attached to farmwork are recently arrived immigrants, long-term migrants, and settled green-card workers who came to the United States during the Bracero Program or afterward. The group of potentially available workers most strongly opposed to doing farmwork consists of bilingual or English-speaking teenagers, most of whose parents were farmworkers. This suggests that the U.S. farm labor force will not reproduce itself. The entire social context and the social processes of immigrant-dominated industries such as farmwork have adapted so well to immigrants that they cease to be attractive to U.S. workers, even to those Mexican-American workers who might be able to function in the Spanish-speaking environment of contemporary agriculture (Commission on Agricultural Workers 1993a:50).

Several factors are responsible for this. First, language and education helped move them out of farmwork. While many first-generation immigrants, even after thirty years of living in the United States, speak only limited English, and their attachment to farmwork is strong, the same cannot be said of their children. Although the school experience of the second-generation Mexican Americans growing up in Texas or California during the 1960s or 1970s left a great deal to be desired, many graduated from high school, community college, or college. Even those who dropped out were, by then, bilingual and oriented toward "American" values. At the very least, they had overcome the main hurdle of language ability that would prevent them from escaping the occupational segregation of farmwork.

At the same time, the 1960s and 1970s constituted an era of cultural, social, and political renaissance based on ethnic pride for Mexicans in the Southwest—the era of Chicanismo, Raza consciousness, and a flourishing farm labor organizing movement. Just as the expansion of civil rights helped African Americans and Puerto Ricans seek employment outside of the agricultural sector, in the West these same developments helped Chicanos. Locally, Fresno State College was an important center of the movement, which included Parlier in the sweep of its influence. The Parlier City Council, formerly dominated by Anglo and Japanese representatives, was taken over by Chicanos in 1972. While the labor market experience of the residents of Parlier today is certain to include a fair measure of residual occupational discrimination, the visible institutional participation and success of second-generation Mexican Americans has an important and tangible effect on the occupational aspirations of all.

A related development, tied to the expansion of occupational opportunities and the transition from the rural Mexican economy to the U.S. economy, is the rapid drop in family size among Mexican Americans. While persons born in Mexico often have seven to ten siblings in each generation, second-generation family sizes are much lower. While farmwork encourages families to employ virtually all family members of working age, the same is not true of jobs that pay by the hour instead of the piece. Also, decreases in fertility are tied to the length of time in school, age of marriage, and occupational aspirations. Dwindling family size influences farm labor recruitment. While network recruitment can still be used effectively with smaller families, it must more rapidly move to friends and distant relatives of current workers, weakening the reciprocal obligations between new workers and the workers who recruited them.

Education, linguistic ability, changing aspirations, and dwindling family size all contribute to the lack of attachment to farmwork we find among the children of Mexican American farmworkers. In short, they aspire never to be involved in farmwork again. Despite this, their occupational horizons are likely to be constrained by difficulties in making the transition to college, and for some young adults farmwork may once again be the employment of last resort. The American dream is beyond the reach of many Chicanos. As Oscar Lewis (1957) has observed in explicating the meaning of "the culture of poverty," the key element is not low income but immigrants' perceptions regarding their lack of occupational mobility and the bitterness that stems from experiencing employment barriers in the midst of a social system that extols abundance and consumption. In Parlier, as in other traditional farm labor supply towns, immigrants' hopes for better lives for their children are becoming frustrated as changes in the U.S. economy reduce the occupation chances of poorly educated or poorly trained workers (e.g., Bluestone and Harrison 1982). The future faced by this younger generation of Mexican Americans who are socially, but not economically, part of the mainstream of California is an extremely uneasy one.

At the other end of the age spectrum, older Mexican-born workers continue to work in agriculture well beyond the age that most U.S. workers retire. This stems not only from cultural outlook but from a lack of income that will allow them to retire. While we found a variety of entrepreneurial activities that supplement decreased farmwork, older workers still tend to continue working as long as their health permits. Even after suffering injuries, many farmworkers continue to work. For example, Teresa Rios, who came to the United States at the age of forty-nine in 1985, continues to work in the orange harvest, dumping bags of oranges in the bin for an older man she works with. Her arthritis makes it difficult for her to pick tree fruit. Also, *mayordomos* are reluctant to have older women (or even men who are not in top physical shape) climbing ladders with full bags of oranges. Unfortunately, as is often the case of people coming from low-income backgrounds, 15 percent of the Parlier labor force has some physical limitations (10 percent overall classified as "serious") preventing their working in farmwork (Griffith, Valdés Pizzini, and Johnson 1992). In Parlier in the coming years, a crucial issue facing the key farm labor supply will not be the SAW exit rate, but the aging of the most productive and experienced workers.

In summary, the labor market behavior of each subpopulation of Parlier residents is markedly different. Language, education, time of immigration, legal status, and personal values are among the many factors internally segmenting the farm labor force. Recently immigrated workers (both legal and illegal) face tremendous constraints in their job mobility, including access to housing, transportation, and cash-flow problems. Specialized support services that have evolved to meet the needs of recent immigrants incorporate services in ways that make the services part of the job package. These services represent varying mixtures of altruism, traditional systems of reciprocity, and monetarized social transactions.

The farm labor contractor system, in particular, has evolved so as to provide a self-funding system that provides critical support services to recently immigrated workers quite efficiently. At the same time, this system creates powerful ties that bind workers to the labor contractor, allowing him access to a reserve pool of workers needed to accommodate rapid fluctuations in labor demand.

The seasonality of the agricultural labor market in the Fresno–Tulare area makes access to employment a more important factor in workers' economic strategies than the exact rate of earnings. Only workers who have managed to overcome the key structural barriers of language, access to housing, and transportation are in a position to explore somewhat more complicated economic strategies. These strategies include combinations of entrepreneurial activities (renting rooms, garages, houses, becoming a *raitero*) with wage labor, mixes of wage and nonwage benefits, and moving in and out of agricultural labor. Many workers who have experience in the nonagricultural labor market are aware of the increased employment stability and benefits offered there and even if they have extensive farmwork experience are not likely to return to farmwork.

Overall trends in use of hired farm labor suggest that the availability of high-quality supervisors is an important factor in meeting labor demand in California. Bad supervision results in workers leaving jobs without warning, because badly supervised workers are less productive and because bad supervision results in higher costs due to a higher incidence of work injuries. The limited availability of skilled supervisors, however, is a "bottleneck" in efforts to increase agricultural productivity. The predominant path to supervisory positions is through work experience, not through learning supervisory skills. Yet the growing use of labor contractors has further eroded the quality of workplace supervision. The primary function of the labor contractor has been to maintain a labor force of casual workers and to deal with the difficulties of hiring that labor force, not to improve supervision or labor productivity. Farm labor contractors, like growers themselves, have rather thin operating margins. As an industry, labor contractors have a history of improving profit margins by cutting the cost of operations and by extending services to workers as a source of revenue, rather than by raising prices to growers. Agriculture continues to be a business environment in which cost containment is a major concern. The persistent problem is how to make the transition to a labor-contracting system in which quality labor management becomes profitable. High-quality labor management would pay off in increased productivity, yet labor contractors will not be able to market higher-quality services successfully as long as small, informal, low-quality, and lower-cost labor contractors continue entering the field.

Conclusion

The data from Parlier, and from the other transnational communities featured in this volume, suggest that policy and program decisions based on standard concepts of residence, family life, job search, and economic strategies cannot adequately respond to either the socioeconomic dynamics of communities such as Parlier or the complex functioning of the farm labor market. Until farm labor policy analysis and program planning reflect the social and economic realities of farm labor supply communities, policymakers will find it difficult to devise policy strategies or public services that respond meaningfully to the circumstances of this population. Currently, however, if not completely "invisible," farmworkers are, at best, perceived by policymakers only through the distorted lens of assumptions about standard work behavior and life strategies.

The changing dynamics of migration from Mexico, the distinctive ties between family relationship and farmwork, the maturing of family support networks to assist new migrants, and the development of artificial support networks for migrants from new sending areas all overshadow the relatively weak forces of laws and regulations. These may function well in many regions of the United States, but not in Parlier and the farm labor market. The image of Parlier as a backwater town reflects the limited spectrum of mainstream perceptions when confronted with the reality of a transnational community operating within a social and economic context much broader than the proximate geographical one. The importance of viewing the dynamics of Parlier both cross-sectionally and over the course of time, with a particular emphasis on migration dynamics, is that it represents a paradigm for many of the transnational communities in California. These, in turn, provide a paradigm for understanding the occupational experience and personal dilemmas of Latinos in rural California and the western United States.

PART III

The Community Studies in Theoretical Perspective

Chapter 9

Characteristics of the Farm Labor Market

A Comparative Summary

In these last two chapters, we consider eight key findings from the community studies of farmworkers in the United States and offer some insight into the factors driving change and promoting stability in the farm labor processes. Those findings we consider most important for the development of theory and policy derive from the issues outlined below.[1]

Composition of the farm labor force. The farm labor force has become dominated by foreign-born workers, most of whom are from Mexico and other Latin American countries, leading to the Latinization of farm labor (see Mines, Gabbard, and Samardick 1989; Commission on Agricultural Workers 1993a). This has lent a distinctive cultural flavor to the farm labor market, based on Latin American patterns regarding employer–employee relations, supervision, labor recruitment, and ideas about race, ethnicity, class, and gender.

The key social-structural types found in the labor force are unaccompanied men (men who are living and working in the United States without their families) and family workers, with the former slowly increasing in proportion to the latter. This has been accompanied by increasing levels of cyclical migration between the United States and Mexico, as well as increasing "pioneering" migration within the United States.

Farm labor supply. The farm labor force contains too many workers. Some growers experience sporadic labor shortages during their peak labor demand periods, but most enjoy surplus labor. There is no evidence that immigration reform has affected farm labor supplies. Increased immigrant awareness of the possibility of working in agriculture without legal documentation, along with easier access to support networks, has facilitated the arrival of new immigrants. Increased competition among new arrivals for limited amounts of farm employment may, eventually, damp the migration flow, but we have documented no such occurrence.

Housing. Farmworker housing is inextricably linked to immigration patterns and efforts to balance farm labor supply and demand. Migrant and seasonal family farmworkers withstand high levels of underemployment and seasonal unemployment in part because of their access to very low-cost housing in home-based communities in the United States or Mexico.

In the United States, farmworkers' home-base communities are characterized by overcrowded dormitories, rooming houses, trailers, garages, and sheds. The quality of housing in the labor supply communities affects migration patterns in that those workers with higher-quality, stable housing are less likely to enter migrant streams than those who occupy dwellings under tenuous arrangements.

In the migrant labor demand regions of the north, the availability of housing influences the quality and reliability of farm labor. Employer-provided housing attracts skilled workers, yet few agricultural employers have made the investments required to maintain and upgrade accommodations for field workers. As a result, the quality of free worker housing varies widely.

Occupational mobility among farmworkers. Workers vary according to their attachment to farmwork. Workers legalized as special agricultural workers (SAWs) are more willing to do farmwork than U.S.-born workers. This is not simply a case of their being first-generation immigrants with few labor market alternatives, although the recent immigrant status of these workers certainly plays a part in their mobility (see Goldring 1990). Nevertheless, the labor market behavior of previous groups of immigrant farmworkers suggests that significant numbers of immigrant farmworkers remain attached to farmwork for long periods after coming to the United States. For many families, leaving farmwork is a multigenerational process, related less to legal status than to one's general incorporation into U.S. society.

Farmworker employment, unemployment, and underemployment. Farmworkers experience extensive underemployment during the peak harvest seasons and seasonal unemployment, with consequent low annual incomes. U.S. agriculture makes extremely inefficient use of its farmworkers. While this may suffice in a climate of labor surpluses, underemployment serves to decrease farmworker attachment to the farm labor force and hastens the flight of more-productive workers from farmwork. Thus, the farm labor market must be constantly replenished with new, usually foreign workers, leading to the ethnic succession observable in the labor force today.

Farmworker decision making. Almost as important as considerations about wage rates, many farmworkers attempt to maximize the amount and stability of work available to them and their families during the season. Because agricultural job offers typically involve complex arrays of task assignments, housing arrangements, and social ties, farmworkers cannot consider only rates of pay when weighing the costs and benefits of different jobs. The uncertainty of accepting unfamiliar job offers in unfamiliar regions underlies the continued reliance on labor intermediaries as well as the importance of informal "switchboards," namely, friends, roommates, and kin, who relay information on the job market.

Networks and recruitment. The primary means by which agricultural employers recruit farmworkers and by which workers seek employment are networks based on personal, family, neighborhood, and village contacts. As in other low-wage labor markets, these networks compensate for some of the inefficient use of farm labor by serving a number of functions, including communicating information about jobs; facilitating worker supervision and task assignment; establishing ties among growers, crew leaders, and workers; and responding quickly to changing market conditions. Despite this, there appear to be upper limits to the number of workers it is possible to recruit via a given extended family or neighborhood network, perpetuating the need for labor contracting.

Farm labor contracting. Farm labor contractors play an important role in all of the labor markets in the study. Over three-fourths (78 percent) of current farmworkers in Parlier and over one-third (36 percent) of both Immokalee and Weslaco farmworkers had worked for a labor contractor at least once during the previous year. Although few Puerto Rican farmworkers are labor contractors, reliance on labor intermediaries such as Glassboro Services has been a feature of Puerto Rican labor recruitment since the 1920s. In the labor demand areas of the north, labor contractors facilitate the employment of recently immigrated, often undocumented, workers.

In this chapter, we consider the first three issues, which we consider descriptive. In Chapter 10, we consider the last five, in the context of a theoretical discussion that raises some pressing issues facing anthropology, rural sociology, agricultural economics, and other related disciplines today.

Composition of the Farm Labor Force

Two adjectives can be used to describe most of the farm labor in the United
States: Latin and immigrant. It should be obvious by now that the farm labor
force is overwhelmingly Spanish-speaking, with ties to either Mexico or Central America. The surveys we conducted in Immokalee, Weslaco, and Parlier
showed very low levels of farm labor market participation by U.S.-born workers. In Parlier, only 17 percent of the current farmworkers were U.S.-born, and
in Immokalee only 19 percent. In Weslaco, the community in the continental
United States with the largest domestic farm labor force, slightly less than
half of the current farmworkers (46 percent) were U.S.-born. Only in Puerto
Rico, an area declining as a supplier of workers to agriculture, do we find that
most of the farmworkers working in the continental United States are citizens;
we encountered relatively few current farmworkers in the low-income Puerto
Rican neighborhoods we selected for study, reflecting the declining role of
Puerto Rico as a farm labor supply region generally. Because of this, we
exclude Puerto Rico from most of the comparative discussion.

The community surveys also showed that many current farmworkers are
recent immigrants. Over half (54 percent) of the current farmworkers in Parlier
and more than three-fourths (77 percent) of the current farmworkers in Immokalee immigrated to the United States in the 1980s. They supplemented a farm
labor workforce made up in large measure of aging farmworkers who arrived
in the United States during the 1950s, 1960s, and 1970s. This aging workforce
was most prominent in Weslaco, where 40 percent of the current farmworkers
had immigrated before 1975 and only 14 percent had immigrated in the 1980s.
Older, green card workers from the Bracero era are also an important group
in Parlier. In Immokalee, many of these earlier farmworkers have become
farm labor contractors.

Strong flows of international migrants continue to enter the farm labor
force. Most of these workers are Mexican, but Guatemalans, Salvadorans, and
other Central American immigrants make up the stream as well. Additional
waves of immigrants come from Haiti and other parts of the Caribbean, although many of these workers move quickly into packing, food processing,
and other jobs (see Richman 1992). Many Mexican migrants, moreover, are
coming from new immigrant sending regions within Mexico, while Puerto
Rican farmworkers—despite their Spanish-speaking abilities and historical
importance in many eastern crops and regions—are declining in the United
States farm labor force.

Along with the decline of Texas-based and other Mexican American workers in agriculture, the lower rates of Puerto Rican participation in the farm labor force offer an interesting comment on the interplay of culture, citizenship, linguistic ability, and the changing social relations of agricultural production. In our case study of Mayagüez, we attributed the decline in Puerto Rican farmwork in part to the restructuring of the insular economy from agriculture to manufacturing and tourism. This constitutes only half of the explanation for decline, however, commonly known as the "supply side" of the issue. Changing labor demand in the agriculture of the continental United States has also played an important role in this process. Puerto Ricans and Mexican Americans speak Spanish; they are not, therefore, barred from the farm labor force on linguistic grounds. Indeed, the notion of the "colonization" of labor markets would suggest that they are particularly predisposed to participate in farm labor (Martin 1989). Yet the evidence suggests that they may be discouraged from farm labor because of cultural and citizenship characteristics. Simply, citizenship has become a liability for them in terms of finding work in agriculture. Their status as citizens affords them powers and rights that impede the current "efficiency" of the agricultural labor process—an efficiency based on disinformation, unequal power relations between workers and their employers, and a variety of "kickbacks" and expenses borne by farmworkers for the privilege of working.[2] This point emerges again in our discussion of new migrants versus old.

Recent Changes in the Composition of the Farm Labor Force

Our discussion in Chapter 1 of the history of farm labor establishes that core sending areas of Mexico have been an important source of workers for U.S. agriculture since the 1920s. Our surveys indicate that migration from traditional sending regions continues to be the primary component of Mexican immigration into the U.S. farm labor force. At the same time, immigration flows in the 1980s have altered labor force composition in a number of regions. In particular, the labor force now includes increasing numbers of marginalized indigenous groups with "new" migration networks. Most important here have been refugees from Guatemala—mostly Kanjobal, Chuj, Aguacatec, Quiché, and other Native American groups from the northwest departments— and Mixtec immigrants from southwestern Mexico (Zabin et al. 1993). Haitian workers have entered the farm labor force but in many areas have fallen from grower favor because of litigious activity. Each new wave of Haitian refugees, however, has been tapped into by growers and utilized as a new source of labor; the so-called Guantánamo Haitians—those detained at Guantánamo

Bay, Cuba, by the Bush administration in 1992—represent the most recent wave. Again, however, many Haitians have moved through the farm labor market relatively quickly (Stepick and Stepick 1990; Richman 1992).

Many workers from new sending regions speak primary languages other than Spanish, despite their national origins. Quite often they are fleeing politi cal violence or economic crises (Upton and Williams 1983; Burns 1993). Most, as well, are culturally less "Hispanic" or "Latin" than they are tied to Native American, often extremely local (village) traditions. Attachment to villages is true for Haitians as well, to the extent that businesses have developed in southern Florida specifically to facilitate "transnational" ties (see Richman 1992). Yet new migration networks also include a growing stream of urban, relatively well educated Mexican workers. Migration flows from these new sending areas, both urban and rural, augment migration from the traditional, core sending areas such as Michoacán, Jalisco, Guanajuato, and Zacatecas. We see this especially in Parlier and Immokalee, where 41 percent and 24 percent of the current farmworkers, respectively, come from new immigrant sending regions, while 42 percent of the Parlier farmworkers, 57 percent of the Immokalee farmworkers, and 54 percent of the Weslaco farmworkers come from traditional sending regions. By contrast, 46 percent of Weslaco's, 17 percent of Parlier's, and 19 percent of Immokalee's farmworkers were U.S. born.

The composition of international migration flows into U.S. agriculture has important implications for projections of farm labor supply. The relatively well educated immigrants from urban areas of Mexico, Central America, and the Caribbean are likely to assimilate into U.S. society more rapidly than traditional campesinos and move out of agriculture more rapidly than previous immigrants. The strong contribution of new migration networks to U.S. farm labor supply means, however, that the large numbers of workers from these rural areas, like earlier immigrants, will probably remain strongly attached to farmwork. Comparing migrants from two areas of Mexico, Goldring (1990) found that migrants who have settled into annual cycles of migration between specific United States crops and Mexican villages are more likely to remain attached to farmwork than those who migrate to a number of locations and spend long periods in the United States. She, too, discovered that attachment to farmwork was enhanced by access to inexpensive, government-subsidized housing in California receiving areas. This suggests that selective pressures exist that favor utilizing cyclical international labor migrants instead of long-term migrants, contributing to the idea of Mexican villages acting as "labor reserves" (Burawoy 1976).

Diffusion of Immigrant Farmworkers Within the United States

Networks established by migrating to different crops expand the potential for immigrant workers to move into new, unfamiliar locations throughout the United States. Work histories of Immokalee respondents, the community with the highest level of secondary migration, suggest that diffusion from one home base to another is facilitated by crop specialization. We encountered cases of Mixtec tomato pickers from northern San Diego County, for example, migrating to pick tomatoes in Immokalee and Guatemalans coming to Florida via Arizona citrus. These movements are often engineered by farm labor contractors and *raiteros* with established links to growers in labor demand regions and specialized hauling and other equipment.

Perhaps the most striking effect of this diffusion has been the increase of Mexican and Central American workers along the eastern seaboard. There, the Latinization of the farm labor market is a much more recent phenomenon than in the West, dating back only thirty to forty years. Our ethnographic interviews revealed repeated cases in which migration pathways pioneered by earlier, Texas-based Mexican immigrants led new immigrants to farmwork in Florida and then to destinations in the north supplied by Florida communities. Again, labor contractors engineered many of these migrations, although others relied on family and network ties. Institutional processes also played a part: H-2A recruiting, labor contractors' contacts with local employment service offices, and direct recruiting in southern Texas by East Coast growers all contributed to the formation of new migrant pathways. Two of these developments just mentioned describe part of the state's role in shaping labor markets and migration pathways. State involvement in the H-2A program is obvious, but the state has also played a part in the growth of labor contracting through its tacit withdrawal from farm labor placement as fewer and fewer growers relied on the employment service to recruit workers. Contractors filled the void left as the employment service withdrew.

During the 1980s, immigrant families, originally part of the network of Texas-based migrants in the 1960s and 1970s, settled out into nonagricultural occupations in the Midwest and the Pacific Northwest. New flows of immigrants from Mexico filled the openings, which were usually field-work jobs. Families who first came from Central Mexico to Weslaco in the 1950s now have branches in Texas, Washington, and California. Networks of more recent immigrants are equally ubiquitous. In Florida, for example, we interviewed a group of unaccompanied Oaxacan males who, in the past five years, had worked in California and Canada as well as in Florida.

One result of these transnational and transregional migrations and connections is that Mexican immigrants have largely replaced groups such as African Americans and Puerto Ricans in the farm labor force of the eastern seaboard. For example, in Florida citrus, a crop previously dominated by African American farmworkers, an estimated 60 percent of the labor force was made up of Texas migrants as early as 1975 (Hudson 1979). Most of these workers originally emigrated from Mexico's traditional core sending areas. Similar processes of ethnic displacement and replacement have been documented in the Pennsylvania mushroom industry (Smith 1991; Garcia 1993) and the North Carolina tobacco, apple, pickle cucumber, and vegetable industries (Griffith 1988; North Carolina Migrant Council 1992).

Regional Differences in Immigration Flows

The changing composition of the farm labor force can be seen simply from the changing rate of overall immigration flows into different labor supply communities over time. Immokalee and Parlier continue to be northern destinations of international migration networks, while Weslaco has ceased to draw immigrants as it did in the past. Mayagüez continues to attract Dominicans, but few of these enter farmwork networks (Grasmuck and Pessar 1991). Specifically, 81 percent of the foreign-born farmworkers in Immokalee ($N = 124$) and 64 percent in Parlier ($N = 106$) entered the United States during the 1980s, compared with only 42 percent of Weslaco's foreign-born farmworkers ($N = 42$). By contrast, 38 percent of Weslaco's foreign-born farmworkers entered during the 1970s, compared with only 26 percent in Parlier and 11 percent in Immokalee, and over one-third of Weslaco's foreign-born (36 percent) entered prior to 1970.

These figures reflect the common immigrant practice of following previous waves of immigrants after the latter become firmly rooted in U.S. society. While first-generation immigrants may never become part of mainstream U.S. social life, they may nevertheless leave the farm labor force. Parlier's workforce had a high representation of Texas-based migrants (most of whom were born in Mexico) during the 1960s and 1970s, but this group is no longer the major component of the workforce. By 1990, we found that the largest single group in the farm labor communities of Florida and California was composed of recent immigrants and cyclical migrants who travel directly from Mexico or Guatemala to labor demand areas and return regularly to their home villages.

Immigration Flows and the Changing Composition of the
Farm Labor Force

The continuing influx of immigrants into traditional farm labor supply communities has had effects that reach far beyond places like Immokalee and
Parlier. As we note throughout this work, Immokalee and Parlier—as well
as other, similarly situated farm labor towns (e.g., Homestead, Florida, or
Watsonville, California)—continue to be northern points on international migration networks. From these areas, migrants move into new regions throughout the United States, initially entering farming regions but gradually setting
out into nonagricultural occupations and more permanent neighborhoods. In
Immokalee, at least 24 percent of the current farmworker population consists
of unauthorized immigrants; in Parlier, 28 percent of the workers are recent
and unauthorized. This is consistent with other data on farm labor, which
shows that Latino farmworkers are pioneering new settlement areas throughout parts of rural America where labor-intensive agriculture is being practiced
(Mines, Gabbard, and Samardick 1989, 1990).

The development of northern destinations has not occurred with equal intensity in other areas we think of as traditional farm labor supply communities.
Mexican immigration to the lower Rio Grande Valley of Texas is low, in part
because of the decreasing availability of winter work in southern Texas and
the increasing availability of winter work in southern Florida and central California. Latinos, of course, continue to flow *through* the lower Rio Grande
Valley yet tend to move on to other destinations, particularly Florida, California, and the Southwest.[3] This change is reflected in the harvests of the northern
labor demand regions. The midwestern labor supply, once dominated by
Texas-based migrants, now relies increasingly on recently emigrated Mexican-born farmworkers based in Florida.

Ethnic Composition of the Current Farm Labor Force

As with immigrant flows, regional differences emerge in the ethnic composition of the workforce. While West Coast and midwestern harvests are now
nearly completely Latinized, East Coast harvests contain vestiges of the earlier
farmworker groups—Jamaican, Haitian, and African American workers. Even
the H-2A program, which has long been dominated by British West Indians,
has turned to Mexico as its labor supply source in areas such as North Carolina
and Kentucky (Heppel and Torres 1993). Our study of the previously Puerto

Rican–dominated New Jersey nursery industry also shows extensive active recruitment of Mexicans, and this has occurred in nearby growing regions as well (see Heppel and Amendola 1992: 109). Our analysis of the ethnicity of the different labor supply communities reveals that Immokalee has a much more diverse farm labor force than the predominantly Latin labor forces of Parlier and Weslaco (Table 9.1).

The difference in ethnic composition of the farm labor force reflects the reliance on extended-family and village networks in farm labor recruitment (see Bach et al. 1990), which results in ethnic clustering and the institutionalization of immigration flows to different communities (Massey et al. 1987; Goldring 1990). Although labor market dynamics and geography play important roles in the processes by which immigration flows become institutionalized, federal and local government participation in the construction of the agricultural labor force often proves more powerful than either the market or geography.

Subgroups of Farm Workers: Family Workers and
Unaccompanied Males

In addition to the ethnic division within the farm labor force, important subgroups characterized by social-structural attributes internally segment the farm labor force. With the decline of Weslaco and other Texas towns as farm labor supply communities, we are witnessing a transformation of the social-structural composition of farm labor. The "family workers" who composed

TABLE 9.1 Ethnicity of Current Farmworkers in Traditional U.S. Farm Labor Supply Communities

Ethnic Group	Immokalee (N = 123)	Parlier (N = 101)	Weslaco (N = 28)
Mexican	34%	74%	54%
Mexican American	9	17	46
Mixtec	5	9	0
Guatemalan	21	0	0
Haitian	17	0	0
African American	3	0	0
Anglo	3	0	0
Puerto Rican	2	0	0
Other[a]	5	0	0
Total	99	100	100

Note: Percentages may not total 100 because of rounding.

[a]Includes Jamaican, Cuban, and other Latino.

most of the farm labor force of the 1960s and 1970s are being replaced by unaccompanied-male immigrants, including both cyclical migrants and those who remain in the United States indefinitely. Comparisons between Immokalee, Parlier, and Weslaco confirm this process: the only community with low current rates of immigration, Weslaco has comparably few unaccompanied-male-immigrant farmworkers, reflecting deteriorating agricultural job opportunities in Texas (Table 9.2). Every winter, a stream of international migrants from Mexico passes through southern Texas on its way to other labor demand communities in Florida and California. In the spring, Mexican migrants pass through again, but this time en route to northern labor demand regions in Michigan, Illinois, Iowa, Ohio, and other regions. Connections made in these northern regions then feed back into labor supplies in Florida and California, as summer migrants return to these southern home-base locations.

Mines and Martin (1983) found that in the early 1980s about one-third (30 percent) of unaccompanied male migrants were young, single "pioneers," while about two-thirds (60 to 70 percent) were older, married men migrating without their wives. Our findings suggest that the unaccompanied men in the farm labor force of today are somewhat younger. If we examine only the single-male migrants in Table 9.2, excluding from our calculations the family farmworkers and female household heads with children, we can see that more than half of the Parlier and Immokalee unaccompanied men are under twenty-five.

Groups of unaccompanied-male migrants interviewed were most often friends and relatives from a village migrating north together—a typical group might include an older man, one or two of his nephews or sons, and several close family friends or in-laws. Most unaccompanied migrants interviewed had an informal leader—the most socially skilled, linguistically accomplished,

TABLE 9.2 Unaccompanied Men and Other Subgroups in the Farm Labor Force

Farmworker Subgroups	Immokalee		Parlier		Weslaco	
Young, pioneer, men (≤25 yrs. old)	22%	(27)	27%	(27)	—	
Older male migrants (>25 yrs. old)	34	(42)	27	(27)	14%	(4)
Family farmworkers	38	(47)	45	(45)	71	(20)
Female heads of household with children	6	(7)	2	(2)	14	(4)
Total	100	(123)	101	(101)	99	(28)

and outgoing member of the group—who negotiated with prospective employers and shaped group consensus about courses of action.

Cyclical migrants from Mexico or Guatemala form the largest group among the unaccompanied migrants (43 percent of unaccompanied male migrants in Immokalee; 72 percent of those in Parlier), yet those who have settled, at least semipermanently, remain an important group. The Immigration Reform and Control Act (IRCA) may have led to increases in cyclical migration for two reasons. First, migrants who legalized as SAWs can travel back to their home villages more cheaply and safely than when they were illegal because they no longer need to pay fees to *coyotes*. Second, cyclical migration encourages new immigrants to come to the United States as they gain information and impressions about the United States from SAWs (Commission on Agricultural Workers 1993a).

The differences between Immokalee and Parlier regarding the proportion of unaccompanied men who are cyclical migrants and those who are settlers reflect primarily ecological factors. Southern Florida's longer growing season results in stronger winter labor demand than central California's season does, making Florida more attractive for farmworkers who wish to remain in the United States year-round. Also, of course, the distance and travel costs to return to Mexico or Guatemala are higher from Florida than from California. Among California-based immigrants, cyclical migration is a highly rational economic strategy, allowing workers to avoid high U.S. costs of living when work is slow and return when they can expect more stable work and higher earnings. Yet this behavior also contributes to the formation and maintenance of Mexican communities as labor reserves for U.S. agribusiness, undermining the extent to which workers invest their labor in production at home and contributing to seasonal labor scarcity and its associated problems (Collins 1988).

Three main factors underlie the increasing presence of unaccompanied males and cyclical migrants in the farm labor market: the continuing influx of international migrants; increasingly "formalized" corporate strategies for recruiting, hiring, and deploying harvest workers; and the cost, availability, quality, type, and regulation of migrant housing.

The distribution of immigrant farmworkers by immigration status provides one means of estimating the rate at which supplies of immigrant workers who leave agricultural work are being replenished by new immigrants. Among unaccompanied-male migrant farmworkers, a large group qualified as SAWs, but many are also long-term immigrants who were legalized under other programs, are green-card immigrants, or are refugees. The unaccompanied-male population also includes recent unauthorized international migrants. Yet the ratio of employment-authorized unaccompanied-male workers to undocumented immigrants varies among the communities. In Weslaco, we encountered no undocumented immigrants, while in Immokalee, 17 percent admitted to being undocumented, and in Parlier, 38 percent. Of course, these are probably underestimates; surely many undocumented workers reported being employment-authorized out of fear of deportation.

The work patterns and labor force participation of unaccompanied males are as closely linked to the economies and traditions of their home villages as they are to farm labor demand in the United States. In the traditional sending villages, northward migration has become so institutionalized that it is likely to continue even in the face of modest improvements in Mexican economic conditions (Massey et al. 1987). It is more likely that improvements in local economic conditions in Mexico will affect migrants from the new sending networks (e.g., urban-manufacturing and service industry workers coming north to do farmwork) more strongly than those of sending areas where a strong tradition of migration has already been established. The networks supporting migration from these new sending areas are not so well established, making travel north, separation from families, and job search in the United States less attractive. Also, the more urbanized communities have a wider range of occupational options than the more rural, traditional sending areas. Recent immigrant workers interviewed include policemen, teachers, truckdrivers, lab technicians, veterinarians, and factory employees. Many of these workers came north in search of farmwork only reluctantly, leaving their families behind.

Fewer than half (42 percent) of the SAWs in Parlier, and one-quarter (24 percent) of those in Immokalee are family workers whose wives and children are now living in the United States with them. Yet we estimate that slightly more than half (56 percent) of the unaccompanied men in Immokalee and more than one-third (42 percent) of those in Parlier who were legalized under IRCA are likely to have wives and children still in Mexico or Guatemala. Surely many of these wives and children will of necessity enter the farm labor force, suggesting that the state, through immigration law, has actively helped to shape labor force composition and labor supplies. The exact way this process occurs may not conform to the intent of those writing and enacting laws but depends on factors ranging from the opportunity costs of leaving Mexico to the availability of housing in receiving communities. Future farm labor supply in traditional labor supply communities such as Immokalee and Parlier will be affected by continuing developments in immigration law, regulations, and implementation. One example of this changing legal environment resulted from a court settlement revising criteria for determination of political refugee status. This case, called the ABC settlement (for American Baptist Council— see Upton and Williams 1983; Burns 1993), is likely to have a significant impact on labor supply in Immokalee, since it allows for legalization of Guatemalans whose asylum applications were denied and for renewed applications by Guatemalans previously deterred by the strict criteria.

Increasing labor market saturation by unaccompanied males tends to undercut the quality of working conditions. This group is less concerned about quality of housing and stability of earnings than it is about the amount of money that can be earned in a season. Thus, high concentrations of unaccompanied-male immigrants probably serve to hold down piece-rate wages. Because young male workers of prime ability set the pace, marginal workers (e.g., older, physically handicapped workers or very young teens) earn below the minimum wage because of their relatively low rate of production. Our data do not support the proposition that recently immigrated undocumented workers are regularly paid subminimum wages, yet they suggest that continuing labor surpluses prevent increases in piece-rate offers.

The spread between unaccompanied males' and other farmworkers' *weekly* earnings in farmwork was 18 percent in Immokalee and 5 percent in Parlier, indicating that there are not very significant differences between them and other workers in their ability to obtain work. Since farmworkers' weekly earnings are a function of hours worked and wage rate, weekly earnings data demonstrate how effectively artificial networks, constructed by crew leaders, can function. Foremen use both the mass shape-up and driving from house to house to provide recently arrived workers with the same access to farmwork as that available to extended-family networks.

In Immokalee, time spent in the United States appears to be a slightly better predictor of earnings than family composition is. Unaccompanied men who arrived in 1989–90 had mean earnings of $153 per week and a mean wage of $3.83 per hour; unaccompanied men who had arrived prior to 1986 had mean earnings of $174 per week and earnings of $4.29 per hour. In Parlier, there was no significant difference among immigration cohorts (pre-IRCA, 1986–88, and 1989–90): for all groups, the mean weekly wage was at or near $217. Because of the high variance in earnings within each subgroup, the differences in earnings between subgroups are not statistically significant in either community.

Several countervailing forces appear to be at work here. While immigrant workers' networks generally improve over time, the existence of informal but structured labor market institutions (i.e., the shape-up, drive-by hiring, and professional recruiters) serves to decrease the handicaps experienced by newly arrived workers. Yet some migration networks are more developed than others, allowing some recent immigrants to find more work than others. The similarities between new immigrants and residents in terms of earnings and amount of work indicate two features of the farm labor market itself. First, the heavy reliance on farm labor contractors and shape-ups reflects the farm labor market's development in a historical context of new immigration. Second, its capacity to absorb, continually, new immigrants has restricted upward mobility within agriculture, so that "seniority" tends to have little or no effect on earnings.

In the more volatile labor markets, recruitment of recently immigrated, illegal, unaccompanied men provides a means of *labor control,* since this group is the least likely to have access to such basics as transportation and housing. In central California, for example, labor contractors establish the "total" institutional contexts for recently immigrated, unaccompanied-male workers' participation in the labor market, providing housing, transportation, work tools, and plans for workers' movement among crops and tasks. They also manage to ensure that the workers themselves pay the cost of the housing, transportation, and tools. Through their own personal networks, farm labor contractors in Florida fill similar functions, controlling farmworker housing by having their mothers, sisters, and other consanguineal kin own and operate labor camps.

Labor contractors often receive income from services they provide to the workers, much like the "company store" of the days of debt peonage in the U.S. South. One of the more infamous manifestations of the labor contractor's power over the crew is known as "the line." Simply, this is a form of consumer credit in which usurious interest has been replaced by high retail prices. In the scenario that follows, reconstructed from the testimony in a case against a North Carolina labor contractor (*James E. Leach et al. v. Albert B. Johnston and Thomas Alexander Sr.,* 1991), there are two "bills" associated with the line: the weekly bill and the cash bill. The former is for charges between noon Saturday, when the workers are paid, and Thursday evening, the evening the labor contractor figures the payroll. The cash bill is for purchases from the line from Friday morning to Saturday noon.

Q. What do you understand a line to be?
A. The cook would give them like beer and wine. In the morning it was wine or half a pint. Sometimes they were close to the camp, you get a beer or half pint and it—at dinnertime they get a pint or two beers.

Q. Anything else? Were cigarettes ever given?

A. Cigarettes in the mornings.

Q. Now, would you make a record of what you had given each worker?

A. Yes.

Q. What would you write if they got a beer, what would you do, how would you . . . ?

A. Well, it's according to what size beer. You got dollar beers and you had dollar-and-a-half beers. Twelve ounce was a dollar, sixteen ounce was a dollar and a half.

Q. Now, what would you, . . . you kept writing these charges down on the tablet. What did you finally do with the tablet when you finished for a week writing down the charges? What did you do with the tablet?

A. Give it to Thomas [the labor contractor].

Q. Now, when the worker was handed his or her wages by Thomas Alexander, Sr., had any money been deducted from the wages?

A. Yes.

Q. What had been deducted?

A. The weekly bill.

Q. The weekly bill consisting of the charges from the line?

A. Right.

Q. Let's take John Doe, worker. He walks in, he gets his money from Thomas Alexander after Mr. Alexander has taken out for the food and the weekly bill.

A. Uh-huh.

Q. How long is it from the time he receives his money from Thomas until he pays his cash bill to you? Is it a matter of minutes, hours, seconds, what?

A. Minutes. Just walk over to me and pay me.

Q. And what if they didn't pay their cash bill?

A. I imagine he put it on next week's bill, I guess.

Q. That never happened?

A. No.

From other testimony in the same case, we learn that the labor contractor, a migrant himself, was able to shop around from state to state for the cheapest wine, beer, and cigarettes to sell workers, striking a balance between making a profit and providing a service. While the practice of running a line is not nearly as common as using housing as a labor control mechanism, the line is important to the current discussion because it highlights the debt relations between workers and labor contractors. Farmworkers submit to the line; most do not resist it, and this may derive from the complexity of the line as a labor control mechanism. Along with being a form of power, the line contains a hint of benevolence: it is—like housing, job contacts, transportation, and so forth—a service the labor contractor provides to the workers, and the more services the labor contractor provides for the crew, the greater his or her potential for power over workers, because each service provided can be a service withheld. Since the revenues stemming from provision of services can amount to approximately 30 percent of worker earnings, the economic benefits of providing services to workers is a substantial factor in structuring the farm labor market.

The kinds of services provided to workers vary with the institutional context of farmworkers' living and working arrangements. In the eastern United States, increasing formalization of the agricultural labor market often entails the construction of labor processes resembling the "total" institutional contexts found in the southern Florida sugar-growing regions and the Virginia and West Virginia apple harvests, both dominated by H-2A workers (Griffith 1987). In these settings, nearly everything is provided for workers, often at costly terms of trade.

In southern Florida, the provision of housing, cooked food, liquor, and entertainment to unaccompanied-male migrants is an economic activity that rivals agricultural employment itself in importance, providing economic opportunities for residents of towns like Immokalee. Similar situations exist in Parlier, as the case of Guti Gonzalez demonstrates. Guti was able to capitalize on the seasonal influx of workers by opening a boardinghouse. At the same time, this house served the additional function of anchoring her social network in Parlier.

The labor control mechanisms that derive from providing services to workers are, if anything, enhanced in situations of migration within the United States. Not surprisingly, unaccompanied males are more likely to have migrated to a northern labor demand area in the United States than are family farmworkers. In Parlier, 32 percent of the unaccompanied males were interstate migrants in 1989, while only 12 percent of the other farmworkers had migrated. In Immokalee, 61 percent of the unaccompanied males were interstate migrants, compared with 46 percent of other farmworkers. Unaccompanied males also expressed more willingness than other farmworkers to migrate in search of work. Because unaccompanied males are available to migrate, they represent a more flexible labor force than family workers, both for "formalized" agricultural operations (e.g., H-2A) and for crewleaders wanting to coordinate the movement of workers from one region to another.

Differences in willingness to migrate among different farmwork subgroups pose some dilemmas for worker recruitment and for farmworker policy. Increasing reliance on larger organizational units of multicrop or multisite production provide new opportunities and incentives to smooth labor demand by moving workers from one crop or region to another in a carefully planned fashion. However, coordinated regional movement of workers either requires the provision of family housing (a strategy adopted by several exemplary producers in Michigan, New Jersey, and Maryland) or results in the preferential hiring of unaccompanied-male migrants. Our research suggests that the latter is occurring.

Many of the "formalized" labor recruitment, supervision, and deployment approaches used by large producers, usually in conjunction with labor contractors, have the potential of significantly decreasing the employment uncertainty and casualness of farm labor. Yet such efforts are usually structured toward recruitment of unaccompanied-male workers because of the variety of advantages associated with them. Most obviously, these workers cost less to transport and house than family workers and are easier to supervise. In particular, the barracks-style housing typical of many camps makes it increasingly difficult for family workers to compete with unaccompanied men for jobs.

The increasing reliance on unaccompanied-male workers has both short- and long-term implications. Adaptations in agricultural-labor processes to better utilize unaccompanied-male migrants inevitably create structural barriers to hiring family farmworkers. Also, unaccompanied men are more likely to alter the face of migration. The population of unaccompanied-male migrants contains high proportions of cyclical migrants (72 percent in the Parlier area and 43 percent in Immokalee). Legal changes (e.g., in marital status, and the natural processes of aging, family formation, and network developments will encourage settlement among these migrants. Without substantial structural changes in the farm labor market, the dwindling supply of legalized unaccompanied men will need to be replenished with new, unauthorized immigrants.

Reliance on recently immigrated, illegal, unaccompanied-male migrants also appears to subtly shift labor management emphasis away from worker productivity (rate and quality of work) and toward worker compliance and labor control (willingness to accept marginal working conditions and reluctance to leave an employer). Such a shift in labor management emphasis is dysfunctional in terms of industrial competitiveness. Under this system, savings stemming from the ease of recruiting and retaining the most compliant workers are traded for lower productivity.

Farm Labor Supply

The movement of international migrants into U.S. agriculture increased and diversified through the 1980s, despite concerted political attempts, particularly IRCA, to control illegal immigration. Instead, almost perversely, IRCA accelerated the migration flow. Worker surpluses we observed in Immokalee, Parlier, and Weslaco stem both from the availability of new, recently immigrated workers and from the strong attachment to the farm labor force among SAWs and other previous immigrants. Although there always has been attrition from the farm labor force over time, the surpluses we witnessed suggest that new immigrant farmworkers are more than adequately replacing workers who leave agriculture.

In-depth interviews with workers revealed several causes for heightened immigration. First, there is a growing awareness in Mexican and Guatemalan sending villages of the widespread availability of bogus documents and the ease with which they can be used, as well as the general lack of Immigration and Naturalization Service (INS) enforcement. As in border scenes in the comedy *Born and Raised in East L.A.*, the false-document market has moved from the backroom to the flea market. Second, greater ease in crossing borders and elimination of fees paid to *coyotes*, facilitated by SAWs, increases the frequency of contact between young men returning to sending villages and U.S. migrant destinations. Brothers and cousins can now come north with their SAW relatives in private automobiles or by public transportation.

Third, the growth in farm labor contracting also facilitates the continued influx of illegal and legal immigrants. Specifically, increased reliance on labor contractors by growers has strengthened the informal institutions that provide newly immigrated workers with the ability to find work even in areas where they have only rudimentary job contacts. This occurs in the context of building artificial networks. Farm labor contractor recruitment of recently arrived workers from Los Angeles, Chicago, Houston, and other urban centers strengthens urban–rural network ties while facilitating the employment of even relatively inexperienced workers in peak-season harvest work.

Ironically, the same support networks that provide means for new-immigrant workers to enter and move around in the United States contribute to labor surpluses that diminish migrants' chances for finding work. During the height of harvest seasons, a high percentage of workers have been able to find work, yet the sporadic stringing together of jobs from season to season feeds continued underemployment and continued demand for formal and informal support networks. Households of unaccompanied males, dormitories, labor shape-up areas, and the work sites themselves provide switchboards for exchange of information and misinformation about work, border patrol enforcement, and forums to discuss different courses of action for finding more work. Such areas also provide convenient recruitment sites for labor contractors.

Households of unaccompanied males also facilitate the process by which underemployed lone males band together to "pioneer" a new work destination. Faced with labor surpluses, workers often pool gas money so they can travel to new, riskier labor demand areas. This process helps explain the diffusion of Latino farmworkers throughout labor-intensive U.S. agriculture. In Parlier, for example, informants reported that the growing labor surplus in 1990 made tasks such as apple thinning in Washington, berry picking in Oregon, and olive harvesting in northern California options worthy of consideration, despite involving long trips and the risk of finding no work. Yet the alternative was boredom and dwindling savings during the midseason slowdown. In Florida and Texas, the December freeze of 1989 stimulated similar pioneering behaviors, as migrants moved north to recover some losses in income. These pioneers were similar to those fleeing the dust bowl of the 1930s or those who left Florida City after Hurricane Andrew in 1992. Whether driven by boredom or crisis, once pioneers forge new links between regions, crops, and tasks, these links tend to result in network formation and continued migration into the new areas. Along the eastern seaboard, for example, the increasing flow of Guatemalans into southern Florida is an example of migration networks maturing from the efforts of earlier groups of pioneers. In this case, however, they were primarily young Chuj, Kanjobal, or other Maya peasants fleeing the violence of the 1978–85 period (Burns 1993). The degree of political stability in Guatemala in the 1990s, as in Haiti, will have a significant impact on future labor supply (Richman 1992).

Added to these labor sources are those of new networks, such as those mentioned in Chapter 8, based in indigenous areas of Mexico (e.g., in the Pacific southwestern sierra of Oaxaca and Guerrero). These networks began their development well before the mid 1980s yet later than the communities in traditional Mexican sending areas. Migrants belonging to the new network of Oaxaca–California–Oregon began to take jobs that had been held by U.S. workers until the late 1970s. The growing Mixtec presence in the California farm labor market was facilitated by the existence of internal migration patterns that familiarized *campesino* workers with U.S.-style mass production of vegetable crops in the Sinaloa and Baja California tomato production areas (Zabin et al. 1993).

Farm labor surpluses are not surprising, given that continuing migration occurs as part of a transnational labor market whose workers have grown to expect intermittent employment. As long as the well-known push factors exist in Mexico, Central America, and the Caribbean (low wages relative to those in the United States, chronic underemployment, political turmoil, shrinking peasant land bases and other resources), emigration from these areas will occur in response to U.S. demands for low-wage labor despite legal sanctions against illegal immigration. On the receiving side, legal sanctions against employment of nonauthorized immigrant workers has so far been largely ineffective in controlling immigration.

Future analysis of migration needs to examine factors other than political mechanisms that influence international migration. Apparent increases in immigration in 1989 and 1990 reflect not only the maturing of rural migrant networks but also a constantly changing social and economic context. Incentives for workers to migrate northward include, in addition to prospective earnings, aspirations regarding access to services (e.g., health care, education, entertainment), satisfaction or dissatisfaction with quality of life and future prospects in the home village, and other nonpecuniary factors. In terms of the farm labor market, among the factors making work possible is the availability, quality, and character of housing.

Housing

Housing has been a central component of the farm labor market for decades. In the South after the Civil War, sharecropping and tenant farming bound a newly freed labor force to the land in part through the provision of housing. Ranch hands throughout the western states were housed in the bunkhouses made famous in films and novels of the West. Today, on the Great Plains and throughout the Corn Belt, hired hands often receive a farmhouse in partial compensation for their labor. Housing remains a cornerstone of maintaining a farm labor force, particularly one capable of fanning out across the United States as migrant farmworkers. In our study, we found that housing in the labor demand regions of the North differs in significant ways from housing in the traditional farm labor supply communities of California, Florida, and Texas.

Migrant Housing in Labor Demand Areas

The amount and type of housing available in a labor demand area strongly affect the adequacy and composition of the labor force. Most summer harvest labor demand areas have housing for migrant families and barracks-style housing for occupancy by unaccompanied men, although usually some workers are forced to find housing on their own. Areas that provide housing for family workers are able to recruit U.S. and employment-authorized workers. Areas that provide no housing or housing designed only for unaccompanied males inevitably become dominated by new immigrant workers. We found, for example, that between one third and one-fifth of the migrant farmworkers interviewed were not provided free housing in the North. Fully 35 percent of migrants from Parlier, 23 percent of those from Weslaco, and 21 percent of those from Immokalee had to find their own housing when they migrated to northern regions.

Workers forced to rent temporary quarters in summer harvest areas often share crowded housing. Success in sharing available housing space (either in rented housing or employer-provided housing) is an important element in determining the feasibility of migrating. Both family workers and unaccompanied men find it preferable, but not always possible, to share housing with compatible relatives. Larger migrant camps with workers from various unrelated family and village networks suffer from greater tension than smaller ones consisting entirely of one closely or loosely knit network.

The quality of the housing observed in northern areas varies greatly but is, in most cases, marginal, leading to particular problems (e.g., colds and other ailments) for those workers who remain north for late fall crops such as apples in Michigan. Its marginal condition usually derives from age. Inadequate investment in maintenance of migrant housing has led to a decrease in housing stock as older dwellings are abandoned. Much of the current housing is dilapidated. Used mobile homes are widely utilized as replacements for older housing, both because of their low cost and because they can be used by groups of unaccompanied-male workers or by families.

Virtually all farmworkers we interviewed considered availability of housing to be a serious consideration in deciding whether to migrate. In each community, more than four-fifths of the heads of households considered access to housing a "very important" factor in migration decisions. Although quality of housing was not as important a consideration, the provision of higher-than-average quality housing is recognized by migrant workers, growers, and farm labor managers as an important fringe benefit in recruiting the most productive and experienced workers. Many employers in California, New Jersey, Maryland, and Michigan reward core workers responsible for general, year-round farmwork, worker recruitment, or supervision with particularly desirable housing. In areas with labor surpluses (e.g., California, southern Florida, Washington), however, employer-provided housing is usually available only for key supervisory or technical personnel. In all areas with a restricted supply of farmworkers, employer-provided housing is seen as an important tool to induce workers to remain with the employer throughout the season. The situation experienced by Maryland nursery workers described here represents one common style of labor management on the East Coast.

Single migrant workers still make up most of [the] nursery's labor force. The company recruits them from the Mexicali, Mexico, area through Arizona agencies. . . . Single workers receive pay advances for bus fare from the border; if they finish out the season, [the nursery] pays their way home. Upon arrival at the nursery, each worker is assigned a sleeping area in the dorm, whose rooms hold four to 12 workers apiece. . . . The camp's workers range in age from 21 to 65. "The older ones help keep the younger ones in control." Paternal and fraternal relationships are common, with up to three generations of a family represented. (*American Nurseryman Magazine,* November 15, 1989, 87–97)

Indeed, providing housing to valuable migrant workers is an extension of the common practice of providing housing to year-round workers on farms across the United States.

There are, however, few economic incentives for agricultural employers to construct family housing, since it is cheaper to house unaccompanied-male workers. Without active public-sector involvement, migrant housing will come to be dominated by barracks, modular housing, and trailer housing, making it increasingly difficult for family workers to participate in the migrant labor force. Where public housing for migrant farmworkers is available, however, it provides a good locus for integrated service delivery initiatives, allowing for the development of multiservice programs providing child care, educational opportunities, English classes, and other high-demand services.

Until provision of housing is recognized as a key "marketing" initiative to attract premium workers, housing will continue to deteriorate. Provision of amenities that are seen by many agricultural employers as "luxuries" (e.g., television sets, laundry facilities, private toilets and showers, play areas for children, and common rooms for parties, educational activities, or child care) are cost-effective in recruiting productive workers and reducing worker turnover. Until current flows of immigrant workers diminish, however, it is not likely that U.S. labor-intensive agriculture will focus on the role played by housing in promoting the development of a stable, productive farm labor force.

Housing in Homebase Communities

Traditional U.S. farm labor supply communities are characterized by several neighborhoods of low-cost housing. Much of this housing is extremely crowded, dilapidated, and minimally affected by zoning, making possible the construction of informal additions or adaptations to allow further crowded housing. The U.S. home-base communities for farmworkers are similar to Mexican sending communities in that extended families have been able to cluster in groups or neighborhoods, facilitating the networking that underlies farm labor recruitment. As these neighborhoods come to be saturated, residential dispersion weakens the links of extended-family networks.

The housing infrastructure of rented rooms, garages, shacks, and trailers that has developed in towns such as Parlier and Immokalee provides a means of clustering single-male workers together, facilitating drive-by recruitment by labor contractors. In many cases, labor contractors or their relatives are landlords, making it easy to keep their rental units occupied while supplying workers to their crews. At the same time, sharing housing with immigrants from other villages serves to expand workers' contacts and information about new and unfamiliar labor demand areas. Crowded housing and chronic labor surpluses help the most recently arrived immigrants "discover" new migration destinations. These dense networks combine with intense competition for farm jobs to motivate the most underemployed workers, out of desperation, to risk migrating further.

Accommodating the housing problem is made possible by the formation of complex, crowded households where rent is shared among different individuals or families. The extent to which crowded shared housing can accommodate a constant surplus of farm labor is limited, however. Communities such as Immokalee and Parlier are already supersaturated. The average farmworker household size in Parlier is 7.3 persons; in Immokalee, 5.2 persons. The largest household in Parlier had 23 persons, in Immokalee, 13 persons, Little more crowding is possible. Even Weslaco, the least crowded of the labor supply communities, had an average of 4.5 persons per household. These household sizes are 25 to 40 percent larger than the average U.S. household size.

In each of the home-base communities, shared housing is a necessary adaptation for the low-income farmworker population. Shared-housing arrangements include extended-family households consisting of parents, their adult children, and grandchildren; multiple nuclear families or nuclear families with singles (e.g., cousins, or brothers- or sisters-in-law); and "dormitory households" of large numbers of recently immigrated unaccompanied males. In Immokalee, 76 percent of the current farmworkers live in crowded, "complex" households. In Parlier, 60 percent share housing, and in Weslaco, 39 percent. In Parlier and Immokalee, the mean farmworker household size is larger than in Weslaco because of the extremely crowded dormitory households.

Earnings from renting crowded housing in Parlier and Immokalee are an important source of income for the permanent residents of home-base towns. Housing densities of about ten persons per mobile home, eight per one-bedroom apartment, and fifteen to twenty-five per two-bedroom house, garage, or backyard "camp" can provide property owners with cash incomes of fifteen thousand to thirty thousand dollars a year, allowing rapid amortization of the costs of purchasing old houses or mobile homes. Many of these transactions occur underground, letting property owners avoid income taxes while allowing them to make adjustments for seasonal and weekly fluctuations in work. Unaccompanied workers are able to afford steep rents with weekly rental installments and flexible allowances for credit during slow periods of work.

Such arrangements allow communities such as Parlier and Immokalee to maintain very large surpluses of recently immigrated workers. Although the cost of housing is exorbitant in relation to the quality of accommodations, it is the only feasible alternative for recently arrived migrants for whom the cost of rental and cleaning deposits and standard lease terms is prohibitive. In Immokalee, an average of 23 percent of workers' earnings are spent on housing, and average housing costs run around $144 per month; in Parlier, 20 percent of earnings are spent on housing, which averages $161 per month; yet in Weslaco, only 10 percent of earnings go to housing, which averages $46 per month, reflecting the high degree of home ownership. The special "underground market" in rented space in crowded housing is, in fact, an effective but expensive mechanism for brokering house sharing.

The housing supply in farmworker towns like Immokalee and Parlier constitutes a barrier to entering the farm labor market. Persons without either network contacts or the social skills or willingness to agree to crowded housing are seriously disadvantaged in traditional farm labor supply communities. Access to informal sources of credit (family members, landlords, or labor contractors) is essential to life below the poverty level and continued participation in the farm labor force.

From the labor demand side, we have noted, crowded neighborhoods facilitate labor recruitment and labor control, partially supplanting the traditional morning shape-ups. In Parlier, the proprietors of some rooming houses serve as labor brokers, helping their renters find work. In other cases, such as that of the Guerrerenses living in a cluster of small shacks in Parlier, labor contractors drop by each evening to fill out their crews. In Immokalee, although the bus station shape-up area provides a location for recruitment of hundreds of daily casual workers, other workers find employment through household networks.

Although all home-base communities studied have built low-income housing and continue to actively promote further public-housing efforts, public housing accommodates only a small proportion of the towns' inhabitants. The design of most public housing also makes it less than amenable for farmworkers' complex extended-family households.

Conclusion

Few social scientists have directly addressed the dynamic that exists among housing, employment, and migration. The need for free or low-cost, off-peak-season housing stems in part from the chronic cash-flow difficulties that farmworkers suffer. The above-mentioned percentages of income spent on housing are calculated for months when farmworkers are working close to full time, since interviews were conducted during peak-employment seasons. The availability of housing for twenty-five dollars a week in communities such as Immokalee and Parlier appears to reflect the upper boundary of unaccompanied-male farmworkers' ability to pay for housing during slow periods of work.

Home ownership (in Mexico, for example) allows migrant farmworkers to adopt economic strategies by combining six to eight months of intense work with three or four months of "resting," home repairs, car repairs, and casual work. This is similar to the cycles of injury and therapy noted among low-income workers in a variety of settings (Gouviea 1992; Griffith, Valdés Pizzini, and Johnson 1992). Off-season social events serve not only as entertainment but as a means of cementing network relations. Supplementing peak-season work with local, winter employment then becomes desirable but not obligatory. In Puerto Rico, the government's housing programs have allowed migrants to work during half the year and return to Puerto Rico during the winter.

The development of a stable, apparently domestic, labor force of migrant workers during the period 1950–75 in southern Texas required cheaper land, cheaper building materials, and a longer farmwork season than are now available. Mexican families continued to migrate into southern Texas during and after the Bracero era because of the availability of a harvest season including crops that fitted well together, aggressive financing of small residential lots, and strong winter demand for labor in citrus. The newly immigrated families developed a specialized and successful economic strategy based on migration and seasonal employment, using their "resting time" to build, expand, and improve their homes.

These conditions have changed. Mechanization of cotton and sugar beets shortened the harvest season in the United States and created gaps in migrant itineraries. Increased land costs, material costs, and zoning and credit eligibility requirements have made home ownership increasingly difficult to achieve. Increasing regulatory enforcement and social disapproval are making it more difficult for families to rely on working teenagers to contribute to family income. Pressure from local government to "improve" the infrastructure of the *colonias* through annexation and development of city services threatens to increase the tax burden on farmworker homeowners.

In summary, the unique and flexible adaptations that made it possible for migrant families to survive on extremely low annual incomes require a laissez-faire regulatory context and cheap inputs, making the value added by personal investments of labor very attractive. These conditions, formerly available in many rural areas of the United States, are increasingly available only in Mexico and other sending communities outside the nation's borders. These housing trends, then, contribute significantly to the growing tendency for growers and crew leaders to recruit cyclical migrants instead of settlers to produce the nation's food.

Chapter 10

The Poverty of Conventional Thought
Social Theory and the Working Poor

The words we use to describe the nation's farmworkers are loaded with images of misfortune: "foreign-born," "immigrant," "ethnic minority," "alien," "unauthorized." The agriculture industry's ability to employ such workers, to rely on their abilities to live in poverty and work under authoritarian methods of labor control, has succeeded in keeping food prices low while insuring the profit margins that have attracted corporate capital to agriculture. In this age of an increasingly service-and-information-based economy, agriculture remains a capital-absorbing enterprise capable of generating profits. Even in the shadow of free trade with Mexico, investment in agriculture continues. We have long known that the quality and quantity of labor is a central ingredient in the equation of successful agricultural production. Gaining control over all facets of the labor process has become institutionalized in agriculture to the extent that poverty, injury, and inhumanity are now common features of putting food on America's table.

Perhaps—as socially conscious Americans—we continue to tolerate this because the nation's two million to three million farmworkers constitute a very small proportion of the total labor force. We are a democracy, after all, where percentages count. On top of their relatively small numbers, farmworkers work in settings quite unlike those experienced by the majority of the nation's working people. They work on a seasonal basis, often migrate from job to job through the year, and usually earn annual incomes far below federally established poverty levels. Usually, too, they live in isolated rural settings, far down dirt roads, hidden inside scrub woods, or in unsightly slums or concrete-block labor camps on the fringes of small towns. Quite frequently they exist under housing and transportation arrangements that are so tightly controlled they could have been designed by some department of corrections. This reduces their access to the consumer markets—department stores, groceries, malls—enjoyed by most people. And if these factors are not enough to set most farmworkers apart from the bulk of the nation's labor force, we could point out that most farmworkers are foreign-born, many are not citizens, and many others—the notorious "undocumenteds," "illegals," or "aliens"— have no legal grounds for being in the country at all. Given these attributes of the farm labor force, how can we justify the title of this chapter? How can we imply that a study of a strange, neglected corner of the U.S. labor force could have any more than remote relevance to labor market theory, policy, or economic thought?

Despite extreme differences between farmworkers and others in the labor force, their behaviors speak to important bodies of social, cultural, and economic theory and method because they are among the nation's working poor. Their behaviors are adaptive responses to social and economic conditions that, in many ways, reflect the direction that many of the world's nation-states have been moving in recent decades. Unless the international divisions of labor change significantly over the next generation, farmworkers provide a window looking out over not only the working poor but also over future labor processes. Like the labor processes at work in U.S. agriculture, the nation's labor processes, increasingly, span international borders, as with the manufacturing of textiles and components for the electronics industry (Nash and Fernández-Kelly 1983). More and more, they draw upon labor forces segmented by factors such as ethnicity, gender, race, and legal or citizenship status (Burawoy 1976; Gordon, Edwards, and Reich 1982). Internal labor markets based on these social and cultural factors are reinforced by the structural characteristics of agriculture: specifically, subcontracting, or the use of labor intermediaries for recruitment and supervision, sustains segmentation by breaking up work groups into small units with differential access to work, working conditions, and power. Similarly, in many industrial settings, subcontracting out portions of the production process (often called "out-sourcing") has been increasing in domestic and international production contexts (Nash 1989). This practice gives companies the opportunity to phase back on production in their unionized shops by having pieces of their main product manufactured in nonunionized shops, establishing competitive relations between shops for more pieces of the company's product. Fragmenting production in this way also allows firms to shop around for places where regulations covering occupational health and safety, unemployment insurance, social-security taxes, transportation, wages and working conditions, and so forth are fewer or less strictly enforced. In cases such as sharecropping or subcontracting, responsibility for enforcing such regulations shifts from the firm to the worker. Particularly dirty, demanding, and hazardous production operations may be done in locations with low numbers of OSHA inspectors, while public-relations departments may be housed in spacious carpeted offices where employees offer coffee in delicate china cups.

Many of these changes allow employers and supervisors to control labor with disguised slavery, debt peonage, paternalism, patron-client ties, and relations of power inherent in families, ethnic groups, networks, and communities (Griffith 1993a). This continues to displace or erode the power of labor unions and facilitates the separation of extremely wealthy families of professionals and executives from the working poor. This gap has come to the foreground in many communities where plants have either closed or firms have won wage concessions from workers (Wallace 1978; Hage and Klauda 1988; Nash 1989; Stull, Broadway, and Griffith, in press). Yet divisions between rich and poor are hardly restricted to the industrial settings of company towns. In agriculture, such a widening gap reflects the so-called disappearing middle known to rural sociologists, which refers to farms becoming either larger or smaller over the past eighty years, with farms in the midsized range disappearing (U.S. Department of Commerce 1987; Gladwin and Zulaut 1989; see also Bartlett 1987). Those at the smaller end of the continuum have retreated into part-time or "gentleman" farming, supplementing agricultural production with off-farm employment, while those at the large end have either become corporate farms or have entered into production subcontracts with other, usually larger corporate operations.

A similar separation has occurred in the political arena, with international trade policy being forged at high levels of federal government and domestic policy being reinterpreted and enforced at the state and local government levels (Gouviea 1992). While international compacts like GATT (the General Agreement on Tariffs and Trade) and NAFTA (the North American Free Trade Agreement) are negotiated with pomp and circumstance at high levels of government, pieces of legislation relevant to the well-being of the working poor fray into the shabby, partitioned hallways of state and local offices. In the present context, the enforcement of occupational health and safety regulations, minimum-wage laws, transportation and insurance requirements, immigration policies, and environmental legislation often fall to inspectors who have long been part of their local communities and whose sympathies lie with management rather than labor. The legal weapons available to the few regulatory personnel committed to the fundamental mission of protecting workers' rights are dysfunctional and cumbersome. The currently ineffective regulatory programs are funded at ridiculously low levels.

These developments call for a rethinking of conventional notions about labor and labor unionism, about capital accumulation, about relationships between wages and consumption, about the inabilities of the workforce to reproduce itself without government assistance, and about the role of the working poor in the changing world order. How difficult is it to grasp that great political and economic disparities exist between management and labor when farmworkers live in rusting trailers without the basic rights of citizens while the heads of the companies that employ them drive $50,000 automobiles and send Christmas gifts to Capitol Hill? In light of such conspicuous consumption practices and consumptive business practices, how can anyone keep a straight face while arguing that corporate farms cannot raise wages or improve working conditions because profit margin considerations would drive them out of business? Is farming truly a marginal enterprise? If so, are American business leaders so stupid or irrational that corporations with fleets of accountants continue to expand their presence in agriculture, buying and leasing land, planting fruits and vegetables, growing timber and raising livestock? Would corporations remain in agriculture if it were not, in fact, an extremely lucrative venture?

Theoretical Significance of the Community Studies

Recent theoretical and methodological strides concerning the working poor have come primarily from sociology and anthropology. Yet the continued domination of labor market theory and method by the discipline of economics, particularly microeconomics, precludes in-depth consideration of those features of labor processes that cannot be easily modeled with conventional analytical techniques.

In particular, analytical techniques relying on standard aggregate data sets based on survey methodologies provide a misleading view of a domain characterized by a rich social ecology. Such techniques, in essence, reify viewing the U.S. labor market in ethnocentric terms during a period when the labor market is becoming increasingly multicultural. The very syntax of standard economic models rests on ethnocentric concepts such as "hourly wage," "job," "fringe benefits"—each of which must be interpreted differently for the working poor. The working environment in which America's immigrant working poor spend their days is part of a global economy—an agora overlaid with multiple social and conceptual geographies—literally and figuratively a polyglot workplace.

The subtle relations of power and resistance that structure labor market dynamics and become essential attributes of labor processes are especially likely to elude representation by standard methods. By converting workers' lives into discrete units of time, reducing them to values in the same way one estimates the cost of wheat, and reifying mathematical relationships as "analytical," traditional economists cannot help glossing over fundamental social and cultural foundations of labor processes. Their methodological elegance conceals their inadequacy in identifying the underlying causes of workers' behaviors.

The complexity that economic science has failed to represent underscores the significance of our treatment of farmworkers as a window overlooking the working poor. Four major subject areas examined in this study are interrelated: the labor process and labor market structure, especially the role of the state in maintaining and reproducing the quality and quantity of labor needed by the agricultural community; immigration and immigration policy; agricultural decision making and land use; and the emerging role of informal economic activity and subcontracting in the economy. Theories about the behaviors of low-wage workers often include propositions about the behaviors of immigrants, the growing importance of the informal economy and "domestic" production and reproduction, and subcontracting. Changing land-use patterns entail different seasonal labor needs and different migrant itineraries, and stimulate changing relations between farm and nonfarm sectors in rural areas. In our discussion of Puerto Rico, we reported that changing uses of land and labor associated with the decline of the sugar industry had a number of consequences for Puerto Rico as a labor supply region for agriculture in New Jersey and the Northeast. In the wake of unemployment stemming from sugar's decline, the Puerto Rican government began development projects designed to house the unemployed and underemployed, soliciting political patronage while simultaneously defusing labor unrest. At the same time, using special tax incentives, Puerto Rico began attracting mainland investors to the island to build manufacturing plants. Together, housing development and employment opportunities removed two principal motives for Puerto Ricans to migrate to the mainland: finding a job and building a house. The latter is probably the main reason for international labor migration and return migration throughout the entire Caribbean and for much of the developing world. The Puerto Rican case thus illustrates how changing uses of land and labor in one region can affect the demographic characteristics of the labor force in another.

Similar points were made for other areas. We noted how changes associated with the civil-rights movement, tourism, and construction in Florida caused many central Florida growers to turn from African American to Mexican and Mexican American workers, and how this subsequently affected changes in farm labor markets throughout the eastern United States. Simultaneous changes, rooted in ethnic and national differences between these groups of workers, occurred in farm labor contracting, crew assembly and supervision, and housing and transportation. The mechanization of cotton harvesting so disrupted migrant itineraries in Texas that many domestic farmworkers had to leave farmwork, stimulating increased demand for illegal immigrant workers from Mexico.

Observations such as these point to the difficulty of discussing the four relevant bodies of theory and method separately. The following discussions must be viewed, then, as arbitrarily separated for the purposes of organization. It is inevitable that some repetition will occur. Our four divisions are but convenient tools for calling upon the theoretical materials that apply to each of the subject areas.

Labor Markets and the Labor Process

By definition, the working poor work in jobs that provide incomes below the amount necessary to feed, clothe, and shelter oneself and one's dependents. The demand for labor for such jobs cannot be satisfied solely through market mechanisms and economic incentives. To accept these jobs, workers need to agree to extremely low standards of living, to have additional means of support, or to have been coerced somehow. Low-income labor markets tend to be supplied by workers possessing one or more of these characteristics. Like teenaged workers earning ''spending money'' at Burger King or K-Mart, farmworkers may be young and somewhat carefree, unencumbered by family responsibilities. Or like working spouses who flesh out household incomes by supplementing another, principal wage earner's income, farmworkers may come from domestic settings in which a number of individuals pool incomes. Or they may be forced into farmwork—pushed out of their villages because of economic or political hardship and drawn into farmwork through relations of debt, family obligation, or network affiliation.

Workers coming from any of these backgrounds, either desperate or able to accept lower wages than workers supporting families, tend to engage in highly competitive struggles with one another for work. Because of this, in the parlance of labor market segmentation theory, the agricultural labor market has attracted social-scientific attention as a "competitive" labor market, in contrast to labor markets that have long been dominated by labor unions (Gordon, Edwards, and Reich 1982). Union-dominated labor markets contain internal labor markets, job ladders, and hierarchical structures based on long-term political struggles between labor and management; in these so-called primary labor markets, wages, working conditions, promotions, pensions, health benefits, and other attributes of the labor process are highly structured and predictable. Hiring, supervision, occupational health issues, other working conditions, and firing become subject to intense scrutiny by committees of workers and managers or their representatives, protecting workers from whimsical or unfair treatment in the workplace.

The benefits of these kinds of jobs accrue to the communities in which primary-sector workers live as well as to the workers themselves. Most obviously, such jobs provide workers with the means to support local merchants, financial services, real-estate markets, churches, builders, and so forth. Higher-paid jobs also generate greater tax revenues for roads, policy, teachers, and other public goods and services. Less obviously, workers in the primary labor market place less of a strain on local public and private support systems, such as subsidized health care, soup kitchens, or food giveaway programs. Over the long term, too, they make contributions to their communities by educating their children, sometimes sending them to college, and taking an active interest in the sports, civic clubs, libraries, and other institutions in which their children become involved.

Competitive labor markets tend not to provide either workers or communities with such security. Workers in these markets may be fired without warning or reason, pay may be withheld for dubious reasons, supervision may involve physical and mental abuse, exposure to hazardous conditions or materials may occur without proper safeguards, and so forth. Workers also become susceptible to competition from workers with lower expectations, different attitudes toward child labor, or reduced consumption needs. This generally occurs when native U.S. workers compete with new-immigrant workers or workers willing to put their entire families to work to flesh out household incomes. The community suffers from the presence of such labor markets by absorbing the damages and losses that low-income industries generate. In particular, workers injured or laid off from competitive-sector industries tend to have little or no health insurance; the costs of their injuries and periods of unemployment must be borne by themselves and the communities in which they live. Other costs involve the increasing incidence of homelessness, abject poverty, and crime. School dropout rates tend to increase in such settings, for a number of reasons. With growing social distance between those in highly skilled, well-paid positions and those in the low-income labor force, convincing students of education's value as a tool for upward mobility becomes more difficult (Willis 1982). With high rates of occupational injury, older children must take up some of the responsibility of primary wage earners to feed, clothe, and maintain the household, undermining their ability to achieve as students. With poor nutrition, increased disease, overcrowded homes, and other consequences of poverty, studying becomes difficult or impossible.

As labor unions in the United States become less powerful or undergo reorganization, more labor markets assume the structural characteristics and human behavior attributes of the agricultural labor market, with corresponding problems at the community level. While remaining highly competitive, the agricultural labor market has grown increasingly internally differentiated or segmented. The character and basis of its internal differentiation, however, are quite distinct from the occupational ladders and other forms of internal labor markets found in union-dominated industries. Agricultural labor markets become differentiated through a complex of factors related to refugee movements, international migrations, language, national origin, ethnicity, race, gender, and legal status. They become further differentiated by network relations with other farmworkers and farm labor contractors. The diverse segments of the farm labor market, interacting with various qualitative and quantitative features of labor demand, then assume even more distinctive forms as they adapt to specific regions and working conditions within regions. The internal components of the labor force are not simply different from one another, not merely interesting for unique cultural practices, racial characteristics, or linguistic behaviors. Each of the internal components of the labor force also involves some access to power and some capacity for resistance. Each, in short, offers a set of rights, obligations, and allegiances that colors its members' experiences in the farm labor market and the neighborhoods, labor camps, and communities in which they live, even if only for a short while.

Throughout this volume, we have documented the existence of important subgroups of workers. Differences noted between workers include legal status, ethnicity, network type, family type, time of arrival in the United States, and whether or not they use a farm labor contractor. In each of the case studies, we have seen that growers and farm labor contractors have been able to utilize these characteristics to accomplish many of their labor needs. They can select for the most willing, docile, and productive workers, determining who, when, and under what conditions various farmworkers become attached to their firms. Of course, a worker's degree of attachment to the firm directly affects his or her quality of life and work. In labor markets such as those depicted in this volume, where employment security, transportation, and housing become as important as rates of pay and working conditions, the opportunities are too great for workers to fall from full-time employment to casual work and then join the ranks of the unemployed. This process proceeds most quickly under the very conditions we have documented in the farm labor market: seasonal fluctuations in labor demand and substantial labor surpluses. Under these conditions, without real or perceived alternative employment opportunities, it is in a worker's best interests to attach himself or herself as firmly as possible to specific growers and farm labor contractors.

Yet there are costs associated with attaching oneself too tightly to a grower or farm labor contractor. In much of the case material, we have seen that workers who attach themselves to farm labor contractors often must submit to costly terms of trade. For example, workers assured of access to free or low-cost housing, or housing with flexible terms of occupancy, may also have to tolerate consumer credit schemes, high transportation costs, and miscellaneous demands on their spare time. Faced with such tradeoffs, workers respond in one of a few common ways, each of which carries implications for the extent and nature of the farmworker's attachment to the farm labor force, level of employment, and consequent income and well-being. We discuss four common adaptations among the working poor here; although we refer to them as workers' adaptations, each of these adaptations implies somewhat distinct uses of a low-wage, largely immigrant labor force by growers and farm labor contractors. The responsibility for the development of these adaptations does not, we emphasize, rest solely on the shoulders of either workers or employers but constitutes joint informal negotiations in which varying degrees of power and resistance come into play. These adaptations develop, in other words, on both the supply and the demand sides of the labor market. We refer to these adaptations as the upward mobility model, the labor reserve model, the transnational model, and the entrepreneurial model.

The Upward Mobility Model

Farmworkers may attempt to improve their positions in the farm labor market by moving from a secondary or tertiary position to the core of a firm's (grower's or farm labor contractor's) labor force. This is, simply, the way farmworkers move up the occupational ladder within the farm labor force, even though a worker's status as a core, secondary, or tertiary worker may change over the course of the years as he or she travels from job to job, firm to firm. Rising in the ranks of farmwork like this may involve adopting a supervisory role; if nothing else, one may be given some authority over other members of one's family or network. At the very least, this usually involves assuming some of the responsibility for recruiting new workers, which opens the door for upwardly mobile workers to represent new workers to growers. Subsequently, the performance of these new workers reflects upon the worker or workers who recruited them. We noted that, especially in the northern labor demand regions, growers often use core workers for labor recruitment and that those recruited into the operation tend to come from the worker's family and network connections. This creates the opportunity for growers and farm labor contractors to draw upon a group of individuals who are similarly situated in society as well as share cultural features such as language and dialect, tastes in food and music, dress, gender relations, religion, and so forth. In this model, the tendency has been for the quality of the linkage between growers and their workers to mimic a familial tie. The potential for paternalism is great, and while this usually implies asymmetrical power relations, it need not imply excessive levels of exploitation and surplus extraction. A great potential exists, however, for the grower or farm labor contractor to transfer responsibility from his or her own shoulders to the core worker or workers. Not only recruitment, but task assignment, supervision, and even arrangements for food, documents, shelter, and transportation may be assigned to key core employees, without much more compensation than greater employment security and preferred housing. This arrangement also allows employers to distribute a number of hidden costs of operating over the recruited networks. The costs of maintaining workers during slow or "wet" times, as well as reproductive and social security costs, are borne by workers themselves. Farmworkers are able to meet these costs, in part, by utilizing the social services available to them but also meet them through the consumption concessions that make them the working poor.

In our case studies, we found that the upwardly mobile model was most often followed by Mexican nationals and Mexican Americans, less often by Puerto Ricans and African Americans, and rarely by either Haitians or the new indigenous workers from Mexico and Central America, such as the Mixtec and Kanjobal populations.

The Labor Reserve Model

We have documented three developments that suggest that the labor reserve model is becoming the principal worker adaptation to farm labor processes: the increasing proportions of unaccompanied-male workers; the related increase in cyclical migration, especially movement between regions with a low cost of living and labor demand regions (e.g., between Oaxaca and Immokalee); and the evidence that cyclical unaccompanied-male migrants are younger than they were ten to fifteen years ago.

This model of worker adaptation has been thoroughly analyzed in a number of settings. Alejandro Portes and John Walton's (1981) analysis of South African labor markets, Michael Burawoy's (1976) comparison between South African and U.S.-immigrant-dominated labor markets, Michael Piore's (1979) analysis of Mexican immigration, and other studies (e.g., Griffith 1985, 1993a; Sticter 1985) have all noted the common dimensions of the labor reserve model. Most important, the separation of productive from reproductive labor is so extreme that the costs of reproducing and maintaining workers during youth and old age are borne in separate geographical regions and often separate political entities.

Added to the well-known phenomenon of transferred reproductive and maintenance costs, the labor reserve model undermines workers' attempts at assimilation and the power assimilation brings. Clearly, numerous advantages accrue to workers from maintaining this cultural integrity, especially in terms of the ease with which they adjust to new work settings and return regularly to their home regions. Yet assimilation refers not only to adopting new eating habits or dressing like performers on television but also to learning the ropes of empowerment and economic opportunity and developing the social skills necessary to marshal collective resistance. The movement between production settings and reproductive arenas, between Immokalee and Oaxaca, facilitates the development of social and physical infrastructures that select for workers who are not likely to put down roots. Housing becomes dormitory- or barracks-style, and labor contractors assemble what we have called artificial networks, creating total institutional contexts. In the most extreme cases of this, the state endorses the labor reserve model by issuing highly restrictive work-authorization visas.

The Transnational Model

Like the labor reserve model, the transnational model involves movement, or at least sustained, regular communication, between two or more regions, nations, or cultures. The principal distinction between this and the labor reserve model is that transnationalism is a family rather than individual process. Transnational movement involves establishing roots, colonizing neighborhoods, creating ethnic enclaves in receiving regions and cultures of emigration and return migration in sending regions.

More important, the transnational model constitutes collective resistance among a people, especially against those forces (legal status, INS enforcement, unemployment) that would "jettison" members of their communities during times of reduced employment. Every year at the end of the harvest, in Parlier, in Immokalee, and in similar communities, some workers engage in a collective attempt to remain in these communities. It is not an overtly political resistance, yet it involves establishing alliances with existing organizations (e.g., legal aid, churches) that could help in their claim to remain in the receiving region. Quite often women drive the growth of transnational communities, and quite often their motives for this lie in the welfare of their children. Their association with school and church programs for children often draws them into socially conscious and activist circles, underscoring the importance of joining reproductive and child-care issues with labor force issues in theory and policy domains.

The Entrepreneurial Model

The least common worker adaptation to farm labor processes is the entrepreneurial model. Yet this model interests us because the specific forms it assumes feed sympathies for worker resistance as well as sympathies for compliance. In this model, workers adapt by filling a niche in the farm labor market. Sharecropping, pinhooking, and labor contracting are the three most commonly mentioned in the preceding chapters, and the three most commonly encountered.

As forms of resistance, these adaptations involve gaining independence, not from the farm labor market so much as from direct supervision, whether by growers or labor contractors. In the case of Immokalee tomato pinhooking, for example, pinhookers assemble their own crews and negotiate with growers on the per-box price of tomatoes; take their crews into the field, using their own buckets, boxes, and other tools; and then pay the grower or the grower's supervisor as they leave the field. They then sell these tomatoes themselves, usually in farmers' markets.

Pinhooking is similar to sharecropping and labor contracting in that it is based on subcontractual or subcontractual-like relations between growers and pinhookers rather than on direct employee–employer relations. It has become so widespread an adaptation in southern Florida that, though still absorbing a relatively small proportion of the labor force, it has spawned two political developments. First, the Florida Tomato Committee attempted to unify tomato growers against pinhookers, arguing that because the fruit pinhookers sell to consumers is sprayed and unwashed, it might cause illness and a consequent backlash against all Florida tomato growers. This was, at least, their stated reason for objecting to pinhookers. Their "secondary" motive, of course, was to give the packer–growers (their members) more control over the tomato market. The effort failed because pinhookers fill a valuable niche in the market and because tomato growers are difficult to unify against an adaptation they perceive is in their own short-term economic interests.

The second political development has been for firms to structure pinhookers into their farming operations in a capacity that is only nominally a subcontractual relationship. This has established, in short, a group of false pinhookers, creating the image of independent contracting while still maintaining a high degree of control over the labor process. In this respect, pinhooking is similar to the internal structure of farm labor contracting, which we discuss in detail. Pinhooking, whether "false" or real, transfers a significant amount of responsibility for labor from growers to pinhookers, including the business of labor recruiting, supervising, checking documents, paying into tax and insurance funds, and insuring occupational safety.

These four models are not exclusive of one another. We find evidence of all four in places like Immokalee and Parlier and may even observe workers moving among these adaptations over the course of their lives or from season to season throughout the year. Many features of these adaptations, however, are especially well suited to labor forces that contain large immigrant, foreign-born, and culturally distinct ("other") populations. The reasons for this become clear in the next section.

Immigration and Migration Studies

The second body of theory we engage in this work deals with internal and international labor migration (Froebel, Heinrichs, and Kreye 1977; Nash and Fernández-Kelly 1983; Sanderson 1985). Our work, the Commission on Agricultural Workers studies (1993a, 1993b, 1993c), and that of the more statistically representative *National Agricultural Worker Survey* (Mines, Gabbard, and Samardick 1991) all find that the agricultural labor force is dominated by foreign-born workers.

The foreign character of this workforce raises questions about the role of U.S. agriculture in demographic change in the sending countries and the recipient U.S. communities. Immokalee, Parlier, Weslaco, and Mayagüez have all been altered by the growth of Latin and Caribbean transnational communities. Developments taking place in Puerto Rico are particularly interesting, given that the island has long been a source of cheap labor for U.S. mainland fields and factories yet has, quite recently, experienced a slowing of emigration from the island into U.S. agriculture and increasing immigration from the Dominican Republic (Duaney 1992:50). Along with the differences between the Mexican and Puerto Rican migrations into and out of U.S. agriculture, the migrations of Dominicans into Puerto Rico have alerted many scholars to the complexity *within* the Latin population. This has severely weakened the utility of the term "Hispanic," calling into question Census Bureau labeling behavior. The problems with the use of the term "Hispanic" illustrate the problems of developing national policies without the means to implement those policies differentially at local and regional levels. Are linguistic programs oriented toward Mexicans living in Los Angeles applicable to Puerto Ricans living in Chicago or Cubans in Miami? Would the same job-training or enhanced recruitment efforts work among Dominicans in New York as work among Chicanos in southern Texas or Guatemalans boning chicken breasts in northern Georgia poultry plants?

Migration as a Network Phenomenon

Ethnic and regional differences within Latin American, Caribbean, and other immigrant and native populations underscore the uneven character of immigration. Our community studies testify to the ways immigrants cluster or become geographically concentrated, as noted by earlier studies (see Portes and Bach 1985; Papademetriou et al. 1989:47–55). At the same time, we document some of the key ways the agricultural labor market facilitates or forces "pioneering" behaviors among immigrants and refugees. Along with many others (e.g., Piore 1979; Portes and Bach 1985; Massey et al. 1987; Portes and Börözc 1989), we have noted the importance of networks and network building in the migration experience. Our observations build upon much of the earlier work on immigrant adjustment behaviors and migration yet depart from this work in a few subtle ways.

We have noted the practice, common among farm labor contractors, of the conscious building of networks of unrelated or partially related, usually single-male, workers. We call these networks "artificial" for two reasons. First, they tend not to be based on any natural or social process such as kinship, village residence, long association, or friendship. Second, they tend to be fragile, their linkages capable of being severed for a number of reasons related to labor market developments. They are constructed as mirror images of "natural" networks, however, in that they function in a way similar to natural networks: in particular, they are designed to provide a wide range of services to network members in an informal or semiformal manner, occasionally flavored with familial gestures such as unwritten loans, shelter guarantees, and travel advances. Their theoretical importance derives from the fact that they provide new-immigrant workers with the means, however basic or crude, of entering labor markets with ease, of surviving through periods of unemployment, and of behaving in ways similar to immigrants with well-developed ties of kinship or friendship. Contrary to Douglas Massey and colleagues (1987), these artificial networks demonstrate that network building need not be accompanied by a permanent process of settlement but may be a temporary adaptation to conditions of fluid employment and housing. They further suggest that networks do not in all cases acquire a momentum, a density, growing beyond the conditions that spawned them, but that they may be constructed in close correspondence with labor demand and dissolved rather quickly with changing economic circumstances. Artificial networks, we noted earlier, often accompany the labor reserve model discussed above.

Recruiting labor based on workers' networks is neither a unique method of labor recruiting among the working poor nor confined to the so-called competitive labor markets. Mark Granovetter's (1977) well-known observation about "the strength of weak ties," for example, illustrates that network relations influence job search and hiring decisions even among white-collar sectors of the economy. In a labor market composed of a significant proportion of immigrants, as among the working poor in general, networks acquire an additional significance because the line between one's home life and one's work life becomes blurred by the multifunctional character of workers' networks. The use of networks for labor recruitment becomes particularly crucial to the maintenance of existing farm labor processes under these conditions. At the same time, this practice assures lower exit rates from agriculture. One further consequence is that it also assures continued poverty among network members, though this poverty is distributed, unevenly, over the network.

Network recruitment feeds two of the above worker adaptations—upward mobility and entrepreneurial behavior—in ways that benefit growers and farm labor contractors, redistributing costs of recruitment and supervision in particular. Yet it also feeds the process of transnationalism, which has both short-term advantages and long-term disadvantages for growers and farm labor contractors, especially in cases where transnationalism has created ethnic enclaves that become enclaves of resistance to the power of growers and farm labor contractors. We have witnessed this, to some extent, among Haitian immigrants based in southern Florida. Whether working for or against grower interests, however, the functional importance of network recruitment here is its potential for gathering together people of socially and culturally similar groups, facilitating organization. This organization, of course, may be used to subordinate groups of workers to employers' needs, or it may enable workers to resist the power of employers. Where the organizational capacity of network recruitment points depends on developments in the wider community of immigrant and native workers.

Our case studies illustrated, again and again, the close relationship between housing and work in the farm labor market. Equally important, although perhaps not elaborated on as much in our case studies, are the relationships that exist between work and neighborhoods. Whether network formation is accompanied by family formation and a process of building a neighborhood, an ethnic enclave or a community of immigrants departs from this close correspondence between work and housing in the labor market. Where housing is closely controlled by farm labor contractors or growers, the growth of artificial support networks providing a total institutional and social context for work is facilitated. While farmworker advocates often see grower-provided housing as a progressive social policy, in the context of network-based reciprocal transactions "free housing" implies social and economic control. By contrast, in areas such as Weslaco, where cheap land and minimal housing regulation make it possible for immigrants to build their own housing, the labor market assumes more of an "open" configuration. In communities where immigrants have secured a foothold of land ownership and control of housing stock, artificial networks become less effective as the initial immigrant settlers begin to develop an infrastructure of crowded, affordable rental housing, restaurants, bars, dance halls, and stores catering to newly arriving immigrants. During this transitional phase, the labor market turns to the street-corner hiring that prevailed in Weslaco in the 1950s and 1960s and that now prevails in Immokalee at the bus station, where workers congregate to work with one of scores of labor contractors. In these communities, labor contractors who effectively control the entire existence of their workers coexist side by side with other labor contractors who hire from the street-corner labor pool. These street-corner labor markets make it feasible for newly arrived migrants to compete with established settled immigrants without relying entirely on an intermediary. Ultimately, the most mature immigrant communities strike a balance between settled immigrants and newcomers, between life as a U.S. community and life as a transnational community.

Migration and Transnationalism

Concentrations of immigrants in selected regions, cities, communities, and neighborhoods has encouraged the development of transnationalism, the spanning of two or more nations, through constant exchanges of information, goods, remittances, and so forth. The very concept of transnationalism suggests that these U.S. communities undergo changes in concert with "sister" communities in Mexico, Central America, Puerto Rico, Haiti, and other sending regions, giving a foreign-policy dimension to the process of agricultural production. In particular, transnationalism involves allegiances that differ from those inspired, solicited, and even demanded by nation-states. The allegiances that emerge in transnational contexts tend to be based less on territory and citizenship than on expressive culture: language, religious beliefs, music, art, tastes in food, and literature. It is no simple coincidence that these also constitute the raw materials of ethnicity.

Foreign workers migrating into and through the United States cannot help but create ethnic-relations problems, especially when they move into jobs and neighborhoods already occupied by native minorities and other immigrant groups. Recently, many of us have been impressed with the resurgence of ethnicity in what was formerly the Soviet Union and its satellite Eastern European nations. As we write, fighting continues between ethnic groups in what used to be Yugoslavia, with Serbian troops shelling cities in Bosnia–Herzegovina. Long-term, less well publicized ethnic strife mars the social faces of Sri Lanka and parts of India, South Africa, Kenya, Indonesia, and Myanmar (Burma). Ethnic conflicts have become an integral part of the social landscapes of state formation and dissolution in the New World as well as the Old. The farm labor market has received refugees from conflicts in Guatemala, Haiti, El Salvador, and other regions, in addition to those "economic" refugees from Mexico and Puerto Rico that have been a central, even defining part of the farm labor force since the early part of this century. These groups have entered the workplaces and living spaces of native groups of Anglo and African American farmworkers, farm labor contractors, and managers, increasingly pushing individuals from these ethnic backgrounds both up and out of the farm labor market.

The growth of immigrant labor from primarily Spanish-speaking countries has underwritten a complex cultural process of Latinization, also called "Hispanicization" and "Mexicanization." These terms refer most explicitly to the growth of enclaves of Spanish speakers, yet the process implies transformations that reach into the recesses of rural communities in sometimes unpredictable ways. Supermarkets begin making Mexican sausages, and the odors of pork frying in corn oil permeate low-income neighborhoods. Clinics need bilingual staff members. Churches begin holding services in Spanish. Television stations broadcast *Simplemente Maria* and other Latin programming. Household composition changes, and new demands are placed on the structures throughout rural townships. This process is far advanced in California, where relationships between sending villages in Mexico and recipient crops, cities, and labor camps in the Central Valley have become so institutionalized that children grow up in Mexico with California farm labor assuming a prominent position in their lifetime occupational plans (Goldring 1990). In many parts of the East, such as Florida, the current form of Latinization, that dominated by Mexicans, dates back only to the mid 1970s, although Florida has experienced earlier Latin immigrations with Cubans, Puerto Ricans, and others from the Spanish-speaking Caribbean. Some of the labor demand regions of the North witnessed the huge increases in Latins in the early 1990s. Nevertheless, nearly any rural U.S. county with significant acreage of labor-intensive crops is bound to import at least a few Mexicans or Guatemalans during the peak of the harvest.

The state—through its immigration policies—has been anything but passive in the development of transnationalism. The failure of legislative programs has been that, instead of creating a foundation for citizenship and a decline in the use of undocumented workers, it has fueled the cyclical migration processes (the labor reserve model) that often serve as stepping stones to the growth of transnational communities. While we do not view this as an inherently socially disruptive process, given the changing and weakening nature of the nation-state throughout the world, it is certain to lead to reactionary policies and private initiatives, including an expansion of labor certification programs, an extension of the authoritarian methods of labor control that accompany the construction of artificial networks, and the growth of nativism, racism, and vigilante forces (Griffith 1993a).

Farm Labor, Agricultural Decision Making, and Resource Use

For the field of rural sociology, our observations concerning the relationships among labor, decision making, and the use of resources should be a welcome addition to a discipline that has all but ignored farmworkers relative to other elements of rural society. This is not by accident. The discipline has been bribed into its ignorance. Research in rural sociology, generally funded by the powerful system of land grant colleges, has focused almost exclusively on the plights of farmers and farming communities, paying little or no attention to those who actually work in the fields in perishable-crop agriculture. This is particularly unfortunate in light of labor's importance in land-use decisions. In our case study of family farming on the Delmarva Peninsula, for example, we found that the availability and docility of labor has been a major factor in shifting from labor-intensive to low-labor enterprise mixes. In Michigan, we observed that some farmers had adopted cropping strategies specifically to keep workers working and hence less likely to leave the farm, planting less lucrative crops in "windows" of time between their main farm operations. In another study, Pfeffer (1992) traced a relationship between labor availability and chemical use.

Our case studies are particularly relevant to two areas of rural sociology: relationships between labor and structural change in agriculture, and relationships between labor and resource use. The "disappearing-middle" literature discusses both structural change in agriculture and changes in the ways farms and farm families combine farmwork with off-farm employment. As the gap increases between large, full-time farming and small, part-time farming, two related developments occur that affect the demand for labor. First, some smaller, part-time farmers tend to shift to less labor-intensive enterprise mixes, such as livestock and grain production. Second, the corporate presence in agriculture—at the large, full-time extreme—opens the door for increased capital investment in food production and processing. This creates a business environment favorable to using labor to add value to farm produce, or an environment for labor-intensive production.

We noted in Chapter 1 that since the 1920s the changes in structure and cropping decisions implied by the disappearing middle have altered the character of farm labor. Where Theodore Roosevelt's 1909 Country Life Commission could advocate the construction of a stable, resident (and sober) farm labor force, Franklin Roosevelt's La Follette Commission of the early 1940s would have been hard-pressed to justify such a recommendation. Local labor supplies have constricted along with the drying up of the multiple and varied farm employment opportunities that a variety of farms provide. As Pfeffer (1992:349) notes:

> The supply of farm labor is no longer readily recruited in the local community. The farm population has long ceased to be the insular community depicted in nostalgic accounts of rural life. Farmers and farmworkers are part of larger labor markets. Employment opportunities are bounded by the effective commuting range to work and the reach of inter-regional and international migration streams, not by local networks.

Yet with the increasing importance of fresh fruits, vegetables, nuts, and ornamentals in modern lifestyles, many middle-sized growers have not abandoned or have returned to labor-intensive agriculture. These growers, along with larger corporate operations and farmworkers, have become increasingly ingenious in their labor relations. Among their solutions to labor supply problems have been the practice of either entering into subcontractual relations or "partnerships" with larger corporate firms. Such relations have created interesting new linkages in two directions. First, contract growing has linked local family farms to larger, multistate corporate enterprises. In typical cases, local growers use seed varieties and cultural practices approved by the corporation and oversee the growth of the crop, using their own small groups of workers to tend to the varied tasks of planting, weeding, pruning, and so forth. The corporation brings crews of workers from fields and packing facilities in other states to harvest, pack, market, and ship the produce, confirming Fischer's (1953) notion of the harvest being regarded as an enterprise separate from other farming operations.

In addition to contract growing, linkages have been established between growers and innovative, entrepreneurial groups of workers, as discussed in the section above. These linkages are more various than the familiar pattern of contract growing. The best-known of these grower–farmworker linkages are those involving labor contracting. Farm labor contracting has become increasingly complex in the past two and a half decades and receives more detailed attention in the following section. Lesser-known arrangements to emerge between growers and farmworkers include pinhooking and sharecropping (Wells 1990). Although associated with coercive and uneven power relations in the aftermath of slavery in the South, sharecropping has been increasing among Mexican farmworkers in California as a means for enterprising strawberry pickers to gain access to land and manage their own farming operations. Miriam Wells (1987, 1990) has documented the recent growth of sharecropping as a form of entrepreneurial behavior among farmworkers as well as among small farmers.

Pinhooking, sharecropping, and labor contracting represent means by which farmworkers attempt to gain more control over their own labor power. At the same time, however, they represent structural changes taking place within the farm labor force that have emerged as growers attempt to circumvent many of the legal responsibilities of dealing with farm labor. As in many subcontractual arrangements, we again emphasize, this constitutes a redistribution of risk from growers to enterprising workers, sometimes forcing workers into the informal or underground economy, where a lack of legal protection creates the potential for the abuse of power by farm labor contractors and others who hire workers.

Subcontracting, Power, and the Informal Economy

Many attributes of the farm labor market encourage informal or unregulated economic transactions. Most important, the heavy reliance on network recruiting among immigrant populations has created social settings in which simply helping oneself, one's friends, and one's relatives survive may be against the law. The existence of comparatively high proportions of illegal immigrant workers in the farm labor market means that nearly everyone—growers and workers alike—will at some time have occasion to help an illegal farmworker work, hide, find housing, attend church, buy food, use a clinic's services, and so forth. While this simple fact encourages illegal transactions to occur, perhaps more significant in today's political economic climate is the proliferation of subcontracting arrangements between farmworkers and growers and within the population of growers. Subcontracting encourages not only participation in an informal or semiformal economy but also allows uneven power relations to emerge behind masks of independence and interdependence.

Subcontracting has been an important part of food production in the United States at least since the 1860s. As noted above, subcontracting involves one individual or firm providing one or more services to a second firm that integrates a variety of phases of the production and marketing of a product or range of products. In agriculture, the "showcase" example of subcontracting occurs in the broiler industry, where every six or so weeks broiler growers raise around forty-five thousand chickens for a broiler-processing facility (Reimund, Martin, and Moore 1981). A single processing facility relies on a number of growers, and the growers usually also produce other crops and livestock as well. Often considered less coercive and more legitimate than production relations such as sharecropping or service tenure, subcontracting appears to establish a relationship between two independent or interdependent business entities. While subcontracting a portion of the production has been the norm in the poultry industry since the 1950s, recent research has shown an increase in subcontracting in other livestock production and aquaculture (Broadway 1992; Grey 1992; Heffernan and Constance 1992). Perishable-crop agriculture has known subcontracting since Chinese workers worked the fields of California during the nineteenth century, as labor contractors (subcontractors) were needed to provide linguistic and cultural brokerage services (Mines 1974; Meister and Loftis 1977; Kissam and Griffith 1991; Heppel and Amendola 1992). In none of these cases do subcontracting arrangements cover all phases of production, yet their increase has created more opportunities for firms to circumvent laws regulating record keeping, standards for wages and working conditions, immigration, and health and safety.

The increases we have seen in labor contracting in agriculture have created new opportunities for extension of employers' power and workers' resistance in the farm labor market. This has occurred for two reasons. First, some farm labor contractors have been driven "underground," into the informal economy, because of increased regulations associated with farm labor contracting and the differential enforcement of those regulations between states and regions of the United States. Operating underground has also been encouraged by the sanctuary individual growers and corporate farms have found in subcontracting arrangements: because growers can hold farm labor contractors responsible for laws governing the treatment of farm labor, enforcement agencies have shifted their attention from growers to farm labor contractors. Under these conditions, enforcement becomes a greater problem because farm labor contractors are more mobile than growers; often assemble and dismantle crews of various sizes through the year; change addresses; and possess technologies, such as CB radios and pickup trucks, that allow them to avoid legal attention.

Second, changing crew compositions with regard to network types, family types, immigration statuses, and migrants' communities of origin have created the potential, within contract crews, for farm labor contractors to increase their control over workers and the various ways that they extract value from relations with workers. Together, these two developments have "criminalized" some labor contracting, laying the social foundation for employers and workers to adopt new methods for exercising and resisting power. The entrance of farm labor contractors into the underground economy constitutes resistance to the power of the state, while the expansion of the mechanisms by which they control and extract value from farmworkers constitutes an extension of farm labor contractor power. Farmworkers, in turn, resist farm labor contractor power.

Labor contracting is most often used in perishable-crop agriculture, which includes crops such as fruits, nuts, vegetables, flowers, and horticultural products. The increase in subcontracted labor, as opposed to directly hired labor, has coincided with structural changes in agriculture and with the increasingly dormant role of U.S. employment service branches in labor recruitment for agricultural labor. Since the 1970s, although we have seen an absolute decline in reported numbers of hired farmworkers throughout the United States, the proportion hired through farm labor contractors has increased (U.S. Department of Commerce 1987). In many of the perishable crops along the eastern seaboard, farm labor contractors supply the majority of the harvest labor. Based in either Florida or Texas, these contractors act as a crucial organizational and supervisory buffer between growers and the farmworking population, at the same time providing linguistic and cultural brokerage services. At the very least, farm labor contractors assemble work crews, enter into a verbal or written contract with a grower, make sure the crews accomplish the necessary tasks, and see that crew members get paid. Beyond this simple arrangement, however, a number of relations between farm labor contractors and crew members usually develop that might appear to be tangential to the business of accomplishing agricultural tasks (Vandeman 1988). Usually it is in these tangential realms that criminally abusive behaviors occur: excessive authoritarianism, exploitation, credit- or debt-peonage schemes, betrayals and abandonments, and cross-country treks at costs more exorbitant than first-class air travel. All of these have become part of farmworker lore about farm labor contractors.

Two of the more important features of the exercise of such power are that it is highly varied and it is unevenly distributed within and between worker populations. Its variation derives from the ability of farm labor contractors to anchor their power in relations based on family and network ties, ethnicity, gender, and race, and features of workers that are sociologically important at the time of the exercise of power (e.g., legal status, skills, education, age). This is, of course, in addition to the power that derives from the farm labor contractor's position as "boss." Because many of the realms in which farm labor contractor power becomes so effective are tangential to the labor market (although part of the labor process) farm labor contractors are not restricted by the terms of the job or the social definitions of work in the exercise of their power.

In addition to the example of the line, presented in Chapter 9, another typical case of excessive abuse illustrates how farm labor contractor power depends on factors internal and external to the labor market. Court cases involving farm labor contractors are crowded with judgments against them for withholding social security, workers' compensation, and other "safety-net" taxes from workers' pay envelopes yet failing to pay into these funds on behalf of the workers (e.g., *Louise Jackson et al v. Otis Clayton* 1989). For workers with incomes below federally established poverty guidelines, the practice of "withholding withholding" deprives them of portions of their safety nets reducing or closing off access to resources for staying alive and healthy during less productive or unproductive periods. Lack of access to social security, workers' compensation, and other webs of the safety net encourages low-wage workers to establish and maintain relations of interdependence between their own and others' centers of domestic production and reproduction (households, networks, ethnic groups, etc.). Through this process, too, the practice of withholding withholding itself comes to depend on relations, beliefs, and customs that allow workers to participate in low-wage jobs without assurances that they will be supported during times of crisis, injury, old age, and so forth. These relations, beliefs, and customs then become components of the practice of withholding withholding, or, in other words, an accomplice to the crime. In many situations, this helps disguise the crime itself by embedding it in a set of gender, network, or ethnic relations. For example, women with young children often may enter the workforce only if they have someone—usually a mother or grandmother—to care for their child. She enters the workforce towing the older woman's labor behind her. Her participation in the labor force depends on the gender relations and expectations inherent in the arrangement, embedded in it, disguised by it. The connection is strengthened, more deeply tangled, by the worker's contribution to the maintenance of her child and the person caring for her child. Discussing California cannery workers of the 1930s, Vicki Ruiz (1987:1b) notes, "For widows or divorced women, a reciprocal economic relationship developed between mothers and daughters. They took care of each other and maintained their own household without the assistance of men."

The examples documented in our case studies demonstrate the varied forms the exercise of farm labor contractor power takes and how it may become hidden or disguised in other relations. They also illustrate submission and acquiescence as components of power. As important as the varied character of power is its uneven distribution within and between populations of agricultural, food processing, and other low-income workers. While the varied and sociologically grounded nature of power gives it a hidden or disguised character as well as increases the opportunity for its occurrence, its uneven distribution encourages linkages among the power to abuse, the maintenance and reproduction of structural characteristics of the labor market, and the labor process itself. A brief discussion of the structure of the agricultural labor market will help clarify this point.

Throughout this century, observers of agricultural labor have noted different segments within the farm labor force. Different positions in the labor force entail differential access to such things as high wages, preferred tasks, suitable housing, and the power to bargain for improved circumstances or to resist the abusive treatment of growers, foremen, and farm labor contractors. Literature on agricultural labor noted differences between workers based on their long-term aspirations and attachment to the production enterprise. Those usually referred to as "hired hands" considered farmwork an apprenticeship, unlike seasonal and casual farmworkers, who had no such hopes, chances, or aspirations. We noted in the opening chapter that the Country Life Commission (1909:41–42) described a transition from hired hand to tenant to landowner among a segment of the labor force in one of the first national studies of agriculture. The distinction between hired hands and other, usually seasonal, workers remains an accurate characterization today. Beyond this distinction, a variety of other factors divide the labor force into more and less vulnerable, more and less powerful, groups of workers.

Writing in 1945, Schwartz recognized three groups of seasonal workers in addition to those more regularly employed as hired hands: workers supplementing nonfarm incomes with occasional farmwork; family members of farmers and farmers who occasionally work for neighboring farmers as wage workers, and migrants who move from crop to crop through the year (1945:10–11). He points out that this last group is differentiated by whether or not they work for farm labor contractors, by ethnicity, by family and immigration status, and so forth. Mines (1974) discusses segments within the California farm labor force based on their propensity to join labor unions (see also Meister and Loftis 1977). He identified at least ten groups ranging from year-round hired hands that were loyal to their employers to the "fruit tramps" who had worked in agriculture since coming from Arkansas and Oklahoma as dust bowl refugees during the 1930s. Mines's study, focusing on the AFL–CIO drive in agriculture during the late 1950s and early 1960s, differentiated between groups based on two factors: their attachment to agricultural labor and their loyalty to their employers. Similar groupings of farmworkers emerge from a variety of works on agriculture and farm labor throughout this century (Reuss, Landis, and Wakefield 1938; Holley, Winston, and Woofter 1940;

Commission on Migratory Labor 1951; Metzler 1955; Currant and Martinez Infante 1959; Fite 1984). We discovered similar segments within the farm labor force in our study communities. For example, we noted that growers in Maryland hire, directly, families or groups of workers year after year for jobs of two to three months' duration yet would subcontract with farm labor contractors for additional, short-term, harvest labor jobs that would last a few days or weeks. From our interviews in New Jersey and the Delmarva Peninsula, as well as interviews with growers in Virginia and North Carolina apple harvests, we discovered that the internal segmentation of the farm labor force has been facilitated also by stricter transportation guidelines. With mandated vehicle and liability insurance requirements placed on farm labor contractors, increasing the cost and risk involved with transporting large crews, crew sizes have diminished in the northern harvests and more "in-stream" recruiting has been occurring. Each phase of recruitment creates the potential for new and different segments within an entire crew.

Conclusion

Since the mid-1970s, structural changes in agriculture, food processing, and other parts of the U.S. food system have increasingly reinforced three components of the labor process: the development of internal segments or labor markets, the use of subcontracting, and reliance on labor intermediaries (Reimund, Martin, and Moore 1981; U.S. Department of Commerce 1987; Heffernan and Constance 1992; Griffith 1993a, 1993b). Each of these developments has created opportunities for the emergence of new forms of power and has further complicated those forms that already exist. These structural developments lay the groundwork for enlisting culture in the exercise of power. In the current social climate, this occurs in part because of opportunities created by immigration since 1975. U.S. food producers have taken advantage of refugee flows from Southeast Asia, from Haiti, from Central America, and from Cuba. They have also been able to take advantage of immigrant flows from Mexico, other parts of Latin America, and the Caribbean to an extent that has been unprecedented since the 1920s (Greenwood and McDowell 1990). Taking advantage of the need for cultural and linguistic brokerage services, labor intermediaries have been able to enter into subcontractual arrangements that effectively insulate components of the production process from one another, insulating the groups of people involved in those processes from one another at the same time. By these means, cultural "sanctuaries" are established, where customary forms of hierarchy and authority based on gender, age, family ties, and so forth provide the raw material for labor intermediaries to exercise their power. How effective resistance becomes in these contexts depends on the abilities of labor intermediaries to access other segments of the working poor or harness other forms of power. As long as the labor market remain saturated, as long as immigration reform fails to have the effect of controlling the influx of new immigrants, labor intermediaries will enjoy the upper hand in this balance of resistance and power.

Appendix

Methods, Sampling, and the Rationale for the Community Study Approach

The core of this work consists of seven studies of agricultural production regions in the United States. These studies were originally conducted on behalf of the U.S. Department of Labor, which was interested in the effect of the Immigration Reform and Control Act of 1986 (IRCA) on farm labor supplies. Understanding the effects of IRCA, however, involved understanding the dynamics of farm labor processes, especially the factors influencing the supply and recruitment of farm labor.

The Case Studies in Relation to the Overall Farm Labor Market

To capture the diversity of U.S. fruit, vegetable, and horticultural production and to examine differences in labor market dynamics among the major migrant streams, we included case studies of farmworker communities in four traditional farm labor supply regions and in three labor demand regions of the north (summer harvest regions) that correspond with each of the labor supply communities (Table A.1).

The labor supply communities chosen represent paradigm cases of farm labor supply areas, although each community has a unique and complex history with regard to farm labor. Similarly, the labor demand areas are representative of several types of labor-intensive agriculture. The mainland U.S. com-

TABLE A.1 Case Study Labor Supply Communities and Corresponding Crops/Regions

Labor Supply Region Study Community Area County Community	*Labor Demand Area* State Region	*Labor-Intensive Crops Studied*
Eastern Region 1		
South Florida	Delaware, Maryland, Virginia	Irish potatoes, staked
Collier County	Delmarva Peninsula	tomatoes, melons, apples,
Immokalee		vegetables, citrus
Middle/Midwestern Regions		
South Texas	Michigan	Strawberries, cucumbers,
Lower Rio Grande Valley	Berrien, Van Buren, Cass	apples, peaches, tomatoes,
Weslaco	Counties	blueberries
Eastern Region 2		
Western Puerto Rico	New Jersey	Container and field nurseries
Mayagüez	Monmouth, Cumberland,	(ornamental)
El Mani, Sabalos	Burlington Counties	
Western Region		
Central California	Central California	Peaches, nectarines, plums,
East San Joaquin Valley	Fresno, Tulare Counties	table grapes, raisin grapes
Parlier		

munities are all partially linked by migrant networks and provide good insight into the means by which similar dynamics operating under distinct local conditions can give rise to a variety of labor market behaviors.

This research design derived from the recognition that the U.S. farm labor market is not a monolithic one but rather a mosaic consisting of various regional and local market segments. Patterns of labor demand are determined by specific crop production activities in specific geographic areas. The community study approach allowed us to develop in-depth profiles of the labor pool of current and potential farmworkers in the labor supply communities and to explore the differences and similarities in the responses of workers of these communities to farm labor demand in "linked" labor markets.

The U.S. farm labor force is not only diverse. Even its most basic characteristics, such as size and composition, are not well known. There are serious deficiencies in standard data sources relating to the distribution of migrant and seasonal farmworkers, their demographic characteristics, labor market behavior, and earnings. Some of these difficulties stem from the fact that aggregate data obscure many of the most significant features of a population that is highly mobile and heterogeneous. Other difficulties stem from the "snap-shot" a particular survey or administrative data source captures. For example, the inaccuracy of the U.S. Census's April 1 count of farmworkers has been widely discussed, yet no satisfactory alternative has been developed. This made it necessary for us to select case study communities purposively, choos-ing those known to be traditional labor supply areas. We sought communities sensitive to changing farm labor supply and demand conditions. Choosing communities with a strong tradition of farmwork served to ensure that respon-dents were familiar with farmwork and as likely as possible to have some connection to existing farm labor recruitment networks.

Labor supply and labor demand areas are nodes in migration and labor recruitment networks, not separate ends of discrete pathways. This is because farm labor recruitment rests so heavily on the dynamics of natural networks of social interaction. Southwestern Michigan is an important destination for southern Texas farmworkers, but so is Washington State; conversely the south-western Michigan labor market relies heavily on southern Texas for its labor supply, but southern Florida is also an important source. Thus, the labor de-mand areas chosen for this study do not correspond perfectly to the labor supply communities. Their partial correspondence do, however, represent some of the strongest flows of farm labor migration in the United States.

Representativeness of the Study

The inadequacies of available data sources for estimating the character of the farmworker population in the United States make deriving reliable estimates of the farmworker population distribution for sampling purposes impossible. The labor force dynamics we observed reflect the general characteristics of the major regions of the U.S. farm labor market. The demographic characteris-tics of the farmworker population we surveyed are similar to the population surveyed by the *National Agricultural Worker Survey* (Mines, Gabbard, and Samardick 1991); however, our study includes more recently arrived unac-companied-male workers than this survey does.

Our survey of current and potential farmworkers represents the potential and current farmworker labor pool in rural labor supply areas of major home-base regions of the United States (i.e., areas where farmworkers spend the winter). It less accurately reflects the composition, dynamics, and labor mar-ket behavior of current and potential farmworkers residing in urban areas (e.g., Philadelphia, Los Angeles, Chicago) and in isolated communities in summer harvest states. Our ethnographic work confirms earlier research indicating that urban, immigrant receiving areas include many urban workers who occasionally participate in the farm labor force.

Using three alternative sets of administrative data that provide some indication of the distribution of the U.S. farm labor force (Table A.2), the Florida, Texas, and California labor supply case study areas can be compared with the overall U.S. farm labor market. These data sets are the 1987 Census of Agriculture, Bureau of the Census tabulations of Employment Security Administration form 92 (ESA-92) reports by agricultural employers regarding numbers of days worked by SAWs by quarter, and Immigration and Naturalization Service (INS) tabulations of SAW (I-700) applications. These data indicate that the case study labor supply areas we studied include, at a minimum, 5 to 20 percent of the U.S. farm labor population.

None of these data sets provides an unequivocal representation of the numbers or distribution of farmworkers in the United States by residence. The Census of Agriculture data represent only the distribution of hired farm labor by work site. Consequently, these data do not definitively profile the subset of seasonal agricultural service workers, nor do they accurately represent farmworker residence patterns. For example, although the Census of Agriculture data on the lower Rio Grande Valley show significant employment of hired and contracted farmworkers (because of winter work in vegetables and citrus), they do not reflect the importance of the region as a home-base area for the large numbers of migrants whose only farmwork is outside of Texas.

TABLE A.2 Farm Labor Supply Study Areas and the National Farm Labor Market

	Wages 1987 Census of Agriculture[a]	Person-Days 1989 ESA-92 Tabulations[b]	SAW Applications May 1990 I-700 Tabulations[c]
Southern Florida	$11.8 million (0.9%)	488.3 (6.8%)	9,335 (0.7%)
Southern Texas	$72.0 million (0.6%)	52.1 (0.7%)	14,562 (1.1%)
Central California	$408.4 million (3.2%)	3,601.0 (50.0%)	61,872 (4.8%)
U.S. Total	$12,709.0 million	7,197.0	1.3 million

Note: Percentages are those of the total for the United States.

[a]1987 expenditures, hired and contract labor.

[b]ESA-92 tabulations include only reported SAW workdays. Data here are for "peak quarter" of year for each defined region: third quarter (July–September) for California, and fourth quarter (October–December) for Florida and Texas.

[c]I-700 tabulations include both approved and pending I-700s.

The ESA-92 data provide information on where SAWs are working and might be a good indicator of the distribution of the overall U.S. farm labor force, because migration networks tend to cluster new arrivals in areas already populated by earlier immigrants. However, the proportion of SAWs in the farm labor force varies from region to region (e.g., southern Texas has very few SAWs, while California and Florida have many). Also, because the data are sorted according to the two-digit zip code level, the zip code regions corresponding to our study areas are larger than the actual study areas.

The I-700 data provide an excellent picture of the distribution of SAW applicants at the time they submitted their legalization application to the INS; however, it is not known what proportion of applications were submitted by SAWs while they were living in a home-base community versus those submitted by SAWs while they were migrating. Also there are probably variations in the proportion of bona fide and fraudulent I-700 applications.

Each labor demand crop/region we studied represents an important segment of the U.S. national market. All have relied extensively on migrant labor for at least the past twenty years. The three-county area of southwestern Michigan is the second largest producing area for pickling cucumbers in the United States, with an estimated value over $20 million. The area is also among the top ten apple-producing regions in the country and the top twenty-five regions in strawberry and in tomato production. New Jersey's nursery production is the seventh highest in the nation. Crop production in the Delaware–Maryland–Virginia area is so diversified that no single crop predominates.

The labor supply case study areas are all in regions that, themselves, generate high local demand for farm labor as well as employment in agricultural-support industries such as fruit and vegetable packing and processing. The crops of the Parlier case study labor demand area, primarily nectarines, peaches, table grapes, and wine grapes, have a value of $810 million, and Fresno County has the largest hired farm labor payroll in the country. As can be seen from the hired and contract labor data, hired farm labor demand in the local regions surrounding the study towns of Immokalee in southern Florida and Weslaco in southern Texas is also substantial. Collier County, where Immokalee is located, ranked fourth in the nation in tomato production, twenty-second in the nation in orange production, and twenty-fourth in grapefruit. Hidalgo County, where Weslaco is located, ranked second in the nation's cucumber production, close behind the southwestern Michigan area; twenty-fourth in oranges; seventh in grapefruit production (which was, however, wiped out in the 1989 freeze); and second in watermelon production. While the summer harvest labor supply areas have relatively sharp peaks of labor demand, two of the supply study areas, central California and southern Florida, have relatively strong year-round labor demand, and the third, Weslaco, has a winter labor demand peak.

The case studies provide interesting bases for comparative analysis, since we focused on two dynamic farm labor supply communities (Parlier and Immokalee) and two (Weslaco and Mayagüez) that are declining in importance as suppliers of farm labor to other communities and regions in the United States. While Parlier and Immokalee continue to draw new immigrants from new and old sending areas in Mexico, Central America, and the Caribbean, Weslaco and Mayagüez have witnessed the development of low-wage manufacturing industries in the wake of a declining agricultural sector. The compositions of summer migrant labor crews in the Midwest, the Pacific Northwest, and parts of the eastern and northeastern United States reflect these changes, with new groups of single-male migrants displacing both family workers from Texas and single-male Puerto Ricans. New refugee and immigrant workers from Central America, Haiti, and Mexico have been critical in these changes, stimulating new processes of network recruitment and network formation. On the East Coast, for example, the familiarity of growers with Latino workers has caused radical declines in the proportions of African Americans and Puerto Ricans in the migrant streams. In Michigan, some Anglo workers from Appalachia and African American workers from nearby cities work in the blueberry harvests, yet because of the Latin flavor of the work environment in other crops they have not been successful in competing with Mexican workers.

The Labor Supply Community Survey

The methodology adopted in studying the labor supply communities derives from ethnosurvey techniques, which have been used successfully in important migration studies (e.g., Massey et al. 1987). The approach was designed to achieve maximum insight into the dynamics of various personal, social, and economic interactions underlying farm labor market behavior. This approach, at the same time, provides a quantitative framework to describe those patterns.

Labor supply communities were mapped block by block, and a two-stage random sample of dwellings was drawn from low-income neighborhoods. Restricting sampling to low-income neighborhoods (based on key informants' perceptions and drive-by observations of each block) served to exclude most, but not all, high-income households, whose residents were extremely unlikely to be part of the farm labor force. Within the low-income neighborhoods, dwellings were selected using a stratified random-sampling approach. Thus, the community survey respondents are representative of the current and potential farm labor force in the labor supply communities. This approach provided a means of analyzing the labor market behavior of the entire potential labor force in each community, not simply a subgroup of workers. Thus, the survey provides the cross-sectional framework necessary for analyzing the perspectives of both current and potential farmworkers.

Surveys were conducted in the home-base communities from February through May 1990, the time when the largest number of migrants were living in the towns. Eligible respondents included all persons fourteen years and over in the household, with the exception of disabled or elderly adults. The labor supply community surveys provided the basis for our discussion of the labor force and community characteristics of Parlier, Weslaco, Immokalee, and Mayagüez reported here. Slightly less than one thousand residents of labor supply communities were interviewed in the course of the study—heads of households, their spouses, and teenaged children, as well as single young adults living on their own. Unless otherwise specified, data presented in this volume refer to respondents who are heads of household.

Ethnographic Observations

Survey data were supplemented with ethnographic observations focused on generating more in-depth data and understanding of key issues such as the development of migration networks, worker strategies for combining farmwork and nonfarmwork, worker and management strategies used by employers and labor contractors, and the occupational outlooks of different groups of workers. Project staff in each labor supply community included interviewers with close ties to the farmworker community who were able to provide additional background on community history, mores, and interactions among different groups. In Parlier, Immokalee, and Mayagüez, staff ethnographers resided in the study community areas throughout the course of the project.

The ethnographic work also included extensive informal discussions, observations, and dialogue with local residents, human-service providers, farmworkers, crew leaders, labor contractors, agricultural employers, community leaders, recent immigrants, housewives, small-business proprietors, and experts representing a broad range of perspectives.

The research approach in summer harvest labor demand areas (California, Delaware, Michigan, New Jersey, Oregon, and Virginia) involved informal but carefully structured discussions with different groups of migrant workers, labor contractors, agricultural employers, service providers, and experts such as extension personnel. Because the emphasis of this facet of the project was on labor demand, priority was given to employer and labor market intermediary interviews. Senior project staff conducted interviews during the summers of 1989 and 1990 in California, Delaware, Maryland, Michigan, New Jersey, Oregon, and Virginia. Additional interviews in the winter harvest labor demand areas of California, Florida, and Texas took place during the winter of 1989–90.

Notes

CHAPTER 2: Waves of Ethnicity

1. The most recent estimates available during the field research period stated that the farmworker population fluctuated from a high of 19,161 in December to a low of 4,567 in July (Florida. Collier County 1988). Farmworkers are notoriously difficult to count, however; these estimates are surely low and probably do not include those who work extremely sporadically in the fields and live in the shadows. In particular, of course, new-immigrant workers tend to be underrepresented in these estimates.

2. The agricultural development that has taken place, moreover, is expected to increase agricultural tax revenues. For example, Hendry County's tax base will rise from the current $61,383 per year to $3,683,578 per year, or an increase of sixty times. While substantial portions of this increase should be used for farmworker housing, historically, most tax revenues in these counties have been used to improve those parts of the infrastructure that make farming more efficient, namely, roadways and irrigation systems.

3. Mean annual earnings for the survey population were $10,531, with a large standard deviation of $8,898, and mean weekly earnings were $230. These are well under federally established poverty guidelines.

4. Colonization of public housing has been well documented by Luin Goldring (1990), who demonstrates a close relationship between labor market behavior and access to low-cost state housing in Watsonville, California, among immigrants from a village in Mexico. In that case, "outsiders" (people not from the Mexican village) are forced from the subsidized units through daily harassment such as stealing their laundry.

5. Under the 1986 Immigration Reform and Control Act (IRCA), individuals who could prove that they had performed at least ninety days of farmwork over the previous three years were classified, by the Immigration and Naturalization Service, as seasonal agricultural workers (SAWs) and allowed to continue working in the United States legally. The SAW provisions of IRCA became one of the primary arenas for immigration fraud; because the forms were shorter and the proof needed was less burdensome, they were heavily utilized by individuals who had never performed farmwork.

6. We use nationality here as a gloss for ethnicity. This results in some inaccuracy, because within the "ethnic" category of Guatemalan, for example, are Kanjobal, Chuj, Quiché, Aguacatec, and a variety of other groups that only in the United States would consider themselves Guatemalan or even Mayan. Nevertheless, these groupings reflect the ways in which different groups in the farm labor market are perceived by employers and farm labor contractors and the differential treatment they receive.

7. Longtime Immokalee residents earned an average of $17,424 per year, and U.S. citizens from Texas (mostly Mexican Americans) earned an average of $16,764 per year. This compared with pre-1975 immigrant earnings of $8,445, new immigrants from traditional sending areas earnings of $5,838, and new immigrants from new sending regions of $7,562. While the new immigrants from new sending regions appear to make more than the new immigrants from traditional sending regions, the range of earnings for the former is far less than that for the latter. We found that Guatemalans, the newest of immigrants from the newest of sending regions, were the most poorly paid (see Griffith and Camposeco 1993).

8. The expansion of legal-alien labor programs has not been confined to the farm labor market but to other low-wage labor markets as well. Recently, "H-2" visas, the visa issued to people admitted into the United States to work on a temporary basis, have been issued to people working such jobs and locations as hotels and restaurants in Michigan, crab pickers and other seafood-processing workers in Maryland and North Carolina, shrimp boat deckhands in Texas, stable workers in California, and quarry workers in Idaho. At the same time, more agricultural producers, such as tobacco and pickle cucumber growers in North Carolina, have been given access to temporary alien workers from Mexico.

9. Workers coming from El Salvador, Guatemala, and other countries ruled by repressive regimes know the necessity of carrying "papers" in the form of *cedulas* (birth certificates), made famous in Oliver Stone's movie *Salvador*. As in Nazi Germany, these population-monitoring instruments are methods of controlling people's work, political activity, and so forth.

10. According to employment service personnel, the crushing blow to the role of the employment service in farm labor came during the 1970s, when the farm labor offices were found to be discriminatory and forced to consolidate their placement services with main offices. At more or less the same time, pieces of legislation, such as the Migrant and Seasonal Agricultural Worker Protection Act, ushered in a period of heightened public awareness of the plight of domestic farmworkers and stricter guidelines regarding transportation, housing, record keeping, and controls regarding new leadership. In particular, growers who used the employment service came under increased scrutiny regarding the terms of occupancy and conditions of their housing, and farm labor contractors who transported workers were forced to insure themselves, their vehicles, and their workers more heavily. Although the system of labor recruitment and crew organization had already been heavily privatized in the decades before the 1970s, the laws passed during this period gave farm labor contractors and growers

even less cause to utilize the employment service. This also contributed to the criminalization of many practices associated with crew assembly, transport, and supervision (e.g., withholding wages).

11. Throughout this work, the names of informants are pseudonyms, to protect their privacy.

CHAPTER 3: Migrant Workers on the Delmarva Peninsula

1. Each of these entrepreneurial niches is variable in terms of the extent to which it benefits workers. Some of them have been encouraged by growers as a way of passing responsibilities (for checking documents, maintaining field sanitation, providing housing, keeping tax records) from their own shoulders to those of workers. We discuss this in some detail in the concluding chapter.

2. We do not mean to suggest that the workforce, even though primarily African American, remained stable throughout this period. Changes occurred, principally in the social-structural components of the workforce. O. F. Larson and E. F. Sharp's (1960) study in New York (a terminal point for many migrants based in southern locations) compared the changes that took place in migrant crews from Florida from 1953 to 1957, finding that the proportions of single, "unattached," males had increased relative to family migrants and that Florida's and Georgia's roles as the primary sending states had been supplemented by Alabama and the Carolinas. It may have been during this period that the current pattern of in-stream recruiting became common.

3. Howard Rosenberg (1993) has documented the process of "packaging" the Mexican worker for locals in Kentucky, where growers' associations have actively propagated the view of Mexicans as industrious, family-oriented workers rather than knife-wielding criminals.

4. The relationship between the availability of labor and farmers' cropping strategies is a complex one that has not received adequate attention from either rural sociologists or agricultural economists. Max Pfeffer's (1992) work on chemical use and labor availability is a notable exception to this. We confess that in this book we give this subject less attention than it deserves, despite our brief discussion in the concluding chapter. Here we mention, however, that while the replacement of labor-intensive crops with low-labor grain crops has occurred on the peninsula, this is not a one-way process; in some cases, the reverse has occurred, as cheap or easily controlled labor has become readily available (Schwartz 1945).

CHAPTER 4: Domestic Farmworkers in America's Heartland

1. This balancing act of spreading oneself thin over many social resources, thereby creating ties of interdependence, is well documented in the anthropological literature

on Mesoamerican and Caribbean peasant communities that supply workers to U.S. agriculture.

CHAPTER 5: Labor Demand in Southwestern Michigan

1. The "explosive" element derives in part from the "bonds" created by the fictive-kin relationship. In some cases, these have led to violence, as seen in the Haitian case presented in Chapter 2.

2. Again, this process of displacement/replacement of Anglo workers by Mexicans is not clear cut but varies from case to case, despite attempts by many scholars to explain it at an abstract theoretical level (see Borjas and Tienda 1987; Papademetriou et al. 1989; Bach and Brill 1991; Waldinger and Bailey 1992).

3. Asparagus is often bracketed with strawberries as "the other" early crop. Peak demand for labor is in May and June, but asparagus does not provide a great deal of work in the southwestern Michigan area. Cucumbers provide some hourly nonharvest labor (hoeing) during the early part of the season, and the cherry harvest, although mostly mechanized, also provides some work in June. Another minor early-season crop is raspberries.

4. Michigan State University production cost estimates (which exclude the costs of family labor and capital costs such as depreciation, insurance, interest, and taxes) indicate that hired harvest labor costs make up about 35 percent of strawberry production costs. Nonharvest operating costs appear to make up another 35 percent of production, leaving an operating margin of 30 to 35 percent. While individual production costs vary substantially, farmers do not perceive strawberries as being a very profitable crop. Further wage increases will likely be among the slowest in agriculture.

5. These kinds of organized migrations are common among firms that produce under contract with growers in a number of regions (see Chapter 3).

6. We do not know to what degree the actual variation in piece rate for different varieties captures the presumed variation in difficulty/speed of harvesting the different crops, but we believe the piece rates are likely to have represented quite reasonable adjustments.

7. This emerged as a major complaint of farm labor contractors interviewed in Florida during 1982 (Griffith and Camposeco 1993).

8. Services include primary health care (the MARCHA network of clinics), child care and health services for preschoolers (Headstart and in-camp), migrant education for elementary-school-aged children (various school districts), night school for working teenagers (Eau Claire school district), legal assistance (Michigan Migrant Legal Action Project), advocacy (Bishop's Committee for Migrants), legalization assistance (individual community volunteers), Aid to Families with Dependent Children and food stamps (county social-service departments), and farmwork job referrals (Michigan Employment Security Commission).

CHAPTER 6: Offshore Citizens as a Supply of Farm Labor

1. This project was funded by the National Science Foundation (BNS 8718670) and involved examining the wage-labor behavior, including farmwork, among small-scale fishermen in Puerto Rico. We include material from that study here because a high proportion of the informants from that study had spent time in the eastern United States as farmworkers.

CHAPTER 7: A Labor Force in Transition

1. This goes against recent statistics on farm concentration throughout the United States. While acreages have increased and numbers of farms have dwindled over the past fifty years, the U.S. Department of Agriculture noted a leveling of this trend *during the 1980s* (see Brooks, Kalbacher, and Reimund 1990).

2. The northern region includes Bergen, Essex, Hudson, Hunterdon, Morris, Passaic, Somerset, Sussex, Union, and Warren counties; the central region includes Burlington, Mercer, Middlesex, Monmouth, and Ocean counties; and the southern region includes Atlantic, Camden, Cape May, Cumberland, Gloucester, and Salem counties.

3. Puerto Ricans do not necessarily come from Mayagüez, but from communities and neighborhoods similar to the *caserios* and *parcelas* discussed in the previous chapter (see Pfeffer 1992).

CHAPTER 8: Northward out of Mexico

1. It is not uncommon to see teenaged youths speaking English to Spanish-speaking adults, the adults answering in Spanish yet obviously, understanding the English and the children continuing, stubbornly, to respond in English.

2. The bearing acreage of raisin grapes increased from 202,481 acres in 1976 to 243,341 acres in 1985, then declined to 234,427 acres by 1989. The bearing acreage of table grapes increased from 28,707 acres in 1976 to 34,517 acres in 1985, then declined to 31,208 acres by 1989. The bearing acreage of wine grapes increased from 71,207 acres in 1976 to 88,214 acres in 1985, then declined to 81,537 acres by 1989. The total grape acreage thus increased by 63,677 acres, or 21 percent, in the three counties 1976–85, but 18,900 acres were removed 1986–89, leaving the 1989 acreage about 15 percent above the 1976 figure. Breaking that down, over the whole period, table-grape acreage increased 9 percent, wine-grape acreage increased 14.5 percent, and raisin-grape acreage increased 16 percent.

3. These conclusions, moreover, do not include "wet time" (rain delays) and other time spent waiting for work or riding to and from work. If these were included, the hourly wage rates of most farmworkers would fall below the minimum.

CHAPTER 9: Characteristics of the Farm Labor Market

1. We are not alone in these observations. During the research, analysis, and writing of this project, two major parallel research efforts were under way, both of which we have referred to many times in this volume. Most important were the case studies and hearings sponsored by the Commission on Agricultural Workers around the country (1993a, 1993b, 1993c), and in particular the work of Monica Heppel and Luis Torres on the commission's final report. A second important study was the *National Agricultural Worker Survey* conducted by Mines, Gabbard, and Samardick (1991).

2. Indeed, the status of Puerto Ricans as citizens has encouraged the development of a labor union called El Comite de Apoyo a los Trabajadores Agricoles (CATA—the Committee to Aid Agricultural Workers).

3. This contradicts, to some extent, the current emphasis on network building. While Weslaco's farmworkers built complex networks during and immediately after the Bracero era, these networks did not achieve the kind of momentum described in often-cited works on migration (e.g., Portes and Bach 1985; Massey et al. 1987).

References

Abu-Lughod, Lila. 1990. ''The Romance of Resistance: Tracing Transformations of Power Through Bedouin Women.'' *American Ethnologist* 17(1):41–55.

Adams, Robert. 1979. *Crucifixion by Power*. Austin: University of Texas Press.

Alarcón, Rafael. 1988. ''Los Migrantes de la Crisis: The Changing Profile of Mexican Labor to California in the 1980s.'' Typescript.

Amendola, Sandra, David Griffith, and L. Gunter. 1993. ''Labor in the South Carolina and Georgia Peach Industries.'' In *Appendix I: Case Studies and Research Reports, 1989–1993,* Commission on Agricultural Workers, Washington, D.C.: U.S. Government Printing Office.

Association of Farmworker Opportunity Programs (AFOP). 1988. ''Partnerships: Helping Migrant Farmworkers Help Themselves.'' AFOP Report, Washington, D.C.

Bach, Robert, and Howard Brill. 1991. ''The Impact of IRCA on the U.S. Labor Market and Economy.'' Final Report to the U.S. Department of Labor, Washington, D.C.

Bach, Robert, Howard Brill, Tom Bailey, Norma Chinchilla, David Griffith, Jaqueline Hagan, Nora Hamilton, James Louky, Terry Repak, Nestor Rodriguez, Cheryl Schechter, and Roger Waldinger. 1990. ''The Impact of IRCA on the U.S. Labor Market and Economy.'' Report prepared for the Institute for Research on Multiculturalism and International Labor, State University of New York, Binghamton.

Bailey, Thomas. 1987. *Immigrant and Native Workers: Contrast and Competition.* Boulder, Colo.: Westview Press.

Barry, D. Marshall. 1990. ''The Adverse Impact of Immigration on Florida's Farmworkers.'' Occasional Paper no. 3, Center for Labor Research and Studies, Florida International University, Miami.

Bartlett, Peggy. 1987. ''The Crisis in Family Farming: Who Will Survive?'' In *Farmwork and Fieldwork: American Agriculture in Anthropological Perspective,* edited by Michael Chibnik. Ithaca, N.Y.: Cornell University Press.

Beechert, Edward. 1985. *Working in Hawaii: A Labor History.* Honolulu: University of Hawaii Press.

311

Benson, Janet. 1990. "Households, Migration, and Community Context." *Urban Anthropology* 19(1–2):9–30.

Bernstein, Bruce. 1986. "Migration, Health, and Nutrition: Haitian Farmworkers in Immokalee, a South Florida Farmworker Town." Ph D diss., Department of Anthropology, University of Connecticut.

Bluestone, Barry, and Bennet Harrison. 1982. *The Deindustrialization of America.* New York: Basic Books.

Bonilla, Frank, and Ricardo Campos. 1981. "A Wealth of Poor: Puerto Ricans in the International Division of Labor." *Daedalus* 110:133–76.

Borjas, George. 1989. "Economic Theory and International Migration." *International Migration Review* 23(3):457–85.

Borjas, George, and Marta Tienda. 1987. *Hispanics in the United States.* New York: Academic Press.

Boyd, Monica. 1989. "Family and Personal Networks in International Migrations." *International Migration Review* 23(3):638–70.

Briody, Elizabeth. 1987. "Patterns of Household Immigration into South Texas." *International Migration Review* 21(1):27–47.

Broadway, Michael. 1992. "Recent Changes in the Structure and Location of the Meat- and Fish-Processing Industry." Paper presented at New Workers in Old Farming Communities, April, at Aspen Institute, Wye Conference Center, Queensland, Md.

Brooks, Steven, Don Kalbacher, and Donald Reimund. 1990. *Structural Change in Agriculture, 1980–89.* Washington, D.C.: U.S. Government Printing Office.

Buitrago Ortiz, Carlos. 1973. *Esperanza: An Ethnographic Study of a Peasant Community in Puerto Rico.* Tucson: University of Arizona Press.

Burawoy, Michael. 1976. "The Functions and Reproduction of Migrant Labor: Comparative Material from South Africa and the United States." *American Journal of Sociology* 81:105–87.

Burns, Allan. 1988. "Immigration, Ethnicity, and Work in Indiantown, Florida." Occasional Paper no. 8, Center for Latin American Studies, University of Florida.

———. 1993. *Maya in Exile: Guatemalans in Florida.* Philadelphia: Temple University Press.

California. Economic Development Department. 1988. *Fresno County Grape Harvest Wage Survey, 1988.* Sacramento: Operation Reports Group, Employment Data and Research.

———. 1990. *Seasonal Labor in California Agriculture: Labor Inputs for California Crops.* Sacramento: Operation Reports Group, Employment Data and Research.

Charns, Alex. 1983. "Slaves Are Free at Last, in North Carolina." *Washington Post,* August 13, sec. A.

Chavez, Leo. 1988. "Settlers or Sojourners? The Case of Mexicans in the United States." *Human Organization* 47(2):95–108.

———. 1990. "Coresidence and Resistance: Strategies for Survival Among Undocumented Mexicans and Central Americans in the United States.'' *Urban Anthropology* 19(1–2):31–62.

Cobb, James. 1982. *The Selling of the South: The Southern Crusade for Industrial Development, 1936–1980.* Baton Rouge: Louisiana State University Press.

———. 1984. *Industrialization and Southern Society.* Lexington: University Press of Kentucky.

Code of Federal Regulations (CFR). 1980. ''Services of the Employment Service System.'' 20 *CFR* chap. 5, 653, subpart B (''Services for Migrants and Seasonal Farmworkers'').

Collins, Jane. 1988. *Unseasonal Migrations: The Effects of Labor Scarcity in Rural Peru.* New Brunswick, N.J.: Rutgers University Press.

Commission on Agricultural Workers. 1993a. *Report of the Commission on Agricultural Workers.* Washington, D.C.: U.S. Government Printing Office.

———. 1993b. *Appendix I: Case Studies and Research Reports, 1989–1993.* Washington, D.C.: U.S. Government Printing Office.

———. 1993c. *Appendix II: Hearings and Workshops, 1989–1993.* Washington, D.C.: U.S. Government Printing Office.

Commission on Migratory Labor. 1951. *Migrant and Seasonal Farmworker Powerlessness.* Washington, D.C.: U.S. Government Printing Office.

Conway, Mimi. 1983. ''The Federal Government Is Aiding Slavery in America.'' *Washington Post,* September 18, sec. C.

Cornelius, Wayne. 1976. *Illegal Migration to the United States: Recent Research Findings, Policy Implications, and Research Priorities.* Boston: M.I.T. Migration and Development Study Group.

———. Forthcoming. *The Evolving Role of Mexicans in the U.S. Economy.* San Diego: Center for U.S.–Mexican Relations, University of California.

Cornelius, Wayne, Carmen Inez Cruz, Juanita Castano, and Elsa Chaney. 1982. *The Dynamics of Migration: International Migration.* San Diego, Calif.: Center for U.S.–Mexican Relations.

Country Life Commission. 1909. *The Report of the Country Life Commission.* Washington, D.C.: U.S. Government Printing Office.

Crewdson, John. 1980. ''Thousands of Aliens Held in Virtual Slavery in the U.S.'' *New York Times,* October 19, sec. A.

Currant, Thomas, and Mark Martinez Infante. 1959. ''Migrant Problems Demand Attention.'' Final Report to the State of Oregon Bureau of Labor, Salem.

Danbom, D. 1979. *The Resisted Revolution.* Ames: Iowa State University Press.

Daniel, Peter. 1972. *In the Shadow of Slavery: Debt Peonage in the South.* Urbana: University of Illinois Press.

Delaware. Department of Agriculture. 1989. *1988 Production Statistics for Delaware Fruit and Vegetable Farms.* Dover: Delaware Department of Agriculture.

Duaney, Jorge. 1992. ''Caribbean Migration to Puerto Rico: A Comparison of Cubans and Dominicans.'' *International Migration Review* 26(1):46–66.

Dubofsky, Melvyn. 1988. *We Shall Be All: A History of the Industrial Workers of the World,* 2d ed. Urbana: University of Illinois Press.

DuBois, W. E. B. 1898. *The Negroes of Farmville, Virginia: A Social Study.* Bulletin 14 of the U.S. Department of Labor. Washington, D.C.: U.S. Government Printing Office.

Fernández-Kelly, M. P. 1983. *For We Are Sold, I and My People.* Albany: State University of New York Press.

Fischer, Lloyd. 1953. *The Harvest Labor Market in California.* Cambridge, Mass.: Harvard University Press.

Fite, Gilbert. 1984. *Cotton Fields No More: Southern Agriculture, 1865–1980.* Lexington: University Press of Kentucky.

Florida. Collier County. 1988. ''Comprehensive Farm Worker Housing Plan.'' Immokalee Pocket of Poverty Project, Florida Department of Community Development and Collier County Government, Naples, October 1.

Florida Institute of Government. 1988. ''Immokalee: Pocket of Poverty.'' Report.

Florida Statistical Abstract. 1989. *1989 Statistical Abstract.* Gainesville: Economic and Business Research, University of Florida.

Foner, Nancy, and Richard Napoli. 1978. ''Jamaican and Black-American Migrant Farm Workers: A Comparative Analysis.'' *Social Problems* 25(4):491–502.

Foucault, Michel. 1980. *The History of Sexuality,* vol. 1. New York: Vintage Books.

Friedland, William, and Dorothy Nelkin. 1971. *Migrant: Agricultural Workers in America's Northeast.* New York: Holt, Rinehart and Winston.

Froebel, Folker, Jurgen Heinrichs, and Otto Kreye. 1977. *The New International Division of Labor.* Cambridge: Cambridge University Press.

Galarza, Ernesto. 1964. *Merchants of Labor: The Mexican Bracero Story.* Santa Barbara, Calif.: McNally and Loftin.

———. 1977. *Farm Workers and Agri-business in California, 1947–1960.* Notre Dame, Ind.: University of Notre Dame Press.

Garcia, Victor. 1993. ''Latinos in the Mushroom Industry: Chester County, Pennsylvania.'' Paper presented at the annual meeting of the American Anthropological Association, November, Washington, D.C.

García Passalacqua, J. M., and Jorge Heine. 1983. *The Puerto Rican Question.* New York: Foreign Policy Association, Headline Series, no. 266.

Gelderman, Carol. 1981. *Henry Ford: The Wayward Capitalist.* New York: Dial Press.

General Accounting Office. 1988. *Illegal Aliens: Influence of Illegal Workers on Wages and Working Conditions.* Washington, D.C.: U.S. Government Printing Office.

Gilbert, Elon, James Dean, Sandra Russo, David Griffith, and Art Hansen. 1981. *Production Practices for Squash and Watermelon on Alachua County, Florida, Farms.* Gainesville: Institute of Food and Agricultural Sciences, University of Florida.

Gladwin, Christina, and Carl Zulauf. 1989. ''The Case for the Disappearing Mid-Size Farm in the United States.'' In *Food and Farm: Current Debates and Policies,* edited by Christina Gladwin and Karl Truman. Lanham, Md.: University Press of America.

Glick-Schiller, Nina, Linda Basch, and Christina Blanc-Szanton, eds. 1991. *Towards a Transnational Perspective on Migration: Race, Class, Ethnicity, and Nationalism Reconsidered.* New York: New York Academy of Sciences.

Glick-Schiller, Nina, and George Fouron. 1990. '' 'Everywhere We Go, We Are in Danger': Ti Manno and the Emergence of a Haitian Transnational Identity.'' *American Ethnologist* 17(2):329–47.

Goldring, Luin. 1990. ''Development and Migration: A Comparative Analysis of Two Mexican Migrant Circuits.'' Working Paper no. 37, prepared for the Commission for the Study of International Migration and Cooperative Economic Development, Washington, D.C.

Gonzalez, Nancy. 1971. ''Toward a Definition of Matrifocality.'' In *Afro-American Anthropology,* edited by Norman Whitten and John Swezd. New York: Free Press.

Gordon, David, Richard Edwards, and Michael Reich. 1982. *Segmented Work, Divided Workers: The Historical Transformation of Labor in the United States.* Cambridge: Cambridge University Press.

Gouviea, Lourdes. 1992. ''Global Strategies and Local Linkages: The Case of the US Meatpacking Industry.'' Typescript. University of Kansas, Lawrence.

———. 1992. Personal communication.

Granovetter, Mark. 1977. *Finding a Job.* New York: Academic Press.

Grasmuck, Sherri, and Patricia Pessar. 1991. *Between Two Islands: Dominican International Migration.* Berkeley and Los Angeles: University of California Press.

Green, Hardy, 1990. *On Strike at Hormel: The Struggle for a Democratic Labor Movement.* Philadelphia: Temple University Press.

Greenwood, Michael, and John McDowell. 1990. *Labor Market Consequences of U.S. Immigration: A Survey.* Washington, D.C.: U.S. Department of Labor.

Grenier, Guillermo. 1990. ''Political Attitudes among Cubans in Miami: Immigrant Versus Exile Agendas.'' Paper presented at the annual meeting of the Caribbean Studies Association, May 24, Havana, Cuba.

Grey, Mark. 1992. ''Lao Porkpackers in Storm Lake, Iowa: Implications for Education and Health Provision.'' Paper presented at New Workers in Old Farming Communities, April, at Aspen Institute, Wye Conference Center, Queensland, Md.

Griffith, David. 1983. ''The Promise of a Country: The Impact of the BWI Temporary Alien Labor Program on the Jamaican Peasantry.'' Ph.D. diss., Department of Anthropology, University of Florida, Gainesville.

———. 1985. ''Women, Remittances, and Reproduction.'' *American Ethnologist* 12:676–90.

———. 1986a. ''Peasants in Reserve: Temporary West Indian Labor in the U.S. Farm Labor Market.'' *International Migration Review* 20(4):875–98.

———. 1986b. ''Social Organizational Obstacles to Capital Accumulation among Returning Migrants: The Case of the British West Indies Temporary Labor Program.'' *Human Organization* 45(1):34–45.

————. 1987. "Nonmarket Labor Processes in an Advanced Capitalist Economy." *American Anthropologist* 89(4):838–52.

————. 1988. "Enhanced Recruitment Demonstration Project: Virginia and North Carolina Apple Harvests." Technical report submitted to the Office of the Assistant Secretary of Policy, U.S. Department of Labor, Washington, D.C.

————. 1989a. "Consequences of Immigration Reform for Low-Wage Workers in the Southeastern U.S.: The Case of the Poultry Industry." *Urban Anthropology* 19(1):155–84.

————. 1989b. *The Impact of the Immigration Reform and Control Act's Employer Sanctions on the U.S. Meat and Poultry Processing Industries.* Final report. Binghamton, N.Y.: Institute for Multiculturalism and International Labor, State University of New York.

————. 1993a. *Jones's Minimal: Low-Wage Labor in the United States.* Albany: State University of New York Press.

————. 1993b. "Seasonal Agricultural Recruitment in the Eastern United States: An Overview with Special Attention to the Northeast." In *Appendix II: Hearings and Workshops,* Commission on Agricultural Workers, 1035–46. Washington, D.C.: U.S. Government Printing Office.

Griffith, David, and Jeronimo Camposeco. 1993. "The Winter Vegetable Industry in South Florida." In *Appendix I: Case Studies and Research Reports,* Commission on Agricultural Workers, 579–629. Washington, D.C.: U.S. Government Printing Office.

Griffith, David, Ed Kissam, David Runsten, Anna García, Jeronimo Camposeco, Manuel Valdés Pizzini, and Max Pfeffer. 1991. "Farm Labor Supply Study." Interim report produced for the U.S. Department of Labor, Washington, D.C.

Griffith, David, and David Runsten. 1988. "The Impact of the 1986 Immigration Control and Reform Act on the U.S. Poultry Industry." Technical report prepared for the U.S. Department of Labor, Bureau of International Labor Affairs, Washington, D.C.

Griffith, David, Manuel Valdés Pizzini, and Jeffrey Johnson. 1992. "Injury and Therapy: Proletarianization in Puerto Rico's Fisheries." *American Ethnologist* 19(1):53–74.

Hage, David, and Paul Klauda. 1988. *No Retreat, No Surrender: Labor's War at Hormel.* New York: Morrow.

Hamm, Shannon, Gary Lucier, Vic Oliveria, Glen Zepp, and Jim Duffield. 1993. "Trends in Labor Intensive Crop Supply, Use, and Mechanization." Paper prepared for the WRCC-76 Conference on Immigration Reform and U.S. Agriculture, March, Washington, D.C.

Hansen, Art, David Griffith, and John Butler. 1981. "Farming Systems of Alachua County, Florida." Institute for Food and Agricultural Sciences, University of Florida, Gainesville.

Heffernan, William, and Glen Constance. 1992. "Changing Locations and Structure of Meat and Poultry Processing in the United States.'' Paper presented at New Workers in Old Farming Communities, April, at Aspen Institute, Wye Conference Center, Queensland, Md.

Heppel, Monica. 1983. ''Harvesting the Crops of Others: Migrant Farm Labor on the Eastern Shore of Virginia.'' Ph.D. diss., Department of Anthropology, American University, Washington, D.C.

Heppel, Monica, and Sandra Amendola, eds. 1992. *Immigration Reform and Perishable Crop Agriculture: Compliance or Circumvention?* Lanham, Md.: University Press of America.

Heppel, Monica, and Luis Torres. 1993. ''The Transition from H-2A to Domestic Workers in the West Virginia Apple Harvest.'' Report prepared for the Employment Security Division, West Virginia Department of Labor, Charleston, W. Va.

Hewitt de Alcantara, Cynthia. 1976. *Modernizing Mexican Agriculture.* Geneva: UNRISD Press.

Holley, W. C., Ellen Winston, and T. J. Woofter, Jr. 1940. *The Plantation South, 1934–37.* WPA Research Monograph no. 22. Washington, D.C.: U.S. Government Printing Office.

Hudson, Bruce. 1979. ''The Florida Citrus Labor Market.'' Working Paper no. 35–79, Center for the Study of Human Resources, University of Texas, Austin.

Immokalee, City of. 1989. *Immokalee Population Analysis.* Immokalee, Fla.

Intercultural Development Research Association. 1986. *High School Drop-Outs, Weslaco, Texas, 1985–86.* Austin: IDRA Publications.

Jackson, Louise, Buck Jones, Elijah McClellan, and Andre Robinson v. Otis Clayton. 1989. Civil Action no. 89-115-Civ-Oc-16. Ocala, Fla.: U.S. District Court for the middle District of Florida.

Jamieson, Stuart. 1945. *Labor Unionism in Agriculture.* USDOL Bulletin no. 836. Washington, D.C.: U.S. Government Printing Office.

Jenkins, J. Craig. 1985. *The Politics of Insurgency: The Farm Worker Movement of the 1960s.* New York: Columbia University Press.

Jiobu, Robert. 1988. *Ethnicity and Assimilation.* Albany: State University of New York.

Kalbacher, Don, and Donald Reimund. 1990. *Changing Land Use in U.S. Agriculture.* Washington, D.C.: U.S. Government Printing Office.

Kearney, Michael, and Carole Nagengast. 1981. ''Anthropological Perspectives on Transnational Communities in Rural California.'' Working Paper on Farm Labor and Rural Poverty no. 3, California Institute for Rural Studies, Davis.

Kissam, Ed, and David Griffith. 1991. ''Need for Replenishment of Agricultural Labor in the United States.'' Interim report to the U.S. Department of Labor, Washington, D.C.

Koziara, Karen. 1977. ''Agricultural Labor Relations Laws in Four States. A Comparison.'' *Monthly Labor Review* 100(5):14–19.

''Labor Profile: Chesterfield Nursery.'' 1989. *American Nursery Magazine,* June, 36–43.

La Follette, Robert, Edward Thomas, and David Walsh. 1941. *Violations of Free Speech and the Rights of Labor.* U.S. Congressional report 1150. 77th Cong., 2d sess.

Lamphere, Louise. 1987. *From Working Daughters to Working Mothers: Production and Reproduction in an Industrial Community.* Ithaca, N.Y.: Cornell University Press.

————. 1992. *Structuring Diversity.* Chicago: University of Chicago Press.

Larson, O. F., and E. F. Sharp. 1960. *Migratory Farm Workers in the Atlantic Coast Stream.* Cornell University Agricultural Experiment Station Bulletin 948, Ithaca, N.Y.

Leach, James E., et al. v. Albert B. Johnston and Thomas Alexander, Sr. 1991. Case no. 91-1138-Civ-J-16. Jacksonville, Fla.: U.S. District Court for the Middle District of Florida.

Leibow, Elliot. 1967. *Talley's Corner.* Boston: Little, Brown.

Lewis, Oscar. 1957. "The Culture of Poverty." *Scientific American.*

Lively, C. E., and Conrad Taeuber. 1939. *Rural Migration in the United States.* Research Monograph no. 19. Washington, D.C.: U.S. Government Printing Office.

Lomnitz, Larissa. 1977. *Networks and Marginality: Life in a Mexican Shantytown.* New York: Academic Press.

Long, Norman, and R. Richardson. 1977. "Informal Sector, Petty Commodity Production, and the Social Relations of Small Scale Enterprise." In *The New Economic Anthropology,* edited by John Clammer. London: Frank Cass.

McWilliams, Cary. 1939. *Factories in the Field.* Berkeley and Los Angeles: University of California Press.

Mantejano, David. 1987. *Anglos and Mexicans in the Making of Texas, 1836–1986.* Austin: University of Texas Press.

Marshall, Ray. 1974. *Rural Workers in Rural Labor Markets.* Salt Lake City, Utah: Olympus.

Martin, Philip. 1989. "Immigration and the Colonization of the Labor Market." Working Paper no. 1, Center for Immigration Studies, Washington, D.C.

————. 1990. "Harvest of Confusion: Immigration Reform and California Agriculture." *International Migration Review* 24(1):69–95.

Martin, Philip, and John Mamer. 1982. "Hired Workers on California Farms." *California Agriculture,* September–October, 21–23.

Martin, Philip, and J. E. Taylor. 1990. "Harvest of Confusion: Immigration Reform and California Agriculture." *International Migration Review* 24:69–95.

Martin, Philip, and S. Vaupel. 1984. "Agricultural Labor Relations in California." Working Paper no. 84-2, University of California Department of Agricultural Economics, Davis.

Maryland. Department of Agriculture. 1989. *Production Statistics for Maryland Fruit and Vegetable Farms.* Baltimore: Maryland Department of Agriculture.

Mason, Herbert, Andrew Alverado, and Gary Riley. 1993. "The Citrus Industry in

California and Arizona." In *Appendix I: Case Studies and Research Reports,* Commission on Agricultural Workers, 69–102. Washington, D.C.: U.S. Government Printing Office.

Massey, Douglas, Rafael Alarcon, Jorge Durand, and Humberto Gonzalez. 1987. *Return to Aztlan: The Social Process of International Migration from Western Mexico.* Berkeley and Los Angeles: University of California Press.

Meister, Dick, and Anne Loftis. 1977. *A Long Time Coming: The Struggle to Unionize America's Farm Workers.* New York: Macmillan.

Metzler, William H. 1955. *Migratory Farm Workers in the Atlantic Coast Stream: A Study in the Belle Glade Area of Florida.* Circular no. 966. Washington, D.C.: U.S. Department of Agriculture.

Metzler, William, Ralph Loomis, and Nelson LeRay. 1967. *The Farm Labor Situation in Selected States, 1965–66.* Agricultural Economic Report no. 110. Washington, D.C.: U.S. Department of Agriculture.

Mines, Richard. 1974. "The AFL-CIO Drive in Agriculture, 1958–1960." Master's thesis in agricultural economics, Columbia University.

Mines, Richard, and Ricardo Anzaldúa. 1982. *New Migrants vs. Old Migrants: Alternative Labor Market Structures in the California Citrus Industry.* Monograph no. 9. San Diego: Center for U.S.–Mexican Relations, University of California.

Mines, Richard, and Philip Martin. 1983. "The Demand for Seasonal Farm Labor in California." Working Paper no. 83-9, Department of Agricultural Economics, University of California, Davis.

Mines, Richard, Susan Gabbard, and Ruth Samardick. 1989. *The National Agricultural Worker Survey (NAWS).* Washington, D.C.: U.S. Government Printing Office.

———. 1990. *The National Agricultural Worker Survey (NAWS).* Washington, D.C.: U.S. Government Printing Office.

———. 1991. *The National Agricultural Worker Survey (NAWS).* Washington, D.C.: U.S. Government Printing Office.

Mintz, Sidney. 1956. "Canmelar: A Puerto Rican Sugar Plantation." In *The People of Puerto Rico,* edited by Julian Steward. Urbana: University of Illinois Press.

———. 1971. "Foreword." In *African-American Anthropology,* edited by Norman Whitten and John Swedz. New York: Free Press.

Nash, June. 1989. *From Tank Town to High Tech.* Albany: State University of New York Press.

Nash, June, and M. P. Fernández-Kelly, eds. 1983. *Women, Men, and the New International Division of Labor.* Albany: State University of New York Press.

Nelkin, Dorothy. 1970. "On the Season: Aspects of the Migrant Labor System." ILR Paperback no. 8. New York State School of Industrial and Labor Relations, Cornell University, Ithaca, N.Y.

New Jersey. Department of Agriculture. 1988. *Agricultural Statistics Survey.* Trenton: New Jersey Department of Agriculture.

New Jersey Association of Nurserymen. 1984. *Survey of Nurseries in New Jersey.* Trenton: New Jersey Association of Nurserymen.

Newman, Kathy. 1988. *Fall from Grace: The Experience of Downward Mobility in the American Middle Class.* New York: Free Press.

North Carolina Migrant Council. 1992. "Migrant Farmworker Health in North Carolina." Manuscript. Durham.

Nuckton, Carol. 1985. "An Econometric Analysis of the California Raisin Industry." Giannini Foundation Research Report 339, Oakland, Calif.

Ong, Aiwa. 1987. *Spirits of Resistance and Capitalist Discipline: Factory Women in Malaysia.* Albany: State University of New York Press.

Padilla, Elena Seda. 1956. "Nocorá: The Subculture of Workers on a Government-Owned Sugar plantation." In *The People of Puerto Rico,* edited by Julian Steward et al., 265–313. Champaign-Urbana: University of Illinois Press.

Papademetriou, Demetrious, Robert Bach, Kyle Johnson, Roger Kramer, Briant Lidsay Lowell, and Shirley Smith. 1989. *The Effects of Immigration on the U.S. Economy and Labor Market.* Immigration Policy and Research Report no. 1. Washington, D.C.: U.S. Department of Labor, Bureau of International Labor Affairs.

Parilla, Efrain. 1973. "Migrants under Contract Drop in Ferré Term." *San Juan Star,* December 19.

Pfeffer, Max. 1992. "Labor and Chemical Use on New Jersey Farms." *Rural Sociology.*

Picó, Fernano. 1986. *Historia General de Puerto Rico.* San Juan: Ediciones Huracán.

Piore, Michael. 1979. *Birds of Passage: Migrant Labor and Industrial Society.* Cambridge: Cambridge University Press.

Portes, Alejandro, and Robert Bach. 1985. *Latin Journey: Cuban and Mexican Immigrants in the United States.* Berkeley and Los Angeles: University of California Press.

Portes, Alejandro, and Jozsef Böröcz. 1989. "Contemporary Immigration: Theoretical Perspectives on Its Determinants and Modes of Incorporation." *International Migration Review* 23(3):606–30.

Portes, Alejandro, and John Walton. 1981. *Labor, Class, and the International System.* New York: Academic Press.

Pratts, Saul. 1987. *La Politica Social en Puerto Rico.* Santurce, P.R.: Jay-Ce Printing.

Puerto Rican Departamento de Trabajo. 1987. "Migration to the U.S. Mainland." Typescript. Mayagüez, P.R.

Ramirez, Rafael. 1978. *El Arrabal y La Política.* Rio Piedras, P.R.: Editorial Universitaria.

Rasmussen, Wayne. 1951. *A History of the Emergency Farm Labor Supply Program, 1943–47.* USDA Bureau of Agricultural Economics Monograph no. 13. Washington, D.C.: U.S. Government Printing Office.

Reimund, Donald, J. Martin, and C. Moore. 1981. *Structural Change in Agriculture: The Experience for Broilers, Fed Cattle, and Processing Vegetables.* Technical Bulletin no. 1648. Washington, D.C.: U.S. Department of Agriculture.

Reubens, Edwin P. 1979. *Temporary Admission of Foreign Workers: Dimensions and*

Policies. Special report of the National Commission for Manpower Policy no. 34. Washington, D.C.: U.S. Government Printing Office.

Reuss, Carl, Paul Landis, and Richard Wakefield. 1938. "Migratory Farm Labor and the Hop Industry on the Pacific Coast." Rural Sociology Series in Farm Labor no. 3. Bulletin no. 363. State College of Washington Agricultural Experiment Station, Pullman.

Rhodes, Richard. 1978. "Intra-European Return Migration and Rural Development: Lessons from the Spanish Case." *Human Organization* 37:95–106.

———. 1989. *Farm: A Year in the Life of an American Farmer.* New York: Simon and Schuster.

Richardson, Bonham. 1983. *Caribbean Migrants.* Knoxville: University of Tennessee Press.

Richman, Karen. 1992. "They Will Welcome Me in the House; Haitian Transnationalism." Ph.D. diss., Department of Anthropology, University of Virginia, Charlottesville.

Rosenberg, Howard. 1993. "IRCA and Agriculture in Selected States: California III." Paper presented at the WRCC-76 Conference on Immigration Reform and U.S. Agriculture, Economic Research Service, USDA, Washington, D.C.

Rouse, Roger. 1988. "Mexican Migration and the Social Space of Postmodernism." *Diaspora: Journal of Transnational Studies* 1(1): 8–23.

Rubel, A. 1966. *Across the Tracks.* Austin: University of Texas Press.

Ruiz, Vicki. 1987. *Cannery Women, Cannery Lives: Mexican Women, Unionization, and the California Food Processing Industry, 1930–1950.* Albuquerque: University of New Mexico Press.

Runsten, David. 1993. "The Tomato Industry in California and Baja, California." In *Appendix I: Case Studies and Research Reports,* Commission on Agricultural Workers, 3–64. Washington, D.C.: U.S. Government Printing Office.

Runsten, David, and Philip LeVeen. 1981. *Mechanization and Mexican Labor in California Agriculture.* Monograph no. 6. San Diego: Center for U.S.–Mexican Relations, University of California.

Safa, Helen. 1984. *Migration and Development.* The Hague: Moulton.

Salley, George. 1983. *A History of the Florida Sugar Industry.* Clewiston, Fla.: Florida Sugar Cane League.

Sanderson, Steve, ed. 1985. *The Americas in the New International Division of Labor.* New York: Holmes and Meier.

Schwartz, Harry. 1945. *Seasonal Farm Labor in the United States.* New York: Columbia University Press.

Scott, James. 1985. *Weapons on the Weak: Everyday Forms of Peasant Resistance.* New Haven, Conn.: Yale University Press.

Selma Irrigator. 1882. Various Issues. Selma, Calif.

Sider, Gerald. 1986. *Culture and Class in Anthropology and History: A Newfoundland Illustration.* Cambridge: Cambridge University Press.

Smith, Robert. 1992. "The Mushroom Industry in Chester County, Pennsylvania." In *Immigration Reform and Perishable Crop Agriculture: Vol. 2. Case Studies,* edited by Monica Heppel and Sandra Amendola. Washington, D.C.: Center for Immigration Studies.

Stack, Carol. 1971. *All Our Kin: Strategies for Survival in a Black Community.* Urbana: University of Illinois Press.

———. 1979. *Hanging onto the Lord and the Land.* Athens: University of Georgia Press.

Stepick, Alex, and Alejandro Portes. 1986. "Flight into Despair: A Profile of Recent Haitian Refugees in South Florida." *International Migration Review* 20(2):329–50.

Stepick, Alex, and Carol Dutton Stepick. 1990. "People in the Shadows: Survey Research among Haitians in Miami." *Human Organization* 49:64–77.

Steward, Julian, Sidney Mintz, Elena Padilla, Raymond Scheel, and Eric Wolf. 1956. *The People of Puerto Rico.* Urbana: University of Illinois Press.

Sticter, Sharon. 1985. *African Migrants.* Cambridge: Cambridge University Press.

Stoler, Ann. 1985. *Capitalism and Confrontation in Sumatra's Plantation Belt.* New Haven, Conn.: Yale University Press.

Stull, Donald, Michael Broadway, and David Griffith, eds. In press. *Making Meat: How Meat, Fish, and Poultry Processing Are Transforming Rural America.* Lawrence: University Press of Kansas.

Taller de Formacíon Política. 1982. *¡Huelga en la Caña!* San Juan: Ediciones Huracán.

———. 1988. *No Estamos Pidiendo El Cielo.* San Juan: Ediciones Huracán.

Texas. Department of Commerce. 1990. *1989 Texas Statistical Abstract.* Austin: Texas Department of Commerce.

Texas. Department of Human Services. 1988. *Use of Social Services in Texas, 1987.* Austin: Texas Department of Human Services.

———. 1990. *Use of Social Services in Texas, 1989.* Austin: Texas Department of Human Services.

Texas Employment Commission. 1990. *Texas Employment Data.* Austin: Texas Department of Labor.

Thomas, J. Steven, and Carol Formicella. 1984. "The Shrimp Industry in Bayou La Battre, Alabama." Working Paper, Department of Sociology and Anthropology, University of South Alabama, Mobile.

Thomas, Robert. 1985. *Citizenship, Gender, and Work.* Berkeley and Los Angeles: University of California Press.

Thompson, Gary, Ricardo Amon, and Philip Martin. 1986. "Agricultural Development and Emigration: Rhetoric and Reality." *International Migration Review* 20(3):575–611.

Trujillo, Larry. 1975. *Parlier: The Hub of Raisin America.* Berkeley: Institute for the Study of Social Change, University of California, Berkeley.

Upton, Peter, and Rob Williams. 1983. "Guatemalan Kanjobal Asylum Applicants: Predecisional Brief." Typescript, Florida Rural Legal Services, Immokalee.

U.S. Congress. 1963. *Farm Labor Contractor Registration Act.* 86th Cong. 1st sess.

———. 1965. *Immigration Act of the United States.* 79 Stat. 911, 89th Cong., 1st sess.

———. 1978. *The West Indies (BWI) Temporary Alien Labor Program.* A study prepared for the Subcommittee on Immigration of the Committee on the Judiciary, U.S. Senate, 95th Cong., 2d sess.

———. 1984. *Amendment to the Packers Act of 1921 to Include Poultry.*

———. 1986. *Immigration Control and Reform Act of 1986.* Public Law 99-603, November 6, 1986. 99th Cong.

U.S. Department of Agriculture (USDA). 1991. *1990 Fact Book of Agriculture.* Office of Public Affairs, Miscellaneous Publication no. 1063. Washington, D.C.: U.S. Government Printing Office.

U.S. Department of Commerce. Bureau of the Census. 1987. *Census of Agriculture.* Washington, D.C.: U.S. Government Printing Office.

U.S. Department of Labor. 1986. *Regulations, Part 500: Migrant and Seasonal Agricultural Worker Protection.* Employment Standards Administration, Wage and Hour Publication no. 1455, revised 1986. Washington, D.C.: U.S. Government Printing Office.

Valdes, Dionicio. 1990. ''Roots of the Farmworker Movement, 1945–65.'' Paper presented at the Conference on Labor History, March 10, Madison, Wis.

Vandeman, Ann Marie. 1988. ''Labor Contracting in California Agriculture.'' Ph.D. diss., Department of Agricultural Economics, University of California, Berkeley.

Villarejo, Don. 1988. ''Critique of 'Migrant Farmworkers: Number and Distribution,' by Phillip L. Martin and James S. Holt.'' Typescript. California Institute for Rural Studies, University of California, Berkeley.

Waldinger, Roger, and Thomas Bailey. 1992. ''Primary, Secondary, and Enclave Labor Markets.'' *American Sociological Review* 56(4):432–45.

Wallace, A. F. C. 1978. *Rockdale: The Growth of an American Village in the Early Industrial Revolution.* New York: Knopf.

Wallerstein, Immanuel. 1974. *The Modern World System.* New York: Academic Press.

''Wartime Changes in Agricultural Employment.'' 1945. *Monthly Labor Review* 61(3):442–51.

Webb, John, and Malcolm Brown. 1938. *Migrant Families.* WPA Division of Social Research, Research Monograph no. 17. Washington, D.C.: U.S. Government Printing Office.

Wells, Miriam. 1987. ''Sharecropping in the U.S.: A Political Economy Perspective.'' In *Farm Work and Fieldwork,* edited by Michael Chibnik, 211–243. Ithaca, N.Y.: Cornell University Press.

———. 1990. ''Mexican Farm Workers Become Strawberry Farmers.'' *Human Organization* 49(2):149–56.

Willis, Paul. 1982. *Learning to Labour: How Working Class Kids Get Working Class Jobs.* London: Gower.

Wolf, Eric. 1956. *Sons of the Shaking Earth.* Berkeley and Los Angeles: University of California Press.

Wood, Charles, and Terry McCoy. 1985. "Migration, Remittances, and Development: A Study of Caribbean Cane Cutters in Florida." *International Migration Review* 19(2):251–77.

Woods and Poole Economics. 1990. *1990 State Profile: Texas.* Austin: Woods and Poole.

Wynne, Waller. 1943. *Culture of a Contemporary Rural Community: Harmony, Georgia.* Rural Life Studies no. 6. Washington, D.C.: Bureau of Agricultural Economics, U.S. Department of Agriculture.

Young, Jan. 1972. *The Migrant Workers and Cesar Chavez.* New York: Simon and Schuster.

Zabin, Carol, Michael Kearney, Anna Garcia, David Runsten, and Carole Nagengast. 1993. *A New Cycle of Poverty: Mixtec Migrants in California Agriculture.* Berkeley: California Institute for Rural Studies, University of California.

About the Authors

Jeronimo Camposeco works for the Florida Rural Legal Services and has become deeply involved in legal issues facing illegal immigrants, refugees, and low-income peoples of southern Florida's rural areas. He is one of the founders and a former director of Corn Maya, an organization designed to aid Guatemalan refugees fleeing the violence of Central America's ethnic wars. He contributed the foreword to Allan F. Burns's *Maya in Exile* (Temple University Press, 1993).

Anna García is a researcher working on a wide range of issues related to Mexican immigrant employment in the United States. She has more than twenty years of experience interpreting migration, work, and life patterns across national borders and in interviewing farmworkers, ex-farmworkers, farm labor contractors, growers, industry specialists, and other knowledgeable informants in the key agricultural states in the United States and in Mexico. After being at the Center for U.S.–Mexican Studies at the University of California, San Diego, for nine years, she became an independent researcher. García is currently investigating urban-immigrant issues in Los Angeles and is part of a consortium of researchers examining the impact of national immigration policy on transborder migration.

David Griffith, an anthropologist, has written extensively on the living and working conditions of low-wage workers, immigrants, fishers, peasants, and the rural and urban poor. He has conducted field research in several locations throughout the United States, particularly the U.S. South, and the Caribbean. His recent book, *Jones's Minimal: Low-Wage Workers in the United States,* chronicles strategies of survival and resistance among immigrant, refugee, and minority workers in the seafood and poultry industries, and he has co-edited, with Donald Stull and Michael Broadway, a forthcoming volume on how the

325

beef, pork, fish, and poultry processing industries are reshaping rural America. He currently holds a joint position as an associate scientist in the Department of Anthropology and the Institute for Coastal and Marine Resources of East Carolina University.

Ed Kissam, who holds degrees in philosophy from Princeton University and comparative literature from the State University of New York at Buffalo, now specializes in issues facing immigrants and farmworkers, helping to adapt adult education programs to the special needs of immigrants in California. He has conducted several studies for the State of California, the U.S. Department of Labor, and the Commission on Agricultural Workers, focusing on farmworkers, Mexican Americans, and immigrants from Mexico and Central America. His work has influenced policy decisions at local, state, and national levels. In 1985, he won the Pushcart Prize for best small press translation collection for his book *The Poetry of Aztec Peoples.* With Aguirre International, he is currently engaged in a nationwide evaluation of Americorps.

Manuel Valdés Pizzini is director of the Social Science Research Center at the University of Puerto Rico in Mayagüez, where he also teaches in the social sciences department. Since the late 1970s, Valdés has been active in research on Caribbean issues, studying ethnohistory, coastal populations, natural-resource management, and the wage-labor histories of farmworkers and artisanal fishers. He received his Ph.D. in anthropology at the State University of New York, Stony Brook, and has published widely in such journals as *American Ethnologist* and *Human Organization.*

Max Pfeffer is a sociologist at Cornell University. While involved in the preparation of this book, he was a faculty member at Rutgers University's Department of Human Ecology. His research and teaching span several areas, including agriculture and the environment, rural labor markets, rural-to-urban and international migration, and farmland preservation. One of his most recent articles on farmworkers, "Low-Wage Employment and Ghetto Poverty: A Comparison of African American and Cambodian Day-Haul Farm Workers in Philadelphia," appears in *Social Problems* (February 1993).

David Runsten is an agricultural economist based in Berkeley, California. For several years he has directed the Working Group on Farm Labor and Rural Poverty, California Institute for Rural Studies. He has lectured to a wide variety of audiences in the public and private sectors, including, recently, at the

Carnegie Endowment for International Peace on the effects of the North American Free Trade Agreement on the competitiveness of U.S. agriculture. He coauthored a report in 1993 for the Columbia Basin Institute entitled "Value Added and Subtracted: The Processed Potato Industry in the Mid-Columbia Basin."

Index

African Americans, 42–44, 77–79, 123, 275
Alliance, the, 9
Asian workers, 7, 85, 192–93

Bracero Program, 5, 14, 17–19, 54; and children of immigrants, 105; documentation of workers in, 17, 19; effect of, on migration, 102–3, 268; and families, 133, 136; immigration during, 107; recruitment during, 194; reliance of, on migrant labor, 124; and workers today, 112
Boycotts, 19
British West Indies Temporary Alien Labor Program, 14, 54

Chinese. *See* Asian workers
Citrus industry: decline of, 104; migrant labor and, 53–54; problems associated with growth of, 31; relocation of, to Mexico, 104; World War II and, 101
Civil rights, 6; and demographic changes, 18; and perishable crop laborers, 17
Commission on Agricultural Workers, 22, 70–71
Commission on Migratory Labor, 15; and foreign nationals, 15–16; and Korean crisis, 15; and labor supply, 16; and population changes, 18
Country Life Commission, 7–10

Dedicated Network of Resources (RED), 159
Depression, Great, 11–12

Environmental regulations, 20
Ethnicity, 39; changes in, 174; as a determinant of household formation, 40; and interethnic relations, 41, 46; and reinforcement of identity, 41
Ethnic succession, 17, 29

Farm crisis: and ecological crises, 9, 11, 104–5, 113, 117, 195; and farm families, 4
Farmer's Union, the, 9
Farm labor contracting: and abuse of workers, 58–60, 67; as a career, 146, 281–82; and cash renting, 9; and crew dynamics, 58–64; and family ties of FLCs, 146; and FLCs as ethnic intermediaries, 16; and "hired hands," 13; importance of, 229–30, 237–38, 245, 261, 278; and job service referrals, 148; and labor camps, 145; and labor control, 56–64, 259, 272; and labor pooling, 78, 87, 129; and network recruitment, 147; resistance to, 127; responsibilities of, 81, 145–46; and seasonal agriculture workers (SAWs), 13; and subcontracting, 20; and tenant farming, 8, 9; and wage markups, 145;

329

Farm labor contracting (*cont.*)
 and women as FLCs, 146; and worker
 income, 61
Farm labor force: composition of, 243,
 246–47, 250–51, 291; conditions of, 4,
 12; ethnicity of, 251–52; families and,
 133; job security of, 115, 130, 229;
 labor pools and, 111, 182; and labor
 turnover, 150, 178, 189; legal status of,
 151; marginal workers and, 99,
 110–11; networks of, 115, 117, 130,
 289; occupational migration from, 117,
 122; and reasons for shortage, 108–10;
 service delivery systems of, 130–31;
 subcontracting and, 290–91; supply
 and demand in, 104–6, 134, 138, 149,
 156, 167, 177, 179, 185, 220–27,
 243–44; underemployment and, 114–
 16, 228, 244; unemployment and, 116,
 228, 244; women and, 293
Farm Labor Organizing Committee, 137
Florida Fruit and Vegetable Association,
 16
Florida Tomato Committee, 282

General Agreements on Tariffs and Trade
 (GATT), 272
Glassboro Services Association, 16, 158,
 174
Grange, the, 9

Homestead Act of 1862, 192
Household structure, relationship of, to
 labor markets, 44–45
Housing, 35; access to, 199, 215, 264,
 267; and Bracero workers, 19; conditions of, 32, 141–43, 196, 244, 264,
 266; as a determinant of migration,
 160; economic importance of, 196,
 263, 265–68, 285; immigration patterns and, 244; as an instrument of
 labor control, 32, 140, 197; labor

camps and, 35, 37, 63, 79, 80, 140–41,
 193, 198; and labor supply and demand, 244; private incentives and, 144,
 197; public programs and, 144, 156–
 58, 198, 201, as a recruitment tool, 33,
 158, 184, 199, 268; regulations and
 laws on, 143, 156; rehabilitation programs and, 143–44

Immigration policy: and Bracero Program, 5, 17; Immigration and Naturalization Service and, 16, 261; Immigration Reform and Control Act and, 54,
 205; and Mexican-U.S. migration, 225
Indentured servitude, 14
Industrialization: labor supply and, 167;
 Operation Bootstrap and, 155
Internal labor markets, 14, 182, 277

Labor demand: changes in, 247; demographic changes in, 234–35; housing
 and, 263; and migrant networks, 227;
 regions of, 24; relationship of, to
 household and community, 44; seasonal fluctuations of, 219; supervision
 and, 237; surpluses and, 261–62, 264
Labor management: crop diversification
 and, 128–29; and organization of
 work, 245; supervisors and, 221–22;
 and worker coordination, 183, 187,
 189, 245
Labor markets, 100, 205, 271, 274–77
Labor reserves, 280
Labor unions: among farmers, 9, 13;
 among farmworkers, 12–13; among industrial workers, 11–12; structural
 characteristics of, 277. See also Migration, migrant labor
LaFollette Commission, 12
Land grant colleges, 20, 288
Laurel Auction Block, 73